Social Democratic Capitalism

LANE KENWORTHY

OXFORD
UNIVERSITY PRESS

OXFORD
UNIVERSITY PRESS

Oxford University Press is a department of the University of Oxford. It furthers
the University's objective of excellence in research, scholarship, and education
by publishing worldwide. Oxford is a registered trade mark of Oxford University
Press in the UK and certain other countries.

Published in the United States of America by Oxford University Press
198 Madison Avenue, New York, NY 10016, United States of America.

CIP data is on file at the Library of Congress
ISBN 978–0–19–006411–2

1 3 5 7 9 8 6 4 2

Printed by Sheridan Books, Inc., United States of America

The arc of the moral universe is long, but it bends toward justice.
—Martin Luther King Jr.

The legitimate object of government is to do for a community of people whatever they need to have done but can not do at all, or can not do so well, for themselves in their separate and individual capacities.
—Abraham Lincoln

If we keep track of how our laws and manners are doing, think up ways to improve them, try them out, and keep the ones that make people better off, we can gradually make the world a better place.
—Steven Pinker

CONTENTS

1

Sources of Successful Societies

For nations, as for individuals, it's good to be rich. Affluent countries are more likely to be democratic, more likely to have government programs that cushion life's bumps and boost the capabilities and well-being of the less fortunate, and more likely to prioritize personal liberty. Their citizens tend to be more secure, better educated, healthier, freer, and happier.

The world's twenty or so rich democratic countries aren't all alike, and they've changed a good bit over the past century.[1] Their experiences give us helpful clues about what institutions and policies best promote human flourishing. To this point in history, the most successful societies have been those that feature capitalism, a democratic political system, good elementary and secondary (K–12) schooling, a big welfare state, employment-conducive public services, and moderate regulation of product and labor markets.[2] I call this set of policies and institutions "social democratic capitalism."

Social democratic capitalism improves living standards for the least well-off, enhances economic security, and very likely boosts equality of opportunity. It does so without sacrificing the many other things we want in a good society, from liberty to economic growth and much more. Its chief practitioners have been the Nordic nations: Denmark, Finland, Norway, and Sweden. Contrary to what some presume, there is no good reason to think social democratic capitalism will work well only in these countries. Its success almost certainly is transferable to other affluent nations. Indeed, all of those nations already are partial adopters of social democratic capitalism.

The United States, the largest of the world's rich democracies, is one of those partial adopters. If the United States were to expand some of its existing public social programs and add some additional ones, many ordinary Americans would have better lives. Despite formidable political obstacles, there is good reason to think America will move in this direction in coming decades.

Those are my conclusions. This book provides the evidence and the reasoning.

Affluence and Its Consequences

Let's begin with some context. The extent of human progress over the past two centuries is astonishing. The starting point is improvement in economic well-being. Economic historians have estimates of gross domestic product (GDP) per person back to the year AD 1 for France and back a few centuries or more for some other countries. For most of the past two thousand years—and by extension, for virtually all of human history—the quantity of goods and services we produced barely budged.[3] Then, around the middle of the 1800s, nations such as the United States, Germany, France, and a handful of others stumbled upon an institutional framework featuring markets, government provision of property rights and public goods, and the scientific method. This configuration has proved conducive to rapid and sustained economic advance, as we see in Figure 1.1.[4]

As societies get richer, they change in a variety of ways. Among these changes are shifts in what people want and what they prioritize. Three are particularly important.

First, people tend to dislike loss.[5] The higher our income, the more insurance we are willing to purchase in order to minimize potential loss. For some types of insurance, such as insurance against low income in old age, government is the most effective provider. Germany created a public old-age pension program in the late 1800s, and other industrializing countries began to do so in the first half of the twentieth century, with many introducing or expanding them during the Great Depression in the 1930s. While many nations now have this type of

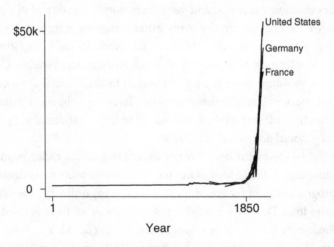

Figure 1.1 GDP per capita. Adjusted for inflation and converted to 2011 US dollars using purchasing power parities. "k" = thousand. The data begin in AD 1 for France, in 1500 for Germany, and in 1650 for the United States. Data source: Maddison Project Database 2018, rug.nl/ggdc.

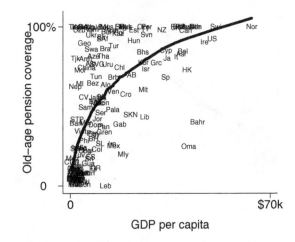

Figure 1.2 Affluence and public old-age pension coverage. Old-age pension coverage: share of statutory pension-age population. 2004–2013. Data source: United Nations Development Program (UNDP), "Human Development Data," using data from the International Labour Office (ILO), *World Social Protection Report*. GDP per capita: converted to 2011 US dollars using purchasing power parities. "k" = thousand. 2005. Data source: UNDP, "Human Development Data." Three small, rich city-states (Andorra, Luxembourg, Singapore) are omitted. The line is a loess curve, calculated with five oil-rich nations excluded.

public program, richer countries tend to have more expansive ones, as Figure 1.2 shows.

Government also plays an important role in the provision of health insurance. As we see in Figure 1.3, public spending on healthcare tends to rise as nations get richer. The same is true for education, as Figure 1.4 shows. (The association in this figure would be even stronger but for the fact that virtually all countries have universal government-funded K–12 schooling, which requires significant expenditure regardless of national wealth.)

Much of what modern governments spend money on is public insurance. Some programs protect against loss of income due to old age, unemployment, illness, disability, family needs, discrimination, and other conditions and circumstances. Other programs ensure widespread availability of schooling, healthcare, housing, job training and placement, transportation, and other services and goods. As a country gets more affluent, the welfare state tends to grow.[6]

A second change in people's desires as they get richer is to want more fairness in their society.[7] Drawing on several decades of public opinion survey data from multiple countries, Ronald Inglehart and Christian Welzel have found that once people can be confident of survival and of a decent standard of living, they tend to shift away from a worldview that emphasizes traditional sources of authority, religious dictates, traditional social roles, and the well-being of

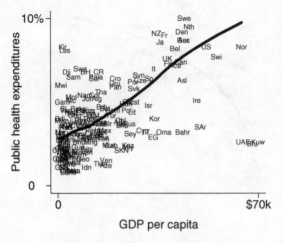

Figure 1.3 Affluence and public health expenditures. Public health expenditures: share of GDP. 2014. Data source: United Nations Development Program (UNDP), "Human Development Data." GDP per capita: see Figure 1.2. 2014. Three small, rich city-states (Andorra, Luxembourg, Singapore) and four small island nations that have very high health expenditures are omitted. The line is a loess curve, calculated with eight oil-rich nations excluded.

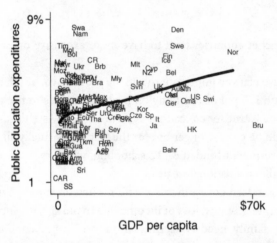

Figure 1.4 Affluence and public education expenditures. Public education expenditures: share of GDP. 2010–2014. Data source: United Nations Development Program (UNDP), "Human Development Data." GDP per capita: see Figure 1.2. 2010. Three small, rich city-states (Andorra, Luxembourg, Singapore) and two small island nations that have very high education expenditures are omitted. The line is a loess curve, calculated with four oil-rich nations excluded.

the group or community rather than that of the individual. A "postmaterialist" or "emancipative" worldview replaces a scarcity orientation.[8] One element of postmaterialism is a desire for basic political rights. Another element is universalistic humanism, which deems all persons, including members of outgroups,

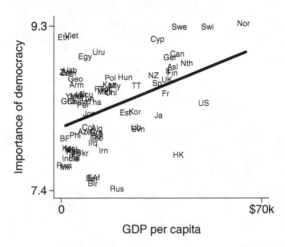

Figure 1.5 Affluence and desire for fairness in politics. Importance of democracy: average response to the question "How important is it for you to live in a country that is governed democratically?," with 1 indicating "not at all important" and 10 indicating "absolutely important." 2005–2014. Data source: World Values Survey. GDP per capita: see Figure 1.2. 2005. Three small, rich city-states (Andorra, Luxembourg, Singapore) and Haiti are omitted. The line is a linear regression line, calculated with two oil-rich nations excluded.

as equally worthy of rights, opportunities, and respect. In the world's rich nations, the shift from a traditional orientation to a postmaterialist one emerged in the generation that grew up after the Great Depression and World War II.[9] As the rest of the world gets richer, we're beginning to observe it there too.[10]

We can see the growing embrace of fairness when we compare nations that have varying levels of economic affluence. The richer the nation, the more important people tend to say it is "to live in a country that is governed democratically," as Figure 1.5 shows. Similarly, a much larger portion of the populace in higher-income nations disagrees that "when jobs are scarce, men should have more right to a job than women," as we see in Figure 1.6.[11] And Figure 1.7 shows a similar pattern when respondents are asked whether "when jobs are scarce, employers should give priority to [native-born] people over immigrants."

A third shift that comes with affluence is a growing emphasis on personal liberty. Most of us want the freedom to choose what to believe, how to behave, with whom to live, and so on. As material well-being increases, this desire for freedom comes to the fore.[12]

Here too we can observe the progress by looking across countries. Figure 1.8 shows that in richer nations more people consider religion, which tends to restrict our beliefs and behaviors, to be not very important in their life.[13] More people say divorce is justifiable, as Figure 1.9 shows. And more people view homosexuality as justifiable, as we see in Figure 1.10.

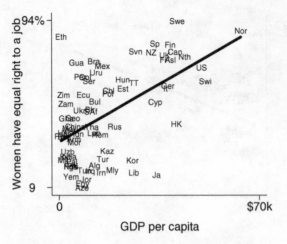

Figure 1.6 Affluence and desire for fairness for women. Women have equal right to a job: share not disagreeing that "when jobs are scarce, men should have more right to a job than women." Other response options: agree, neither agree nor disagree. 2005–2014. Data source: World Values Survey. GDP per capita: see Figure 1.2. 2005. Three small, rich city-states (Andorra, Luxembourg, Singapore) are omitted. The line is a linear regression line, calculated with two oil-rich nations excluded.

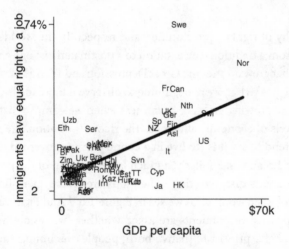

Figure 1.7 Affluence and desire for fairness for immigrants. Immigrants have equal right to a job: share disagreeing that "when jobs are scarce, employers should give priority to [native-born] people over immigrants." Other response options: agree, neither agree nor disagree. 2005–2014. Data source: World Values Survey. GDP per capita: see Figure 1.2. 2005. Three small, rich city-states (Andorra, Luxembourg, Singapore) are omitted. The line is a linear regression line, calculated with two oil-rich nations excluded.

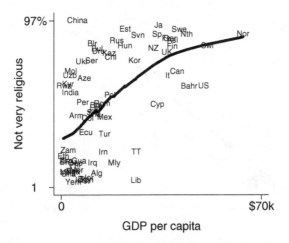

Figure 1.8 Affluence and desire for freedom in personal beliefs. Not very religious: share of the population responding other than "very important" to the question "For each of the following, indicate how important it is in your life: religion." Other response options: rather important, not very important, not at all important. 2005–2014. Data source: World Values Survey. GDP per capita: see Figure 1.2. 2005. Three small, rich city-states (Andorra, Luxembourg, Singapore) are omitted. The line is a loess curve, calculated with three oil-rich nations excluded.

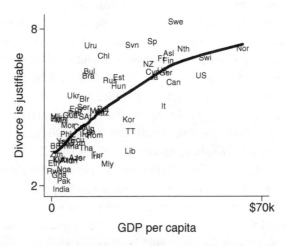

Figure 1.9 Affluence and desire for freedom in personal behavior: divorce. Divorce is justifiable: average response to the question "Please tell me for each of the following actions whether you think it can always be justified, never be justified, or something in between: divorce," where 1 indicates "never justified" and 10 indicates "always justified." 2005–2014. Data source: World Values Survey. GDP per capita: see Figure 1.2. 2005. Three small, rich city-states (Andorra, Luxembourg, Singapore) are omitted. The line is a loess curve, calculated with two oil-rich nations excluded.

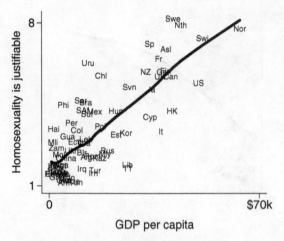

Figure 1.10 Affluence and desire for freedom in personal behavior: homosexuality.
Homosexuality is justifiable: average response to the question "Please tell me for each of the
following actions whether you think it can always be justified, never be justified, or something in
between: homosexuality," where 1 indicates "never justified" and 10 indicates "always justified." 2005–
2014. Data source: World Values Survey. GDP per capita: see Figure 1.2. 2005. Three small, rich city-
states (Andorra, Luxembourg, Singapore) are omitted. The line is a loess curve.

These advances in freedom aren't without cost. As people come to value
freedom more heavily, more choose to divorce or not to marry, so fewer children
grow up with two parents.[14] And as religion fades, a key source of community
weakens.[15] But these developments do enhance individual liberty.

People's value orientations tend to be established in their teen and early
adult years and then persist through the rest of their lives, so at the societal level
changes in attitudes often happen slowly, via new cohorts replacing older ones.
Even so, the attitude shifts are clearly visible in the cross-country patterns in
Figures 1.2 through 1.10. Researchers also find them when comparing across
cohorts within countries and when examining changes over time in the few nations for which attitudinal data are available over a lengthy period of time.[16]

When a country's economic performance weakens, such as during recessions,
the rise in support for public insurance, fairness, and personal freedom sometimes stalls or even reverses. However, such backsliding tends to be temporary.[17]

Together, affluence, its causes (markets, stable and supportive government,
and science), and its consequences (desire for more insurance, fairness, and personal freedom) have produced societies that are not only richer but also more
secure, better educated, healthier, fairer, and freer. Let's take a look at some of the
evidence that makes this clear.[18]

A common way to measure the extent of poverty or material deprivation in
different countries is to pick a minimally-acceptable income level and calculate

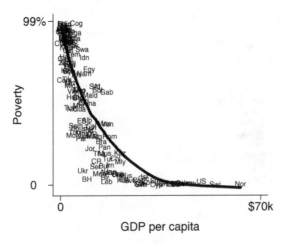

Figure 1.11 Affluence and a decent income floor. Poverty: share of persons living in a household with an income less than $5.50 per day. Incomes adjusted for inflation and converted to 2011 US dollars using purchasing power parities. Average over 2004–2015. Data source: World Bank. GDP per capita: see Figure 1.2. 2010. Three small, rich city-states (Andorra, Luxembourg, Singapore) are omitted. The line is a loess curve.

the share of the population that lives in households with an income below that level. Figure 1.11 shows that if we use $5.50 per day as the threshold, many low-income nations have very high poverty rates, while high-income nations have virtually no poverty. Figure 1.12 shows that school completion tends to be greater in higher-income countries. In Figures 1.13 and 1.14, we see a similarly strong relationship for life expectancy and for homicides.[19]

Fairness outcomes also improve. Richer nations tend to be more democratic, as Figure 1.15 shows. Women in more affluent countries tend to be better off on measures of inclusion, justice, and security, as we see in Figure 1.16. Figure 1.17 shows that immigrants are much happier with their lives in richer countries.

Finally, not only do people *want* more freedom as their societies become wealthier; they often get it. Researchers at a libertarian think tank, the Cato Institute, have compiled data on an assortment of freedoms, including the rule of law, security and safety, freedom of movement, religious freedom, freedom of association, freedom of expression and information, and freedom of identity and relationships. Figure 1.18 shows that a composite index reflecting these personal freedoms tends to rise with countries' GDP per capita.

The formula for progress, then, is straightforward: Put in place the prerequisites for sustained economic growth. Get richer. This brings pressure (from individuals and from organizations representing them, such as labor unions) for government services and supports, for fairness, and for personal

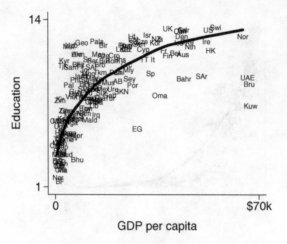

Figure 1.12 Affluence and education. Education: average years of schooling completed. 2015. Data source: United Nations Development Program (UNDP), "Human Development Data." GDP per capita: see Figure 1.2. 2015. Three small, rich city-states (Andorra, Luxembourg, Singapore) are omitted. The line is a loess curve, calculated with eight oil-rich nations excluded.

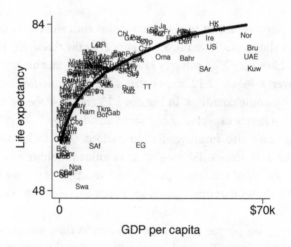

Figure 1.13 Affluence and life expectancy. Life expectancy: years at birth. 2015. Data source: United Nations Development Program (UNDP), "Human Development Data." GDP per capita: see Figure 1.2. 2015. Three small, rich city-states (Andorra, Luxembourg, Singapore) are omitted. The line is a loess curve, calculated with eight oil-rich nations excluded.

freedoms. Together, changes in material well-being and in popular attitudes improve the likelihood of good outcomes.

Achieving sustained economic growth has proved difficult for many of the world's poorer nations. A key challenge for social scientists is to improve our understanding of how to kick-start and sustain economic growth.[20] In the past several

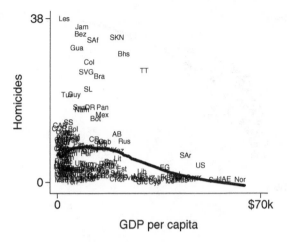

Figure 1.14 Affluence and safety. Homicides: per 100,000 population. 2010–2014. Data source: United Nations Development Program (UNDP), "Human Development Data." GDP per capita: see Figure 1.2. 2010. Three small, rich city-states (Andorra, Luxembourg, Singapore) and three very-high-homicide countries (El Salvador, Honduras, Venezuela) are omitted. The line is a loess curve, calculated with eight oil-rich nations excluded.

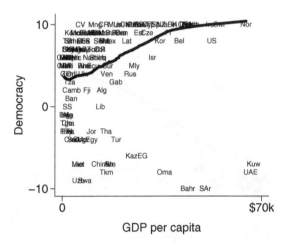

Figure 1.15 Affluence and democracy. Democracy: higher values indicate more democratic. Scale is −10 to +10. 2016. Data source: HumanProgress, "Democracy versus Autocracy Over Time," using data from Polity IV Annual Time-Series. GDP per capita: see Figure 1.2. 2015. Three small, rich city-states (Andorra, Luxembourg, Singapore) are omitted. The line is a loess curve, calculated with seven oil-rich nations excluded.

decades there has been considerable progress: for the first time, poorer countries containing a large portion of the world's population—particularly China and India but some others as well—have been growing rapidly. During this period more people have escaped poverty than ever before in human history.[21]

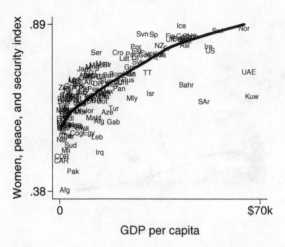

Figure 1.16 Affluence and women's well-being. Women, peace, and security index: a composite measure of inclusion (economic, social, political), justice (formal laws and informal discrimination), and security (family, community, societal) via 11 indicators. Scale is 0 to 1. Data source: Georgetown Institute for Women, Peace, and Security and Peace Research Institute of Oslo, *Women, Peace, and Security Index 2017–18*. GDP per capita: see Figure 1.2. 2015. Three small, rich city-states (Andorra, Luxembourg, Singapore) are omitted. The line is a loess curve, calculated with five oil-rich nations excluded.

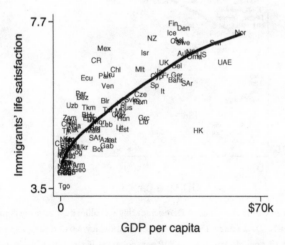

Figure 1.17 Affluence and immigrants' well-being. Immigrant life satisfaction: average response to the question "Please imagine a ladder, with steps numbered from 0 at the bottom to 10 at the top. The top of the ladder represents the best possible life for you and the bottom of the ladder represents the worst possible life for you. On which step of the ladder would you say you personally feel you stand at this time?" 2005–2017. Data source: Gallup World Poll, via the *World Happiness Report 2018*, online appendix. GDP per capita: see Figure 1.2. 2015. Three small, rich city-states (Andorra, Luxembourg, Singapore) are omitted. The line is a loess curve, calculated with six oil-rich nations excluded.

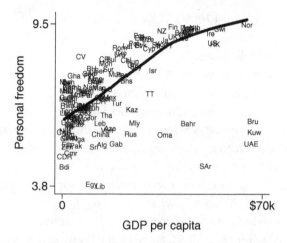

Figure 1.18 Affluence and personal freedom. Personal freedom: average score for rule of law, security and safety, freedom of movement, religious freedom, freedom of association, freedom of expression and information, and freedom of identity and relationships. Scale is 0 to 10. 2015. Data source: Ian Vasquez and Tanja Porcnik, *The Human Freedom Index*, Cato Institute. GDP per capita: see Figure 1.2. 2015. Three small, rich city-states (Andorra, Luxembourg, Singapore) are omitted. The line is a loess curve, calculated with seven oil-rich nations excluded.

While affluence makes progress in other areas more likely, it isn't a precondition. An equally important challenge for social scientists, therefore, is to figure out ways to speed up the implementation of services, cushions, fairness, and freedom even before nations become rich.[22] How can we get more children in good schools for longer? How can we improve health outcomes before a fully modern healthcare system is in place? How can we reduce deep poverty in advance of full-scale national affluence?

Along with addressing climate change and other existential threats, these tasks are the most important ones facing researchers and policy makers, because they affect a large share of the world's people, including its least well-off.

However, they aren't our only challenge. For all of their achievements, the world's rich democratic countries have progressed unevenly toward the good society. These twenty or so nations are similar to one another in some of their institutions and policies, but they also vary quite a bit. And while it isn't always easy to spot in the charts we've looked at so far, they differ significantly on an array of outcomes.

What, according to these countries' experience, is the configuration of institutions and policies most conducive to human flourishing? The historical and comparative evidence suggests that the answer is social democratic capitalism.

Social Democratic Capitalism

Social democratic capitalism consists of democracy, capitalism, education, a big welfare state, and high employment. All rich longstanding-democratic nations have the first three of these—democratic political systems, capitalist economies, and good-quality K–12 schooling. What sets social democratic capitalism apart is the addition of expansive and generous public insurance programs along with aggressive promotion of high employment via public services and modest rather than stringent regulation of product and labor markets.

In Part 1 of this book, I examine social democratic capitalism and its performance. What has it achieved? To what extent does it suffer from tradeoffs? Up to now, social democratic capitalism's chief practitioners have been the Nordic countries: Denmark, Finland, Norway, and Sweden. Is its success generalizable beyond the Nordics? Are there alternatives that can do as well or better?

Chapter 2 looks at the experience of the Nordics and other rich democratic nations. Joining democracy, capitalism, and education together with a big welfare state and high employment has brought the Nordic countries a better standard of living for their least well-off members, greater income security, and very likely more equality of opportunity. And they have gotten these results without sacrificing economic growth, freedom, health, happiness, or any of a large number of other outcomes we want in a good society.

Skeptics discount the Nordics' success on the presumption that these nations have some unique feature that allows them, and only them, to reap the benefits of social democratic policies without suffering tradeoffs. Versions of this story identify the Nordics' secret weapon as an immutable work ethic, superior intelligence, trust, solidarity, small population size, ethnic homogeneity, institutional coherence, effective government, corporatism, a willingness to be taxed, tax compliance, strong labor unions, or low income inequality. I examine these hypotheses in Chapter 3. None holds up to close inspection.

Is there a small-government set of institutions and policies that can match the success of social democratic capitalism? Some believe there is. It consists of low government spending and taxes, strong families and voluntary organizations, private rather than public services, and public transfer programs heavily targeted to the least well-off. As I document in Chapter 4, the experience of the affluent democratic nations over the past half century hasn't been friendly to this hypothesis. Countries with smaller government haven't achieved faster economic growth. Families and voluntary organizations are sometimes less effective and efficient than government programs, they by nature aren't comprehensive in coverage, and they've been weakening over time. They also are nearly or equally as prominent in nations with a big government as in those with a smaller one.

Private provision of services should be welcomed, even embraced, but it is most effective as a complement to public provision rather than a substitute. Relying on heavily targeted government transfers can work, but it may be politically sustainable only in a country with a strong egalitarian ethos, such as Australia. Even there, it hasn't matched the success of social democratic capitalism.

Universal basic income has emerged as a prominent alternative to social democratic capitalism, championed mainly by those on the political left but also by some on the right. We have very little evidence to look to in evaluating the attractiveness of this proposal. What, then, should we make of it? I consider this question in Chapter 5.

Social Democratic America

Part 2 of the book focuses on the United States. The United States is by far the largest of the affluent democratic nations, with about one-third of their total population.[23] Despite being one of the richest in this group, it is among the countries that are farthest from the good society. Too few ordinary Americans have adequate economic security, too few who grow up in disadvantaged circumstances are able to reach the middle class, and too few see their boat lifted when the economic tide rises. I detail the nature and extent of these problems in Chapter 6.

In Chapter 7 I suggest remedies. The problems are big ones, but they are not intractable. The key to a solution? Social democratic capitalism. While we have gradually expanded the size and scope of our public insurance programs and employment-enhancing services over the past century, we need to do more. I offer recommendations to add or improve health insurance, paid parental leave, a child allowance, unemployment insurance and wage insurance, sickness insurance, disability assistance, social assistance, pensions, eldercare, housing assistance, early education, apprenticeships, college, affirmative action, full employment, the minimum wage, the Earned Income Tax Credit, profit sharing, infrastructure and public spaces, and paid vacation days and holidays. After outlining the details for each of these, I turn to how much it will cost and how to pay for it.

Can it happen? I predict yes. In Chapter 8 I explain why. The notion that the United States will further increase the size and scope of its welfare state may seem blind to the reality of contemporary American politics, but a different picture emerges when we step back and consider the long run. The lesson of the past one hundred years is that as the country gets richer, we are willing to spend more in order to safeguard against loss and enhance fairness. Advances in social policy come only intermittently, but they do come. And when they come, they usually last. Building a social democratic America doesn't require a radical break from our historical path. It simply requires continuing along that path. In all likelihood, that is exactly what we will do.

America has come a long way on the road to the good society, but we have many miles yet to travel. Happily, our history and the experiences of other rich nations show us the way forward. The United States is a much better country today than it was a century ago, and a key part of the reason is that government does more to ensure economic security, opportunity, and shared prosperity now than it did then. In the future it will do more still, and we'll be the better for it.

PART 1

SOCIAL DEMOCRATIC CAPITALISM

Social Democratic Capitalism and the Good Society

Social democratic capitalism consists of political democracy plus capitalism plus education plus a big welfare state plus high employment. The experience of the world's affluent nations suggests that this set of institutions and policies is the most likely to yield a coupling of democracy and liberty with income security, a good standard of living for the least well-off, and equality of opportunity.

What exactly is social democratic capitalism? Which nations have embraced it? What is the evidence that it yields good outcomes? Does getting those outcomes require sacrificing other features of a good society? If social democratic capitalism has worked well up to now, will it continue to do so going forward?

Social Democratic Capitalism

Social democratic capitalism has six core elements[1]:

1. Democracy in the political sphere
2. Capitalism: private ownership and markets
3. Basic education: good-quality K–12 schooling
4. Expansive, generous public insurance programs
5. Employment-oriented public services: early education, affordable college, retraining, job placement assistance, individualized monitoring and support, lifelong learning
6. Modest regulation of product and labor markets

The first, second, and third of these are common to all of the world's rich longstanding-democratic nations. Each has a democratic polity, a market-oriented economy with extensive private ownership of firms, and good-quality universal primary and secondary schooling. When it comes to the fourth, fifth, and sixth elements, there is greater variation. Every affluent democratic country has a welfare state, but their expansiveness and generosity differ significantly. Employment-oriented public services and modest product and labor market regulations aim to boost employment, and these too vary widely across countries.

The leading practitioners of social democratic capitalism are the Nordic nations. Denmark and Sweden have embraced this model since roughly the 1970s. Norway has too, but its performance on many outcomes is advantaged by its substantial oil wealth, so we should be cautious in drawing inferences from the Norwegian experience. Finland is a relative latecomer in embracing the full gamut of social democratic policies, so it too isn't quite as useful as Denmark and Sweden in assessing the model.

Social democratic political parties in the Nordic countries have been the prime movers in the adoption of this set of institutions and policies, and it's for this reason that I use the term "social democratic capitalism."[2] Others might prefer a different label, such as "social capitalism," "social investment capitalism," or "flexicurity."[3]

Figures 2.1 through 2.4 help us to see countries' positioning on the fourth, fifth, and sixth elements of social democratic capitalism. On the horizontal axis of Figure 2.1 is a measure of the expansiveness and generosity of public insurance programs: government social expenditures as a share of gross domestic product (GDP). I make a small adjustment for the size of the nation's elderly population and its unemployment rate, because spending is affected not only by the structure and reach of a country's programs but also by the share of the population that needs them.[4] Countries on the right side of the chart tend to have a more generous and/or expansive welfare state. These include the Nordic nations plus the continental European countries Austria, France, Belgium, the Netherlands, and Germany. Norway's position is somewhat misleading: its very large GDP (the denominator in the measure) pushes it farther to the left than it ought to be.

On the vertical axis of Figure 2.1 is a measure of countries' use of employment-promoting government services: spending on active labor market policies such as retraining and job placement and on programs like early education and paid parental leave that help parents balance family commitments with paid work. These kinds of services encourage more people, particularly women and parents, to enter employment, they help persons who lose a job to prepare for and find another one, and they serve as a direct source of jobs for teachers, trainers, caseworkers, and others. Here Denmark and Sweden stand out, followed by Finland and Norway along with France, Belgium, Austria, Ireland, and the UK.[5]

Figure 2.2's horizontal axis has the same measure of public insurance expansiveness and generosity as in Figure 2.1. On its vertical axis is a measure of the

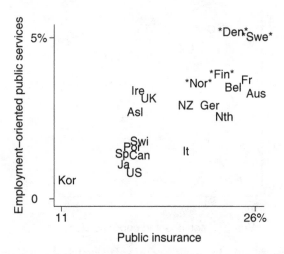

Figure 2.1 Expansive, generous public insurance and employment-oriented public services. Public insurance: public social expenditures as a share of GDP, adjusted for the size of the elderly population and the unemployment rate. The adjustment is as follows: adjusted public social expenditures = public social expenditures + (0.5 × (21.6 − (elderly population share + unemployment rate))). Each percentage point of the elderly share and/or unemployment costs about 0.5 percent of GDP, and 21.6 is the average across all countries and years for the elderly share (14.2 percent) plus the unemployment rate (7.4 percent). 1980–2015. Data source: OECD. Employment-oriented public services: public expenditures on active labor market policy and family (early education, paid parental leave, child allowances and tax credits) as a share of GDP. 1985–2015. Data source: OECD. The asterisks highlight the Nordic countries. "Asl" is Australia; "Aus" is Austria.

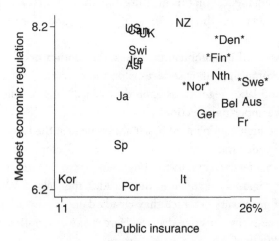

Figure 2.2 Expansive, generous public insurance and modest product and labor market regulations. Public insurance: see Figure 2.1. Modest economic regulation: average score for legal system and property rights, credit market regulations, labor market regulations, business regulations, and freedom to trade internationally. Higher scores indicate less regulation. 1980–2015. Data source: Fraser Institute, Economic Freedom database. The asterisks highlight the Nordic countries. "Asl" is Australia; "Aus" is Austria.

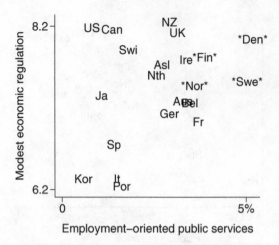

Figure 2.3 Employment-oriented public services and modest product and labor market regulations. Employment-oriented public services: see Figure 2.1. Modest economic regulation: see Figure 2.2. The asterisks highlight the Nordic countries. "Asl" is Australia; "Aus" is Austria.

modesty of product and labor market regulations. This measure is based on each country's average score for its legal system and property rights, credit market regulations, labor market regulations, business regulations, and freedom to trade internationally. The easier it is to start up, operate, and shut down a business, and the more flexible firms can be in hiring and firing workers, the more private firms are likely to be able and willing to boost employment. Denmark is among the countries scoring highest on this measure, together with New Zealand, the United States, Canada, and the UK. Finland, Sweden, and Norway aren't far behind.

Figure 2.3 shows the third combination of these three indicators. Commitment to employment-promoting public services is on the horizontal axis, and modesty of product and labor regulations is on the vertical. The Nordic countries again appear in the upper-right section.

An emphasis on high employment hasn't always been at the forefront for social democrats. (Sweden was committed to pursuit of "full employment" as early as the 1950s, but that referred mainly to a low unemployment rate among men.) As public social programs expanded in the decades after World War II, some reached a level of generosity at which they clearly dampened work incentives, and this wasn't necessarily considered a vice. Here is one description of the situation as of the 1980s, by Gøsta Esping-Andersen:

> Like pensions, sickness and related benefits were originally meant to help only the truly incapacitated. The idea of paid absence from work has undergone a decisive transformation in terms of both quality and

scope. In most European countries, sickness benefits today equal normal
earnings. In some countries, notably Scandinavia, legislation has delib-
erately sought to emancipate the individual from work-compulsion
by extending high benefits for a broad variety of contingencies, including sickness, maternity, parenthood (for mother and father), education, trade union and related involvement, and vacation. Controls
and restrictions have been eliminated or liberalized; waiting days have
been abolished, a medical certificate of illness is required only after one
week, no previous work experience is required to qualify, and benefits
can be upheld for very long periods. . . . When, as in Sweden, on any
given day approximately 15 percent of workers are absent yet paid to
work . . . a very large share of what normally is regarded as labor time is
in fact 'welfare time.'[6]

   Since then, employment promotion has become increasingly central to the
social democratic model.[7] Why the shift? After all, employment isn't always
a good thing. The need for a paycheck can trap people in careers that divert
them from more productive or rewarding pursuits. Work can be physically or
emotionally taxing. It can be monotonous, boring, and alienating. Some jobs
require a degree of indifference, meanness, or dishonesty toward customers
or subordinates that eats away at one's humanity. And work can interfere with
family life.
   Yet employment has significant virtues.[8] It imposes regularity and discipline on people's lives. It can be a source of mental stimulation. It helps to
fulfill the widespread desire to contribute to, and be integrated in, the larger
society. It shapes identity and can boost self-esteem. With neighborhood and
family ties weakening, the office or factory can be a key site of social interaction. Lack of employment tends to be associated with feelings of social exclusion, discouragement, boredom, and unhappiness. In addition, employment
may help to achieve desirable societal outcomes such as economic security
and opportunity.
   So employment has benefits and drawbacks. Some believe policy should
therefore aim to enhance people's freedom to opt in or out of paid work.[9] What
tips the balance in favor of high employment for social democratic capitalism is
the fact that paying for a big welfare state requires a large amount of government
revenue. High tax rates are one way to get that revenue, but capital mobility has
made it more difficult for nations to keep tax rates high, or to increase them.
A larger share of the population in paid work means more taxable income, which
increases tax revenue without necessitating an increase in tax rates. High employment eases the fiscal crunch another way too, by reducing the number of
people fully or heavily reliant on public benefits.

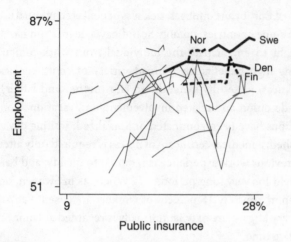

Figure 2.4 Expansive, generous public insurance and high employment. The data points are years, from 1980 to 2015. Solid thick lines: Denmark and Sweden. Dashed thick lines: Finland and Norway. The other countries are Australia, Austria, Belgium, Canada, France, Germany, Ireland, Italy, Japan, Korea (South), Netherlands, New Zealand, Portugal, Spain, Switzerland, United Kingdom, and United States. Public insurance: see Figure 2.1. Employment rate: employed persons aged 25–64 as a share of all persons aged 25–64. Data source: OECD. The lines are loess curves.

Have social democratic employment-promotion policies succeeded? Figure 2.4 once again has public insurance spending on the horizontal axis. The vertical axis has the actual employment rate, rather than policies aimed at boosting that rate.[10] Instead of data for a single point in time, this chart has a line for each country that shows movement over the period from 1980 to 2015. The Nordic countries, highlighted in bold, again are in the upper-right corner. They have been the most successful at achieving and maintaining a large welfare state together with high employment.

How to Identify Social Democratic Capitalism's Effects

How can we assess the hypothesis that social democratic capitalism is the set of policies and institutions that gets us closest to the good society? We look at countries. Examining persons or firms or cities or regions can help, but it won't, in many instances, give us the information we need, because processes at these levels may or may not scale up to full nations.[11]

For countries, the best way to identify causality is via quasi-experimental ("difference in differences") analysis.[12] We measure countries on the hypothesized cause and the outcome at a point in time. Then some countries change more than others on the hypothesized cause; for instance, some countries expand their public insurance programs more than others. Then we compare across the countries to see whether changes in the outcome correlate with changes in the hypothesized cause. This isn't foolproof evidence, but it gets us as close as possible to an experimental design.

Unfortunately, much of the change in public insurance expansiveness and generosity in the world's rich nations occurred prior to the 1980s, and data for many of the outcomes we want in a good society aren't available that far back in time. What we need for a difference-in-differences analysis is sustained, unidirectional changes over time in social policy and differences across countries in the magnitude of that change. It isn't especially helpful to examine year-to-year fluctuations in social program generosity because noteworthy effects on outcomes such as poverty are likely to take a while to show up, and because many things influence short-run changes in outcomes. Instead, we want changes that are large, that are in a single direction (rather than back and forth), that persist for some time, and that vary in size across nations.[13] The 1930s and the 1960s and '70s fit the bill when it comes to public insurance.[14] But we don't have cross-nationally comparable data for those periods on the key outcomes.

The best available option in this circumstance is to turn to other analytical strategies such as static comparison across countries and comparison over time in individual nations.

A Big Welfare State and High Employment Contribute to an "Expanded Rawlsian" Result

In *A Theory of Justice,* John Rawls argued that among the features we should want in a good society, three stand out as especially important: basic liberties, equality of opportunity, and the best possible living standards for the least well-off.[15] I share this view, though I think it needs a clarification and an addition.

Begin with the clarification. For Rawls, basic liberties refer to both democratic political institutions and personal freedoms.[16] All of the world's rich democratic nations have both democratic polities and extensive personal liberties.

Next, the addition. Given what social scientists have learned about loss aversion since *A Theory of Justice* was published in the early 1970s, if Rawls were writing today he likely would include income security as an additional core attribute of a good society. Humans dislike loss, and we're willing to pay substantial sums to avoid it or limit it.[17] As a person's income or assets increase, she will tend to buy more insurance. Similarly, as nations get richer, they tend to allocate a larger portion of their income (GDP) to insurance. Richard Layard puts it as follows: "Many studies have found that a loss hurts roughly twice as much as an equal gain helps. That is why people are so keen to avoid loss, and so unwilling to incur the risk of loss. . . . It is precisely because people hate loss that we have a social safety net, a welfare state. People want the security that these entities provide. . . . If security is what most of us desperately want, it should be a major goal for society. The rich have quite a lot of it and the poor less. A happy society requires a lot of it all round."[18]

We can think of this set of features—a democratic political system, basic personal liberties, the best possible living standards for the least well-off, income security, and equality of opportunity—as an "expanded Rawlsian" result. Social democratic capitalism seems well designed to achieve these aims. Does it succeed in doing so?

Let's begin with the living standards of the least well-off. Even in countries that are quite rich, many people have limited earnings from work. Government transfer programs that cover more risks and do so more generously are likely to boost their income.

The vertical axis of Figure 2.5 has a widely used indicator of the living standards of the least well-off: the relative poverty rate. This is calculated, for each country, as the share of people living in households with an income below 60 percent of the country's median income. On the horizontal axis is public

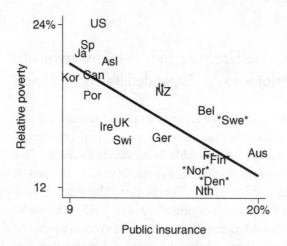

Figure 2.5 Public insurance and relative poverty. Relative poverty: share of persons in households with income below 60 percent of the country's median. 2010–2016. Data sources: Luxembourg Income Study; OECD. Public insurance: public social expenditures as a share of GDP, adjusted for the elderly population share and the unemployment rate. I also subtract spending on health and active labor market policy; because these are services rather than transfers, they aren't counted in household incomes and thus won't affect the poverty rate. 1980–2015. Data source: OECD. The asterisks highlight the Nordic countries. "Asl" is Australia; "Aus" is Austria. The line is a linear regression line. The correlation is –.74.

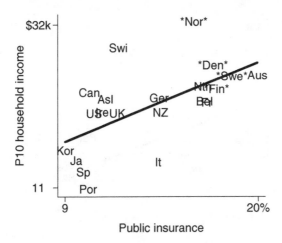

Figure 2.6 Public insurance and 10th-percentile household income. 10th-percentile household income: posttransfer-posttax income. 2010–2016. The incomes are adjusted for household size and then rescaled to reflect a three-person household, adjusted for inflation, and converted to US dollars using purchasing power parities. "k" = thousand. Public insurance: see Figure 2.5. Data sources: Luxembourg Income Study; OECD. "Asl" is Australia; "Aus" is Austria. The correlation is +.59.

insurance expenditures as a share of GDP. (Here I subtract expenditures on health and active labor market policy; these are services, which aren't counted as income and thus can't affect the poverty rate.) There is a strong correlation; countries with a bigger welfare state tend to have lower relative poverty rates.

Some think the living standards of the least well-off are best assessed via an absolute measure, rather than a relative one.[19] The vertical axis in the next chart, Figure 2.6, shows the income of a household at the 10th percentile of the distribution (90 percent of households have larger incomes, and 10 percent have smaller ones). The incomes are adjusted for cost-of-living differences across countries. The incomes of low-end households tend to be higher in nations with more expansive and generous social programs.

A more direct indicator of material well-being is people's responses to questions about their living conditions. Since 2007, the Gallup World Poll has asked a representative sample of adults in each country whether there has been a time in the past year when they didn't have enough money to (a) buy food that they or their family needed or (b) provide adequate shelter or housing. On the vertical axis in Figure 2.7 is the average share of households responding "yes" to these two questions. The share ranges from 5 percent in Denmark to 15 percent in the United States and 20 percent in South Korea.[20] Here too we see a tendency for countries with a bigger welfare state to do better.[21]

So all three indicators of the living standards of the least well-off—the relative poverty rate, 10th-percentile household incomes, and material

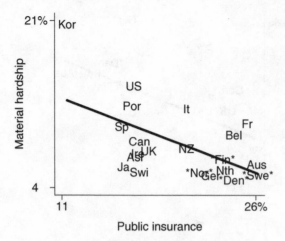

Figure 2.7 Public insurance and material hardship. Material hardship: average share of adults responding yes to the question "Have there been times in the past 12 months when you did not have enough money to buy food that you or your family needed?" and the question "Have there been times in the past 12 months when you did not have enough money to provide adequate shelter or housing for you and your family?" 2007–2017. Data source: Gallup World Poll, via the Legatum Prosperity Index. Public insurance: see Figure 2.1. The asterisks highlight the Nordic countries. "Asl" is Australia; "Aus" is Austria. The line is a linear regression line. The correlation is –.55.

deprivation—suggest that things are better where the welfare state is larger and more generous. This correlation reflects a causal effect.[22] One way we know this is because of over-time patterns. In recent decades increases in income for the least well-off in the rich democratic nations have tended to come mainly from increases in government transfers, not from rising earnings.[23]

A common worry is that government transfer programs will discourage employment, reducing people's market incomes, so that these programs end up reducing poverty that they themselves caused.[24] But while some transfer recipients do work less than they otherwise might, this effect tends to be outweighed by the income boost from the transfers, so the poorest are better off than they would be in the absence of these programs. And countries with greater welfare state expansiveness and generosity don't tend to have lower employment rates.[25]

Another potential problem is that heavy public spending on services might crowd out spending on transfers. Transfers are counted as income whereas services aren't, so crowding out would hinder the ability of a big welfare state to reduce poverty.[26] That hasn't happened, however. Many of the countries that are the biggest spenders on public services have continued to have generous transfer programs.[27]

So a big welfare state helps the least well-off. Does employment help too? People at the low end don't automatically benefit from a higher employment

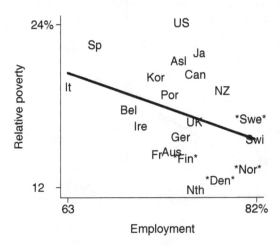

Figure 2.8 Employment and relative poverty. Relative poverty: see Figure 2.5. Employment rate: employed persons aged 25–64 as a share of the population aged 25–64. 2000–2016. Data source: OECD. The asterisks highlight the Nordic countries. "Asl" is Australia; "Aus" is Austria. The line is a linear regression line. The correlation is –.36.

rate.[28] They could end up worse off in a relative sense if the additional jobs go mainly to persons in households that already had middle or high incomes. Even in an absolute sense there may be no gain if a person shifts from receipt of a government transfer to a job with low pay. In the United States, a steady rise in the employment rate during the 1980s and 1990s produced very little increase in the earnings of households in the bottom fifth of incomes.[29] The same appears to have been true for Germany in the 2000s and 2010s.[30] On average, however, employment does help the least well-off. In Figures 2.8, 2.9, and 2.10, we see that nations with higher employment rates tend to have lower relative poverty rates, higher 10th-percentile household incomes, and less material hardship. Increases in employment rates have played a key role in rising low-end incomes in Ireland, the Netherlands, and Spain. And when employment has increased within countries over time, poverty rates have tended to fall.[31]

Next, let's consider income security, which refers mainly to avoidance of large income reductions. A helpful measure here is the average decrease in household income from one year to the next when an individual in the household experiences a large earnings decline. Suppose a person suffers a large earnings drop because she retires, loses her job, or takes time off to deal with a health problem or to have a child. If she is the sole earner in the household and nothing else changes, the household's income will decline by the same amount as the individual earnings decline. But if there is another earner in the household, the fall in household income will be smaller (as a share of the previous year's income). And if the other earner increases his work hours or gets a pay raise, the

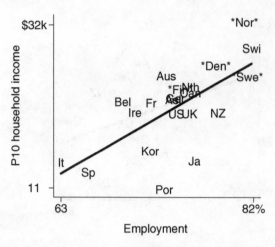

Figure 2.9 Employment and 10th-percentile household income. 10th-percentile household income: see Figure 2.6. Employment rate: see Figure 2.8. The asterisks highlight the Nordic countries. "Asl" is Australia; "Aus" is Austria. The line is a linear regression line. The correlation is +.67.

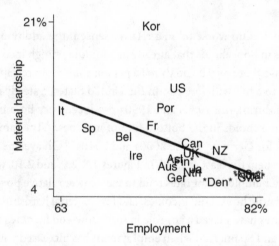

Figure 2.10 Employment and material hardship. Material hardship: see Figure 2.7. Employment rate: see Figure 2.8. The asterisks highlight the Nordic countries. "Asl" is Australia; "Aus" is Austria. The line is a linear regression line. The correlation is –.50.

household's income might not decline at all. The same is true if the household receives unemployment compensation, sickness or disability benefit, parental leave payment, a pension, social assistance, or some other public insurance program payment.

The vertical axis of Figure 2.11 shows the average decline in household income when a member experiences an earnings decline of 20 percent or more from one year to the next. Boosting economic security is a core objective of welfare state programs, so it isn't surprising to see that average income decline tends to be smaller in nations with more expansive and generous public insurance.[32] Income decline also tends to be smaller in countries with a higher employment rate, as we see in Figure 2.12.

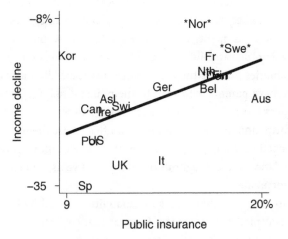

Figure 2.11 Public insurance and income decline. Income decline: average year-to-year household disposable income decline for households in which an individual experiences an earnings decline of 20 percent or more. 2005–2010. Data source: Boris Cournède, Paula Garda, Peter Hoeller, and Volker Ziemann, "Effects of Pro-Growth Policies on the Economic Stability of Firms, Workers and Households," *OECD Economic Policy Papers* 12, 2015, figure 18, using CNEF, ECHP, EU-SILC, and OECD data. Public insurance: see Figure 2.5. The asterisks highlight the Nordic countries. "Asl" is Australia; "Aus" is Austria. The line is a linear regression line. The correlation is +.53.

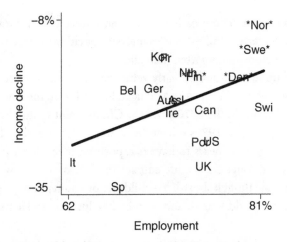

Figure 2.12 Employment and income decline. Income decline: see Figure 2.11. Employment rate: see Figure 2.8. The asterisks highlight the Nordic countries. "Asl" is Australia; "Aus" is Austria. The line is a linear regression line. The correlation is +.44.

The story thus far: A big welfare state and high employment boost the living standards of the poor and improve income security. The Nordic countries, which have generous public insurance programs and high employment rates, have tended to do especially well on these two outcomes.

Let's now look at equality of opportunity. The feature of social democratic capitalism that's most likely to enhance equality of opportunity is provision of accessible, affordable, high-quality early education (childcare and preschool). It does so by improving the capabilities of children from less advantaged homes, pulling those capabilities closer to those of children in the middle and at the top.[33]

Some children have parents who read to them, instill helpful traits such as self-control and persistence, shield them from stress and physical harm, expose them to new information and learning opportunities, assist them with school work, utilize connections to help them get out of trouble or into a good job, remain in a stable relationship throughout the childhood years, and so on. Other children are less fortunate.

Schools help to offset the differences in capabilities caused by families. We know this from two pieces of evidence. First, at kindergarten entry children from poor homes tend to have much lower measurable skills than children from affluent homes. Given the huge variation in home and neighborhood circumstances, we would expect that gap to continue to widen throughout childhood. But it doesn't; it's about the same size at the end of high school as at the start of kindergarten. This tells us that schools have an equalizing effect.[34] Second, during summer vacations, when children are out of school, those from lower-income families tend to fall farther behind compared to those from higher-income families.[35]

Having children enter school earlier in life can reduce the disparity when they arrive for kindergarten. Indeed, some analysts conclude that the impact of schooling is larger before kindergarten than after.[36]

The effects of three high-quality early education programs in the United States—the Perry Preschool Project in Michigan in the 1960s, the Abecedarian Project in North Carolina in the 1970s, and the Child-Parent Center Education Program in Chicago in the 1970s—have been tracked into early adulthood or beyond. Each program appears to have had positive effects for low-income children that persist throughout the life course. That's also the case with Head Start, with a large-scale though short-lived childcare program put in place in the United States during World War II, and with early education in Denmark and Norway.[37]

For the Perry and Chicago programs, gains in test scores faded away but there were long-term gains in labor market success and other outcomes. The same appears to be true for Head Start and for Norway's universal early education program. This suggests that the key improvement is in noncognitive skills rather than in cognitive ability. On the other hand, the Abecedarian Project yielded better long-term behavioral outcomes and sustained gains in test scores. A natural experiment in Denmark also found lasting test-score gains. So early education's benefits for children from less advantaged homes may come via both cognitive and noncognitive skills.

An especially informative test is one that looks at differences across countries in changes over time.[38] If early education helps to equalize opportunity, we would expect a greater equalization over time in countries that adopted universal early education, such as Sweden and Denmark, than in countries that didn't. Gøsta Esping-Andersen has examined the data. He concludes that this is indeed what happened:

> I use the IALS [International Adult Literacy Survey] data to compare social origin effects on the probability of completing upper-level secondary education across birth cohorts. . . . The analyses follow three cohorts, the oldest born in the late 1940s and early 1950s, the youngest in the 1970s. And I compare "social inheritance" trends in the three Nordic countries with Germany, the UK, and the US. The results are very consistent with a "constant flux" scenario in Germany, the UK, and the US. In these countries we see no decline whatsoever in the impact of origins on educational attainment across the cohorts—which is to say, over a half century. . . . In contrast, there is a very significant decline in the association in all three Scandinavian countries, and the drop occurs primarily in the youngest cohort—the first to enjoy near-universal participation in childcare.[39]

There is no straightforward way to measure opportunity, so social scientists tend to infer from outcomes, such as earnings or income. If we find that a particular group fares worse than others, we suspect a barrier to opportunity. It isn't ironclad proof, but it's the best we can do. To assess equality of opportunity among people from different family backgrounds, a common indicator is relative intergenerational mobility—a person's position on the earnings ladder relative to her or his parents' position.[40] If most people end up in a position similar to that of their parents, opportunity probably isn't very equal.

The vertical axis in Figure 2.13 shows the correlation between the relative position of fathers in the earnings distribution and the relative position of their sons at a similar point in the life course. Smaller numbers, which are higher on the axis, indicate a weaker correlation, or greater intergenerational mobility; this suggests that children's earnings aren't determined by the earnings of their parents, which implies greater equality of opportunity. The horizontal axis in the figure shows public expenditures on early education. There is a positive

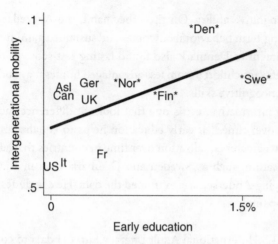

Figure 2.13 Early education and intergenerational mobility. Intergenerational mobility: correlation between the earnings of parents and those of their children, with axis values reversed. Data source: John Ermisch et al., eds., *From Parents to Children*, Russell Sage Foundation, 2012, figure 2.1. Early education: expenditures as a share of GDP. 1980–1995. Data source: OECD, Social Expenditures Database. The asterisks highlight the Nordic countries. "Asl" is Australia. The line is a linear regression line. The correlation is +.60.

association across the countries: those spending more on early education tend to have greater intergenerational mobility.

We can think of opportunity as individuals' capability to choose, act, and accomplish—what Isaiah Berlin called "positive liberty" and Amartya Sen has labeled "real freedom."[41] While critics of big government tend to assume that public social programs reduce freedom, many of these programs are capability-enhancing. They boost people's cognitive and noncognitive skills, increase their employment options, ensure that hard times do minimal damage, and reduce dependence on family and friends. More than a century ago, John Stuart Mill recognized that true freedom to lead the kind of life we want requires education, health, and economic security.[42] More recently, Anu Partanen has highlighted this point in a comparison of her native Finland with her adopted country, the United States. Observing that many Americans don't have access to high quality, affordable health insurance, childcare, housing in good school districts, college, and eldercare, Partanen notes that this diminishes not only Americans' economic security but also their freedom:

> Most people, including myself, assumed that part of what made the United States a great country, and such an exceptional one, was that you could live your life relatively unencumbered by the downside of a traditional, old-fashioned society: dependency on the people you

happened to be stuck with. In America you had the liberty to express your individuality and choose your own community. This would allow you to interact with family, neighbors, and fellow citizens on the basis of who you were, rather than on what you were obligated to do or expected to be according to old-fashioned thinking. The longer I lived in America . . . the more puzzled I grew. For it was exactly those key benefits of modernity—freedom, personal independence, and opportunity—that seemed, from my outsider's perspective, in a thousand small ways to be surprisingly missing from American life today. . . . In order to compete and to survive, the Americans I encountered and read about were . . . beholden to their spouses, parents, children, colleagues, and bosses in ways that constrained their own liberty.[43]

Here too we have no direct measure. A useful indirect measure comes from a question asked by the Gallup World Poll: "Are you satisfied or dissatisfied with your freedom to choose what you do with your life?" We can treat the share responding "satisfied" as an indicator of equality of opportunity, of the degree to which capabilities extend widely across the population. This share is on the vertical axis of Figure 2.14, with public insurance expenditures on the horizontal axis. The pattern across countries is consistent with the hypothesis that an expansive and generous welfare state expands opportunity.

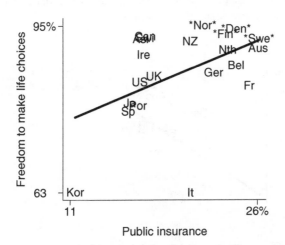

Figure 2.14 Public insurance and freedom to make life choices. Freedom to make life choices: share responding "satisfied" to the question "Are you satisfied or dissatisfied with your freedom to choose what you do with your life?" Average over 2005–2016. Data source: Gallup World Poll, via the *World Happiness Report 2017*, online appendix. Public insurance: see Figure 2.1. The asterisks highlight the Nordic countries. "Asl" is Australia; "Aus" is Austria. The line is a linear regression line. The correlation is +.46.

Employment also should help to equalize opportunity. Where individuals from poor backgrounds have a better chance to get a foothold in the labor market, their disadvantage stemming from parents, school quality, connections, and related factors matters less. Figures 2.15 and 2.16 show that employment rates are correlated with greater intergenerational earnings mobility and with more people feeling satisfied with their freedom to make life choices.

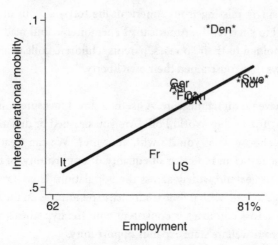

Figure 2.15 Employment and intergenerational mobility. Intergenerational mobility: see Figure 2.13. Employment: see Figure 2.8. The asterisks highlight the Nordic countries. "Asl" is Australia. The line is a linear regression line. The correlation is +.68.

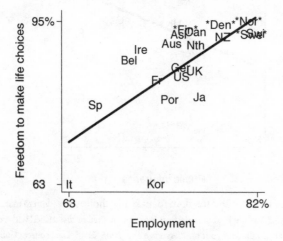

Figure 2.16 Employment and freedom to make life choices. Freedom to make life choices: see Figure 2.14. Employment: see Figure 2.8. The asterisks highlight the Nordic countries. "Asl" is Australia; "Aus" is Austria. The line is a linear regression line. The correlation is +.68.

We should be cautious in drawing inferences from the associations in these equality of opportunity charts. The number of countries with intergenerational mobility data is small, and the data may not be as comparable across nations as we would like.[44] Still, the cross-country patterns are consistent with the hypothesis and with other evidence suggesting a beneficial effect of high-quality, affordable early education, of broader welfare state expansiveness and generosity, and of higher employment rates.

Let's step back and take stock. What have we discovered? All of the world's rich longstanding-democratic nations have democratic polities and extensive personal liberties. The other elements of an expanded Rawlsian result are a high standard of living for the least well-off, income security, and equality of opportunity. The patterns in Figures 2.5 through 2.16 suggest that a large welfare state and high employment help to achieve these outcomes. In statistical analyses not shown here, the associations we see in these charts persist when adjusted for country affluence, the foreign-born share of the population, and collective bargaining coverage.[45] The conclusion that these relationships are causal isn't a slam dunk, because, as I noted earlier, we don't have over-time data that would allow a better test of causality. But the links are compelling on theoretical grounds, and the evidence we do have is supportive.

Is it a mistake to conclude that *both* public insurance programs and employment matter? Might it instead be the case that countries with big welfare states also tend to have higher employment rates, with one or the other doing all of the causal work, rather than both? No. For one thing, welfare state size and employment rates aren't correlated across nations; as we can see in Figure 2.4 above, the Nordic countries are high on both, but some countries are high on one and low on the other. Also, statistical analyses suggest that welfare state size and employment have independent effects on expanded Rawlsian outcomes.[46]

Are the beneficial effects of public insurance and those of high employment interdependent? In other words, does a country need to have both in order to get the benefits of either one? Again, no. The patterns in Figures 2.5 through 2.16 suggest that public insurance helps on its own and so does employment. Social democratic capitalism isn't an interdependent configuration (a "gestalt"). It's a collection of helpful institutions and policies.

How large are the benefits of a big welfare state and high employment? For public insurance programs, the share of GDP spent by nations at the high end is about 10 percentage points greater than the share spent by nations at the low end. Statistical analyses reported in Figure 2.17 suggest that in a country at the high end, the relative poverty rate is expected to be about 7 percentage points lower than in a country at the low end, the income of a 10th-percentile household $7,000 higher, the share of the population experiencing material hardship 4 percentage points lower, the household income decline where an individual

	Public Insurance	Employment
Relative poverty	-7%	-3%
P10 household income	+$7,000	+$10,000
Material hardship	-4%	-6%
Income decline	-10%	-10%
Freedom to make life choices	+7%	+20%

Figure 2.17 Estimated difference in outcome for a country at the high end on public insurance or employment versus a country at the low end. % = percentage points. "+" indicates that a country at the high end on public insurance or employment tends to be higher on the outcome than a country at the low end; "–" indicates that a country at the high end tends to be lower. Public insurance: see Figure 2.5. Employment: see Figure 2.8. Relative poverty: see Figure 2.5. 10th-percentile household income: see Figure 2.6. Material hardship: see Figure 2.7. Income decline: see Figure 2.11. Freedom to make life choices: see Figure 2.14. These estimates are from regressions using various combinations of public insurance expenditures, employment rate, GDP per capita, foreign-born population share, and collective bargaining coverage as predictors.

experiences a large earnings decline 10 percentage points smaller, and the share of the population satisfied with their freedom to choose what to do with their life 7 percentage points higher. For employment, the counterpart numbers are 3 percentage points for relative poverty, $10,000 for low-end household income, 6 percentage points for material hardship, 10 percentage points for household income decline, and 20 percentage points for freedom to make life choices.

To sum up: Democracy, capitalism, and basic education are common across the affluent democratic world. Social democratic capitalism couples these with a large welfare state and with high employment. In doing so it boosts a country's likelihood of achieving an expanded Rawlsian result.

Tradeoffs?

Most of us want more than "expanded Rawls." Even if we agree to privilege democracy, personal liberties, a high living standards floor, income security, and equality of opportunity, we seek additional features in a good society. Does social democratic capitalism get us an expanded Rawlsian result *at the expense of* economic prosperity, community, stable families, good health, happiness, or other desired outcomes?

One tradeoff is baked into the social democratic model: upper-middle-class and rich households forgo cash income in favor of services that they may or may not utilize and in favor of more transfers and services for less well-off households. To fund a big welfare state and employment-oriented services, tax rates need to be fairly high for most of the population. For households in the middle and below, these tax payments are more than offset by the value of services they use and

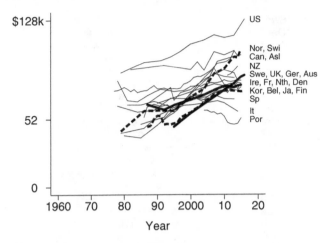

Figure 2.18 Upper-middle-class household income. 90th percentile of the income distribution. Posttransfer-posttax household income. The incomes are adjusted for household size and then rescaled to reflect a three-person household, adjusted for inflation, and converted to US dollars using purchasing power parities. "k" = thousand. Data sources: Luxembourg Income Study; OECD. The lines are loess curves. Solid thick lines: Denmark and Sweden. Dashed thick lines: Finland and Norway. "Asl" is Australia; "Aus" is Austria.

transfers they receive. For those in the top quarter or so (the exact cut-off point varies), particularly those with children, there may be considerable benefit to the services and transfers provided—childcare, preschool, child allowance, free or low-cost college, and more. But most people with high incomes and few or no children will pay a good bit more in taxes than they receive in services and benefits.

The picture in Figure 2.18 is consistent with this tradeoff expectation. It shows household incomes at the 90th percentile of the distribution (90 percent of households have incomes that are lower, and 10 percent have incomes that are higher). Setting Norway aside, we see that incomes for this group in Sweden, Denmark, and Finland are notably lower than in the United States, Switzerland, Canada, and Australia.

What about other tradeoffs? Do countries with social democratic policies and institutions fare poorly when it comes to other things we desire in a good society? Do they have less freedom? Slower economic growth? More government debt? Weaker families or communities? Poorer health? Less happiness?

In assessing the evidence, I'll sometimes use the Nordic countries as stand-ins for social democratic capitalism. But mostly I'll use a social democratic capitalism index, which is shown in Figure 2.19. The index is a composite of four indicators. Two measure the size and generosity of public insurance programs. One of these is public expenditures on social programs as a share of GDP, with an adjustment for the size of the elderly population and the unemployment rate (see Figures 2.1 and 2.58). The other is a measure of replacement rates for

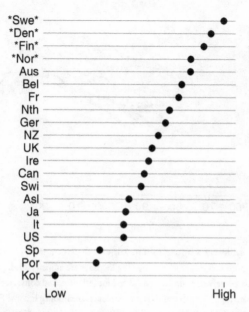

Figure 2.19 Social democratic capitalism index. Average standard deviation score on four indicators: public expenditures on social programs as a share of GDP, replacement rates for major public transfer programs, public expenditures on employment-oriented services, and modest regulation of product and labor markets. The data cover the period 1980–2015. For details and data sources, see Figures 2.1–2.3 and 2.57–2.60. The asterisks highlight the Nordic countries. "Asl" is Australia; "Aus" is Austria.

major public income transfer programs at three stages in the life cycle: child-hood, working-age, and retirement years (Figure 2.57). The other two indicators are for policies that aim to boost employment. One is public expenditures on employment-oriented services (Figures 2.1 and 2.59). The other is modest regulation of product and labor markets (Figures 2.2 and 2.60). I convert each of these four measures to a common metric (standard deviation units) and then calculate the average for each nation over the period from 1980 to 2015.[47]

The country ranking is consistent with what we would expect. The Nordics score highest, with Sweden and Denmark ahead of Finland and Norway. They are followed by five continental European nations that have big welfare states but less public spending on employment-promoting services and heavier regulation of product and labor markets: Austria, Belgium, France, the Netherlands, and Germany. In the lower half of scores are Switzerland, Japan, and the six English-speaking countries, which have smaller welfare states and limited public spending on employment-oriented services. They are joined by the three southern European nations and South Korea, which have medium-sized or small welfare states, little employment-promoting service spending, and heavy product and labor market regulation.

The most straightforward way to assess possible tradeoffs is to see whether nations that score higher on the social democratic capitalism index tend to do worse on other outcomes that we want in a good society. In order to allow you to see the data, I'll show a large number of graphs in the following pages. (If this isn't your cup of tea, just skip over them. I explain what they tell us in the text.) What we're looking for here isn't evidence that social democratic capitalism produces better outcomes; we simply want to know whether or not it contributes to worse outcomes.

Let's begin with freedom. A key element of social democratic capitalism is modest, rather than heavy, regulation of product and labor markets, so with respect to economic freedom the model embraces liberty rather than constricting it.[48] How about personal freedom? One line of conservative thinking, best expressed in Milton Friedman's books *Capitalism and Freedom* and *Free to Choose*, suggests that a big welfare state, and the taxes needed to fund it, will impinge on personal liberty.[49] We saw earlier that social democratic capitalism appears to be conducive to people's ability to choose, act, and accomplish, which is sometimes labeled "positive freedom." At issue here is "negative freedom"—an absence of restrictions on speech, religion, and so on.

Researchers at a libertarian think tank, the Cato Institute, have assembled a "personal freedom index" that measures legal protection, security, freedom of movement, freedom of religion, freedom of association, assembly, and civil society, freedom of expression, and freedom in relationships. Figure 2.20 shows

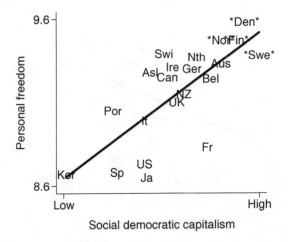

Figure 2.20 Social democratic capitalism and personal freedom. Personal freedom: average score for rule of law, security and safety, freedom of movement, religious freedom, freedom of association, freedom of expression and information, and freedom of identity and relationships. Scale is 0 to 10. 2008–2014. Data source: Ian Vasquez and Tanja Porcnik, *The Human Freedom Index*, Cato Institute. Social democratic capitalism: see Figure 2.19. The asterisks highlight the Nordic countries. "Asl" is Australia; "Aus" is Austria. The line is a linear regression line.

that nations with social democratic policies tend to have more personal freedom, not less.

Next let's look at economic growth. Generous benefits and services, and the high tax rates needed to fund them, can reduce the financial incentive to innovate, invest, create and expand businesses, increase skills, and work hard. At some level of taxes or government expenditures, such responses will be sufficiently widespread and large that they reduce growth. The question is where the tipping point lies, and whether or not existing nations have reached that point.

Over the medium and long run, innovation is the key driver of economic growth. Innovation isn't easy to measure, particularly when the aim is to compare across countries. The best indicator we have is expert judgments. Two influential country rankings are by the Global Competitiveness Report and the Global Innovation Index. The vertical axis in Figure 2.21 shows the average for each nation on these two rankings as of 2015. Finland and Sweden are near the top of the rankings, with Denmark not far behind. Norway is in the middle of the pack. Social democratic capitalist countries don't appear to be lacking in innovation.

The vertical axis in Figure 2.22 has economic growth rates over the period from 1979 to 2016. The pattern suggests no association. Countries with social democratic policies have grown, on average, no slower than others.

Figure 2.23 looks at the long run in a single country: Denmark. In order to do so I switch from the social democratic capitalism index to public social

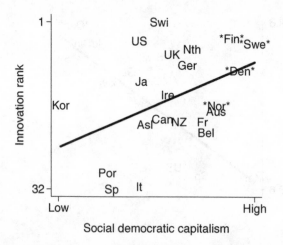

Figure 2.21 Social democratic capitalism and innovation. Innovation rank: average innovation ranking for 2015 according to the Global Competitiveness Report and the Global Innovation Index. Data sources: World Economic Forum, *The Global Competitiveness Report 2015–2016*, pillar 12, table 5; Cornell University, INSEAD, and WIPO, *The Global Innovation Index 2015*, p. xxx. Social democratic capitalism: see Figure 2.19. The asterisks highlight the Nordic countries. "Asl" is Australia; "Aus" is Austria. The line is a linear regression line.

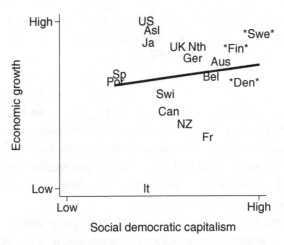

Figure 2.22 Social democratic capitalism and economic growth. Economic growth: average annual rate of change in real GDP per capita, adjusted for initial level (catch-up). 1979 to 2016. Data source: OECD. The line is a linear regression line. Ireland, South Korea, and Norway are outliers and so are omitted. Social democratic capitalism: see Figure 2.19. The asterisks highlight the Nordic countries. "Asl" is Australia; "Aus" is Austria. The line is a linear regression line.

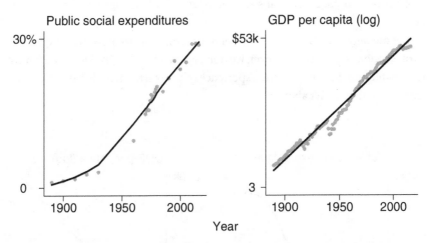

Figure 2.23 Public social expenditures and economic growth in Denmark. Public social expenditures: share of GDP. Data source: Esteban Ortiz-Ospina and Max Roser, "Public Spending," *Our World in Data*, using data for 1890–1930 from Peter Lindert, *Growing Public*, volume 1, Cambridge University Press, 2004, data for 1960–1979 from OECD, "Social Expenditure 1960–1990: Problems of Growth and Control," OECD Social Policy Studies, 1985, and data for 1980ff from OECD, Social Expenditures Database. The line is a loess curve. GDP per capita: natural log of inflation-adjusted GDP per capita. A log scale is used to focus on rates of change. "k" = thousand. The vertical axis does not begin at zero. The line is a linear regression line; it represents a constant rate of economic growth. Data source: Maddison Project Database 2018, rug.nl/ggdc.

expenditures as a share of GDP, a measure of public insurance expansiveness and generosity. Over the past century Denmark's welfare state grew from non-existent to quite large, as the chart on the left indicates. The chart on the right shows the log of GDP per capita. The fact that the data points form a straight line suggests that the Danish economy has grown at a constant rate. If social democratic policies were a hindrance to economic growth, we would expect Denmark's growth rate to have slowed as a result of its welfare state's massive expansion. But that didn't happen. As we see in Figure 2.24, the same is true for Sweden, which, like Denmark, shifted from a nonexistent welfare state to a large one. Figure 2.25 shows that it's also true for the United States, where the welfare state grew from nothing to medium-size.[50]

We also can compare changes across countries. If social democratic capitalism is bad for economic growth, nations with a bigger increase in social democratic policies should experience a smaller increase, or a larger decline, in economic growth. On the vertical axis in Figure 2.26 is change in the average rate of economic growth from the period 1950–1973 (the post–World War II "golden age") to the period 1979–2016. On the horizontal axis is change between these two periods in public social expenditures as a share of GDP. Once again the data give us no reason to conclude that social democratic policies are bad for economic growth.

Let me reiterate: There is *some* level of government size beyond which it will harm economic growth. However, we don't know what that level is, and the most reasonable conclusion from the experience of the world's rich democratic countries is that they aren't above it.

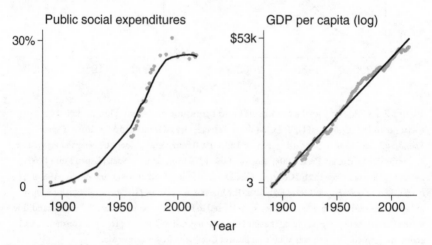

Figure 2.24 Public social expenditures and economic growth in Sweden. For data description and sources, see Figure 2.23.

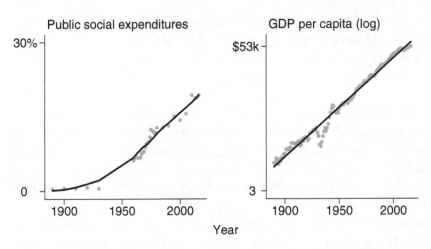

Figure 2.25 Public social expenditures and economic growth in the United States. For data description and sources, see Figure 2.23.

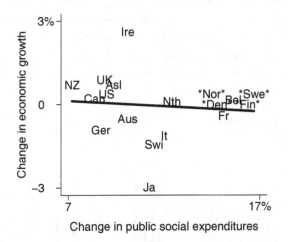

Figure 2.26 Change in public social expenditures and change in economic growth. Economic growth: average annual rate of change in real GDP per capita, adjusted for initial level (catch-up). 1979–2016 minus 1950–1973. Data source: Maddison Project Database 2018, rug.nl/ ggdc. Public social expenditures: share of GDP. 1979–2016 minus 1960. Data source: Esteban Ortiz-Ospina and Max Roser, "Public Spending," *Our World in Data*, using data for 1960–1979 from OECD, "Social Expenditure 1960–1990: Problems of Growth and Control," OECD Social Policy Studies, 1985, and data for 1980ff from OECD, Social Expenditures Database. The asterisks highlight the Nordic countries. "Asl" is Australia; "Aus" is Austria. The line is a linear regression line.

Does social democratic capitalism *boost* economic growth? There are several reasons why it might. By providing an array of cushions for people who fail, it may encourage entrepreneurship. It facilitates employment by women and persons from less-advantaged backgrounds. It allows unemployed workers more time to reskill and choose a productive job. It tends to reduce income in-equality.[51] I don't, however, see support for this hypothesis in the cross-country or over-time data. Social democratic capitalism seems to be no worse for ec-onomic growth than other institutional and policy configurations, but also no better.

In addition to economic growth, we want a reasonable degree of mac-roeconomic stability. The two biggest economic crises of the past century were driven by financial bubbles that popped and spilled over to the broader economy, wreaking havoc on the lives of hundreds of millions of people and causing not just temporary agony but also long-term financial and psycho-logical scarring.[52] Financial crises occur frequently in capitalist economies, as we see in Figure 2.27.[53] However, social democratic policies don't ap-pear to make rich nations more likely to experience such crises, as Figure 2.28 shows.

Let's turn from economic growth and stability to employment. A big welfare state could depress employment by allowing people to live off transfer income rather than earnings. But high employment is a core aim of social democratic capitalism, so policy makers take steps to avoid such disincentives and to offset them with employment-oriented services and modest product and labor market regulations. Figure 2.29 suggests a positive association between social demo-cratic capitalism and employment rates.

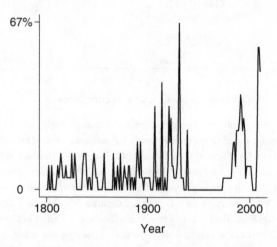

Figure 2.27 Share of rich democratic nations in banking crisis. The countries are Australia, Austria, Belgium, Canada, Denmark, Finland, France, Germany, Ireland, Italy, Japan, Korea (South), Netherlands, New Zealand, Norway, Portugal, Spain, Sweden, Switzerland, United Kingdom, United States. Data source: Carmen M. Reinhart and Kenneth Rogoff, "Dates for Banking Crises, Currency Crashes, Sovereign Domestic or External Default (or Restructuring), Inflation Crises, and Stock Market Crashes (Varieties)," carmenreinhart.com/data.

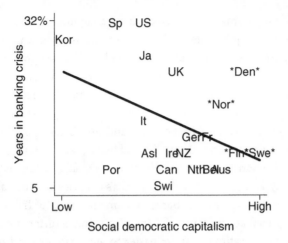

Figure 2.28 Social democratic capitalism and frequency of banking crises. Years in banking crisis: share of years, 1973–2010. Data source: Carmen M. Reinhart and Kenneth Rogoff, "Dates for Banking Crises, Currency Crashes, Sovereign Domestic or External Default (or Restructuring), Inflation Crises, and Stock Market Crashes (Varieties)," carmenreinhart.com/data. Social democratic capitalism: see Figure 2.19. The asterisks highlight the Nordic countries. "Asl" is Australia; "Aus" is Austria. The line is a linear regression line.

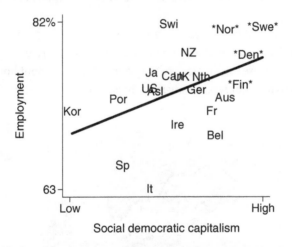

Figure 2.29 Social democratic capitalism and employment. Employment: employed persons aged 25–64 as a share of all persons aged 25–64. 2000–2016. Data source: OECD. Social democratic capitalism: see Figure 2.19. The asterisks highlight the Nordic countries. "Asl" is Australia; "Aus" is Austria. The line is a linear regression line.

Social democratic policies are geared to boost employment across the entire economy, not in each and every geographic area. They don't automatically help places that experience rapid, large-scale job loss—a phenomenon that has become relatively common in the rich democratic countries over the past generation. Employment decline can have a significant ripple effect on small cities and towns. Job losses reduce household income, causing people to cut back on purchases. As a result, retail employers, a key potential source of work for those who have been laid off, are less likely to be able to hire new employees, which lengthens unemployment spells, which further reduces consumer spending.[54]

This problem has contributed to the rise of anti-immigrant "populist" parties in the rich democratic countries. In the United States, worry about jobs was, it appears, one of the contributors to the election of Donald Trump as president in 2016. One analysis found that across America's counties an especially strong predictor of a shift in voting from Barack Obama in 2012 to Trump in 2016 was the share of jobs that are "routine"—those in manufacturing, sales, clerical work, and related occupations that are easier to automate or send offshore.[55] Across Europe, experience of unemployment and exposure to globalization are correlated with support for populist parties.[56]

Decline of manufacturing jobs has been an important source of local job loss. This decline has been a steady one in all affluent democratic nations since the early 1970s, as Figure 2.30 shows. Countries that more fully embrace social democratic capitalism have deindustrialized, but no more rapidly or extensively than others.

One reason we care about economic growth is that it can boost incomes and living standards. As we saw earlier, welfare states that are more expansive and generous tend to increase the incomes of the poor.[57] But what about households in the middle, who may not receive any more in government transfers than they

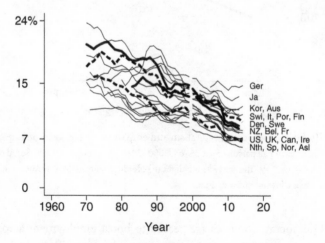

Figure 2.30 Manufacturing employment. Share of the population aged 15–64. The break in the series is due to a change in measurement. Data source: OECD. Solid thick lines: Denmark and Sweden. Dashed thick lines: Finland and Norway. "Asl" is Australia; "Aus" is Austria.

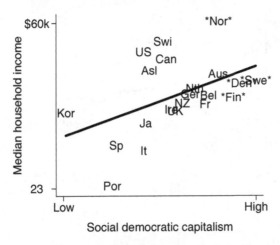

Figure 2.31 Social democratic capitalism and median household income. Median household income: posttransfer-posttax income. 2010–2016. The incomes are adjusted for household size and then rescaled to reflect a three-person household, adjusted for inflation, and converted to US dollars using purchasing power parities. "k" = thousand. Social democratic capitalism: see Figure 2.19. The asterisks highlight the Nordic countries. "Asl" is Australia; "Aus" is Austria. The line is a linear regression line.

pay in taxes? If a large share of economic growth is grabbed by those at the top of the income ladder, or wasted by public-sector bureaucrats, less will be available for households in the middle.[58] Median household income gives us a picture of how those in the middle are faring. The cross-country pattern in Figure 2.31 suggests no reason to think that social democratic policies are bad for middle-class incomes.

How does social democratic capitalism fare when it comes to health outcomes? Life expectancy has increased at about the same pace in all of the rich democratic nations over the past half century—apart from the United States, which has lagged behind in recent decades.[59] Figure 2.32 shows that three of the four Nordic countries are in the middle of the life expectancy pack. Denmark is toward the low end, probably due to the fact that smoking has declined less in Denmark than elsewhere.[60] A helpful complementary indicator is "healthy life expectancy," which is an estimate of how many years a person will live without limitations on usual activities. Norway and Sweden do particularly well here, while Denmark and Finland are toward the bottom, as we see in Figure 2.33. All told, it looks very unlikely that social democratic capitalism has impeded good health outcomes.

Housing unaffordability in large cities is an increasingly important problem faced by rich nations. Economic and social developments have made cities more attractive places to live. Crime rates, a major worry in the 1970s and 1980s, have fallen significantly. Globalization has expanded the quantity and quality of eating

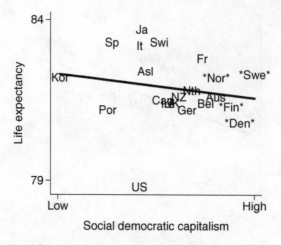

Figure 2.32 Social democratic capitalism and life expectancy. Life expectancy: years of life expectancy at birth. 2014. Data source: OECD. Social democratic capitalism: see Figure 2.19. The asterisks highlight the Nordic countries. "Asl" is Australia; "Aus" is Austria. The line is a linear regression line.

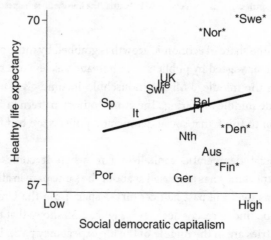

Figure 2.33 Social democratic capitalism and healthy life expectancy. Healthy life expectancy: expected years of life without limitations on usual activities. At birth. 2014. These data are available only for European countries, so Australia, Canada, Japan, Korea, New Zealand, and the United States are missing. Data source: OECD, *Health at a Glance: Europe, 2012.* Social democratic capitalism: see Figure 2.19. The line is a linear regression line. The asterisks highlight the Nordic countries. "Aus" is Austria.

and entertainment options. Public spaces are now cleaner. Public transportation improvements, ride-sharing services, and enhanced biking and walking options have increased accessibility. Perhaps most important, professional-analytical jobs have grown in number and risen in status and pay, and many of these jobs are located in cities. The problem is that in the most attractive cities, demand for

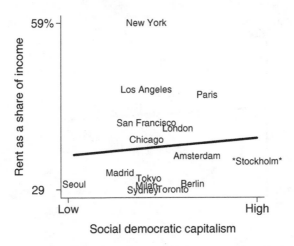

Figure 2.34 Social democratic capitalism and housing cost in large cities. Housing
cost: average rent as a share of median income. 2016. New York is Manhattan only. Data source: Balazs
Szekely, "In Search of the World's Best City for Renters," *RENTCafé* blog, 2017. Social democratic
capitalism: see Figure 2.19. The line is a linear regression line. The asterisks highlight cities in the Nordic
countries.

housing has sharply outstripped supply, which pushes up the cost of buying and
renting. As a result, far fewer people are able to live in these cities than would
like to, and the problem is particularly severe for those with low and middle
incomes. Have social democratic nations exacerbated this problem, perhaps by
overregulating housing construction and thereby limiting its supply?

Figure 2.34 shows average rent as a share of median income in 15 major cities.
The only Nordic city in this group is Stockholm. While Stockholm's housing
is quite expensive, it isn't notably worse than the cities in nations with less of
a social democratic orientation, from the United States and the UK to Japan
and Spain.

What about education? Good-quality schooling is a core element of social
democratic capitalism, but the cushions provided by expansive and generous
public insurance programs could discourage some people from studying hard
or completing a college degree.[61] Also, heavy public spending on childcare and
preschool might divert funds away from K–12 schools and colleges. Do we see
evidence of such tradeoffs? A common measure of national educational performance, shown in Figure 2.35, is fifteen-year-olds' scores on the Program
for International Student Assessment (PISA) reading, math, and science tests.
Finnish students have tended to do quite well on these assessments, though
they've fallen back a bit in recent years. Denmark, Norway, and Sweden have
been average. Sweden's scores were at the bottom of the table in one year, 2012,
but that looks to have been an anomaly. The pattern in the figure suggests no
tradeoff between social democratic policies and good PISA test scores.

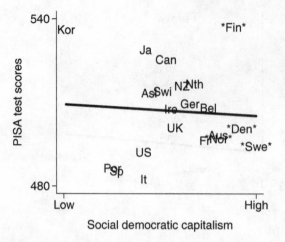

Figure 2.35 Social democratic capitalism and PISA test scores. PISA test scores: average student score on Program for International Assessment (PISA) reading, math, and science tests. 15-year-olds. The PISA tests ask students to solve problems they haven't seen before, to identify patterns that aren't obvious, and to make compelling written arguments. 2006–2015. Data source: OECD. Social democratic capitalism: see Figure 2.19. The asterisks highlight the Nordic countries. "Asl" is Australia; "Aus" is Austria. The line is a linear regression line.

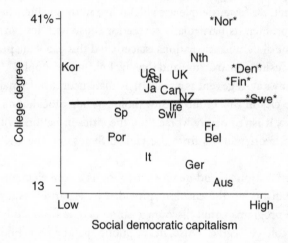

Figure 2.36 Social democratic capitalism and college completion. College degree: bachelor's degree (or bachelor's equivalent) or more. Ages 25 to 34. 1999–2014. Data sources: National Center for Education Statistics, *Digest of Education Statistics*, table 603.30, using OECD data; OECD, *Education at a Glance 2015*, table A1.3a, p. 41. Social democratic capitalism: see Figure 2.19. The asterisks highlight the Nordic countries. "Asl" is Australia; "Aus" is Austria. The line is a linear regression line.

Another common indicator of educational success is the share of people who complete a four-year college degree. Here the Nordic countries have risen to near the top. Figure 2.36 suggests no reason to think that social democratic capitalism's benefits come at the expense of tertiary educational attainment.

Figures 2.37 and 2.38 give us information on safety. The first indicator is the homicide rate. The second is the share of people who say they feel safe walking alone at night in the area where they live. The Nordic nations do well on both measures, apart from the relatively high homicide rate in Finland. Pursuit of social democratic policies doesn't appear to sacrifice safety.

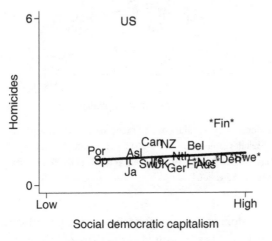

Figure 2.37 Social democratic capitalism and homicides. Homicides: per 100,000 population. 2000–2010. Data source: OECD. Social democratic capitalism: see Figure 2.19. The asterisks highlight the Nordic countries. "Asl" is Australia; "Aus" is Austria. The line is a linear regression line, calculated with the United States excluded.

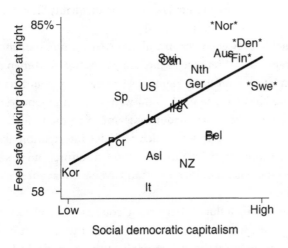

Figure 2.38 Social democratic capitalism and perceived safety. Perceived safety: share responding "yes" to the question "Do you feel safe walking alone at night in the city or area where you live?" 2007–2017. Data source: Gallup World Poll, via the Legatum Prosperity Index. Social democratic capitalism: see Figure 2.19. The asterisks highlight the Nordic countries. "Asl" is Australia; "Aus" is Austria. The line is a linear regression line.

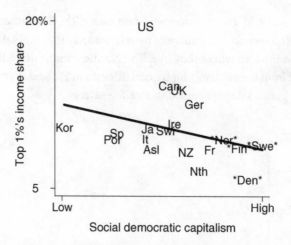

Figure 2.39 Social democratic capitalism and income inequality. Top 1 percent's income share: pretax income. Excludes capital gains. 2000–2015. Data source: World Inequality Database. Social democratic capitalism: see Figure 2.19. The asterisks highlight the Nordic countries. "Asl" is Australia. The line is a linear regression line.

Let's turn to indicators of inequality and inclusion. The vertical axis in Figure 2.39 shows income inequality, measured as the share of income that goes to the top 1 percent of the population. Income inequality has tended to be comparatively low in the Nordic countries. They've experienced increases since 1980, but from a low starting point, so they remain below the norm among rich democratic nations. There is no sign in the data that countries with social democratic policies end up with higher levels of income inequality. The same is true for wealth inequality, as we see in Figure 2.40.

What of inequality between women and men? A common indicator here is the gender pay gap—the difference in median pay between women and men who work full-time year-round. As Figure 2.41 reveals, the countries with social democratic policies have tended to do well at limiting female-male pay inequality. Figure 2.42 shows a broader indicator of women's inclusion: the Women, Peace, and Security Index, which includes information about how women fare in the economy and politics, in law and culture, and in safety and security. Here too there is no indication of an adverse impact of social democratic capitalism.

A key challenge facing affluent democratic countries is embrace and integration of immigrants. Justice considerations oblige the rich nations to welcome some, perhaps many, of the estimated 65 million people fleeing danger, persecution, or severe material deprivation, as well as others seeking better economic opportunity or family reunification.[62] Figure 2.43 shows each country's foreign-born share of the population in years for which comparable

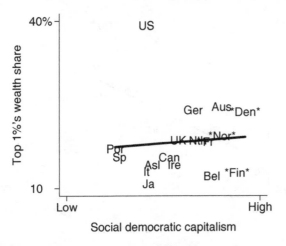

Figure 2.40 Social democratic capitalism and wealth inequality. Wealth = assets minus liabilities. 2009–2015. Data source: OECD. Social democratic capitalism: see Figure 2.19. The asterisks highlight the Nordic countries. "Asl" is Australia; "Aus" is Austria. The line is a linear regression line.

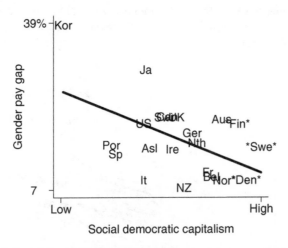

Figure 2.41 Social democratic capitalism and the gender pay gap. Gender pay gap: difference between median full-time male pay and median full-time female pay as a share of median male pay. Data source: OECD. Social democratic capitalism: see Figure 2.19. The asterisks highlight the Nordic countries. "Asl" is Australia; "Aus" is Austria. The line is a linear regression line.

data are available. Denmark and Finland are near the bottom of the pack. Norway has done better, but a significant portion of its immigrants are from other affluent nations, coming for the very high wages. Sweden is alone among the four Nordics in embracing a large inflow of migrants from outside of western Europe. Indeed, it has been perhaps the world's most welcoming country in recent decades.[63]

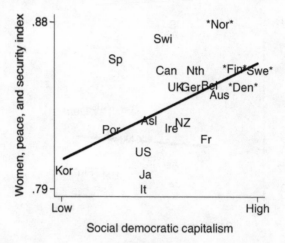

Figure 2.42 Social democratic capitalism and the women, peace, and security index. Women, peace, and security index: a composite measure of inclusion (economic, social, political), justice (formal laws and informal discrimination), and security (family, community, societal) via 11 indicators. Scale is 0 to 1. Data source: Georgetown Institute for Women, Peace, and Security and Peace Research Institute of Oslo, *Women, Peace, and Security Index 2017–18.* Social democratic capitalism: see Figure 2.19. The asterisks highlight the Nordic countries. "Asl" is Australia; "Aus" is Austria. The line is a linear regression line.

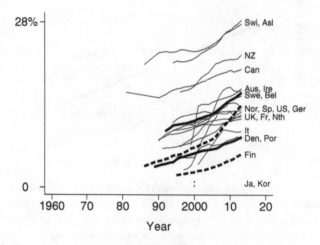

Figure 2.43 Openness to immigration. Foreign-born share of the population. Includes both legal and illegal immigrants. Data source: OECD. Solid thick lines: Denmark and Sweden. Dashed thick lines: Finland and Norway. "Asl" is Australia; "Aus" is Austria.

Even in the best circumstances, genuine assimilation of immigrants often takes multiple generations.[64] In the contemporary age, with its omnipresent media spotlight, countries and their governments are pressured to deliver results in a much shorter time frame. This is a very difficult challenge. And it can create

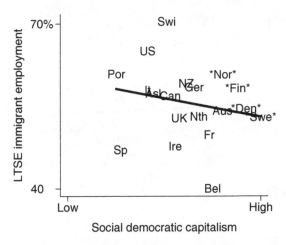

Figure 2.44 Social democratic capitalism and employment among less-educated immigrants. LTSE immigrant employment: employment rate among immigrants with less than secondary education. Age 15–64. 2012. Data source: OECD, *Indicators of Immigrant Integration 2015*, figure 5.2. Social democratic capitalism: see Figure 2.19. The asterisks highlight the Nordic countries. "Asl" is Australia; "Aus" is Austria. The line is a linear regression line.

political strains. In the face of a rapid, large-scale inflow of unfamiliar peoples, a segment of the native-born population in any country will be susceptible to calls for closing the door. In Sweden the anti-immigration Sweden Democrats party, founded in the 1990s, has steadily increased its vote share, reaching 6 percent in 2010, 13 percent in 2014, and 18 percent in 2018.[65] Successful integration and inclusion of immigrants can help to reduce the appeal of anti-immigrant movements and political parties.

One indicator of inclusion is the employment rate of less-skilled immigrants. Figure 2.44 shows that, as of the most recent available data, social democratic capitalist nations may have done less well than others. But if there is a real difference, it is a very small one. Among the Nordic countries, the employment rate is lowest in Sweden. That surely owes partly to its embrace of refugees from the Balkans in the 1990s, Iraq in the 2000s, and Syria in the 2010s. During these decades Sweden has admitted more refugees (relative to population size) than any other rich democratic country, many arriving with not only limited education but also pronounced language and cultural barriers to integration.[66]

Figure 2.45 shows another indicator of inclusion: the relative poverty rate. The performance of the Nordic nations isn't especially impressive.[67] Immigrant households in Norway and Sweden have a fairly low relative poverty rate, but several nations do better. And the immigrant poverty rates in Denmark and especially Finland are among the highest.

A third indicator of immigrant inclusion, subjective well-being, is shown in Figure 2.46. The measure is life satisfaction among foreign-born persons over

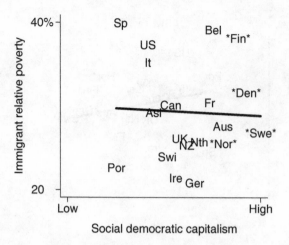

Figure 2.45 Social democratic capitalism and relative poverty among immigrants.
Immigrant relative poverty: share of immigrants living in households with a posttransfer-posttax income below 60 percent of the country median. 2012. Data source: OECD, *Indicators of Immigrant Integration 2015*, table 8.1. Social democratic capitalism: see Figure 2.19. The asterisks highlight the Nordic countries. "Asl" is Australia; "Aus" is Austria. The line is a linear regression line.

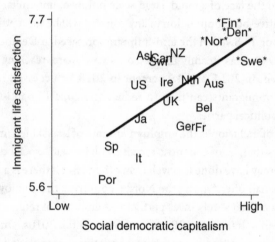

Figure 2.46 Social democratic capitalism and life satisfaction among immigrants.
Immigrant life satisfaction: average response to the question "Please imagine a ladder, with steps numbered from 0 at the bottom to 10 at the top. The top of the ladder represents the best possible life for you and the bottom of the ladder represents the worst possible life for you. On which step of the ladder would you say you personally feel you stand at this time?" 2005–2017. Data source: Gallup World Poll, via the *World Happiness Report 2018*, online appendix. Social democratic capitalism: see Figure 2.19. The asterisks highlight the Nordic countries. "Asl" is Australia; "Aus" is Austria. The line is a linear regression line.

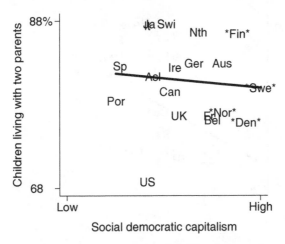

Figure 2.47 Social democratic capitalism and children living with two parents. Children living with two parents: share of all children. 2016. Data source: OECD Family Database. Social democratic capitalism: see Figure 2.19. The asterisks highlight the Nordic countries. "Asl" is Australia; "Aus" is Austria. The line is a linear regression line.

the period 2005–2017. Here the Nordic nations do better. Finland, Denmark, and Norway top the list, with Sweden not far behind.

Taking these three indicators together, it doesn't appear that social democratic policies systematically hinder immigrant integration and inclusion, though they also don't look to be unusually successful.

Next, let's consider family. It's conceivable that by reducing the need to have a partner to help with the breadwinning and childrearing, government services and transfers will cause fewer people to commit to long-term family relationships. Marriage isn't a helpful indicator. While the institution has fallen out of favor in many western European countries, that doesn't necessarily mean there are fewer long-term relationships. A better measure is the share of children that live in a home with two parents.[68] As Figure 2.47 shows, the Nordic countries run the gamut, with Denmark and Norway toward the low end, Sweden in the middle of the pack, and Finland at the high end. Across the affluent democratic countries there is no correlation between the social democratic capitalism index and the share of children living with two parents.

Have social democratic policies encouraged people to stop having kids? According to one hypothesis, expansive and generous public social programs foster a culture in which children are seen as a burden and a distraction from the fun things in life.[69] The data say this is wrong. Fertility rates are lower now than half a century ago in all of the rich democratic nations, but as we see in Figure 2.48, they are higher in the Nordic countries than in many others.

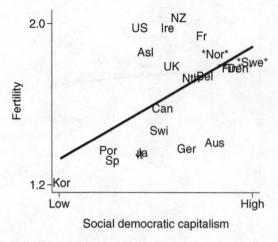

Figure 2.48 Social democratic capitalism and fertility. Fertility: average number of children born per woman. 2000–2015. Data source: OECD. Social democratic capitalism: see Figure 2.19. The asterisks highlight the Nordic countries. "Asl" is Australia; "Aus" is Austria. The line is a linear regression line.

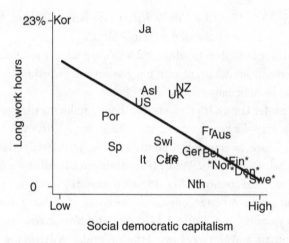

Figure 2.49 Social democratic capitalism and long work hours. Long work hours: share of employed persons whose usual hours of work per week are 50 or more. 2014. Data source: OECD. Social democratic capitalism: see Figure 2.19. The asterisks highlight the Nordic countries. "Asl" is Australia; "Aus" is Austria. The line is a linear regression line.

One reason for the comparatively high fertility rates in the Nordic nations is their array of policies that facilitate women's ability to balance work and family, particularly paid parental leave and affordable high-quality early education.[70] Figure 2.49 points to another possible contributor: in countries that are higher on the social democratic capitalism index, relatively few people have very long work hours, measured here as 50 hours per week or more.

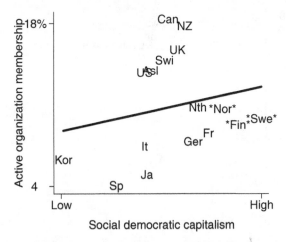

Figure 2.50 Social democratic capitalism and civic participation. Active organization membership: share of the adult population. Average across eight types of voluntary organization: sports-recreation, religious, art-music-education, charitable, professional, labor union, environment, consumer. Question: "Now I am going to read off a list of voluntary organizations. For each organization, could you tell me whether you are an active member, an inactive member, or not a member of that type of organization?" 2005–14. Data source: World Values Survey, worldvaluessurvey. org. Social democratic capitalism: see Figure 2.19. The asterisks highlight the Nordic countries. "Asl" is Australia. The line is a linear regression line.

What about participation in voluntary organizations? Some critics expect that social democratic capitalism will depress such participation, because "progressive social policy . . . has sought to make civil society less essential by assigning to the state many of the roles formerly played by religious congregations, civic associations, fraternal groups, and charities, especially in providing help to the poor."[71] Figure 2.50 shows one measure of civic participation: the share of adults who say they are an active member of a civic group or organization. The pattern across the countries suggests little or no tradeoff between social democratic policies and civic engagement.

A sometimes overlooked element of a just society is openness and support for other peoples. We've already considered openness to migrants. Another aspect is openness to trade. Are countries with social democratic policies tempted to restrict imports in order to match the economic performance outcomes of other affluent nations? The pattern in Figure 2.51 suggests no reason to think so.

A good society won't unduly burden future generations with a large public debt that they will have to repay.[72] It's reasonable to hypothesize that countries with greater public expenditures will tend to accumulate larger debts. But as Figure 2.52 reveals, the Nordic countries, which are among the world's biggest spenders, have studiously avoided running up a debt. They've done so by raising enough in revenue to cover their spending. (Norway isn't shown in the chart. Because of its oil revenue, it has a large government surplus.)

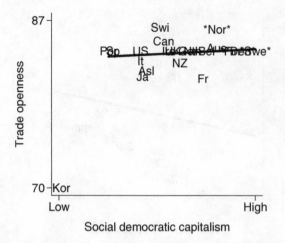

Figure 2.51 Social democratic capitalism and trade openness. Trade openness: scale of 0 to 100, with higher scores indicating greater freedom. The score is based on a country's average tariff rate and the extensiveness of non-tariff barriers to imports. 2005–15. Data source: Heritage Foundation, heritage.org/index. Social democratic capitalism: see Figure 2.19. The asterisks highlight the Nordic countries. "Asl" is Australia; "Aus" is Austria. The line is a linear regression line, calculated with South Korea excluded.

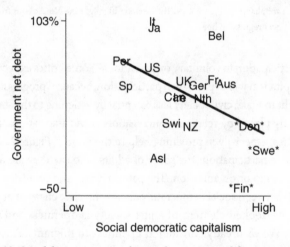

Figure 2.52 Social democratic capitalism and government debt. Government net debt: government financial liabilities minus government financial assets, measured as a share of GDP. Higher on the vertical axis indicates larger debt. 2005–15. Data source: OECD. Social democratic capitalism: see Figure 2.19. The asterisks highlight the Nordic countries. Norway, which has a surplus (negative net debt) of better than 200 percent of GDP, is omitted. "Asl" is Australia; "Aus" is Austria. The line is a linear regression line.

What about environmental fairness? Nearly all climate scientists believe that limiting greenhouse gas emissions is vital to keeping climate change in check.[73] The vertical axis in Figure 2.53 shows countries' per capita carbon dioxide emissions. The Nordic nations vary in their performance, with Finland and Norway

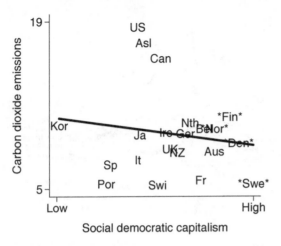

Figure 2.53 Social democratic capitalism and carbon emissions. Carbon dioxide emissions: metric tons per capita. 2000–13. Data source: World Bank. Social democratic capitalism: see Figure 2.19. The asterisks highlight the Nordic countries. "Asl" is Australia; "Aus" is Austria. The line is a linear regression line.

near the high (bad) end and Sweden at the low (good) end. There is no sign of a tradeoff between social democratic capitalism and environmental protection.

Finally, we come to happiness, which some consider the ultimate prize.[74] Skeptics of the social democratic model have sometimes pointed to the Nordic countries' high suicide rates, suggesting that this indicates dissatisfaction with insufficient liberty or excessive collectivism and conformity. As Figure 2.54 shows, half a century ago suicide rates were indeed comparatively high in Denmark, Finland, and Sweden, and that remained true of Denmark and Finland as recently as the mid-1990s. Today, however, the suicide rate in three of the four Nordics is squarely in the middle of the pack among the rich nations, and the fourth, Finland, isn't far from the middle. Figure 2.55, which shows the cross-country pattern, suggests a possible positive association between social democratic policies and suicide rates. But the association is weak and could easily be due to other factors, such as cold, dark winters in nations with higher suicide rates.[75]

What do we see when we turn to survey questions that ask directly about life satisfaction? The Gallup World Poll regularly asks the following question in the rich democratic countries: "Please imagine a ladder, with steps numbered from 0 at the bottom to 10 at the top. The top of the ladder represents the best possible life for you and the bottom of the ladder represents the worst possible life for you. On which step of the ladder would you say you personally feel you stand at this time?" Figure 2.56 shows a strong positive association between the social democratic capitalism index and average responses to this question.[76]

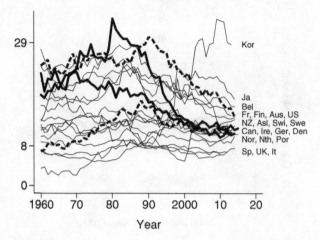

Figure 2.54 Suicides. Suicides per 100,000 population. Data source: OECD. Solid thick lines: Denmark and Sweden. Dashed thick lines: Finland and Norway. "Asl" is Australia; "Aus" is Austria.

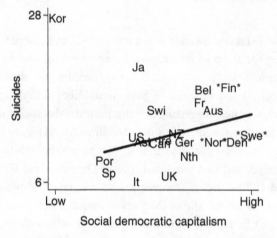

Figure 2.55 Social democratic capitalism and suicides. Suicides: per 100,000 population. 2000–14. Data source: OECD. Social democratic capitalism: see Figure 2.19. The asterisks highlight the Nordic countries. "Asl" is Australia; "Aus" is Austria. The line is a linear regression line, calculated with South Korea excluded.

That's a long walk through a lot of data. What can we conclude? Do we see evidence of tradeoffs? We've looked at personal freedom, innovation, economic growth, banking crises, employment rates, deindustrialization, middle-class incomes, upper-middle-class incomes, life expectancy, urban housing costs, PISA test scores, college completion, homicides, perceived safety, income inequality, wealth inequality, gender inequality, immigrant inclusion, children living with two parents, fertility, long work hours, civic engagement, trade openness,

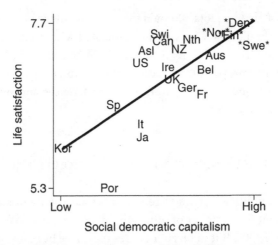

Figure 2.56 Social democratic capitalism and life satisfaction. Life satisfaction: average response to the question "Please imagine a ladder, with steps numbered from 0 at the bottom to 10 at the top. The top of the ladder represents the best possible life for you and the bottom of the ladder represents the worst possible life for you. On which step of the ladder would you say you personally feel you stand at this time?" 2005–2017. Data source: Gallup World Poll, via the *World Happiness Report 2018*, online appendix. Social democratic capitalism: see Figure 2.19. The asterisks highlight the Nordic countries. "Asl" is Australia; "Aus" is Austria. The line is a linear regression line.

government debt, carbon emissions, suicides, and life satisfaction. On most of these indicators social democratic capitalist nations have done neither better nor worse than other countries. On some—personal freedom, employment, perceived safety, income inequality, gender inequality, long work hours, government debt, and life satisfaction—social democratic capitalist nations have tended to do better. On only one of these indicators, upper-middle-class income levels, do we see compelling evidence of a tradeoff.

So does the experience of the world's rich democratic nations suggest that social democratic capitalism sacrifices key elements of the good society in pursuit of expanded Rawlsian outcomes? No, it doesn't.

Details, Details

Social democratic capitalism, as I've defined it here, features political democracy, private ownership and markets, good-quality K–12 schooling, expansive and generous public insurance programs, employment-oriented public services, and modest regulation of product and labor markets. It's worth emphasizing that this general description offers no guidance on a host of important policy details: Should early education be universal or targeted to the poor (or to the poor plus middle)? Should paid parental leave be for six months or one year?

Should it include a "daddy quota"? Should there be a statutory minimum wage? If so, how high? Should low wages be supplemented with a tax credit? How much regulation of hiring and firing is too much? What's the best balance between taxation of income, payroll, and consumption? And many, many more.

Answers to these questions hinge on public preferences and on evidence about what works.

Has Social Democracy Lost Its Electoral Mojo?

Social democratic political parties were dominant electorally in some countries and prominent in a number of others in the decades after World War II and even into the 1990s. But in recent decades they have been less dominant, and in some nations distinctly on the retreat. The Danish Social Democratic Party averaged 37 percent of the vote in elections from 1920 to 2000, but it hasn't reached 30 percent in any election since the turn of the century. In Sweden's 2018 election the Social Democrats received their lowest vote share, 28 percent, since 1908. As of 2019, the Dutch Social Democrats hold just 6 percent of their country's parliamentary seats, the French Socialists just 5 percent. Their counterparts in Germany, the United Kingdom, Italy, and elsewhere also are out of power. Meanwhile, far right and far left "populist" parties have steadily increased their vote share and now are part of the government in some countries.

My interest, however, is in social democratic capitalism's socioeconomic effects, not its electoral popularity. Even so, it's worth noting that part of the reason for the electoral struggles of center-left parties in recent decades is their success in creating and sustaining a generous welfare state. This forces them to campaign as defenders of the status quo rather than advocates for change.

Have the Nordic Countries Been Abandoning Social Democratic Capitalism?

Social democratic capitalism has worked very well for the Nordic countries. But according to some observers, those countries have moved away from it in recent years.[77] Is that true?

Each of the Nordic nations has reduced the generosity of some public transfers, such as pensions, unemployment compensation, and sickness compensation. These cuts have taken various forms: stricter eligibility criteria, lower replacement rates, shorter duration, heavier tax clawbacks. They also have made some changes to services, including increased use of user fees, some partial shifts from universalism to targeting, and allowance or encouragement of private providers.[78]

At the same time, the Nordics have increased the generosity of some benefits and services, most notably parental and family leave, early education, and child allowances.

Figure 2.57 shows replacement rates for major public transfer programs at three stages in the life cycle: childhood, working-age, and retirement years. The scores are averaged across these three stages. Sweden and Finland have pulled back somewhat from the very high levels they had in the 1980s, yet they remain quite generous in comparative terms. In Denmark and Norway we see no downward trend.

Figure 2.58 shows expenditures on public insurance programs—both transfers and services—as a share of GDP. This total has remained constant or increased in each of the Nordic nations since 1980, and Denmark and Finland have moved from the middle of the ranking to join Sweden near the top. Norway appears to be an exception, but that's because its very large GDP hides the true extent of its social program generosity.

In Figure 2.59 we see that spending on employment-oriented public services—active labor market policy and family policy—has increased in three of the four Nordic nations since 1980 and held constant in the other.

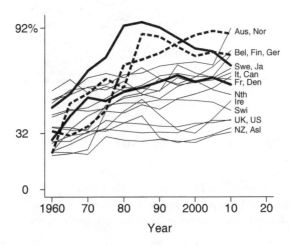

Figure 2.57 Public transfer replacement rates. Average replacement rate for public insurance programs aimed at risks during childhood, working age, and old age. Data source: Simon Birnbaum, Tommy Ferrarini, Kenneth Nelson, and Joakim Palme, *The Generational Social Contract*, Edward Elgar, 2017, using data from the Social Policy Indicators (SPIN) database. Solid thick lines: Denmark and Sweden. Dashed thick lines: Finland and Norway. "Asl" is Australia; "Aus" is Austria.

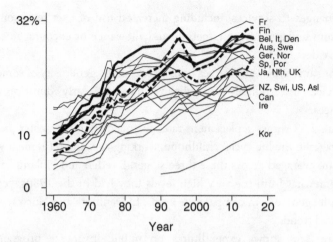

Figure 2.58 Public social expenditures. Share of GDP. Gross public social expenditures. These data aren't adjusted for the elderly population share and the unemployment rate. Data source: Esteban Ortiz-Ospina and Max Roser, "Public Spending," *Our World in Data*, using data for 1960–1979 from OECD, "Social Expenditure 1960–1990: Problems of Growth and Control," OECD Social Policy Studies, 1985, and data for 1980ff from OECD, Social Expenditures Database. Solid thick lines: Denmark and Sweden. Dashed thick lines: Finland and Norway. "Asl" is Australia; "Aus" is Austria.

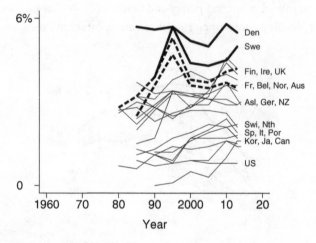

Figure 2.59 Employment-oriented public services. Share of GDP. Public expenditures on active labor market policy and family policy. Data source: OECD. Solid thick lines: Denmark and Sweden. Dashed thick lines: Finland and Norway. "Asl" is Australia; "Aus" is Austria.

Finally, Figure 2.60 shows that all four Nordic countries have kept the stringency of product and labor market regulations roughly constant since 2000, following two decades of steady movement away from heavier regulations.

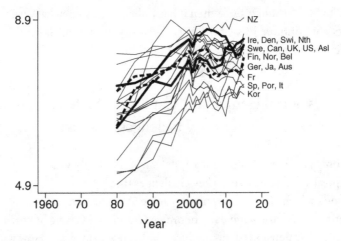

Figure 2.60 Modest economic regulation. Average score for legal system and property rights, credit market regulations, labor market regulations, business regulations, and freedom to trade internationally. Higher scores indicate less regulation. Data source: Fraser Institute, Economic Freedom database. Solid thick lines: Denmark and Sweden. Dashed thick lines: Finland and Norway. "Asl" is Australia; "Aus" is Austria.

So the Nordic countries haven't been abandoning social democratic capitalism. Their public insurance programs now cover more risks than before, though some of that coverage is a bit less generous than it had been. They have introduced some targeting within universalism. They now provide more public services, particularly ones geared toward facilitating employment, and they've increased the generosity of many of those services. And they haven't turned away from flexibility in their regulation of product and labor markets.

Other Rich Democratic Nations are Moving Toward Social Democratic Capitalism

While the Nordic countries have adjusted but not abandoned social democratic capitalism, other rich democratic nations increasingly are embracing it.[79] Many of the continental European nations have had expansive and generous public social programs for a long time. Over the past two decades, some of them—most notably Germany, the Netherlands, and Austria—have added early education, lifelong learning, active labor market policy, and other employment-conducive public services, and some have loosened their product and labor market regulations. Both steps bring these countries into closer alignment with the social democratic model. The United Kingdom also moved in this direction under the New Labour governments headed by Tony Blair and Gordon Brown from

1997 to 2010, though since then it has pulled back somewhat. Even the United States has continued its slow but fairly steady movement toward social democratic capitalism, as I detail in Part 2 of this book.

Is Social Democratic Capitalism Suited for Future Challenges?

Not only has social democratic capitalism worked very well up to now. It also is well positioned to face some key challenges that lie ahead.

One such challenge is population aging. As the elderly population grows due to retirement of the large baby boom generation and rising life expectancy, the cost of public pension programs and healthcare will increase. How will countries pay for this? High employment is likely to be key. The larger the share of the population in paid work, the greater the tax revenue that can be raised from them.

What about capital mobility? Doesn't it hinder governments' ability to raise tax revenues?[80] It can, but we've seen little evidence of large-scale capital flight or a race to the bottom in tax rates.[81] The best way for countries to keep investors at home is to provide a skilled workforce, good services, and product and labor market flexibility, each of which is a hallmark of social democratic capitalism.[82]

Families and voluntary organizations have weakened in most affluent nations over past half century.[83] This is a consequence of women's improved economic position, religion's declining influence, shifting norms, and other developments. This trend seems likely to continue, or at least to not reverse. It is most problematic for the least advantaged—children, single parents, persons with less education or with disabilities. Expansive and generous public services and transfer programs are in many instances an effective substitute. Indeed, because of their wider reach, they may be more effective than families or intermediate organizations.

In the contemporary "postmaterialist" era, many individuals want more ability to choose.[84] The social democratic model already enhances individuals' array of choices and their capacity to take advantage of them by reducing dependence on family, friends, and employers. Critics sometimes portray the model as inherently limiting of choice in service providers, but that's mistaken. The Nordic countries have engaged in a variety of experiments with enhanced choice in public services—giving individuals more options among government providers and allowing private providers to compete with public ones.

Advances in automation and the rise of the "gig" or "platform" economy have increased work flexibility but also precariousness. More people fear losing their jobs, move in and out of jobs, work irregularly, or work multiple jobs. In

this environment, individuals and households will be more economically secure if benefits and insurance are generous and if they come from government
rather than from an employer.[85] Think of a stereotypical member of the modern
precariat, working irregular shifts at a coffee shop and driving for an on-demand
ride service. In the contemporary United States, such a life can be hellish—low
income, unpredictable, at the mercy of finicky managers and customers. Now
imagine it in a country where every person has health insurance, access to good-
quality childcare and preschool, paid parental leave, paid sick leave, free or low-
cost college, a decent pension, and other services and benefits. In this latter
context, while irregular or low-paid employment may still be suboptimal, it will
be noticeably less stressful and problematic.

Finally, there is growing worry that technological advance, globalization, fi-
nancialization, union weakening, and other developments are reducing the
degree to which the economic product ends up in the paychecks of ordinary
workers, because more goes to profits instead of wages and because a growing
portion of wages goes to those at the top. This could significantly reduce consumer demand, in turn reducing economic growth.[86] It's too soon to know
whether this is a real problem, and if so how big it is. Social democratic capitalism won't necessarily solve it, but by transferring more of the GDP to low- and
middle-earning households via government benefits and by boosting the share
of people in paid work, it is likely to help.

A Success Story

Social democratic capitalism features a democratic polity, a capitalist economy,
good primary and second education, a big welfare state, employment-promoting
public services, and modest regulation of product and labor markets. It aims to
combine individual freedom with equality of opportunity, income security, and
a good standard of living for the least well-off. The evidence from the world's
rich longstanding-democratic nations suggests that it achieves these goals. And
it does so without sacrificing other elements of a good society, from economic
growth to health to happiness and much more. It is, to this point in history, the
most successful package of institutions and policies we have devised.

3

Is Its Success Generalizable?

Before advocating widespread adoption of a new product or policy, it's common to try it out on a small group. A company that develops a new medicine will evaluate its benefits and drawbacks via a clinical trial. In the United States, state and local governments frequently experiment with policy ideas before the federal government decides to adopt them. This is, in effect, what has happened with social democratic capitalism over the past several decades. The Nordic countries, its chief practitioners, have served as trial subjects.

The results, as we saw in Chapter 2, are very encouraging. The Nordic nations' coupling of democracy, capitalism, and education together with a big welfare state and high employment have produced a better standard of living for their least well-off members, greater income security, and very likely more equality of opportunity than in other rich democratic nations. And the Nordics have gotten these results without sacrificing economic growth, freedom, health, happiness, or any of a large number of other outcomes we want in a good society.

However, unlike in a trial of a new medicine, the Nordic countries weren't randomly selected from the world's rich longstanding-democratic nations to receive this "treatment." It's conceivable that the Nordics are blessed with attributes that enable them, and only them, to reap the benefits of social democratic policies without suffering tradeoffs. It's possible, in other words, that while social democratic capitalism works quite well, it can do so only in Denmark, Finland, Norway, and Sweden. Varying versions of this hypothesis identify the Nordics' secret sauce as an immutable work ethic, superior intelligence, trust, solidarity, small population size, racial and ethnic homogeneity, institutional coherence, effective government, corporatism, a willingness to be taxed, tax compliance, strong labor unions, or low income inequality.

The question here isn't whether other nations are likely to adopt social democratic policies. They may or may not.[1] Nor is it whether social democratic policies, if other countries do adopt them, will yield a higher standard of living for the least well-off, greater income security, and more equality of opportunity. They almost certainly will. The question is whether other nations that adopt social democratic policies will be more likely than the Nordics to suffer tradeoffs.

Work Ethic and Personal Responsibility

One possibility is that Nordic culture features a deeply ingrained (Viking? Lutheran?) commitment to employment, and this causes people in the Nordic countries to continue to work, and work hard, even in the face of financial disincentives created by public social programs. In the words of one analyst, "The uniquely strong norms associated with personal responsibility and work in the Nordics made these societies particularly well suited for avoiding the moral hazard of generous welfare systems."[2]

Are Nordic citizens more culturally predisposed than others to work hard in the face of monetary disincentives? Three pieces of evidence suggest they probably aren't. The first comes from a World Values Survey question asking whether it is justifiable to claim government benefits to which you aren't entitled. Figure 3.1 shows the share responding that doing so is never justified. A generation ago, this share was comparatively high in Denmark, Norway, and Sweden. That seems consistent with the hypothesis of a deep-seated cultural commitment to employment. In the past two decades, however, there has been a significant shift.

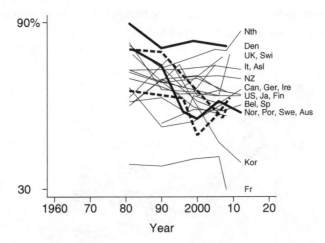

Figure 3.1 Claiming government benefits to which you aren't entitled is never justified. Question: "Please tell me for each of the following actions whether you think it can always be justified, never be justified, or something in between: claiming government benefits to which you are not entitled." The lines show the share responding "never be justified." The vertical axis doesn't begin at zero. Data sources: World Values Survey and European Values Survey. Solid thick lines: Denmark and Sweden. Dashed thick lines: Finland and Norway. "Asl" is Australia; "Aus" is Austria.

In Denmark, a large share continues to say "never justified." But Norway and Sweden have moved from the top of the ranking to near the bottom, joining Finland. They now have comparatively few citizens who feel it's never justifiable to claim government benefits to which you aren't entitled. We shouldn't take this to mean that Finns, Norwegians, and Swedes are lacking in personal responsibility or work ethic, but it does give us reason to doubt that they are uniquely highly endowed with these qualities.

A second piece of evidence is the number of hours worked by people who are employed. Figure 3.2 shows average hours worked per year by employed persons in the rich democratic countries. Here too there is no empirical sign of an overriding commitment to work in the Nordic nations. Denmark and Norway are at the low end of the spectrum, with Sweden and Finland toward the middle but in the lower half.

Third, there are specific policy episodes in the Nordic nations that offer a useful test of the "uniquely strong work ethic" hypothesis. One is Sweden's sickness insurance program in the late 1980s. Jonas Agell describes the circumstances: "According to the rules in place by the end of the 1980s, employees were entitled to a 90 percent compensation level from the first day of reporting sick. Due to supplementary insurance agreements in the labor market, however, many employees had a compensation level of 100 percent. For the first seven days of sickness leave, a physician's certificate was not required." How did Swedes respond? Did they continue to show up for work, ignoring the monetary incentive to be out "sick"? According to Agell, the average number of work days missed due to sickness increased from 13 in the mid-1960s to 25 in 1988,

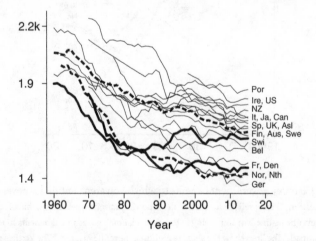

Figure 3.2 Hours worked by employed persons. Average annual hours worked per employed person. "k" = thousand. The vertical axis doesn't begin at zero. Data source: OECD. Solid thick lines: Denmark and Sweden. Dashed thick lines: Finland and Norway. "Asl" is Australia; "Aus" is Austria.

despite an improvement in actual health among the Swedish population.[3] To put this in cross-national perspective, Americans on average miss 5 days of work per year.[4]

Disability programs offer another test. Children of persons who receive disability payments are more likely than others to be aware of the program and to know its eligibility and benefit rules. If those children are more likely than others to end up on the disability program as adults, this suggests some degree of benefit cheating. Norway is a useful case to examine, because its economy has been exceptionally strong during the past generation, with lots of high-paying jobs. It offers plenty of opportunity, in other words, for people to make a good living via employment. A recent study finds that Norwegian children of disability benefit recipients are indeed more likely to become recipients themselves, suggesting that they do respond to incentives.[5]

None of this evidence is definitive, but it leans strongly against the hypothesis that a unique cultural emphasis on work and personal responsibility makes Nordic citizens less likely to succumb to employment disincentives than their counterparts in other affluent countries.

We don't need to look to culture in order to explain high employment rates in the Nordic nations. As we saw in Chapter 2, social democratic capitalism aims to boost employment via work-conducive public services and modest rather than stringent product and labor market regulations. In the event that policy makers go too far with government transfer generosity and create employment disincentives, as they sometimes have, these two elements of social democratic capitalism are likely to offset the damage. These policies, rather than an immutable work ethic or a culture of personal responsibility, are the key cause of high Nordic employment rates. We should expect the same result when social democratic policies are used in other nations.

Intelligence

If people in the Nordic countries have an advantage in average cognitive ability, they might be able to compensate for employment and innovation disincentives by working smarter. We can't directly compare intelligence across countries, but scores on international tests of reading, math, and science are inconsistent with the hypothesis of superior Nordic cognitive ability. As Figure 3.3 shows, high school students in Finland have done quite well on these tests over the past decade, but the scores of their counterparts in Denmark, Norway, and Sweden have been average or below. This isn't what we would expect to see if people in the Nordic countries have an intelligence advantage.

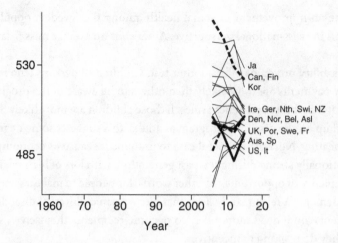

Figure 3.3 PISA test scores, 15-year-olds. Average student score on Program for International Assessment (PISA) reading, math, and science tests. The PISA tests ask students to solve problems they haven't seen before, to identify patterns that aren't obvious, and to make compelling written arguments. The vertical axis doesn't begin at zero. Data source: OECD. Solid thick lines: Denmark and Sweden. Dashed thick lines: Finland and Norway. "Asl" is Australia; "Aus" is Austria.

Trust

Some research suggests that interpersonal trust improves key societal outcomes such as economic growth, educational attainment, health, and safety.[6] The standard measure of trust comes from survey responses to the question "Generally speaking, would you say that most people can be trusted or that you need to be very careful in dealing with people?" The World Values Survey has asked this question since the early 1980s. Figure 3.4 shows the share of the population in each of the rich democratic countries who choose the "most people can be trusted" response. The Nordic nations have tended to feature comparatively high levels of interpersonal trust.[7]

Is trust what enables the Nordics to achieve "expanded Rawlsian" outcomes without suffering tradeoffs?[8] One key question is: How important is trust in achieving good outcomes? Here the supportive evidence is, in my view, quite thin.[9]

Even if trust does contribute to good outcomes, there is little reason to think a high level of trustingness is possible only in the Nordic nations. Figure 3.5 shows the level of trust in Denmark and Sweden according to the World Values Survey and in the United States according to the National Opinion Research Center. The question wording is virtually identical. In the 1960s, Americans appear to have been just as trusting as Danes and Swedes, and perhaps more so.

So Americans apparently can be just as trusting as their Nordic counterparts. What drove the large decline in interpersonal trust in the United States? The

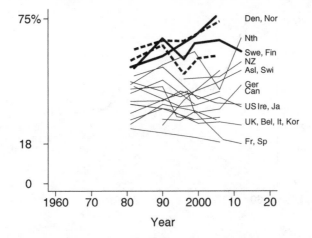

Figure 3.4 Interpersonal trust. Share of adults who believe most people can be trusted. Question: "Generally speaking, would you say that most people can be trusted or that you need to be very careful in dealing with people?" Data source: World Values Survey. Solid thick lines: Denmark and Sweden. Dashed thick lines: Finland and Norway. "Asl" is Australia.

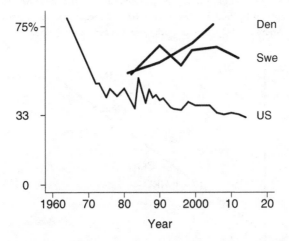

Figure 3.5 Interpersonal trust. Share of adults who believe most people can be trusted. Data source for Denmark and Sweden: World Values Survey. Data sources for the United States: General Social Survey, sda.berkeley.edu/archive.htm, series trust; National Opinion Research Corp.

main cause seems to have been a reduction in trust in government, spurred by the Vietnam War in the 1960s and Watergate in the 1970s. As Figure 3.6 indicates, trust in government correlates very closely with interpersonal trust over time. The pattern across rich democratic nations gives additional reason to think that trust in government is an important determinant of interpersonal trust. As Figure 3.7 shows, the cross-country association is quite strong.[10] Rising

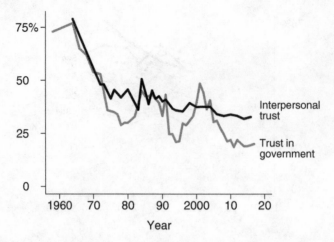

Figure 3.6 Trust in government and interpersonal trust in the United States. Share of adults. Trust in government question: "Do you trust the government in Washington to do what is right always, most of the time, some of the time, or never?" The line shows the share responding "always" or "most of the time." Data source: Pew Research Center, "Public Trust in Government, 1958–2017," using data from assorted surveys. Interpersonal trust question: "Generally speaking, would you say that most people can be trusted or that you can't be too careful in life?" The line shows the share responding "most people can be trusted." Data sources: General Social Survey, sda.berkeley.edu/archive.htm, series trust; National Opinion Research Corp. The correlation is +.85.

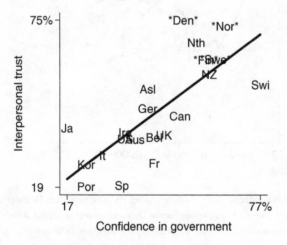

Figure 3.7 Confidence in government and interpersonal trust. Interpersonal trust: Share of adults saying "most people can be trusted." The other response option is "You can never be too careful when dealing with others." Data source: World Values Survey. Confidence in government: Share of adults responding "yes" to the question "Do you have confidence in the national government?" Data source: Gallup World Poll, via the OECD. The asterisks highlight the Nordic countries. "Asl" is Australia; "Aus" is Austria. The line is a linear regression line. The correlation is +.76.

trust in government also appears to have been a key cause of the increase in interpersonal trust in Denmark over the past generation.[11]

If countries can in theory achieve Nordic levels of interpersonal trust, how can they do so in practice? As it happens, a prominent hypothesis, supported by recent findings, holds that an effective route is via an expansive and generous welfare state.[12]

What can we conclude? Interpersonal trust probably isn't vital for good outcomes. Even if it is, high trustingness isn't unique to the Nordic countries; other rich nations might well achieve comparable levels of trust if they were to embrace social democratic capitalism.

Solidarity

For much of the past century, the Nordic countries have had strong labor unions, a tradition of voting for political parties that promote social inclusion, and a commitment to high levels of foreign aid for poor nations. These are frequently seen as expressions of a solidaristic, egalitarian culture, which contrasts with the more individualistic "You're on your own" attitude that dominates in nations such as the United States and the priority attached to the family in southern European countries.

We shouldn't, however, overstate the role of egalitarian sentiments in the Nordic countries. Figure 3.8 shows that in public opinion surveys, the share of Swedes who say freedom and family security are very important to them has consistently been much larger than the share saying equality is very important.

Nor, to my knowledge, is there scholarly research that convincingly links solidaristic or egalitarian culture to better societal performance on outcomes such as economic growth, health, happiness, or others.

Small Size and Homogeneity

The Nordic nations are small in population: Denmark, Finland, and Norway each have 5 to 6 million people and Sweden has 10 million. They also are relatively homogenous: according to a common measure of ethnic heterogeneity, among twenty-one rich longstanding-democratic nations Finland is the eighth most diverse, Denmark sixteenth, Norway seventeenth, and Sweden eighteenth.[13]

Homogeneity and small size very likely played a role in why the Nordics adopted social democratic policies.[14] But do they underlie the Nordic countries' success in achieving expanded Rawlsian outcomes while avoiding tradeoffs? According to Tyler Cowen, "A small country with higher ethnic homogeneity

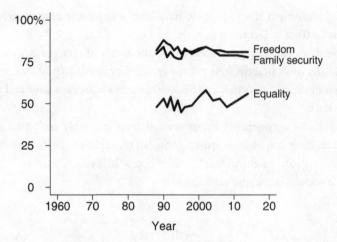

Figure 3.8 Importance of freedom, family security, and equality to Swedes. Share responding "very important" to the question "How important do you consider the following things to be to yourself?" Other response options: fairly important, neither important nor unimportant, not very important, not at all important. Data source: Johan Martinsson, Ulrika Andersson, and Annika Bergström, eds., "Swedish Trends, 1986–2017," SOM Institute, University of Gothenburg, 2018, p. 18.

and with only a few concentrated population centers usually can provide higher levels of social insurance without experiencing the level of system abuse that might occur in the United States."[15] But he doesn't offer any reason why that would be true, nor any evidence suggesting it is. As noted earlier, a comparatively large share of Nordic citizens believe it's okay to cheat, and their work commitment decreases when benefits get too generous.

It's also worth noting that across the rich democratic countries, neither small population size nor homogeneity is associated with faster economic growth or greater affluence.[16]

Institutional Coherence

According to the "varieties of capitalism" hypothesis, the economies of the world's rich democratic nations fall into two groups. Coordination is market-based in "liberal market economies" such as the United States and the United Kingdom. Coordination is based largely on nonmarket or extramarket institutions in "coordinated market economies" such as Germany and Austria. What matters for successful economic growth, in this view, is not the type of economic coordination, but the degree of institutional coherence. Countries with more coherent institutions—those with consistently market-oriented or consistently nonmarket-oriented institutions and policies—should grow more rapidly.[17]

Does institutional coherence account for the Nordic nations' success in coupling the advantages of social democratic capitalism with an absence of tradeoffs?[18] That's unlikely. The Nordic countries' configuration of institutions and policies hasn't been more coherent than those of Germany, Japan, the United States, and some other rich democracies.[19] In any case, the empirical record suggests no association between institutional coherence and economic success; nations with hybrid institutions and policies, or with a mix that changes over time, have performed as well as those with more coherent arrangements.[20]

Effective Government

The Nordic countries have tended to have good government.[21] A common measure is the World Bank's "government effectiveness" index, which attempts to gauge public and expert perceptions of the quality of public services, the quality of the civil service and the degree of its independence from political pressures, the quality of policy formulation and implementation, and the credibility of the government's commitment to such policies. Scores are available beginning in the mid-1990s. As Figure 3.9 shows, the Nordic nations have consistently ranked at or near the top among the rich democracies. A particular strength has been their willingness to experiment and adjust, to be pragmatic rather than bound by dogma. As one observer colorfully puts it, "The streets of Stockholm are awash with the blood of sacred cows."[22]

Have Nordic governments been *uniquely* effective? I'm not aware of evidence that supports such a conclusion. According to the World Bank measure, the level of government effectiveness in Switzerland, New Zealand, and the Netherlands has tended to match that of the Nordic nations, with Japan, Canada, and Germany close behind.

Policy makers in the Nordic countries have made some significant mistakes. In the late 1980s and early 1990s, the governments in Finland and Sweden caused recessions by reducing capital controls rapidly, and both then decided to impose austerity measures, deepening the recessions.[23] The downturns, which ended up lasting from 1990 to 1995, were among the most severe experienced by any rich country since the 1930s. Denmark's government proved no more effective than those of many other rich countries at identifying and preventing a housing bubble in the mid-2000s. And on various occasions Nordic policy makers have overshot in the generosity of public social programs, as I noted earlier.

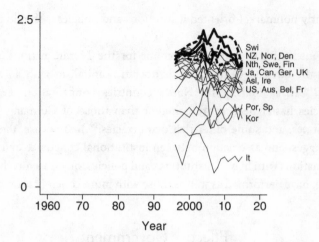

Figure 3.9 Government effectiveness. Government effectiveness attempts to capture perceptions of the quality of public services, the quality of the civil service and the degree of its independence from political pressures, the quality of policy formulation and implementation, and the credibility of the government's commitment to such policies. Data source: Stefan Dahlberg, Sören Holmberg, Bo Rothstein, Anna Khomenko, and Richard Svensson, Quality of Government Basic Dataset, version Jan16, Quality of Government Institute, University of Gothenburg, series wbgi_gee, using data from the World Bank. Solid thick lines: Denmark and Sweden. Dashed thick lines: Finland and Norway. "Asl" is Australia; "Aus" is Austria.

Why might government effectiveness be critical for a country wishing to achieve social democratic capitalist outcomes? A big welfare state is sometimes assumed to require a massive bureaucracy that will inevitably be inefficient, ignorant of on-the-ground needs and complexities, vulnerable to rent-seeking by private interest groups, and more attentive to its own interests than to those of its customers or clients.[24] However, many public insurance programs don't in fact suffer from these problems. Think of pensions, the government transfer program that spends the largest quantity of money. It works very simply: A small tax is regularly deducted from each employed person and from his employer. When the person reaches the age of eligibility, he begins receiving a payment. There are some complicated cases that must be sorted out by government personnel, but this is minor. The administrative cost is low—for Social Security in the United States, just 0.4 percent of total program expenditures.[25] The potential for self-interested bureaucrats to expand their turf is minimal, as is the ability of private actors to grab a share of the money. For the Earned Income Tax Credit, America's next-largest antipoverty program, administrative costs also are less than 1 percent of expenditures.[26] Or consider healthcare. Administrative costs for Medicare, America's government health insurance program for the elderly, are less than 2 percent of expenditures.[27] For Medicaid, which is administered separately by each of the 50 states, they are 4.6 percent.[28] If the United States were to enact a public sickness insurance program or paid parental leave, two policies that every other affluent democratic nation already has, the size and cost of the government administrative apparatus would be smaller than many critics of big government imagine.

Policy experimentation in the Nordic nations and others lightens the burden on the governments of countries that wish to embrace social democratic capitalism. Rather than starting from scratch, they can draw on "best practice" in the Nordics and elsewhere.

Students of economic development in poorer nations increasingly recognize that application of a ready-made template for a particular policy sometimes doesn't work well, because the problem has idiosyncratic features in a particular country or locality, because the needed government administrative capacity doesn't exist, because information is limited, or because the new policy disrupts existing routines and hence fosters resistance by administrators or beneficiaries.[29] But while this can be an issue for some modern public insurance programs, such as active labor market policy, it's of limited relevance for most.

What about government's capacity to correct mistakes? An effective government, Franklin Roosevelt once said, will "Take a method and try it. If it fails, admit it frankly and try another."[30] Might this be a problem for a nation such as the United States, which has an array of governmental veto points that make it difficult to change course? Policy adjustment in the United States is indeed more difficult than in, say, Sweden. Yet the US experience with public insurance programs since the 1930s has been one of frequent adjustment. Every program has been changed a number of times, sometimes in minor ways and other times in major ones.[31] Often these adjustments have been expansions, but sometimes they have involved cuts, and occasionally those cuts have been quite large, such as the mid-1990s "welfare reform." Program adjustment can be difficult in the United States, but it does happen.

Corporatism

Regularized dialogue among organized interest groups and between interest groups and government—known as corporatism or corporatist concertation—can improve government policy making and implementation. Policies are likely to be based on more and better information, to be better coordinated across policy areas, and to be subject to less dispute and resistance once implemented. Some studies have linked corporatism with healthier economic performance: lower unemployment and inflation, faster economic growth, and greater adaptability to economic change.[32]

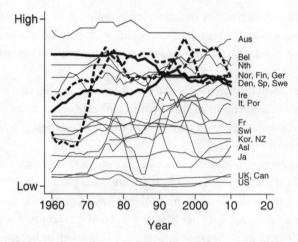

Figure 3.10 Corporatism. A composite measure formed by combining indicators of the involvement of unions and employers in government decisions, the organizational structure of collective actors, the structure of works council representation, the rights of works councils, government intervention in wage bargaining, the dominant level of wage bargaining, coordination of wage bargaining, and mandatory extension of collective agreements. Data source: Detlef Jahn, "Changing of the Guard: Trends in Corporatist Arrangements in 42 Highly Industrialized Societies from 1960 to 2010," *Socio-Economic Review*, 2016. Solid thick lines: Denmark and Sweden. Dashed thick lines: Finland and Norway. "Asl" is Australia; "Aus" is Austria.

While the Nordic countries have been among the most prominent practitioners of corporatism, they aren't exceptional in this regard, as we see in Figure 3.10. Moreover, corporatism's beneficial effects on economic outcomes seem to have dissipated by the 1990s.[33] This, then, is an unlikely candidate for why the Nordic nations have been comparatively successful.

Willingness to Be Taxed

Government debt forces a portion of revenues to go toward interest payments, which means those revenues can't be used for transfers or services. A nation with social democratic policies but stuck with a sizable government debt might, for this reason, be less successful in boosting low-end living standards, improving income security, and equalizing opportunity without experiencing tradeoffs. The Nordic nations have tended to balance their public budget. The result, as we see in Figure 3.11, is little or no government debt.

Is this because Nordic citizens are uniquely amenable to paying high taxes? Figure 3.12 shows tax revenues as a share of GDP in the Nordics and other rich nations going back to the mid-1960s. While Denmark and Sweden had the highest tax revenues from the mid-1980s until around 2010, in prior years their

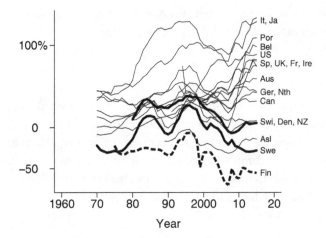

Figure 3.11 Government debt. Government financial liabilities minus government financial assets ("net debt"), measured as a share of GDP. Higher on the vertical axis indicates larger debt. Data source: OECD. Norway, which has a surplus (negative net debt) of better than 200 percent of GDP, is omitted. Solid thick lines: Denmark and Sweden. Dashed thick line: Finland. "Asl" is Australia; "Aus" is Austria.

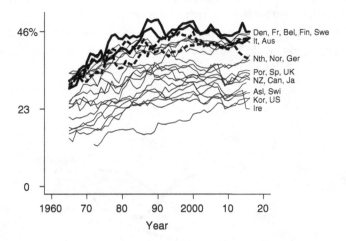

Figure 3.12 Tax revenues. Share of GDP. Includes all types of taxes at all levels of government. Doesn't include nontax sources of government revenue. Data source: OECD. Solid thick lines: Denmark and Sweden. Dashed thick lines: Finland and Norway. "Asl" is Australia; "Aus" is Austria.

revenue levels were similar to those of several continental European nations. That has been true for Finland and Norway throughout the past half century (apart from a brief spell in the early 1990s when Finland's GDP fell sharply), and in recent years it has been the case for Sweden as well. This is thin evidence on which to rest a conclusion that only the Nordic nations can generate a quantity of taxes sufficient to pay for social democratic policies.

Why, then, have the Nordics had lower public debt levels than most other rich nations? The chief reason is their commitment to genuine Keynesianism in fiscal policy. Keynes argued for deficit spending during economic recessions, in order to compensate for a shortfall in private-sector demand.[34] After World War II some policy makers in the rich countries shifted to a view that deficit spending should be used to stimulate the economy on a regular basis, not just during downturns.[35] Nordic social democrats have tended to stick with Keynes's approach, which means running a surplus when the economy is growing in order the keep the budget in balance over the business cycle.[36]

Tax Compliance

Even if Nordic citizens are no more fond of high taxes than their counterparts elsewhere, are they more likely to pay them? The social democratic model requires heavy tax revenues. If too many people react to high tax rates by cheating, the model may run into trouble. Are people in the Nordic countries less prone to tax cheating than citizens in other rich democracies?

One indicator is what people say in response to a survey question. Since the early 1980s, the World Values Survey and European Values Survey have asked

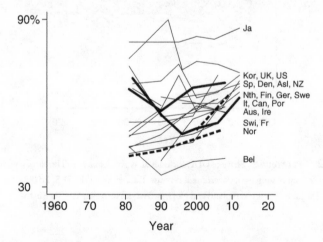

Figure 3.13 Cheating on taxes is never justified. Question: "Please tell me for each of the following actions whether you think it can always be justified, never be justified, or something in between: cheating on taxes." The lines show the share responding "never be justified." The vertical axis doesn't begin at zero. Data sources: World Values Survey and European Values Survey. Solid thick lines: Denmark and Sweden. Dashed thick lines: Finland and Norway. "Asl" is Australia; "Aus" is Austria.

citizens whether they think cheating on taxes "can never be justified, always be justified, or something in between." Figure 3.13 shows the share responding "can never be justified." The Nordic countries are in the middle of the pack. Based on what they say, they don't appear to be less likely to cheat on tax payments than their counterparts abroad.

What about actual behavior? Research on tax cheating suggests it is largely a function of incentives rather than culture or individual virtue.[37] When a person's income is reported to the tax authority by a third party, such as an employer or financial company, the incidence and magnitude of tax cheating tends to be very low. It increases when income is self-reported, as is the case for many people who are self-employed. In Denmark, the tax evasion rate among those with only or mainly self-reported income is about 50 percent. In the United States it is similar, at about 56 percent.[38] This suggests no grounds for believing that the Nordic nations are uniquely able to get their citizenry to comply with heavy taxation.

Strong Unions

The unionization rate is higher in the four Nordic countries than in all other rich democratic nations apart from Belgium, as Figure 3.14 shows. In other countries unionization has been declining, in some cases quite rapidly. Like small population size and ethnic homogeneity, strong labor unions increase the likelihood

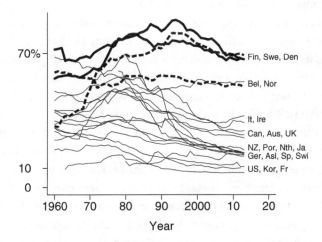

Figure 3.14 Unionization. Union members as a share of all employees. Data source: Jelle Visser, "ICTWSS: Database on Institutional Characteristics of Trade Unions, Wage Setting, State Intervention, and Social Pacts," version 5.1, 2016, Amsterdam Institute for Advanced Labour Studies, series ud, ud_s. Solid thick lines: Denmark and Sweden. Dashed thick lines: Finland and Norway. "Asl" is Australia; "Aus" is Austria.

that a country will adopt social democratic policies.[39] To what extent do they contribute to successful outcomes?

High unionization levels and centralization of union organizations facilitate coordinated wage setting. In the 1970s and 1980s, such coordination encouraged moderate wage increases by workers and thereby contributed to healthy macroeconomic performance—low unemployment together with low inflation. Since then, however, with the advent of independent central banks and restrictive monetary policy, coordinated wage bargaining hasn't been needed to achieve wage restraint.[40]

Indeed, the tables have now turned. A variety of developments— technological advance, globalization, heightened product market competition, the shareholder value revolution in corporate governance, and looser labor markets—have increased firms' incentive to resist wage increases and enhanced their leverage vis-à-vis workers. In this new economic context, the major challenge facing workers is to ensure that wages increase. A high unionization rate is likely to help.

In some countries with moderate unionization, such as the Netherlands and Austria, collective bargaining agreements are extended by convention to non-union sectors and firms. In France this kind of extension is legally mandated. Another alternative is wage setting by a public body; in Australia, tribunals set wages for many occupations. Because of these kinds of compensatory mechanisms, in some countries the share of the work force whose wages are determined by collective bargaining is a good bit larger than the share who are union members, as can be seen in Figure 3.15.

How successful have countries been at securing rising wages in the new economic era? Figure 3.16 shows, for the period from 1995 (the earliest year of available data) to 2013, each country's growth rate of GDP per capita and its growth rate of median compensation. The line in the chart is a 45-degree line; a country will be on the line if its median compensation has grown at the same rate as the economy. The Nordic nations and Belgium have high unionization rates, so it isn't surprising to see them close to the line. France and the Netherlands also are close; as just noted, in France the law requires extension of collectively bargained wage agreements, and the Netherlands has a strong extension norm. Austria, Australia, and New Zealand also have compensating mechanisms, such as Australia's tribunals. These three countries fall somewhat below the 45-degree line, meaning median wage growth has lagged behind that of the economy. The countries with the lowest rates of unionization and no compensating mechanism, such as the United States, sit farthest below the line.

Can a nation like the United States do something to avoid wage stagnation? At the low end of the labor market, one key is a statutory minimum wage that is moderately high and rises in concert with economic growth. Pursuit of high

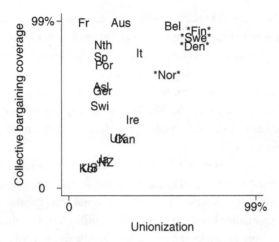

Figure 3.15 Unionization and collective bargaining coverage. 2013. Unionization: union members as a share of all employees. Collective bargaining coverage: share of employees whose wages are determined by a collective agreement. Data source: Jelle Visser, "ICTWSS: Database on Institutional Characteristics of Trade Unions, Wage Setting, State Intervention, and Social Pacts," version 5.1, 2016, Amsterdam Institute for Advanced Labour Studies, series ud, ud_s, adjcov. The asterisks highlight the Nordic countries. "Asl" is Australia; "Aus" is Austria.

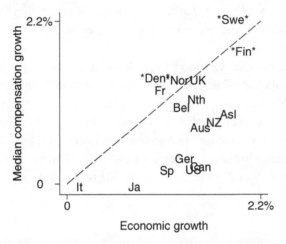

Figure 3.16 Economic growth and median compensation growth. 1995–2013. Median compensation growth: average annual growth rate of median inflation-adjusted compensation (wages plus in-kind compensation plus employees' and employers' social contributions). Data source: Cyrille Schwellnus, Andreas Kappeler, and Pierre-Alain Pionnier, "The Decoupling of Median Wages from Productivity in OECD Countries," *International Productivity Monitor*, 2017, table 1. Economic growth: average annual growth rate of inflation-adjusted GDP per capita. Data source: OECD. The line is a 45-degree line; a country will lie on this line if its median compensation growth rate is equal to its economic growth rate. The asterisks highlight the Nordic countries. "Asl" is Australia; "Aus" is Austria.

employment, a core element of social democratic capitalism, can contribute to wage growth via labor market tightness (a low unemployment rate, often referred to as "full employment"). When employers can benefit from hiring more workers but find it difficult to do so, they are more likely to bid up wages.[41] In addition, countries can use a government subsidy to supplement low earnings and ensure that incomes rise over time. The United States already has such a program, the Earned Income Tax Credit, which could help to fill this need if suitably expanded, as I explain in Chapter 7.

Wage increases aren't the only way in which unions matter. Strong unions are part of the reason the Nordic countries have had moderate increases in income inequality rather than large increases. Solidaristic wage setting compresses earnings, which limits inequality between the upper-middle class and those below. And unions push against skyrocketing executive pay, which helps to contain the gap between the top 1 percent and everyone else.[42]

In the United States, unions are very weak and, apart from the statutory minimum wage, there is no mechanism to compensate for that weakness. At the moment, the United States is an outlier among the rich nations. But that may not be true for long. As we can see in Figure 3.14, unionization rates have been declining in nearly all of the affluent countries. In Germany, once the prototypical "coordinated market economy," collective bargaining has weakened significantly, and it's quite possible other nations will suffer the same fate.[43]

So what outcomes can we expect in weak-union countries that adopt social democratic policies? While most outcomes are likely to be similar to those achieved by the Nordics, wage growth (in the middle and below) is likely to be slower and income inequality higher. It's important to emphasize, though, that this isn't a tradeoff. The point isn't that weak-union nations will be made worse in some way by embracing social democratic capitalism. It's just that social democratic policies won't in and of themselves solve the problems of wage stagnation and rising income inequality.

Low Income Inequality

Over the past decade a growing number of observers have hypothesized that income inequality has harmful effects on a range of outcomes we value, from education to health to economic growth to happiness and more.[44] If it does, the Nordic nations might have an advantage in achieving good outcomes because their other institutions, including strong labor unions, secure low levels of income inequality, as Figures 3.17 and 3.18 show. Some other rich democratic countries also have low inequality and thus might be able to duplicate this

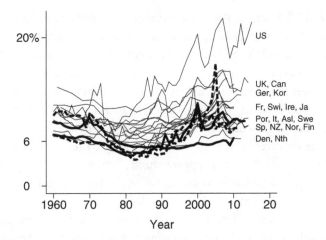

Figure 3.17 Income inequality between the top 1 percent and the bottom 99 percent. Top 1 percent's income share. Pretax income. Excludes capital gains. Data source: World Inequality Database. Solid thick lines: Denmark and Sweden. Dashed thick lines: Finland and Norway. "Asl" is Australia.

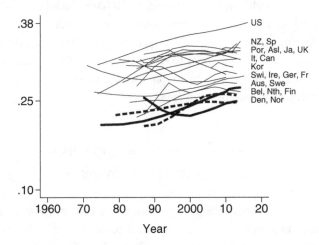

Figure 3.18 Income inequality within the bottom 99 percent. Gini coefficient. Posttransfer-posttax income, adjusted for household size. The lines are loess curves. The vertical axis doesn't begin at zero. Data sources: Luxembourg Income Study; OECD. Solid thick lines: Denmark and Sweden. Dashed thick lines: Finland and Norway. "Asl" is Australia; "Aus" is Austria.

success, but nations such as the United States and the United Kingdom prob-ably wouldn't. The worry is that while a nation such as the United States might benefit from social democratic policies, these benefits would be swamped by income inequality's destructive impact.

Is income inequality harmful? In separate research, I've examined the experiences of the world's affluent democratic countries in the period from

1979 to 2007.[45] Many of the most prominent predictions of harmful effects are supported only weakly or not at all. The evidence suggests that income inequality hasn't slowed the growth of college completion. It either hasn't reduced the increase in life expectancy or the decrease in infant mortality or, if it has, the impact has been small. It looks unlikely to have contributed to the rise in obesity. It hasn't slowed the fall in teen births or homicides since the early 1990s. It hasn't reduced economic growth. It hasn't hindered employment. It isn't systematically linked to the occurrence of economic crises. It hasn't reduced income growth for poor households. It doesn't appear to have affected average happiness. In the United States it has had little or no impact on trust in political institutions, on voter turnout, or on party polarization.

For some outcomes—interpersonal trust, the Great Recession, and household debt—the evidence is ambiguous or it is too soon to make any kind of informed judgment.

On the other hand, the evidence pretty strongly suggests that in the United States income inequality has increased disparities in education, health, family formation, family stability, and happiness, and it has reduced residential mixing. It also has reduced middle-class household income growth.

These findings suggest grounds for cautious optimism about the ability of a country such as the United States to enjoy most of the same good outcomes as the Nordic countries if it were to couple social democratic policies with a relatively high degree of income inequality.

Is Social Democratic Capitalism an Interdependent System?

A final hypothesis worth considering is that the difference between the Nordic nations and other rich democracies when it comes to social democratic capitalism is categorical—a difference not of degree but of kind. Social democratic capitalism, in this view, is an interdependent system, and a country won't enjoy its beneficial effects unless all of social democratic capitalism's component policies and institutions are in place.

As I noted in Chapter 2, the evidence suggests this isn't the case. Expansive and generous public insurance programs improve economic security, the incomes of the least well-off, and equality of opportunity in a linear fashion. High employment rates do the same. And the benefits of a big welfare state are independent of the benefits of high employment; neither requires the presence of the other. This means a country is likely to benefit by moving toward the social democratic model no matter where its starting point, and the benefit can come from expanding public insurance, from boosting employment, or from both.

Social Democratic Capitalism's Success Very Likely Is Generalizable

The Nordic nations have used social democratic capitalism to achieve "expanded Rawlsian" outcomes with little or no sacrifice of other elements of a good society. Skeptics hypothesize that the Nordics have unique attributes that enable them, and only them, to reap the benefits of social democratic policies without suffering tradeoffs. While these hypotheses are plausible, none of them turn out, on close inspection, to be compelling.

Compared to their counterparts in other affluent democratic nations, Nordic citizens don't have a uniquely strong work ethic or personal responsibility norms, they aren't more intelligent, and they aren't less prone to tax cheating. They are more trusting of fellow citizens, but that appears to have little impact on outcomes and in any case can be duplicated via improved confidence in government. It isn't clear that they are exceptionally solidaristic, nor that solidarity matters for successful outcomes. The Nordic nations' small size and homogeneity may well have made it more likely that they would adopt social democratic policies, but it probably hasn't contributed to their ability to get good outcomes. The Nordic countries have had a comparatively high level of government effectiveness, but not a uniquely high level. They have made greater use of corporatism than many other rich democracies, but corporatism doesn't seem to have had much impact on outcomes since the 1990s. They have avoided running up a large public debt despite high levels of government spending, but that owes to a commitment to balancing the budget across the business cycle, not to an abnormally strong willingness of their citizens to be heavily taxed.

One feature of the Nordic nations that *is* likely to matter is union strength. Countries such as the United States, where unions are weaker and there is no other mechanism to expand the reach of collective bargaining, are likely to have slower wage growth for ordinary workers and higher levels of income inequality than the Nordics. In other respects, however, the successful outcomes we observe in the Nordic nations are likely to carry over to other countries that adopt social democratic policies.

Political impediments to full embrace of social democratic capitalism are formidable in some nations. But once those impediments are surmounted, we can be relatively confident in the likelihood of good results.

4

Is There an Attractive
Small-Government Alternative?

As a country gets richer, people become more willing to spend money to insure against loss and to enhance fairness. This is visible when looking across nations at different levels of economic affluence, as we observed in Chapter 1, and we can see it in developments over time in the world's rich democratic nations. In the past century, these nations have gone from spending virtually nothing on public social programs to spending around 25 percent of GDP, on average, as Figure 4.1 shows.

These government transfers and services are a core element of social democratic capitalism. As we learned in Chapter 2, social democratic policies contribute to an "expanded Rawlsian" result—democracy, basic personal liberties, good living standards for the least well-off, income security, and equality of opportunity.

Is there a small-government set of institutions and policies that can do as well as social democratic capitalism? Some believe there is.[1] It consists of the following:

- Low government spending and taxes
- Strong families and voluntary organizations
- Private rather than public services
- Public transfer programs heavily targeted to the least well-off

Here, in principle, is how it would work: Smaller government produces faster economic growth. Even if a disproportionate share of this growth goes to the affluent, over the long run it will boost the living standards of the least well-off. Private actors provide healthcare, preschool, college, and other services via markets, with competition driving quality up and prices down. Families and voluntary organizations are the principal source of support for those in need. Government transfers targeted to the most needy fill in any gaps left by markets, families, and civic groups.

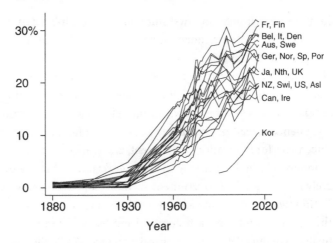

Figure 4.1 Public social expenditures. Share of GDP. Gross public social expenditures. Data source: Esteban Ortiz-Ospina and Max Roser, "Public Spending," *Our World in Data*, using data for 1880–1930 from Peter Lindert, *Growing Public*, volume 1, Cambridge University Press, 2004, data for 1960–1979 from OECD, "Social Expenditure 1960–1990: Problems of Growth and Control," OECD Social Policy Studies, 1985, and data for 1980ff from OECD, Social Expenditures Database. "Asl" is Australia; "Aus" is Austria.

This is plausible in theory. How well is it likely to work in practice?

Before proceeding, let me clarify two bits of terminology. First, some call government "big" if it is a heavy regulator or if it engages in active steering of investment. When I refer to the size of government as large or small here, I mean solely in terms of spending and taxing. Second, "small" must be understood in context. In all of the rich longstanding-democratic nations, total government expenditures and revenues are 25 percent or more of the GDP. Compared to most of the world's nations, that's fairly large. But compared to the norm among the affluent democracies, government taxing and spending at one-quarter or one-third of GDP is on the small side.

Small Government and Economic Growth

Government helps the economy in various ways.[2] When it protects safety and property and enforces contracts, it facilitates economic activity. Antitrust rules enhance competition. Schools boost human capital. Roads, bridges, and other infrastructure grease the wheels of business. Limited liability and bankruptcy provisions encourage risk-taking. Affordable high-quality childcare increases employment among parents and enhances the capabilities of less-advantaged children. Access to medical care improves health and reduces anxiety. Child labor restrictions, antidiscrimination laws, minimum wages, job safety regulations, consumer safety protections, unemployment insurance, and a host of other policies help ensure social peace.

On the other hand, governments with higher taxes and spending may be more prone to adopt policies that stifle business, reduce competition among firms, or waste resources. They may run up debts that channel resources into interest payments instead of productive activity. And high taxes can weaken financial incentives for innovation, investment, and work effort.

An economy will be healthier with some government than with none, but there surely is some level of government spending and taxing at which the balance will tip toward economic harm. It would be nice if social scientists could locate the tipping point with a theoretical model or a computer simulation. Unfortunately, we can't. We need empirical evidence. While there are many potential sources of such evidence, the most informative is the experiences of the affluent longstanding-democratic nations.

The evidence from those countries gives us no reason to think that government spending and taxing up to at least 55 percent of GDP, and perhaps as high as 65 percent, hurts economic growth. In all of these countries, public expenditures and taxation have grown significantly over the past century. If bigger government is bad for economic growth, this should have produced a slowdown in growth rates. But it hasn't. If we compare across the rich democracies, those with lower taxes and government spending haven't had faster economic growth rates. The best test, because it most closely approximates an experiment, is to see if countries that have increased public expenditures and taxes the most have experienced smaller increases (or larger decreases) in economic growth. They haven't.[3]

Civil Society

In the small-government model, families and voluntary organizations carry much of the load in helping children and the less advantaged. In assessing how well this is likely to work, it's worth asking why rich democratic societies turn to government programs at all, when they could leave this task entirely up to families and intermediary organizations.

One reason is that families and voluntary groups aren't comprehensive in their coverage. Many children live with just one parent, and some parents are short on money, time, or parenting skills. Civic groups by nature leave a significant portion of the population uncovered; they help who they can, but some people who need assistance fall through the cracks, and some types of assistance that would help aren't offered.

A second reason is that government programs sometimes are more effective and efficient, due to economies of scale, coordination advantages, reduced administrative costs, and ability to require universal participation. For instance, safety and property protection can be provided by voluntary organizations such as local militias, but it's done more effectively by a government police force (and more fairly, because rules ensure that everyone gets access to the service, the accused have rights, and so on). Voluntary savings clubs could address the problem of people setting too little money aside for retirement, but it's much more effective and efficient to create a public pension program.[4]

An additional problem with families and voluntary organizations is that they have been weakening over the past half century. Consider the United States. Figure 4.2 shows that the share of American adults who are married has declined. Each line is for a cohort. For two of the cohorts marriage rates declined over time, while for the others they've been stable. But across cohorts, from one to the next, the married share has fallen consistently. Among the cohort born between 1925 and 1934, nearly nine in ten were married at age thirty-five to forty-four. Half a century later, among the cohort born between 1975 and 1984, the share of thirty-five-to-forty-four-year-olds who are married is nearly 30 percentage points lower.

Figure 4.3 shows that the share of American children growing up in a two-parent household has fallen by 15 to 20 percentage points over the past half century. This trend owes partly to more married parents splitting up, but even more important has been the increase in having children without being married. As

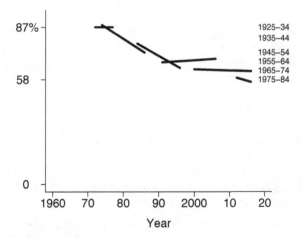

Figure 4.2 Marriage. Share of persons aged 35–44 who are married. Each line is for a cohort, with birth years listed to the right. The lines are linear regression lines. Data source: General Social Survey, sda.berkeley.edu/archive.htm, series marital.

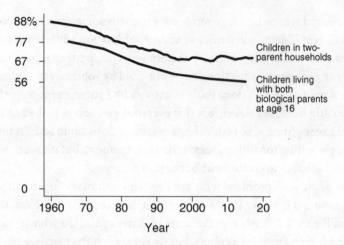

Figure 4.3 Children growing up with two parents. Share of children. The data points for children living with both biological parents are decade averages. Data sources: General Social Survey, sda.berkeley.edu/archive.htm, series family16; Census Bureau, "Living Arrangements of Children," table CH-1.

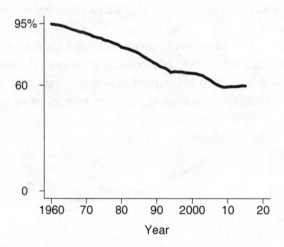

Figure 4.4 Children born to married parents. Share of children born to married women. Data source: National Center for Health Statistics.

we see in Figure 4.4, the share of children born to married parents dropped from 95 percent in 1960 to 60 percent in 2015.

These trends aren't surprising. Historically, marriage has been as much a product of economic necessity and social norms as of love and friendship. As societies get richer, economic circumstances and norms tend to change in ways that reduce the prevalence of marriage. Women become better educated, more likely to be employed, and more likely to earn enough to live independently.

In addition, government benefits allow women with limited labor market prospects to survive without dependence on a husband. So for an increasing share of women, getting married, or remaining in an unsatisfying marriage, becomes a choice rather than a financial necessity. A second change that comes with growing affluence is that people attach greater importance to individual freedom and choice. As a result, norms discouraging divorce, nonmarital cohabitation, and out-of-wedlock childbearing begin to weaken.

In the United States, the decline of marriage and of two-parent childrearing are particularly problematic from the perspective of economic security and equal opportunity because they've been more pronounced among Americans who have less education and income.[5]

Voluntary organizations also have been weakening. Robert Putnam compiled data on membership rates in thirty-two national chapter-based associations that existed throughout much of the twentieth century. Membership in these groups peaked around 1960 and then fell steadily for four decades, as we see in Figure 4.5. We also have two measures of the average amount of time Americans report spending on associational activity. As Figure 4.6 shows, both suggest a substantial decline between the mid-1960s and the early 1990s.

These two indicators are available only up to the turn of the century. Several others—membership and participation in religious organizations and membership in other types of organizations (labor unions, service groups, youth

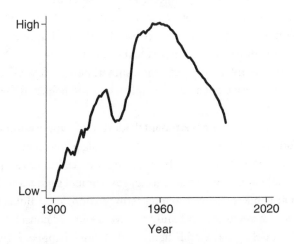

Figure 4.5 Membership in civic organizations. Membership in 32 national chapter-based organizations. Includes the Parent-Teacher Association (PTA), Boy Scouts, Girl Scouts, 4-H, League of Women Voters, Knights of Columbus, Rotary, Elks, Kiwanis, Jaycees, Optimists, American Legion, Veterans of Foreign Wars, the NAACP, B'nai B'rith, Grange, Red Cross, and more. Data source: Robert D. Putnam, *Bowling Alone: The Collapse and Revival of American Community*, Simon and Schuster, 2000, figure 8.

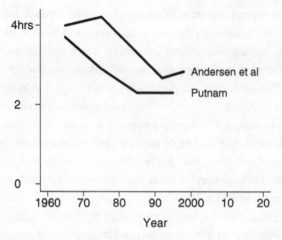

Figure 4.6 Time spent on civic association activity. Per month. Average among US adults. Includes activity such as attendance at community, political, church, or trade union meetings; voluntary tutoring or coaching; paperwork and other organizational work associated with voluntary activities; other voluntary community or political activities, such as demonstrations and providing meals/refreshments. The "Putnam" line excludes activity with religious organizations. Data sources: Robert D. Putnam, *Bowling Alone: The Collapse and Revival of American Community*, Simon and Schuster, 2000, p. 62; Robert Andersen, James Curtis, and Edward Grabb, "Trends in Civic Association Activity in Four Democracies: The Special Case of Women in the United States," *American Sociological Review*, 2006, table 1.

groups, sports clubs, and others)—suggest a similar story of decline in the post-2000 years. There are a few exceptions to the downward trend: volunteering, self-help and support groups, and Internet-based activism. But overall civic engagement has clearly decreased in the past half century.[6]

So families and voluntary organizations sometimes are less effective than public programs, they leave out a lot of people who need help, and they've been weakening over time.

In addition, these two nongovernmental sources of support and assistance are nearly or equally as prominent in nations with big governments as in those with smaller ones. Start with family. By reducing the need to have a partner to help with the breadwinning and childrearing, government services and transfers may cause fewer people to commit to long-term relationships.[7] But is this effect a large one? If so, we might expect family to have weakened considerably when universal K–12 schooling was established, but that didn't happen. Figure 4.7 has the share of children living in a home with two parents on the vertical axis, with government expenditures as a share of GDP on the horizontal axis. The pattern suggests that family isn't weaker in countries with bigger governments.

What about voluntary organizations? Yuval Levin, a prominent conservative thinker in the United States, contends that "progressive social policy . . . has

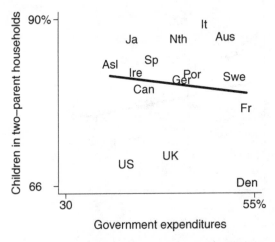

Figure 4.7 Government size and two-parent households. Children in two-parent households: share of children aged 0 to 14 who live in a household with both a mother and father. 2014. Data source: OECD Family Database, table SF1.3.A. Government expenditures: share of GDP. Includes all levels of government: national, regional, local. Average over 2000–2014. Data source: OECD. "Asl" is Australia; "Aus" is Austria. The line is a linear regression line. The correlation is –.12.

sought to make civil society less essential by assigning to the state many of the roles formerly played by religious congregations, civic associations, fraternal groups, and charities, especially in providing help to the poor."[8] In Figure 4.8 we see a negative association across the rich countries between government spending and the share of adults who say they are an active member of a civic group or organization, but the association is quite weak.

Consider the United States and Sweden, two countries that differ significantly in the expansiveness and generosity of their public insurance programs. If big government has the effect of quashing or crowding out civic engagement, we ought to observe a good bit more participation in civic groups by Americans than by Swedes. The World Values Survey asks about active membership in eight types of groups: art-music-education, charitable, consumer, environmental, labor union, professional, religious, and sports-recreation. Each country has been surveyed three times over the past two decades. It turns out the difference between the two countries is fairly small. When we average across these eight types of groups, 10 percent of Swedes say they are active members compared to 14 percent of Americans.

What about family and groups as a source of social support? Yuval Levin suggests that "As the national government grows more centralized, and takes over the work otherwise performed by mediating institutions—from families and communities to local governments and charities—individuals become increasingly atomized."[9] A helpful measure comes from the Gallup World Poll, which regularly asks "If you were in trouble, do you have relatives or friends you

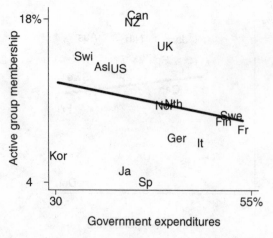

Figure 4.8 Government size and voluntary organizations. Active group membership: share of adults who say they are an active member of a civic group or organization. Average for eight types of organization: religious, sports-recreation, art-music-education, charitable, professional, labor union, environmental, consumer. Question: "Now I am going to read off a list of voluntary organizations. For each organization, could you tell me whether you are an active member, an inactive member, or not a member of that type of organization?" Average over 2005–2014. Data source: World Values Survey, worldvaluessurvey.org. Government expenditures: share of GDP. Includes all levels of government: national, regional, local. Average over 2000–2014. Data source: OECD. "Asl" is Australia. The line is a linear regression line. The correlation is −.21.

can count on to help you whenever you need them, or not?" The comparative pattern, shown in Figure 4.9, offers no indication of an adverse impact of big government.

So what does the evidence tell us about families and voluntary organizations as an alternative route to equality of opportunity, a good standard of living for the least well-off, and income security? They are inherently incomplete in coverage. They've been weakening over the past half century. And they're just as prominent, or very nearly so, in countries with big governments as in those with smaller ones. There is, in other words, little empirical support for this element of the small government model.

Private Services

Our goals for services are universal access, quality provision, cost control, and innovation. In many instances this requires embracing competition from private providers. Service users should be allowed to choose among providers, including private ones.

At the same time, we shouldn't go overboard on choice. For instance, in elementary and secondary schooling there is no need to offer parents a menu of

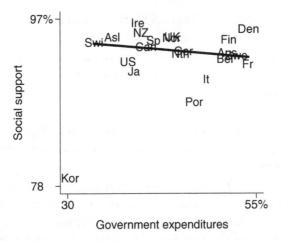

Figure 4.9 Government size and social support. Social support: share responding "yes" to the question "If you were in trouble, do you have relatives or friends you can count on to help you whenever you need them?" Average over 2005–2016. Data source: Gallup World Poll, via the *World Happiness Report 2017*, online appendix. Government expenditures: share of GDP. Includes all levels of government: national, regional, local. Average over 2000–2014. Data source: OECD. "Asl" is Australia; "Aus" is Austria. The line is a linear regression line, calculated with South Korea excluded. The correlation is −.22 (excluding South Korea).

"education plans" with various combinations of subject coverage or different options for sequencing math classes. We should simply allow them to choose which school their child will attend. In healthcare, we should allow people to choose their provider, but it isn't necessary to offer dozens of health insurance plans to choose among. A few options is likely to be enough.

Can we get good outcomes with *only* private service providers? In some instances, yes; think of mobile phones or rental cars. But in others, such as schools, healthcare, transportation, water, sewage, electricity, and Internet access, private providers tend to be unwilling or unable to ensure access to everyone at an affordable price, so government needs to play a role, potentially a large one, in provision.

The comparative experience also has taught us that in the healthcare sector, markets and competition don't give payers enough power to limit the prices charged by providers. Cost control is best achieved if the chief payer is government or a small number of insurers.[10]

Targeted Transfers

In principle, public insurance programs that target the most needy can help the least well-off at limited cost to taxpayers. How well do they work in practice?

Relative to the norm among affluent democratic countries, the US welfare state is small and targeted. It has been a success, but not a rousing one. Measures of material hardship suggest that Americans at the low end of the socioeconomic ladder are less well off than their counterparts in most other rich nations. The US relative poverty rate is among the highest. Tens of millions of Americans with fairly low incomes aren't poor enough to qualify for Medicaid, aren't old enough to get Medicare, but have too little income to buy health insurance on the private market, even with a government subsidy.[11]

Has this approach been more successful elsewhere? Proponents sometimes point to Australia as a success story.[12] On the horizontal axis of both charts in Figure 4.10 is a measure of the degree to which government transfers are targeted to the poor. Countries with greater targeting are to the right; countries that have a more universalistic public safety net, with transfers spread more evenly up and down the income ladder, are to the left. Australia's government transfers are directed toward lower-income households to a greater degree than in any other affluent country. In the first chart, the vertical axis shows public transfers as a share of total household income; here we see that Australia's transfers are highly targeted and that the country spends comparatively little on them. In the second chart, the vertical axis shows the degree to which transfers reduce income inequality; given its low spending, Australia's public transfer system is effective at redistributing income.[13] As a result, Australia's transfer programs boost

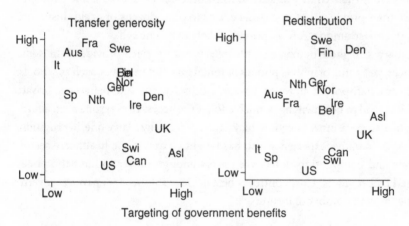

Figure 4.10 Australia's government transfers: heavily targeted, inexpensive, and redistributive. Australia is "Asl." Targeting: concentration coefficient for government transfers; "high" indicates more targeted, "low" more universal. Transfer generosity: government transfers as a share of household income. Redistribution: percentage reduction in inequality of household income (Gini coefficient) when government transfers are added. Data source: Ive Marx, Lina Salanauskaite, and Gerlinde Verbist, "For the Poor, but Not Only the Poor: On Optimal Pro-Poorness in Redistributive Policies," *Social Forces*, 2016, using Luxembourg Income Study data.

the incomes of its poor citizens more than America's do, and it has less poverty and material deprivation.

Yet Australia's success shouldn't be overstated. As we saw in Chapter 2, it has a higher incidence of material hardship and a higher relative poverty rate than a number of other affluent countries.[14]

In any case, it isn't clear that the Australian model would be feasible in a country such as the United States. Social scientists have long questioned the durability of a public safety net that relies on heavy targeting. Because a limited segment of the population receives benefits, political support for targeted programs can be tenuous.[15] The continued popular support for Australia's targeted transfers may owe to the country's exceptionally egalitarian culture. For instance, Australian retirees with high incomes receive little pension. If Social Security in the United States were restructured so that few upper-middle class or affluent Americans received any benefits, its political support might weaken significantly.

This isn't to say that all social transfer programs need to be universal. In the United States, some targeted programs such as Medicaid and the Earned Income Tax Credit have been expanded over time rather than retrenched. And Denmark, which has one of the world's most expansive public safety nets, has moved toward greater targeting.[16] The point is simply that it may be difficult for other countries to duplicate the Australian model.

Indeed, it isn't clear that Australia will be able to continue relying on this model. One element of Australia's heavily progressive government transfers has been a generous benefit to single mothers, whether they are employed or not and regardless of the age of their children. But since the early 2000s Australian policy makers have gradually reduced these benefits. Some solo parents have compensated by increasing paid work, but hardship has increased among this group as a whole.[17]

Swiss Lessons?

Switzerland is perhaps the most successful small-government country.[18] It is prosperous, free, orderly, and pleasant. It also does fairly well in income security and the decency of its income floor—not as well as the Nordic countries, but better than a number of other small-government nations.[19]

However, Switzerland isn't a useful case for assessing the attractiveness and viability of a small-government model. For several centuries, Switzerland has positioned itself as a financial safe-haven. This has brought in large amounts of foreign money, which has spilled over into economic growth, significant financial-sector employment, and high wages. In this sense, Switzerland is like Norway with its oil resources—a genuine success story, but not one from which we should draw inferences for other countries.

The Libertarian Fallback

So the evidence doesn't support the hope for a small-government model that can do as well as social democratic capitalism. For some small government proponents, that isn't a problem, because the real justification for small government is that individual freedom trumps other considerations.[20]

This libertarian notion has few adherents. Virtually everyone supports government paternalism in the form of property protection, traffic lights, and food safety regulations, to mention just a few examples. And many people support public social programs. When basic needs are met, we tend to prefer more security, broader opportunity, and confidence that living standards will improve over time. We are willing to allocate some of our present and future income to guarantee these things, and we are willing to allow government to take on that task. That's a key reason why public social programs tend to expand in scope and size as nations grow richer.

What's more, recent evidence from the world's rich democratic nations suggests that having a smaller government may not offer any advantage when it comes to personal freedom.[21] Researchers for the Cato Institute, a libertarian think tank, have assembled a "personal freedom index" that measures legal protection, security, freedom of movement, freedom of religion, freedom of association, assembly, and civil society, freedom of expression, and freedom in relationships. The pattern in Figure 4.11 suggests no incompatibility between big government and individual liberty.

An additional source of information about freedom is public opinion surveys. Since 2005 the Gallup World Poll has asked a representative sample of adults in various countries whether they are satisfied or dissatisfied with their freedom to choose what they do with their life. As we saw in Chapter 2, in countries with bigger welfare states a larger, not smaller, share say they are satisfied with their freedom to choose.

The "Government Failure" Fallback

The most common arguments in favor of small government point not to good outcomes they will achieve, but rather to the likelihood that government efforts will do worse.

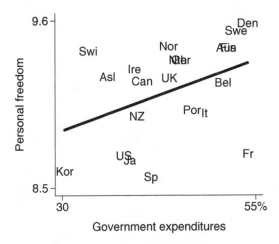

Figure 4.11 Government size and personal freedom. Personal freedom: average score for rule of law, security and safety, freedom of movement, religious freedom, freedom of association, freedom of expression and information, and freedom of identity and relationships. Scale is 0 to 10. 2012. Data source: Ian Vasquez and Tanja Porcnik, *The Human Freedom Index*, Cato Institute, 2015, table 2. Government expenditures: share of GDP. Includes all levels of government: national, regional, local. Average over 2000–2014. Data source: OECD. "Asl" is Australia; "Aus" is Austria. The line is a linear regression line. The correlation is +.40.

One such argument suggests that government's size is inversely related to its effectiveness: the bigger a government gets, the worse its performance will be. This could happen because the more a government spends and taxes, the more it invites lobbying by interest group for favors and the more opportunity and incentive it creates for policy makers and other public officials to dispense such favors. Also, larger governments may create more layers of bureaucracy, impeding effective decision making.[22]

What does the cross-country experience tell us about this hypothesis? There are various ways to measure the quality of government.[23] A common measure is the World Bank's "government effectiveness" indicator, which attempts to gauge public and expert perceptions of the quality of public services, the quality of the civil service and the degree of its independence from political pressures, the quality of policy formulation and implementation, and the credibility of the government's commitment to such policies. Figure 4.12 shows the relationship between countries' level of government spending and their score on this measure. There is no noteworthy association. Countries with bigger governments don't tend to have less effective ones.[24]

Another potential problem with government policy is excessive complexity— complicated public programs with an array of overlapping rules, benefits, and exemptions.[25] The United States, for instance, has an assortment of programs

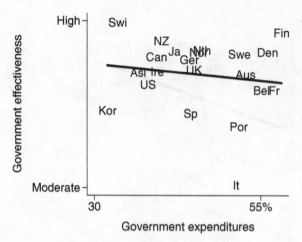

Figure 4.12 Government size and government effectiveness. 2014. Government
effectiveness attempts to capture perceptions of the quality of public services, the quality of the civil
service and the degree of its independence from political pressures, the quality of policy formulation
and implementation, and the credibility of the government's commitment to such policies. The data
set includes most of the world's countries, so "moderate" and "high" government effectiveness are
relative to this larger group. Data source: Stefan Dahlberg, Sören Holmberg, Bo Rothstein, Anna
Khomenko, and Richard Svensson, Quality of Government Basic Dataset, version Jan16, Quality of
Government Institute, University of Gothenburg, series wbgi_gee, using data from the World Bank.
Government expenditures: share of GDP. Includes all levels of government: central, regional, and
local. Data source: OECD. "Asl" is Australia; "Aus" is Austria. The line is a linear regression line. The
correlation is −.14.

and regulations that facilitate access to medical care: Medicare, Medicaid,
S-CHIP, the Veteran's Administration, tax breaks for employer contributions
to employee health insurance, healthcare exchanges run by the federal and state
governments in which private insurers compete for customers, a requirement
that private insurance plans don't exclude people with preexisting conditions, a
requirement that private plans allow parents to include their children up through
age twenty-five, and much more. America's tax system, with its multitude of
specific provisions and exemptions, is equally complex. The IRS Taxpayer
Advocate Service estimates that the direct and indirect costs of complying with
the US tax code total more than $150 billion a year, about 1 percent of GDP.[26]
The chief beneficiaries are industries, firms, and affluent individuals who lobby
for and are best positioned to take advantage of deductions and exemptions.
Simpler would be better.

However, policy complexity in the United States is a result more of
government's structure than of its size. The policy making process is ridden
with veto points that allow legislative opponents and interest groups to in-
sert loopholes and special benefits in exchange for allowing proposed

policies to go forward. The fact that the United States has multiple layers of government—federal, state, local—adds an additional layer of complexity. And since the 1970s congresses and presidents, eager to reduce the number of federal government employees ("shrink the bureaucracy"), have increasingly delegated the implementation of new or expanded programs to state and local governments, private contractors, and nonprofit agencies.[27] This too has tended to increase complexity.

But aren't larger government programs inherently more complex? No. Social Security is one of America's biggest government programs, but it also is very simple. A "Medicare for All" healthcare system would increase government expenditures' share of GDP, but it would be much less complex than the current hodgepodge. A tax system with fewer loopholes could raise more revenue and also be simpler.

Another common argument suggesting that government does more harm than good contends that bigger governments weaken competition, thereby reducing innovation and economic dynamism. According to Luigi Zingales, "When government is small and relatively weak, the most effective way to make money is to start a successful private-sector business. But the larger the size and scope of government spending, the easier it is to make money by diverting public resources. After all, starting a business is difficult and involves a lot of risk. Getting a government favor or contract is easier, at least if you have connections, and is a much safer bet."[28]

What do we observe when we compare across rich nations? The vertical axis of Figure 4.13 has an indicator of the degree of competition in product markets. The measure combines the degree of intensity of local competition, the degree to which corporate activity is spread across many firms rather than dominated by a few, the degree to which anti-monopoly policy effectively promotes competition, and the absence of barriers to imports, with the scoring for each of these elements based on a survey of executives conducted by the World Economic Forum. The figure shows that nations with bigger governments are just as likely as those with smaller governments to have competitive product markets.

Why don't bigger governments tend to reduce competition? One reason is that firms and other economic actors may care more about shaping government regulations in their favor than about getting government money. Consider the United States. Government taxes and spends less in the United States than in most other rich countries, and Americans embrace competition. Yet the US economy is riddled with rules, regulations, and practices that inhibit competition or privilege particular firms and industries. Half-hearted antitrust enforcement allows corporate behemoths to maintain market

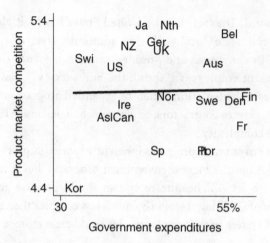

Figure 4.13 Government size and product market competition. The data are for 2014. Product market competition: average responses by executives in each country to four questions: (1) How would you assess the intensity of competition in the local markets in your country? 1 = limited in most industries; 7 = intense in most industries. (2) How would you characterize corporate activity in your country? 1 = dominated by a few business groups; 7 = spread among many firms. (3) To what extent does anti-monopoly policy promote competition in your country? 1 = does not promote competition; 7 = effectively promotes competition. (4) In your country, to what extent do tariff and non-tariff barriers limit the ability of imported goods to compete in the domestic market? 1 = strongly limit; 7 = do not limit. Data source: World Economic Forum, *The Global Competitiveness Report 2014–15.* Government expenditures: share of GDP. Includes all levels of government: central, regional, and local. Data source: OECD. "Asl" is Australia; "Aus" is Austria. The line is a linear regression line. The correlation is +.03.

share and profitability despite little innovation. Patents limit competition in pharmaceuticals, computer software, entertainment, and a slew of other product markets.[29] Licensing, credentialing, and certification requirements for occupations or particular types of businesses dampen competition in product markets ranging from medical care to legal services to education to taxi transportation to hairdressing and beyond.[30] Zoning restrictions and historic preservation designations limit expansion of housing units in large cities by imposing building height restrictions and preventing new construction on much of the land.[31] The federal government's practice of allowing some banks to become "too big to fail" gives those banks an advantage over competitors (they can engage in riskier strategies, with potentially higher profit margins, than can others).[32]

A second reason is that firms' efforts to get money from government include lobbying for preferential tax treatment. When they succeed, the result is less government revenue, not more—a smaller government rather than a larger one.

Third, the hypothesis that big government results in less competition fails to consider the types of programs on which government spends money. Public insurance programs mainly transfer money to individuals; they offer little opportunity for firms or interest groups to grab a piece of the pie. That is largely true of government provision of services as well. Opportunity for large-scale diversion of public resources is present mainly in government service programs that rely on private provision, such as the US military or Medicare's prescription drug benefit.

Hypotheses about government failure are perfectly plausible in theory. But when we look across the existing rich democratic nations, we find no support for the contention that bigger governments perform less effectively or inhibit competition more than smaller ones.

The Small-Government Mirage

Social democratic capitalism has proved effective at generating "expanded Rawlsian" outcomes—democracy, basic personal liberties, a high living standards floor, income security, and equality of opportunity—without sacrificing economic growth or other features of a good society. Is there a small-government set of institutions and policies that can achieve the same thing? Some conservative thinkers, researchers, and policy makers believe there is. It relies on markets and small government to achieve rapid economic growth, some of which trickles down to the least well-off. Families and voluntary organizations provide income, services, and other types of support to those who need it. Services are offered by private providers. Targeted government transfers fill in the gaps.

The record of the world's affluent democratic nations over the past half century doesn't support this hypothesis. Countries with smaller government haven't had faster economic growth. Families and voluntary organizations aren't comprehensive in coverage; they sometimes are less effective and efficient than government programs; they've been weakening over time; and they are nearly or equally as prominent in nations with a big government as in those with a smaller one. Private provision of services should be welcomed, even embraced, but it is most effective as a complement to public provision rather than a substitute. Relying on heavily targeted government transfers can reduce poverty and insecurity, but not as well as social democratic capitalism; and it may be sustainable only in a country with a strong egalitarian ethos, such as Australia.

Conservatives who are willing to treat small government as merely one goal among many, rather than their be-all and end-all, can help improve social policy in a variety of ways, such as increasing choice and competition in the delivery of services, enhancing supports for employment, reducing regulatory obstacles to employment (such as occupational licensing requirements and zoning restrictions), and improving government efficiency and effectiveness (for instance, by fostering more consistent use of evidence in policy making).[33] In some of the rich democratic nations, this is what conservatives now tend to do. In the United States, on the other hand, many on the right, including much of the leadership of the Republican Party, remain wedded to the small-government illusion.

5

Why Not a Basic Income?

A universal basic income would give individuals a regular cash payment. Eligibility wouldn't be conditional on need or employment status. The idea originated centuries ago, with proponents such as Thomas More in the 1500s and Thomas Paine in the 1700s. It had a small but prominent group of supporters in the late 1800s and early 1990s, including John Stuart Mill, Henry George, and Bertrand Russell. Milton Friedman and James Tobin popularized it in the 1960s (as a "negative income tax"), and US policy makers gave a version of it serious consideration in the early 1970s.[1] Today it has advocates on both the left and right sides of the political spectrum.[2]

On the left, supporters highlight the potential enhancement to freedom—specifically, freedom from work. In the words of Philippe Van Parijs:

> A basic income would serve as a powerful instrument of social justice: it would promote freedom for all by providing the material resources that people need to pursue their aims. . . . A UBI [universal basic income] makes it easier to take a break between two jobs, reduce working time, make room for more training, take up self-employment, or join a co-operative. And with a UBI, workers will only take a job if they find it suitably attractive. . . . If the motive in combating unemployment is not some sort of work fetishism—an obsession with keeping everyone busy—but rather a concern to give every person the possibility of taking up gainful employment in which she can find recognition and accomplishment, then the UBI is to be preferred.[3]

For proponents on the right, the chief advantage is reduction in the deadweight costs of public social programs. If the government simply cuts a check to each person, there is no need for caseworkers or bureaucratic oversight.

A third attractive feature of a universal basic income is that because it would go to everyone, recipients will face no stigma.

There are important details to be worked out. Should the payment go to all individuals, to all residents, to all citizens, or to all adults? Should it be paid out monthly or once a year? What should be the amount? Should the amount be the same or different across geographic regions in a country and across age groups?

At the generous end of the spectrum, Philippe Van Parijs and Yannick Vanderborght argue for all permanent fiscal residents as recipients (this excludes undocumented migrants and tourists but doesn't presuppose citizenship).[4] The amount would be one-fourth of a country's per capita GDP, which in the contemporary United States would be about $15,000 per year. At the lower end, Charles Murray argued, a decade ago, for $10,000 per adult, with a requirement that $3,000 of this be put toward health insurance.[5]

Despite its potential advantages, I don't think a basic income grant is a good idea for the world's rich democratic nations at the moment. The last three words in that sentence are important. In the future, artificial intelligence may advance to a point at which robots are able to perform complex in-person service tasks—preschool teacher, elderly caregiver, yoga instructor—as well as humans do. Robots don't get sick or show up late for work, so it's likely that as consumers we will prefer them over humans. (Some might favor humans because they're quirky, but presumably robots can be programmed to have that feature too.) In this scenario there may be few jobs that we're willing to pay other humans to perform. A basic income would then be a necessity.[6]

The question, though, is whether it would be good to move to a basic income in advance of that future scenario. I think not, for four reasons.

First, for many basic income proponents, a major advantage is the libertarian element—the idea of letting people choose what to do with the help they receive from government. This does have an appealing quality. On the other hand, a key purpose of government is to help individuals to do things they should but otherwise wouldn't, or to do those things for them. Government builds roads, ensures clean air and water, and protects us from physical harm. It educates us, provides access to medical care, and forces us to save for retirement. It encourages us to take time off during the first months of a child's life, offers parenting advice, and helps to monitor the health of newborns and their parents. Caseworkers for active labor market programs and social assistance help us to see what types of professions or jobs might be a good choice, how to develop the right kind of skills, and how to get hired.

These types of services and public goods improve lives. They are worth spending money on.[7] In part because of their value, the share of people doing this kind of work—advising, educating, organizing, managing—and the share of income spent on purchasing such services, is likely to increase going forward. The fact that some public sector bureaucrats do their job poorly, or that some people would prefer to be left alone rather than instructed, guided, cajoled, or pressured by a caseworker, doesn't mean we should turn away from providing such support to the individuals and families who need or want it. Paternalism has a place in a good society.[8]

Second, the likely reduction in employment produced by a basic income could be economically and politically problematic. Let's stipulate that a basic income grant worth discussing would be large enough to allow people to opt out of employment. For many proponents, that is one of its chief virtues. Some supporters suggest that the drop in employment might nevertheless be small or nil because current social assistance recipients would no longer face a withdrawal of benefits if they were to work more, because budding entrepreneurs would create more new firms given the greater cushion in the event of failure, and because people would have more freedom to choose a job they truly want and to get the skills needed to succeed in it.[9] Even so, we should expect some loss of employment.[10]

How much? We have little useful information for prediction. Perhaps the best is a three-year basic income experiment conducted in a small Canadian town in the 1970s. Labor force participation dropped by about 10 percentage points.[11] For a basic income that is permanent and more generous, as proponents would like, we might anticipate a larger drop.

Suppose the decline amounts to 15 percentage points. How problematic would this be? An optimist might point out that since 1970 the employment rate among prime-working-age (age 25–54) men has dropped by about 10 percentage points in many of the rich democratic nations, and this hasn't been especially problematic.[12] But that's mainly because the employment rate among women has risen more rapidly than it has fallen among men. A decline in the *overall* employment rate of 15 percentage points could have troubling consequences. We need high employment to ensure a tax base large enough to pay for generous social programs and government's other functions.[13]

Moreover, reciprocity norms are unlikely to disappear, so a policy that significantly reduces employment might lead to a polarizing political divide.[14] Here is one prediction, by Paul Krugman, of how that is likely to play out in the United States:

> Britain, pre-Thatcher, had an unemployment benefit system that effectively allowed you to decide to live on the dole. There was even a song, "I'm going down to Liverpool to do nothing, with UB40 in my hand." That ended up being a very unpopular system, even in Britain, where the politics are much less racially polarized than they are here. It's going to take a long, long time to persuade a significant block of American voters that a system in which you can simply choose not to work is okay.[15]

Here is another, by Robert Frank:

> A moment's reflection reveals that a payment large enough to sustain an urban family of four at the official government poverty threshold (about $25,000 today) would quickly doom the program politically. Imagine, for example, that a group of ten families formed a rural commune and supplemented their $250,000 in cash grants with the untaxed fruits of gardening and animal husbandry. If they located in Colorado or Washington, they could also grow marijuana, both for sale and for personal consumption. Their mornings would be free to drink coffee and engage in extended discussions of politics and the arts. They could hone their musical skills. They could read novels, write poetry, play nude volleyball. Is it far-fetched to imagine that at least some groups would forsake paid employment in favor of leading lives like these at taxpayer expense? Once such groups formed, wouldn't it be only a matter of time before journalists found them and created an eager audience for reports of their doings? And wouldn't most voters react angrily once footage of the reveling commune members began running on the nightly news?
>
> Of course they would, and who could blame them? An Indianapolis dentist with varicose veins rises at 6:00 each morning and drives through heavy traffic on a snow-covered freeway to spend the rest of his day treating patients with bad breath who take offense if they're charged a fee for breaking an appointment without notice. How could such a person not be indignant at the sight of able-bodied people living it up on his tax dollars?
>
> In short, it is a pipe dream to imagine that an income grant large enough to lift an urban family from poverty could win or sustain political support for long. Voters might support a cash grant if it were far too small to support comfortable living in groups. But the proposal would then fail by definition as an effective social safety net.[16]

To make matters worse, the existence of a UBI might reduce public pressure on government to provide jobs and full employment. That could add to the employment loss that results directly from the basic income.

In their 2017 book *Basic Income*, Van Parijs and Yannick Vanderborght propose a UBI of one-quarter of a country's per capita income, which in the contemporary United States would mean about $15,000. This would go to each individual, including children. A couple with four children would thus have an employment-free family income of $90,000, which would go a long way in many parts of the country. The incentive to have more children in order to boost one's grant would add another dimension to the potential hostility.

The third reason I don't favor a universal basic income at this moment is that it very likely would have to replace some existing public insurance programs, and in doing so it would reduce our ability to allocate resources according to differing needs and circumstances.[17]

Consider the Van Parijs and Vanderborght proposal. They recommend a basic income grant equal to one-fourth of GDP per person, which means total spending on the UBI would amount to 25 percent of GDP. If we set aside healthcare, that's more than any rich democratic nation (including the Nordics) currently spends on public transfers and services.[18] So the political feasibility of such a grant would hinge on getting rid of some, perhaps most, other public insurance programs. Suppose we go with a less expensive version, proposed in several recent popular books, of $1,000 per month for each adult.[19] In the United States, that means $12,000 per year for the 250 million adults, which totals about 17 percent of GDP. Adding that to our existing public social programs would still put the United States well above the total public social expenditures of any other affluent democracy.

We then would have little or no ability to address differential need. If I'm a single adult earning $50,000 a year who gets downsized from my job, I would be much better off receiving 80 percent of that salary in unemployment compensation rather than $15,000 (to again use the US amount) from a basic income. If I have a disabled child who needs daily support and special educational services, the cost will be much greater than the $30,000 I would get for my basic income plus that of the child. And so on. Public insurance programs have been put in place over time to address specific and varied risks and needs. Losing this would, in my view, outweigh what we would gain from the simplicity of a basic income.

Van Parijs and Vanderborght advocate for starting with a smaller UBI. If we do that, it wouldn't be necessary to reduce spending on other programs. UBI would be a complement to the existing welfare state, rather than a substitute. The hope is that once established, it could grow over time alongside those other programs.[20] However, as we get richer, policy makers would need to decide whether additional money should go to the UBI or to other benefits and services. Because of differences in needs and the advantage of programs that cater to those differences, policy makers might reasonably tend to favor increasing spending on those programs rather than on the UBI. This makes it hard to envision the path to a UBI large enough to give people the freedom from employment that advocates desire.

The fourth reason, and the most important one, why I don't favor a shift to a universal basic income at this moment is that we know social democratic policies yield very good outcomes, whereas basic income's effects are uncertain.[21] If and when modern societies get to a point where artificial intelligence is producing widespread joblessness, we probably will have no alternative to a basic income. But today we do, and that alternative is an attractive one.

PART 2

SOCIAL DEMOCRATIC AMERICA

6

America Is Underachieving

A good society will ensure a decent standard of living for its least well-off. It will reduce people's vulnerability to large income declines and large unanticipated expenses. It will aggressively curtail inequality of opportunity. And it will ensure that economic growth is broadly shared among the population rather than confined to those at the top.

The United States isn't doing as well as it should in meeting these challenges. The incomes and living standards of Americans at the bottom of the socioeconomic ladder are too low. Too many Americans experience significant income declines from year to year or month to month, and too many are vulnerable to a large unanticipated medical expense. Too few who grow up in disadvantaged circumstances are able to reach the middle class. And too few see their boat lifted when the economic tide rises.

A Decent Floor

The United States has done less well by its poor than a number of other affluent nations. The reason is straightforward. Like their counterparts abroad, America's least well-off have been hit hard by shifts in the economy since the 1970s, but whereas some countries have ensured that government supports rise as the economy grows, the United States hasn't.

Think of the income distribution in the United States as a ladder with five rungs, each of which holds 20 percent of the population. Among the 25 million households on the bottom rung, the average income as of 2016 was just $22,000.[1]

Income data are never perfect. However, these data, compiled by the Luxembourg Income Study, are quite good. They include earnings, government cash and near-cash transfers, and other sources of income. Tax payments are subtracted. These data give us a pretty reliable picture of the incomes of American households.

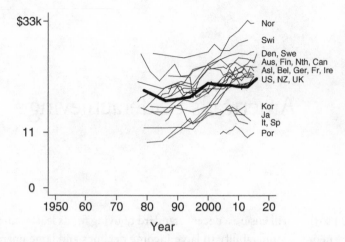

Figure 6.1 10th-percentile household income. Posttransfer-posttax household income.
The incomes are adjusted for household size and then rescaled to reflect a three-person household,
adjusted for inflation, and converted to US dollars using purchasing power parities. "k" = thousand.
Data sources: Luxembourg Income Study; OECD. Thick line: United States. "Asl" is Australia;
"Aus" is Austria.

Figure 6.1 puts this in comparative context. It shows that, despite America's
affluence, household income at the 10th percentile of the income ladder—the
middle of the bottom 20 percent—is lower in the United States than in many
other wealthy nations. It's only a little below some of the other countries, but
$5,000 to $10,000 below the leaders. That's a sizable difference.

What if we look at a more direct measure of living standards, such as material
hardship? Two OECD researchers, Romina Boarini and Marco Mira d'Ercole,
have compiled material deprivation data from surveys in various nations.[2] Each
survey asked identical or very similar questions about seven indicators of material hardship: inability to adequately heat one's home, constrained food choices,
overcrowding, poor environmental conditions (noise, pollution), arrears in payment of utility bills, arrears in mortgage or rent payments, and difficulty making
ends meet. Boarini and Mira d'Ercole create a summary measure of deprivation
by averaging, for each country, the shares of the population reporting deprivation in each of these seven areas. As Figure 6.2 indicates, the United States fares
just as badly on this measure.[3]

How Poor Are the Poor?

Are low-income Americans genuinely poor? Most have clothing, food, and
shelter. Many have a car, a television, heat and air conditioning, and access to
medical care.[4] But making ends meet on an income of $22,000 is a challenge.

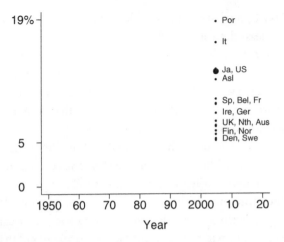

Figure 6.2 Material hardship. Average of the deprivation rates (share of households experiencing deprivation) in the following seven areas: inability to adequately heat home, constrained food choices, overcrowding, poor environmental conditions such as noise and pollution, arrears in payment of utility bills, arrears in mortgage or rent payment, difficulty in making ends meet. Measured in 2005. Data source: OECD, *Growing Unequal?*, 2008, pp. 186–88, using data from the Survey on Income and Living Conditions (EU-SILC) for European countries, the Household Income and Labour Dynamics in Australia survey (HILDA) for Australia, and the Survey of Income and Program Participation (SIPP) for the United States. Large dot: United States. "Asl" is Australia; "Aus" is Austria.

That comes out to $1,833 a month. If you spend $700 on rent and utilities, $350 on food, and $250 on transportation, you're left with just $533 each month for all other expenses. It's doable. Tens of millions of Americans offer proof of that. But this is a life best described as "scraping by."[5]

There are important caveats. First, since $22,000 is the average among these 25 million households, about half have an income above this amount, and for them making ends meet will be a little easier. But it still won't be easy. And the other half have incomes below the $22,000 average. Some solo adults make do with an income of $10,000 or $5,000. Some families with one or more kids get by on $15,000 or even less. About 1 percent of families with children and 4 percent of those without children have, for at least three months during a year, an income of less than $2 a day—an astonishingly low amount.[6] (That includes food stamps [Supplemental Nutrition Assistance Program, or SNAP], EITC payments, and housing support.) As Kathryn Edin, Luke Shaefer, Matthew Desmond, and others have documented, some of these Americans live in abysmal conditions and engage in demeaning or dangerous activities in order to subsist.[7]

Second, some of these households have assets that reduce their expenses or provide a cushion in case expenses exceed income in a particular month or year. Some, for example, own a home outright and therefore have no rent or mortgage payments. But many aren't saved by assets. Approximately 26 percent of

Americans are "asset poor," meaning they don't have enough assets to replace their income for at least three months.[8]

Third, these data very likely underestimate the true incomes of some households at the bottom. The data come from a survey in which people are asked what their income was in the prior year. People in low-income households tend to underreport their income, perhaps out of fear that accurate disclosure will result in loss of a government benefit they receive.[9]

A fourth caveat is that some of these 25 million households have a low in- come for only a short time. Their income may be low one year because the wage earner leaves her job temporarily to have a child, is sick, or gets laid off. By the following year, the earner may be back in paid employment. Some low earners are just beginning their work career. Five or ten years later, their earnings will be higher, or perhaps they will have a partner whose earnings add to household income. On the other hand, some who move up the economic ladder will later move back down. Shuffling in and out of poverty is common. Using a data set known as the Panel Study of Income Dynamics (PSID), which tracks the same set of households over time, Mark Rank, Thomas Hirschl, and Kirk Foster cal- culate that 10 percent of Americans spend ten or more years with an income below 1.5 times the US government's official poverty line (about $18,000 for a single adult and $37,500 for a household of four as of 2017) between the ages of twenty-five and sixty.[10]

Fifth, some of these households are made up of immigrants from much poorer nations. They are better off than they would have been if they had stayed in their native country, though that doesn't change the fact that they are scraping by.

How much should these qualifiers alter our impression of low-end living standards in the United States? It's difficult to say. Suppose the truly poor consti- tute only half of the bottom fifth. That's still 10 percent of American households, quite a large share for a nation as rich as ours.

Since the early 1990s the Survey of Income and Program Participation (SIPP) has asked a representative sample of Americans about their living conditions. Here's what the most recent survey, in 2011, found for households in the bottom fifth of incomes:

- 54 percent don't have a dishwasher.
- 47 percent don't have a computer.
- 31 percent don't have a clothes washer.
- 22 percent report two or more of the following: unmet essential expenses, unpaid rent or mortgage, unpaid utilities, disconnected utilities, discon- nected phone, insufficient amount of food to eat, didn't see a doctor when needed, didn't see a dentist when needed.
- 11 percent say their neighborhood is unsafe.[11]

Americans with incomes in the lowest income quintile are much more likely than those with higher incomes to experience stress, worry, and sadness, as Figure 6.3 shows.

Perhaps we should measure low income in another way. We could, for example, identify the minimum income needed for a decent standard of living and then see how many households fall below this amount. A team of researchers at the Economic Policy Institute did this, estimating "basic family budgets" for metropolitan and rural areas around the country and calculating the share of families with incomes below these amounts in 1997–1999.[12] They concluded that approximately 29 percent of US families could not make ends meet. More recently, researchers for United Way have calculated household "survival budgets" in six states—California, Connecticut, Florida, Indiana, Michigan, and New Jersey—as of 2012. Their estimates for a family of four range from $46,000 in Indiana to $65,000 in Connecticut, and they find that 35 percent or more of the households in each of the six states had an income below the needed amount.[13] Researchers with Wider Opportunities for Women and the Center for Social Development at Washington University have calculated basic-needs budgets for various household types as of 2013. They estimate that to meet basic expenses, a single adult needed, on average, about $30,000, and a household with two adults and two children needed about $71,000. According to their calculations, 45 percent of American households fell below the threshold.[14]

This helps us understand a striking finding in a 2014 study by the Federal Reserve. Among 5,000 American adults asked how they would pay for a

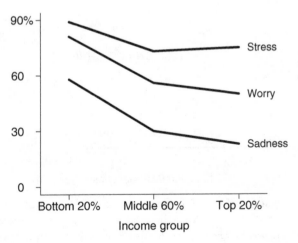

Figure 6.3 Income and psychological well-being. Share of respondents who say they experienced a given emotion yesterday. 2008–2013. Data source: Carol Graham, *Happiness for All? Unequal Hopes and Lives in Pursuit of the American Dream*, Princeton University Press, 2017, figure 4.1, using Gallup data.

hypothetical emergency expense totaling $400, 37 percent said they would be unable to pay for it with cash or money in their bank account.[15]

How Do Rich Countries Lift Up the Poor?

Historically, economic growth has tended to benefit all households, and that continues to be the case in many of the world's developing nations.[16] But the fruits of economic growth don't automatically trickle down to everyone. In many affluent countries, a host of developments over the past generation—economic globalization, the proliferation of computers and robots, shareholder obsession with short-term profits, union decline, and more—have reduced the likelihood that economic growth will boost the incomes of the least well-off.

Figure 6.4 shows that the United States has been particularly ineffective at lifting up the poor since the late 1970s. Many other rich democracies achieved larger increases in the incomes of low-end households (vertical axis) despite smaller increases in GDP per capita (horizontal axis).[17]

Why is that? We often think of the trickle-down process as one in which economic growth produces rising earnings via more work hours and higher wages. But in many of these countries, the earnings of low-end households have increased little since the late 1970s. Instead, it is increases in government transfers that have tended to drive increases in incomes.[18]

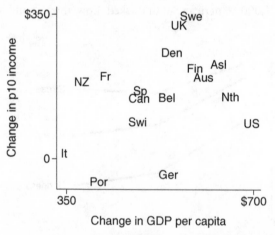

Figure 6.4 Economic growth and 10th-percentile household income growth. Change is per year, over the period 1979–2015. Because the actual years vary somewhat depending on the country, change is calculated by regressing household income or GDP per capita on year. Household incomes are posttransfer-posttax, adjusted for household size (the amounts shown are for a household with three persons). Household incomes and GDP per capita are adjusted for inflation and converted to US dollars using purchasing power parities. Ireland and Norway are omitted; both would be far off the plot in the upper-right corner. Data sources: OECD; Luxembourg Income Study. "Asl" is Australia.

Sometimes increasing government transfers requires no explicit policy change, as benefit levels tend to rise automatically as the economy grows. This happens when, for instance, pensions, unemployment compensation, and related benefits are indexed to average wages. Increases in other transfers, such as social assistance, typically require periodic policy updates. That's true also of tax reductions for low-income households.

In the United States, only one of our main government transfer programs, Social Security, is structured in such a way that benefit levels automatically increase when the economy grows. Social Security retirement benefits are indexed to average wages, so they have tended to rise more or less in concert with GDP.

Unemployment benefit levels are determined by state governments. In many instances, the benefit level is a "replacement rate," which means the payment is a certain fraction of the unemployed person's former wage or salary. Because real wages in the bottom half of the distribution have not increased in the past several decades, unemployment benefits for Americans in low-wage jobs have failed to keep up with growth in the economy. Other programs, such as the Earned Income Tax Credit (EITC), the Supplemental Nutritional Assistance Program (SNAP, formerly called the Food Stamp Program), Social Security Disability Insurance (SSDI), and Supplemental Security Income (SSI), are indexed to prices. This means they keep up with inflation, but not with economic growth. Temporary Assistance for Needy Families (TANF, formerly AFDC) payments are determined by state policy makers; there is no automatic increase, not even for inflation. AFDC-TANF benefit levels have fallen in inflation-adjusted terms for nearly half a century.

If most of the poorest Americans were Social Security recipients, the United States probably would be a good bit higher on the vertical axis in Figure 6.4. But in the United States, as in many other countries, many of the least well-off aren't retirees.[19] The fact that most of our other government transfers have only kept up with inflation rather than with the economy, coupled with the decline in AFDC-TANF benefits, is a key cause of slow income growth at the bottom in the United States.

Should we bemoan the fact that employment and earnings haven't been the key trickle-down mechanism in recent decades? Not necessarily. At higher points in the income distribution, they do play more of a role.[20] But for those at the low end there are limits to what employment can accomplish. Some people have psychological, cognitive, or physical conditions that limit their earnings capability. Some are constrained by family circumstances. At any given point in time, some will be out of work due to structural or cyclical unemployment. And some are retirees. We surely can do better at helping able adults get into (or back into) employment, but we shouldn't pretend that paid work is a realistic route to guaranteeing rising incomes for everyone.[21]

Why So Little Progress for America's Poor?

Let's look more closely at over-time developments in the United States. Figure 6.5 shows average income among the bottom fifth of US households between 1979 and 2016. It increased by about $3,500. That's a small improvement for a period of nearly four decades, especially given that for much of this time the American economy was growing at a healthy clip.[22]

Why has this happened? There are two main sources of income for low-end households: earnings and government transfers. And there are two main ways for households to increase earnings: more employment (increasing work hours or adding a second earner) and higher wages. So progress for the poor depends on increases in wages and/or employment and/or government transfers.

Low-end wages rose steadily from the mid-1940s through the end of the 1960s. We don't have reliable data for this period on wages at the 10th percentile, but a substitute indicator is the statutory minimum wage. As Figure 6.6 shows, the minimum wage (adjusted for inflation) increased sharply in the 1940s, 1950s, and 1960s and then decreased a bit in the 1970s. Since then it has been flat, as has the 10th-percentile wage level.

The pattern for employment is similar. Here a good measure is the average number of employment hours among low-income working-age households, shown in Figure 6.7. In the 1980s and 1990s, hours rose during periods of economic growth, but they then decreased so precipitously during recessions

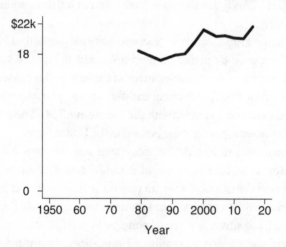

Figure 6.5 Average income of households in the bottom 20 percent. Posttransfer-posttax income. The income measure includes earnings, government cash and near-cash transfers, and other sources of cash income. Tax payments are subtracted. The incomes are adjusted for household size and then rescaled to reflect a three-person household. The incomes are in 2016 dollars; inflation adjustment is via the CPI-U-RS. Data source: Luxembourg Income Study, series dhi.

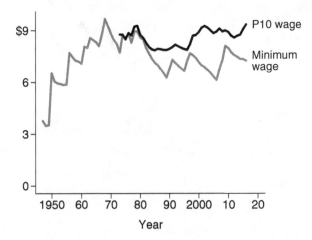

Figure 6.6 Low-end wages. The wage levels are in 2016 dollars; inflation adjustment is via the CPI-U-RS. Data sources: US Department of Labor; Economic Policy Institute, "Wages by Percentile."

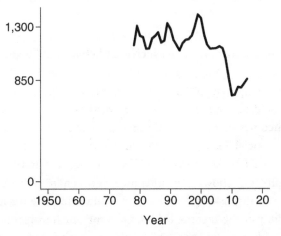

Figure 6.7 Employment hours in low-income households. Average annual hours worked in working-age ("head" aged 25–64) households in the bottom quintile of the pretransfer-pretax income distribution. Data source: calculations by Keith Bentele using Current Population Survey data (IPUMS March Extracts).

that there was little or no net gain. In the 2001–2007 upturn, economic growth produced no rise in the country's overall employment rate[23] or in average employment hours for low-end households. Hours then fall sharply during the great recession in 2008–2010, and they remain well below their 1979 level.

As a result of these two trends since the 1970s—flat wages and flat or declining employment—low-end households have seen little increase in inflation-adjusted earnings. Figure 6.8 shows that market income among households on

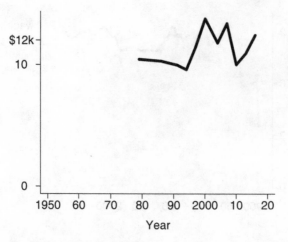

Figure 6.8 Average market income of households in the bottom 20 percent. Pretransfer-pretax household income among households in the bottom fifth of posttransfer-posttax incomes. The incomes are adjusted for household size and then rescaled to reflect a three-person household. The incomes are in 2016 dollars; inflation adjustment is via the CPI-U-RS. Data source: Luxembourg Income Study.

the bottom fifth of the income ladder increased between 1979 and 2016, but only slightly.

With wages and employment failing to increase, we're left with government transfers. As I noted in the previous section, this has been the key source of rising low-end incomes in a number of other affluent countries, but less so in the United States. Social Security benefits increased, as did the Earned Income Tax Credit. But social assistance (AFDC-TANF) coverage and benefit levels decreased.[24] Figure 6.9 shows the difference between market (pretransfer-pretax) income and disposable (posttransfer-posttax) income for households on the bottom fifth of the income ladder. Government transfers have helped America's poor, adding $7,000 to $10,000, on average, to their incomes. And they've played a particularly important role in propping up incomes during economic downturns. But their relatively small increase since the late 1970s, coupled with stagnant wages and stagnant employment, means there has been little rise in the incomes of low-end households.[25]

The United States could have done better. An instructive comparison case is the United Kingdom. Like the United States, its public insurance programs are moderately generous, and it too was governed in the 1980s and early 1990s by a conservative party devoted to rolling back the welfare state. In 1997 a New Labour government was elected, headed by Tony Blair and Gordon Brown, and a year later Prime Minister Blair committed the government to ending child poverty in the UK within a generation. That led to a raft of policy initiatives that significantly boosted incomes among Britain's least well-off.[26] As Figure 6.10

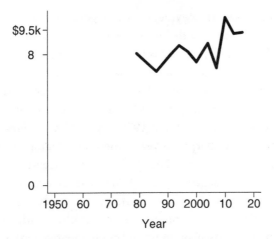

Figure 6.9 Net government transfers to households in the bottom 20 percent. Average posttransfer-posttax income minus average pretransfer-pretax income among households in the bottom fifth of posttransfer-posttax incomes. The incomes are adjusted for household size and then rescaled to reflect a three-person household. The amounts are in 2016 dollars; inflation adjustment is via the CPI-U-RS. Data source: Luxembourg Income Study.

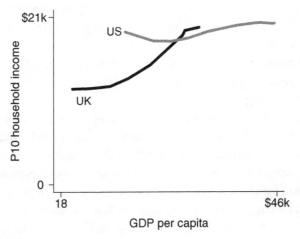

Figure 6.10 GDP per capita and 10th-percentile household income in the US and the UK. The data points are years, from 1979 to 2013. The lines are loess curves. Household incomes are posttransfer-posttax, adjusted for household size and then rescaled to reflect a three-person household. Household incomes and GDP per capita are adjusted for inflation using the CPI and converted to US dollars using purchasing power parities. "k" = thousand. Data sources: OECD; Luxembourg Income Study.

shows, household income at the 10th percentile rose much more in the UK than in the United States, despite similar increases in per capita GDP.

What about the argument that overly-generous social policy is the cause of slow income growth for the poor? According to this argument, economic growth has failed to boost employment because government benefits reduce the incentive for Americans with limited skills to take a low-paying, not-very-satisfying job.[27] This hypothesis is inconsistent with three key pieces of evidence. First, social assistance benefits in the United States—mainly AFDC-TANF and food stamps—have never been particularly generous, and their generosity has decreased steadily since the mid-1970s.[28] Second, we see in Figure 6.7 above that in the 1980s and 1990s employment hours in low-end households did rise quite sharply in years when the economy was growing. Ironically, it was in the period from 2001 to 2007, after incentives for employment were significantly enhanced by the 1996 welfare reform, that we see no rise in work hours during an economic growth phase. The demographic group that was the focus of welfare reform, poor single mothers with children, did experience a jump in employment hours and consequently in market incomes during this period.[29] However, more employment for this group didn't translate into more employment for America's poor overall. Third, the cross-country evidence suggests that countries with generous social policies have done just as well on employment and economic growth as those, like the United States, that have a smaller public safety net.[30]

The core of America's strategy for alleviating poverty over the past generation has been to encourage more paid work among the poor by making sure that government transfers aren't very generous. This strategy has not been a success, in part because during this same period the economy has changed in ways that make it more difficult for people at the low end of the labor market to get more work hours and/or rising wages.

The experience of other rich democratic nations suggests that the social democratic approach would be more effective. Increase benefit levels, and ensure that they rise over time in concert with growth of the economy. Encourage employment by providing an array of services and supports—paid parental leave, good-quality low-cost childcare and preschool, training and job placement assistance, and individualized monitoring and cajoling. Ensure that wages, too, rise over time. In the Nordic countries this is achieved by strong unions; in the United States, where unions are much weaker, it must be done via the statutory minimum wage.

Income Security

To be economically secure is to have sufficient resources to cover your expenses. One key, which we've just looked at, is to have a decent income. But that may not suffice if you experience a sizable income decline or a large unanticipated expense.

Americans care a good bit about the stability of their income and expenses. The Pew Research Center and the U.S. Financial Diaries Project have each asked a sample of low- and middle-income Americans "Which is more important to you: financial stability or moving up the income ladder?" In both surveys, two-thirds or more chose financial stability.[31]

Though we don't have hard data to confirm it, from the mid-1940s through the mid-1970s the incidence of large income drops and large unanticipated expenses very likely decreased for most Americans. Incomes grew steadily for most households, reducing the share with low income and facilitating the purchase of private insurance. More Americans became homeowners, thereby accumulating some assets. And a raft of new government laws and programs—limited liability law, bankruptcy protection, Social Security old-age benefits, unemployment insurance, the statutory minimum wage, AFDC (Aid to Families with Dependent Children, which later became TANF), Social Security disability benefits and Supplemental Security Income (SSI), Medicare and Medicaid, food stamps, the EITC, and disaster relief, among others—provided a safeguard against various financial risks, from business failure to job loss to poor health to old age.[32]

Since the 1970s, America's economy and society have changed in ways that are likely to have reduced income security.[33] Competition among firms has intensified as manufacturing and some services have become internationalized. Competitive pressures have increased even in sectors not exposed to competition from abroad, such as retail trade and hotels, partly due to the emergence of large and highly efficient firms such as Walmart and Amazon. At the same time, companies' shareholders now demand constant profit improvement rather than steady long-term performance.

These shifts force management to be hypersensitive to costs and constraints. One result is less job security, as firms restructure, downsize, move offshore, or simply go under. Another is enhanced management desire for flexibility, leading to greater use of part-time and temporary employees and irregular and unstable work hours. This increases earnings instability for some people and may reduce their likelihood of qualifying for unemployment compensation, paid sickness leave, and other supports. Employers also have cut back on the provision of benefits, including health insurance and pensions.

Private insurance companies are subject to the same pressures. And they now have access to detailed information about the likelihood that particular persons or households will get in a car accident, need expensive medical care, or experience home damage from a fire or a hurricane. As a result, private insurers are more selective about the type and extent of insurance coverage they provide and about the clientele to whom they provide it.[34]

Family protections against income instability also have weakened. Having a second adult in the household who has a paying job (or can get one) is a valuable asset in the event of income loss, but the share of American households with two adults has decreased, particularly among those with less education and income.[35]

The period since the 1970s also has witnessed commitments by some prominent American policy makers to ensure that, in Bill Clinton's expression, "the era of big government is over." Apart from AFDC-TANF, America's social programs haven't shrunk or disappeared. But they haven't increased very much.[36]

A survey in 2007 found more than 25 percent of Americans saying they were "fairly worried" or "very worried" about their economic security, and a similar survey in 2016 found 23 percent of Americans saying they feel "not financially secure." According to the latter poll, 17 percent are frequently anxious about their financial situation and 30 percent lose sleep over it.[37]

What do the data tell us about the incidence of large income declines and unanticipated expenses in the United States?

Large Income Decline

A large income decline can be problematic even if it is temporary. Consider two households with the same average income over ten years. In one, the income is consistent over these years. The other experiences a big drop in income in one of the years, but offsets that drop with higher-than-average income in one or more later years. The latter household may be worse off in two respects. First, a loss tends to reduce our happiness more than an equivalent gain increases it.[38] Second, a large decline in income may force a household to sell assets, such as a home, in order to meet expenses. Even if the income loss is ultimately offset, the household may be worse off at the end of the period due to the asset sell-off.

It turns out, however, that income declines often aren't temporary. Stephen Rose and Scott Winship have analyzed data from the Panel Study of Income Dynamics (PSID) to find out what subsequently happens to households experiencing a significant income decline.[39] According to their calculations, among households that experience a drop in income of 25 percent or more from one year to the next, about one-third do not recover to their prior income level even a full decade later.

There are various reasons for this. Some people own a small business that fails and don't manage to get a job that pays as much as they had made as entrepreneurs. Others become disabled or suffer a serious health problem and are unable to return to their previous earnings level. Still others are laid off, don't find a new job right away, and then suffer because potential employers view their jobless spell as a signal that they are undesirable employees. And some are a product of early death of a partner; about 10 percent of American twenty-five-year-olds won't live to age sixty-five, and 30 percent of Americans don't have life insurance.[40]

So income decline is a problem for those who experience it. How many Americans are we talking about? Several researchers have attempted to estimate the frequency of sharp income drops. Rose and Winship find that in any given year, 15 to 20 percent of Americans experience an income decline of 25 percent or more from the previous year.[41] Using a different data source, the Survey of Income and Program Participation (SIPP), Winship estimates that during the 1990s and 2000s approximately 8 to 13 percent of households suffered this fate each year.[42] A study by the Congressional Budget Office matches data from the Survey of Income and Program Participation (SIPP) with Social Security Administration records and gets a similar estimate of approximately 10 percent during the 1990s and 2000s.[43] A team of researchers led by Jacob Hacker uses a third data source, the Current Population Survey (CPS), covering the mid-1980s through 2012, and comes up with an estimate of 15 to 20 percent.[44]

These estimates vary, but not wildly. In any given year, approximately 10 to 20 percent of working-age Americans will experience a severe income drop.

Has the incidence of large year-to-year income decline increased over time? Yes, according to calculations by Jacob Hacker's team and by Scott Winship. These estimates, shown in Figure 6.11, suggest a rise in sharp year-to-year income decline of perhaps three to five percentage points since the 1970s or the early 1980s.[45] This isn't a massive increase, but it might cumulate into a more substantial one.

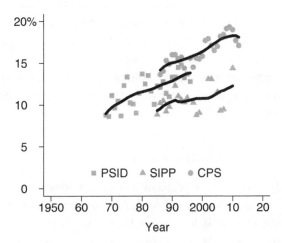

Figure 6.11 Households experiencing an income decline of 25 percent or more from one year to the next. The lines are loess curves. PSID and SIPP: posttransfer-pretax income, for households with a "head" aged 25–54. PSID is the Panel Study of Income Dynamics. SIPP is the Survey of Income and Program Participation. Data source: Scott Winship, "Bogeyman Economics," *National Affairs*, 2012, figure 1. CPS: posttransfer-pretax income, for households of all ages. CPS is the Current Population Survey. Data source: Economic Security Index.

What's the bottom line? In my read, the data tell us that sharp declines of income among working-age American households are relatively common and that their incidence has increased over the past generation.

We need to keep in mind that some of these declines are voluntary. A person may leave a job or cut back on work hours to spend more time with children or an ailing relative. A couple may divorce. Someone may quit a job to move to a more desirable location without having another job lined up. Still, we don't know what portion of income drops are voluntary, and I don't think we should presume that most are.

How should we assess the trend? One perspective is to view it as unavoidable. The American economy has changed since the 1970s. It's more competitive, flexible, and in flux. Even though this is bad for some households, it can't be prevented unless we seal the country off from the rest of the world and heavily regulate our labor market. In this view, we should be happy that the increase in income volatility hasn't been larger.

A different take is disappointment. There are ways to insure against income decline. We could have improved our porous unemployment compensation system, added a public sickness insurance program, and created a wage insurance program so that someone who loses a job and gets a new, lower-paying one receives some payment to offset the earnings loss. We could have done more, in other words, to offset the impact of economic and family shifts.

Figure 6.12 offers cross-country rationale for this view. It shows the average year-to-year income decline of households in which an individual experiences a large (20 percent or more) decrease in earnings. In the United States the average drop in income is 28 percent. In most other rich nations it is smaller, and in some it is *much* smaller. The cross-country difference owes partly to the likelihood of having a second employed person in the household whose earnings cushion the loss and partly to the scope and generosity of public insurance programs that compensate for lost earnings.

Month-to-Month Income Variability

Income instability isn't solely a problem if it occurs across years. Instability *within* a year—from month to month—also can put a strain on households, particularly if their income is low or moderate. As Jonathan Morduch and Rachel Schneider put it, "Without a steady income, planning is much more complicated, and accumulating savings for unexpected expenses—not to mention major purchases such as a car or down payment on a home, or college or retirement—is quite difficult. At a more basic level, uncertainty about how often and how much income will arrive each month adds to the challenge of creating a basic spending plan for how to buy groceries and pay household bills."[46]

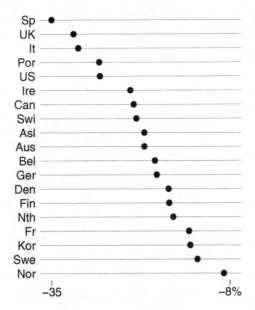

Figure 6.12 Household income decline. Average year-to-year household disposable income decline for households in which an individual experiences an earnings decline of 20 percent or more. 2005–2010. Data source: Boris Cournède, Paula Garda, Peter Hoeller, and Volker Ziemann, "Effects of Pro-Growth Policies on the Economic Stability of Firms, Workers and Households," OECD Economic Policy Papers 12, 2015, figure 18, using CNEF, ECHP, EU-SILC, and OECD data.

For some households, employment and/or work hours vary from month to month as one or more adults in the household moves between jobs or takes time off due to sickness or family constraints. And some jobs—seasonal ones, temp work, "platform economy" positions—are inherently irregular.[47] Even when employment is stable, pay can vary. This has always been true for taxi drivers and waitresses, but uncertain pay is no longer exceptional. Recent studies estimate that 2.6 percent of employed Americans are on-call workers, 1.5 percent are temp agency workers, 3.1 percent are workers provided by contract firms, and 0.5 percent are workers who provide services through online intermediaries such as Uber and Task Rabbit. Around 10 percent have irregular or on-call shifts.[48] As many as 33 percent engage in freelance work of various kinds.[49]

The U.S. Financial Diaries Project collected detailed cash flow and financial data from 237 low- and middle-income families over the course of a year. On average, about one-third of the income of these families came from a job without a regular wage or salary. In 40 percent of these families, one or both adults worked more than one job. Among those with low income, about half reported that it was difficult to predict what the household's income would be during the month.[50]

Large month-to-month income fluctuations are much more common among Americans in the lowest fifth of incomes than among those with middle incomes.[51] Households deploy myriad strategies to deal with unsteady income: working an additional job, borrowing from a credit card or money lender, borrowing from family or friends, paying some bills but not others, pawning possessions, selling blood, selling drugs.

Large Unanticipated Expense

A sharp drop in income causes economic insecurity because we may have trouble meeting our expenses. A large unanticipated expense can produce the same result.

In the United States, the most common large unexpected expense is medical. About one in ten Americans doesn't have health insurance. Others are underinsured, in the sense that they face a nontrivial likelihood of having to pay out of pocket for healthcare if they fall victim to a fairly common accident, condition, or disease.

Of course, many of the uninsured and underinsured won't end up with a large healthcare bill. And some who do will be able to pay it (due to high income or to assets that can be sold), or will be allowed to escape paying it because of low income or assets, or will go into personal bankruptcy and have the debt expunged. Yet in a modern society, we should consider most of the uninsured and some of the underinsured as economically insecure, in the same way we do those with low income or unstable income.[52] They are living on the edge to a degree that should not happen in a rich nation in the twenty-first century. After all, every other affluent democracy manages to provide health insurance for all of its citizens without breaking the bank.

This form of economic insecurity decreased sharply with the spread of employer-provided private health insurance after World War II and then with the creation of Medicare and Medicaid in the mid-1960s. As Figure 6.13 shows, the share of Americans without private health insurance fell steadily from the mid-1940s until the mid-1970s. But then it leveled off, and in the 1980s it began rising. The share without either public or private insurance was essentially flat from the mid-1970s until full implementation of the Affordable Care Act (ACA) beginning in 2014.

The ACA is expected to eventually reduce the uninsured share to perhaps 6 to 8 percent. That would be a substantial improvement in economic security, but it will still leave us well short of where we could be, and where every other affluent nation has been for some time.[53]

Figure 6.13 understates vulnerability to a large medical expense in two respects. First, these data capture the average share of Americans who are

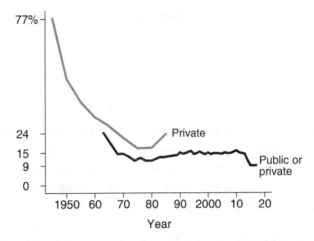

Figure 6.13 Persons without health insurance. Share of the population. 1964: Medicare and Medicaid created. 1998: S-CHIP enacted. 2010: Affordable Care Act passed. Data sources: Michael A. Morrisey, *Health Insurance*, 2nd edition, 2013, exhibit 1.2; Council of Economic Advisors, "Methodological Appendix: Methods Used to Construct a Consistent Historical Time Series of Health Insurance Coverage," 2014, using data from the National Health Interview Survey and other surveys.

uninsured at a given point during a year. (This share is very similar to the share who are uninsured throughout the entire year.[54]) If we instead ask how many are uninsured at *any* point during a year or two, the figure is larger. The Lewin Group has estimated that during the two-year period of 2007 and 2008, 29 percent of Americans lacked health insurance at some point.[55]

Second, it isn't only the uninsured who are insecure. Some Americans have a health insurance policy that is inadequate.[56] One in ten Americans lacks health insurance, but six in ten say they worry a great deal about the availability and affordability of healthcare.[57] Out-of-pocket expenses allowed by insurance plans sold on the national health insurance exchanges can be as high as $13,700 a year for a family.[58] In a survey by the Commonwealth Fund, 29 percent of American adults aged 19 to 64 who had health insurance throughout the year reported that they had outstanding medical debt, had trouble paying medical bills, were contacted by a collection agency for unpaid medical bills, or had to alter their way of life in order to pay medical bills.[59] And a survey by the Kaiser Foundation and the *New York Times* found that "while insurance may protect people from having medical bill problems in the first place, once those problems occur the consequences are similar regardless of insurance status. Among those with medical bill problems, almost identical shares of the insured (44 percent) and un- insured (45 percent) say the bills have had a major impact on their families."[60]

About one-quarter of Americans who file for bankruptcy do so mainly be- cause of a large medical bill.[61] Personal bankruptcy filings increased steadily from 1980 through the mid-to-late 2000s. Since 2010 they have decreased, perhaps in part because of the expansion in health insurance via the Affordable Care Act.[62]

Wealth as a Backstop?

A large income decline or a large unanticipated expense will be less problematic for a household that has assets it can use to replace the lost income or to pay the expense. But several pieces of evidence suggest that this helps only a small share of Americans who experience these types of economic insecurity.

First, the bottom 40 percent of Americans have virtually no wealth. From 1983 (the first year of reliable data) through 2007, average net worth among this group was just $2,000. In 2010, 2013, and 2016, the three most recent years in which data were collected, it was *negative* $10,000.[63] Second, studies regularly find that about one in four Americans don't have enough wealth to replace 25 percent of their income.[64] Third, the Economic Security Index team headed by Jacob Hacker has calculated the share of Americans who experience an income drop from one year to the next of 25 percent or more *and* who don't have enough liquid assets to cover that loss. According to their estimates, taking wealth into account does reduce the incidence of this type of insecurity, but only by one percentage point.[65]

Equality of Opportunity

Americans believe in equal opportunity. Surveys consistently find 90 percent of the public agreeing that "our society should do what is necessary to make sure that everyone has an equal opportunity to succeed."[66] This level of support is rare.[67] It suggests policy makers ought to put equality of opportunity at or near the top of the list of goals they pursue.

True equality of opportunity is unattainable. Equal opportunity requires that each person has equivalent skills, abilities, knowledge, and noncognitive traits upon reaching adulthood, and that's impossible to achieve. Our capabilities are shaped by genetics, developments in utero, parents, siblings, peers, teachers, preachers, sports coaches, tutors, neighborhoods, and a slew of chance events and occurrences. Society can't fully equalize, offset, or compensate for these influences. In fact, if we think about it carefully, few of us would want equal opportunity, as it would require massive intervention in home life and probably also genetic engineering. Moreover, if parents knew everyone would end up with the same skills and abilities at the end of childhood, they would have little incentive to invest effort and money in their children's development, and that would result in a lower absolute level of capabilities for everyone.

What we really want is for each person to have the most opportunity possible. We should aim, in Amartya Sen's helpful formulation, to maximize people's capability to choose, act, and accomplish.[68] Pursuing that goal requires providing greater-than-average help to those with less advantageous circumstances or conditions. That, in turn, would move us closer to equal opportunity, even if, as I've just explained, full equality of opportunity isn't attainable.

Americans have tended to believe that ours is a country in which opportunity is plentiful. This view became especially prominent in the second half of the nineteenth century, when the economy was shifting from farming to industry and Horatio Alger was churning out rags-to-riches tales.[69] It's still present. On the night of his election in 2008, Barack Obama, the country's first African American president, began his victory speech by saying "If there is anyone out there who still doubts that America is a place where all things are possible . . . tonight is your answer."

There's more than a grain of truth in this sentiment. One of the country's major successes in the past half century has been its progress in reducing obstacles to opportunity stemming from gender and race. Today, women are more likely to graduate from college than men and are catching up in employment and earnings.[70] The gap between whites and nonwhites has narrowed as well, albeit less dramatically.[71]

When we turn to family background, however, the news is disappointing. Americans growing up in less advantaged homes have far less opportunity than their counterparts from better-off families, and this opportunity gap hasn't narrowed in recent decades. If anything, it may have widened.

Family Background and Unequal Opportunity

There is no straightforward way to measure opportunity, so social scientists tend to infer from outcomes, such as employment or earnings. If we find that a particular group fares worse than others, we suspect a barrier to opportunity. It isn't ironclad proof, but it's the best we can do. To assess equality of opportunity among people from different family backgrounds, we look at relative intergenerational mobility—a person's position on the income ladder relative to her or his parents' position.[72]

Think of the income distribution as a ladder with five rungs, with each rung representing a fifth of the population. In a society with equal opportunity, every person would have a 20 percent chance of landing on each of the five rungs and hence a 60 percent chance of landing on the middle rung or a higher one. The reality is quite different. An American born into a family in the bottom fifth of incomes between the mid-1960s and the mid-1980s has roughly a 30 percent chance of reaching the middle fifth or higher in adulthood, whereas an American born into the middle fifth has a 66 percent chance of ending up in the middle fifth or higher and one born into the top fifth has an 80 percent chance.[73]

Figure 6.14 offers a more precise way to see the degree of inequality of opportunity. It uses data from a large sample of Americans born since 1970 and their parents. On the horizontal axis is the parents' income rank—their income relative to the incomes of other parents. On the vertical axis is the average income ranking of the children of those parents when the children are in young adulthood. The dot farthest to the left, for instance, shows the average income rank of children whose parents were in the lowest income percentile.

In a society with perfectly equal opportunity, the data points in this chart would form a flat line—children's income position in adulthood would, on average, be the same no matter what their parents' income position was. Instead we see a line that slopes sharply upward. Among people whose parents were on the bottom rungs of the income ladder, the average income ranking in young adulthood is relatively low. Among those whose parents were in the middle, the average is in the middle. And persons whose parents' income was at the high end tend to end up at the high end themselves.

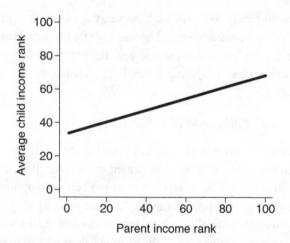

Figure 6.14 Children's income rank by their parents' income rank. Horizontal axis: Parents' household income rank when the child is in her or his late teens, in 1994–2000. Vertical axis: Child's average household income rank at age 31–37, in 2014–2015. The sample is children born in the years 1978–1983. The income data are from tax filings merged with Social Security records. Data source: Raj Chetty, Nathaniel Hendren, Maggie R. Jones, and Sonya R. Porter, "Race and Economic Opportunity in the United States: An Intergenerational Perspective," Working Paper 24441, National Bureau of Economic Research, 2018, online appendix figure 1. The slope is .35.

There is some movement. Among children whose parents were in the lowest income percentile, the average ranking is the 33rd percentile. That means some end up at the bottom, some end up in the middle, and perhaps a few end up even higher. Similarly, among children whose parents were at the top of the income distribution, the average income ranking is around the 68th percentile, which means many of them don't stay at the very top. Even so, the correlation between parents' income position and children's income position is quite strong.

The causes of this stark inequality of opportunity are multiple and interlinked, from genes to family structure to parenting to household income to neighborhood to schooling and more.

Children in low-income homes tend to start behind right from birth, due to differences in genetics and developments in utero.[74]

Poorer children are less likely to grow up in a home with both of their original parents, and kids from single-adult households tend to fare worse on a host of outcomes, from school completion to staying out of prison to earning more in adulthood.[75]

Low-income parents aren't able to spend as much on goods and services aimed at enriching their children, such as music lessons and other extracurricular activities, travel, and summer camp.[76]

Parents with less education and income tend to read less to their children and provide less help with schoolwork. They are less likely to set and enforce clear rules and routines. And they are less likely to encourage their children to aspire to high achievement in school and at work. Low-income parents also are more likely to be anxious and stressed, which may affect the general home atmosphere and hinder their ability to provide emotional support to their children.[77]

Children in low-income families are more likely to grow up in neighborhoods with high crime, with few employed adults, and with weak institutions and organizations (civic groups, churches, sports leagues).[78]

In the prekindergarten years, children of affluent parents often attend high-quality education-oriented preschools, while kids of poorer parents are more likely to be left with a neighborhood babysitter who plops them in front of the television.[79]

Elementary and secondary schools help to equalize opportunity, and as disparities in funding across public K–12 school districts have diminished, they've become more effective at doing so. Yet large differences in the quality of schools persist, and the poorest neighborhoods still tend to have weaker ones.[80]

The equalizing effects of college are striking. Among Americans whose family incomes during childhood were in the bottom fifth but who get a four-year college degree, 53 percent end up in the middle fifth or higher, which is pretty close to the 60 percent chance they would have with perfectly equal opportunity.[81] But children from poor backgrounds are less likely than others to enter and complete college, partly because they lag behind at the end of high school, partly because college is so expensive, and partly because many colleges don't have adequate supports in place.[82]

When it comes time to get a job, the story is no better. Low-income parents tend to have fewer valuable connections to help their children find good jobs.[83] Some people from poor homes are further hampered by a lack of English language skills. Another disadvantage for the lower-income population is that in the 1970s and 1980s, the United States began incarcerating more young men, including many for minor offenses. Having a criminal record makes it more difficult to get a stable job with decent pay.[84] A number of developments, including technological advances, globalization, a loss of manufacturing employment, and the decline of unions, have reduced the number of jobs that require limited skills but pay a middle-class wage—the kind of jobs that once lifted poorer Americans into the middle class.[85]

Finally, not only do those from better-off families tend to end up with more schooling and higher-paying jobs. They also marry (or cohabit with) others like themselves, which magnifies the impact of gaps in skills, jobs, and pay among individuals.[86]

Has the Opportunity Gap Widened?

From the mid-1800s to the 1970s, differences in opportunity based on family circumstances decreased.[87] As the farming-based US labor force shifted to manufacturing, many Americans joined the paid economy, allowing an increasing number to move onto and up the income ladder. Elementary education became universal, and secondary education expanded. Then, in the 1960s and 1970s, school desegregation, the outlawing of discrimination in college admissions and hiring, and the introduction of affirmative action opened economic doors for many Americans.

What has happened since the 1970s? It's too soon to tell, as most Americans born after the 1970s are still relatively young, making it difficult to know where on the income ladder they will end up. But there is reason to suspect that America's progress in reducing inequality of opportunity based on family background has stalled, and perhaps even reversed. A few trends favor enhanced mobility: racial discrimination has continued to decrease, health insurance coverage for the poor has expanded due to changes in Medicaid in the 1980s and the late 1990s, we removed lead from gasoline beginning in the 1970s, violent crime has decreased sharply since the early 1990s, and in many states the gap in school funding between low-income districts and high-income districts has been reduced. However, a number of the key determinants of attainment— family structure, parents' income, parenting styles and behaviors, education, employment and earnings, and partner selection—have moved in a direction that is likely to have widened the opportunity gap.[88]

The collapse of the two-parent family has been most pronounced among parents with less than a college education. The same appears to be true of parental instability, which some experts believe is more consequential for children than the number of parents in the home.[89]

Inequality in incomes has increased since the 1970s.[90] Over the same period we've seen a rise in inequality of families' expenditures on their children, particularly between the top and the middle.[91]

With the advent of the modern intensive-parenting culture, class differences in parenting styles and traits seem to have increased.[92]

As care of preschool-age children has shifted from stay-at-home mothers to out-of-home providers, it's likely that the gap in the quality of care and education received by low-income kids versus high-income kids during these years has widened.

According to data compiled by Sean Reardon, the gap in average test scores between middle-school children from high-income families versus low-income families has risen steadily. Among children born in 1970, those from high-income homes scored, on average, about three-quarters of a standard deviation higher on math and reading tests than those from low-income homes. For children born in 2000, the gap has grown to one and a quarter standard deviations. Most of the increase in the test score gap, according to Reardon, has occurred between children from high-income families and those from middle-income ones.[93]

Households with different incomes increasingly live in different communities, as residential segregation by class has increased. Education and income gaps in participation in schools, civic organizations, churches, and other institutions have widened. And compared to their higher-income peers, children from low-income families have become less and less likely to participate in school-based extracurricular activities, from clubs to band to sports teams.[94]

The gap in college completion also has widened. College completion has increased among all groups, but the lower the parents' income, the smaller the rise.[95]

Finally, Americans increasingly tend to marry or partner with someone who has similar educational attainment.[96] This shift toward greater marital homogamy is likely to have further reduced the chance that someone starting at the bottom will end up in the middle or higher.

Though it's too early to draw a confident conclusion about whether equality of opportunity has changed since the 1970s, some studies have attempted to do so. Five conclude that equality of opportunity, measured as relative intergenerational income mobility, hasn't changed.[97] Three others, however, conclude that it has declined.[98]

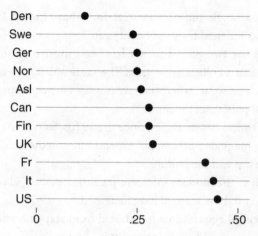

Figure 6.15 Inequality of opportunity in 11 rich nations. Correlation between the earnings of parents and those of their children. A larger correlation indicates less relative intergenerational mobility and hence less equality of opportunity. Data source: John Ermisch, Markus Jäntti, and Timothy Smeeding, eds., *From Parents to Children: The Intergenerational Transmission of Advantage,* Russell Sage Foundation, 2012, figure 1.1.

How Does the United States Compare to Other Affluent Countries?

From 1865 to 1970, the United States probably had more relative intergenerational mobility than other rich countries. But that may no longer be the case. Figure 6.15 shows the degree of earnings mobility in the United States and ten other countries according to one set of estimates. Along with Italy and France, the United States has the least mobility. On the other hand, two recent studies find no difference in mobility between the United States, Canada, Sweden, and Germany.[99]

These calculations are limited by the fact that they focus on the *earnings* of the parent (father) and the child. This is a partial, and potentially misleading, indicator of household income. Moreover, this causes these studies to leave out Americans who grow up in a single-mother household—a group that includes a nontrivial share of those on the lowest rung of the income ladder. Learning from other countries' experiences is an important tool for improving policies and institutions. We need more and better data on intergenerational mobility.[100]

Shared Prosperity

In a good society, those in the middle and at the bottom ought to benefit significantly from economic growth. When the country prospers, everyone should prosper.[101] I examined the least well-off earlier in this chapter. Now let's take a look at households in the middle.

America's Great Decoupling

Figure 6.16 shows median household income in the United States and other affluent democratic nations since the late 1970s. Middle-class households in the United States are richer than their counterparts in most other countries. But they are below Norway and Switzerland, and their income has increased only modestly since the 1970s, so other nations have been catching up.[102]

Is the slow growth of household incomes in the middle since the late 1970s due to slow growth of the economy? Figure 6.17 suggests that the answer is no. The figure shows trends since the late 1940s in GDP per capita along with three indicators of income in the middle. Each series is displayed as an index set to equal 1 in 1947. In the period between World War II and the mid-to-late 1970s, economic growth was good for Americans in the middle. As GDP per capita increased, so did family income at the 80th percentile, the 50th percentile (the median), and the 20th percentile. Indeed, they moved virtually in lockstep. Since the 1970s, however, household income has become decoupled from economic growth. As the economy has grown, relatively little of that growth has reached households in the middle, particularly those in the lower-middle.[103]

We also can see the decoupling of middle incomes from economic growth if we compare across countries. Figure 6.18 shows change in median household income by change in GDP per capita in the United States and thirteen other rich democratic nations since the late 1970s. Median income increased less in the United States than in most of the other nations. That's not because the US

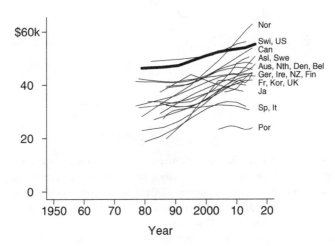

Figure 6.16 Median household income. Posttransfer-posttax household income. The incomes are adjusted for household size and then rescaled to reflect a three-person household, adjusted for inflation, and converted to US dollars using purchasing power parities. "k" = thousand. Data sources: Luxembourg Income Study; OECD. Thick line: United States. "Asl" is Australia; "Aus" is Austria. The lines are loess curves.

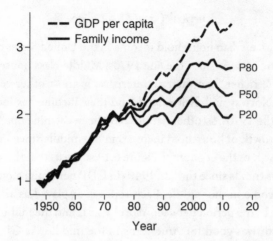

Figure 6.17 GDP per capita and middle-class family income. Each series is displayed as an index set to equal 1 in 1947. Inflation adjustment for each series is via the CPI-U-RS. P20 is the 20th percentile on the income ladder; P50 is the 50th percentile (median); P80 is the 80th percentile. The family income data are posttransfer-pretax. Data source for GDP per capita: Bureau of Economic Analysis, "National Income and Product Accounts Tables," table 1.1.5. Data source for family income: Census Bureau, "Historical Income Data," tables F-1, F-5.

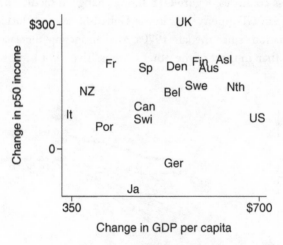

Figure 6.18 Economic growth and median household income growth. Average per-year change, 1979 to 2015. Because the actual years vary somewhat depending on the country, change is calculated by regressing household income or GDP per capita on year. Household incomes are posttransfer-posttax, adjusted for household size (the amounts shown are for a household with three persons). Household incomes and GDP per capita are adjusted for inflation and converted to US dollars using purchasing power parities. Ireland and Norway are omitted; both would be far off the plot in the upper-right corner. Data sources: OECD; Luxembourg Income Study. "Asl" is Australia; "Aus" is Austria.

economy grew less rapidly; in fact, its increase in per capita GDP was comparatively large. The problem is that less of America's economic growth reached middle-class households.[104]

High and rising top-end income inequality looks to have been a key cause of the decoupling of middle-class household income growth from economic growth. Figure 6.19 shows that the share of household income going to those in the top 1 percent decreased slowly during the decades after World War II, but since the late 1970s it has increased sharply.

How do we know this has contributed to slow income growth for middle-class households? First, the two are arithmetically related. If the top 1 percent get a large share of the household income, less of the income growth is available for households in the middle. The top 1 percent's large share could conceivably come at the expense of the near-rich or the poor rather than at the expense of the middle. It also is possible that a high level of top-end income inequality will yield faster economic growth, so that its large (and perhaps rising) share of the pie is offset by rapid expansion of the pie. But these are mere possibilities. In the United States, income inequality does not appear to have increased economic growth.[105] Nor does it seem to have come at the expense of the poor.[106]

Second, the timing fits. As Figure 6.17 above shows, during the period from the end of World War II through the 1970s, when top-end income inequality was moderate and declining, income growth in middle-class households kept pace with growth of the economy, whereas after 1979, when top-end income

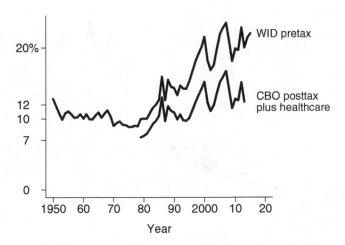

Figure 6.19 Top 1 percent's income share. Top 1 percent's share of income. Income data includes capital gains. Data sources: World Inequality Database (WID); Congressional Budget Office (CBO). The "WID pretax" data can be considered an upper-bound estimate of the top 1 percent's share. The "CBO posttax plus healthcare" is a lower-bound estimate.

inequality was high and rising, income growth for middle-class households lagged well behind economic growth.

Third, a key hypothesized causal path, wages, has moved as the hypothesis predicts. Figure 6.20 shows an estimate of wages in the top 1 percent and in the bottom 90 percent going back to the mid-1940s. Since the late 1970s, wages for Americans at the top of the distribution have grown very rapidly, faster than GDP per capita, while wages for those in the middle have grown very slowly. In addition, among the rich nations for which we have data on wage trends, the United States has had the slowest growth at the median.[107]

What else besides income inequality might have caused slow income growth in the middle? One alternative possibility is a fall in the share of value-added in the economy that goes to labor. That share did fall, but the decline was fairly minor, and smaller than in many other rich nations.[108]

Another possibility is that a growing portion of compensation has gone to nonmonetary benefits such as healthcare. However, the share of employee compensation accounted for by nonwage benefits has been essentially flat since the late 1970s, so this is likely to have played at most a very small role.[109] Healthcare costs have increased, but the share of employees covered by an employer healthcare plan has fallen, and employer contributions to pensions have decreased.

How much income has the post-1979 inequality-driven decoupling cost middle-class American households? Figure 6.21 offers an estimate. The solid line is actual median household income. The dashed line shows what the trend in median household income would have been had it kept pace with GDP per

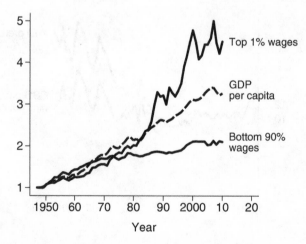

Figure 6.20 GDP per capita and wages. Each series is displayed as an index set to equal 1 in 1947. Inflation adjustment for each series is via the CPI-U-RS. Data source for GDP: Bureau of Economic Analysis, "National Income and Product Accounts Tables," table 1.1.5. Data source for wages: Lawrence Mishel et al., *The State of Working America*, 12th edition, wages dataset.

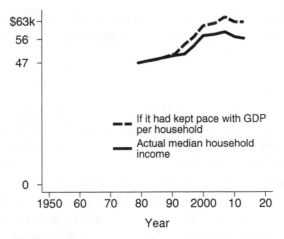

Figure 6.21 How much income has decoupling cost the median US household? Posttransfer-posttax income, in 2015 dollars. Inflation adjustment for each series is via the CPI-U-RS. "k" = thousand. Data source for median and mean household income: Luxembourg Income Study. Data source for GDP: Bureau of Economic Analysis, "National Income and Product Accounts Tables," table 1.1.5. Data source for number of households: Census Bureau, "Historical Income Data," table H-5.

household. Using GDP per household rather than GDP per capita (person) adjusts for the fact that the number of households has increased faster than the number of persons since the late 1970s.[110] The actual median household income was $47,000 in 1979 and $56,000 in 2016. Had it kept pace with GDP per household since 1979, median household income would instead have been around $63,000.

"It's Better Than It Looks"

In the view of some, this picture of slow middle-class income growth is too pessimistic. They argue that incomes or broader living standards actually have grown relatively rapidly, keeping pace with the economy.[111] Let's consider several versions of this view.

1. The income data miss upward movement over the life course. The income data shown in Figures 6.17 and 6.21 are from the Current Population Survey, which each year asks a representative sample of American adults what their income was in the previous year. But each year the sample consists of a new group; the survey doesn't track the same people as they move through the life course.

If we interpret Figures 6.17 and 6.21 as showing what happens to typical American families over the life course, we will conclude that they see very little increase in income as they age. That's incorrect. In any given year, some of those with below-median income are young. Their wages and income are low because they are in the early stages of the work career and/or because they are single. Over time, many will experience a significant income rise, getting pay increases or partnering with someone who also has earnings, or both. Figures 6.17 and 6.21 miss this income growth over the life course.

Figure 6.22 illustrates the point. The lower line shows median income among families with a "head" aged twenty-five to thirty-four. The top line shows median income among the same cohort of families twenty years later, when their heads are aged forty-five to fifty-four. Consider the year 1979, for instance. The lower line tells us that in 1979 the median income of families with a twenty-five-to-thirty-four-year-old head was about $58,000 (in 2013 dollars). The data point for 1979 in the top line looks at the median income of that same group of families twenty years later, in 1999, when they are forty-five to fifty-four years old. This is the peak earning stage for most people, and their median income is now about $91,000.

In each year, the gap between the two lines is roughly $33,000. This tells us that the incomes of middle-class Americans tend to increase substantially as they move from the early years of the work career to the peak years.

Should this reduce our concern about the over-time pattern shown in Figures 6.17 and 6.21 above? No, it shouldn't. Look again at Figure 6.22. Between the mid-1940s and the mid-1970s, the median income of families in

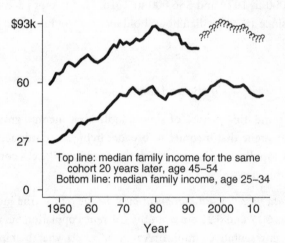

Figure 6.22 Median income within and across cohorts. For each year, the lower line is median income among families with a "head" aged 25–34 and the top line is median income for the same cohort of families twenty years later. In the years for which the calculation is possible, 1947 to 1993, the average increase in income during this two-decade portion of the life course is $32,500. The data are in 2013 dollars; inflation adjustment is via the CPI-U-RS. "k" = thousand. Data source: U.S. Census Bureau, "Historical Income Data," table F-11.

early adulthood (the lower line) rose steadily. In the mid-1940s median income for these young families was around $27,000; by the mid-1970s it had doubled. Americans during this period experienced income gains over the life course, but they also tended to have higher incomes than their predecessors, both in their early work years and in their peak years. That's because the economy was growing at a healthy clip and the economic growth was trickling down to Americans in the middle.

After the mid-1970s, this steady gain disappeared.[112] From the mid-1970s to 2010s the median income of families with a twenty-five-to-thirty-four-year-old head was flat. They continued to achieve income gains during the life course. (Actually, we don't yet know about those who started out after the mid-1990s, as they're just now beginning to reach age forty-five to fifty-four. The question marks in the chart show what their incomes will be if the historical trajectory holds true.) But the improvement across cohorts that characterized the period from the mid-1940s through the 1970s—each cohort starting higher and ending higher than earlier ones—disappeared.

Income for many Americans rises during the life course, and this is indeed hidden by charts such as Figures 6.17 and 6.21. But that shouldn't lessen our concern about the decoupling of household income growth from economic growth that has occurred over the past generation. We want improvement not just within cohorts, but also across them.

2. Demographic changes. The size of the typical American household has been shrinking since the mid-1960s, when the "baby boom" ended. Some will therefore say we don't need income growth to be so rapid any more. But this shrinkage in household size probably shouldn't alter our interpretation of slow income growth. Incomes have become decoupled from economic growth because a large and rising share of economic growth has gone to households at the top of the ladder. Yet household size has decreased among the rich too; they don't need the extra income more than those in the middle and below do.

Also, more people are in college or retired. The income data in Figures 6.17 and 6.21 are for families with a "head" aged fifteen or older. The share of young Americans attending college has increased since the 1970s, and the share of Americans who are elderly and hence retired has risen. These two developments have reduced the share of families with an employed adult head. However, this doesn't account for the slow growth of family income relative to the economy. The trend in income among families with a head aged twenty-five to fifty-four, in the prime of the work career, is very similar to that for all families.[113]

A third demographic change is that immigration into the United States began to increase in the late 1960s. The foreign-born share of the American population, including both legal and illegal immigrants, rose from 5 percent in 1970 to

13 percent in 2015.[114] Quite a few have come with limited labor market skills and little or no English, so their incomes tend to be low. For many such immigrants, a low income in the United States is a substantial improvement over what their income would be in their home country, so if this accounts for the divorce between economic growth and median income growth over the past generation, perhaps we shouldn't worry. But immigration actually is a relatively small part of the story. The rise in median family income for non-Hispanic whites, which excludes most immigrants, has been only slightly greater than the rise in median income for all families shown in Figures 6.17 and 6.21.[115]

3. *Consumption has continued to rise rapidly.* Some consider spending a better indicator than income of people's standard of living. Even though the incomes of middle- and low-income Americans have grown slowly, they may have increased their consumption more rapidly by drawing on assets (equity in a home, savings) and/or debt.

But that isn't the case. According to the best available data, from the Consumer Expenditures Survey (CES), median family expenditures rose at the same pace as median family income in the 1980s, 1990s, and 2000s.[116]

4. *Wealth has increased sharply.* Income and consumption growth for middle-income Americans may have lagged well behind growth of the economy, but was that offset by rapid growth of wealth (assets minus debts)?

Yes, it was, but only temporarily. We have data on wealth from the Survey of Consumer Finances (SCF), administered by the Federal Reserve every three years. Figure 6.23 shows the trend in median household wealth along with the trend in median household income. The wealth data are first available in 1983. What we see is a sharp upward spike in median wealth in the second half of the 1990s and the first half of the 2000s. The home is the chief asset of most middle-class Americans, and home values jumped during this period. But then the housing bubble burst and median wealth fell precipitously, erasing all of the gains.[117] And for those who lost their home during the crash, things are even worse than what is conveyed by these data.[118]

Even before the bubble burst, not everyone benefited. Of the one-third of Americans who don't own a home, many are on the lower half of the income ladder. For them, the rise in home values in the 1990s and 2000s did nothing to compensate for the slow growth of income since the late 1970s.

5. *There have been significant improvements in quality of life.* A final variant of the notion that income data understate the degree of advance in living standards focuses on improvements in the quality of goods, services, and social norms. It suggests that adjusting the income data for inflation doesn't do justice to the enhancements in quality of life that have occurred in the past generation.[119]

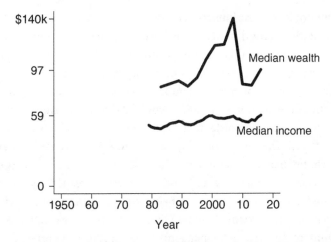

Figure 6.23 Median household income and median household wealth. 2016 dollars. "k" = thousand. Median wealth: Household net worth, calculated as assets minus liabilities. Data source: Urban Institute, "Nine Charts about Wealth Inequality in America," using Survey of Consumer Finances data. Median income: Posttransfer-pretax household income. Data source: US Census Bureau, "Historical Income Tables."

Fewer jobs require hard physical labor, and workplace accidents and deaths have decreased. Life expectancy rose from seventy-four years in 1979 to seventy-nine years in 2015. Cancer survival is up. Infant mortality is down. An array of new pharmaceuticals now help relieve various conditions and ailments. MRIs, CT scans, and other diagnostic tools have enhanced physicians' ability to detect serious health problems. Organ transplants, hip and knee replacements, and LASIK eye surgery are now commonplace. Violent crime has dropped to pre-1970s levels. Air and water quality are much improved.

We live in bigger houses; the median size of new homes rose from 1,600 square feet in 1979 to 2,400 in 2017. Cars are safer and get better gas mileage. Food and clothing are cheaper. We have access to an assortment of conveniences that didn't exist or weren't widely available a generation ago: personal computers, printers, scanners, microwave ovens, TV remote controls, digital video recorders, digital cameras, five-blade razors, home pregnancy tests, home security systems. Product variety has increased for almost all goods and services, from cars to restaurant food to toothpaste to television programs.

We have much greater access to information via the Internet, Google, travel guides, mapping apps and GPS, smartphones, and tablets. We have a host of new communication tools: cell phones, voicemail, email, Skype, Facebook, Twitter, Instagram. Personal entertainment sources and devices have proliferated: cable TV and streaming video, high-definition televisions, home entertainment systems, the Internet, MP3 players, CD players, DVD players, Netflix, satellite radio, video games.

Last, but not least, discrimination on the basis of sex, race, and more recently sexual orientation have diminished. For women, racial and ethnic minorities, and LGBTQ Americans, this may be the most valuable improvement of all.

There is no disputing these gains in quality of life. But did they occur because income growth for middle- and low-income Americans lagged well behind growth of the economy? In other words, did ordinary Americans need to sacrifice income growth in order to get these improved products and services?

Some say yes. They point out that returns to success soared in fields such as high tech, finance, entertainment, and athletics, as well as for CEOs. These markets became "winner-take-all," and the rewards reaped by the winners mushroomed. For those with a shot at being the best in their field, this increased the financial incentive to work harder or longer or to be more creative. According to the argument, this rise in financial incentives produced a corresponding rise in excellence—new products and services and enhanced quality.

Is this correct? To begin, consider the case of Apple and Steve Jobs. Apple's Macintosh, iPod, iTunes, MacBook Air, iPhone, and iPad were so different from and superior to anything that preceded them that their addition to living standards isn't likely to be adequately measured. Did slow middle-class income growth make this possible? Would Jobs and his teams of engineers, designers, and others at Apple have worked as hard as they did to create these new products and bring them to market in the absence of massive winner-take-all financial incentives?

It's difficult to know, but Walter Isaacson's comprehensive biography of Steve Jobs suggests that he was driven mainly by a passion for the products, for winning the competitive battle, and for status among peers.[120] Excellence and victory were their own reward, not a means to the end of financial riches. In this respect Jobs mirrors scores of inventors and entrepreneurs over the ages. So while the rise of winner-take-all compensation occurred simultaneously with surges in innovation and productivity in certain fields, it may not have caused those surges.

For a more systematic assessment, we can look at the preceding period—the 1940s, 1950s, 1960s, and early 1970s. In these years the incomes of ordinary Americans grew at roughly the same pace as the economy and as incomes at the top. Did this squash the incentive for innovation and hard work and thereby come at the expense of broader quality-of-life improvements?

During this period the share of Americans working in physically taxing jobs fell steadily, as employment in agriculture and manufacturing was declining. Life expectancy rose from sixty-five in 1945 to seventy-one in 1973. Antibiotic use began in the 1940s, and open-heart bypass surgery was introduced in the 1960s.

In 1940, only 44 percent of Americans owned a home; by 1970 that jumped to 64 percent. Home features and amenities changed dramatically, as the following list makes clear. Running water: 70 percent in 1940, 98 percent in 1970. Indoor flush toilet: 60 percent in 1960, 95 percent in 1970. Electric lighting: 79 percent in 1940, 99 percent in 1970. Central heating: 40 percent in 1940, 78 percent in 1970. Air conditioning: very few (we don't have precise data) in 1940, more than half in 1970. Refrigerator: 47 percent in 1940, 99 percent in 1970. Washing machine: less than half in 1940, 92 percent in 1970. Vacuum cleaner: 40 percent in 1940, 92 percent in 1970.

In 1970, 80 percent of American households had a car, compared to just 52 percent in 1940. The interstate highway system was built in the 1950s and 1960s. In 1970 there were 154 million air passengers, versus just 4 million in 1940. Only 45 percent of homes had a telephone in 1945; by 1970 virtually all did. Long-distance phone calls were rare before the 1960s. In 1950, just 60 percent of employed Americans took a vacation; in 1970 that had risen to 80 percent. By 1970, 99 percent of Americans had a television, up from just 32 percent in 1940. In music, the "album" originated in the late 1940s, and rock-n-roll began in the 1950s. Other innovations that made life easier or more pleasurable include photocopiers, disposable diapers, and the bikini.

The Civil Rights Act of 1964 outlawed gender and race discrimination in public places, education, and employment. For women, life changed in myriad ways. Female labor force participation rose from 30 percent in 1940 to 49 percent in 1970. Norms inhibiting divorce relaxed in the 1960s. The Pill was introduced in 1960. Abortion was legalized in the early 1970s. Access to college increased massively in the 1960s.

Comparing these changes in quality of life is difficult, but I see no reason to conclude that the pace of advance, or of innovation, has been more rapid in recent decades than before.[121]

The bottom line? Yes, there have been significant improvements in quality of life in the United States since the 1970s. But that shouldn't lessen our disappointment in the fact that incomes have been growing far more slowly than the economy.

"It's Worse Than It Looks"

Rather than understating the true degree of progress for middle- and low-income Americans, the income trends shown in Figures 6.17 and 6.21 above might overstate it.[122]

1. Income growth is due mainly to the addition of a second earner. The income of American households in the lower half has grown slowly since the 1970s. But it might not have increased at all if not for the fact that more households came to have two earners rather than one. From the 1940s through the mid-1970s, wages rose steadily. As a result, the median income of most families, whether they had one earner or two, increased at about the same pace as the economy. Since then, households with a single adult have seen no income rise at all.[123]

It's important to emphasize that most of this shift from one earner to two has been voluntary. A growing number of women have sought employment as their educational attainment has increased, discrimination in the labor market has dissipated, and social norms have changed. The transition from the traditional male-breadwinner family to the dual-earner one isn't simply a product of desperation to keep incomes growing.

Even so, as more two-adult households have both adults in employment, more are struggling to balance the demands of home and work. Good-quality childcare and preschool are expensive, and elementary and secondary schools are in session only 180 of the 250 weekdays each year. The difficulty is accentuated by the growing prevalence of long work hours, odd hours, irregular hours, and long commutes. By the early 2000s, 25 percent of employed men and 10 percent of employed women were working 50 or more hours per week.[124] And 35 to 40 percent of Americans were working outside regular hours (9 a.m. to 5 p.m.) and/or days (Monday to Friday).[125] Average commute time rose from 40 minutes in 1980 to 50 minutes in the late 2000s.[126]

2. *The cost of some key middle-class expenses has risen much faster than inflation.* The income numbers in Figures 6.17 and 6.21 are adjusted for inflation. But the adjustment is based on the price of a bundle of goods and services considered typical for American households. Changes in the cost of certain goods and services that middle-class Americans consider essential may not be adequately captured in this bundle. In particular, because middle-class families typically want to own a home and to send their kids to college, they suffered more than other Americans from the sharp rise in housing prices and college costs in the 1990s and 2000s. Moreover, as middle-class families have shifted from having one earner to two, their spending needs may have changed in ways that adjusting for inflation doesn't capture. For example, they now need to pay for childcare and require two cars rather than one.[127]

Consider a four-person family with two adults and two preschool-age children. In the early 1970s, this family probably would have had one of the adults employed and the other staying at home. By the 2000s, it's likely that both were employed. Here is how their costs for these big-ticket expenses might have differed.[128] Childcare: $0 in the early 1970s, $12,500 in the mid-2000s. Car(s): $5,800 for one car in the early 1970s, $8,800 for two cars in the mid-2000s. Home mortgage: $6,000 in the early 1970s, $10,200 in the mid-2000s. When the children reach school age, the strain eases. But when they head off to college it reappears; the average yearly cost of tuition, fees, and room/board at public four-year colleges rose from $6,500 in the early 1970s to $12,000 in the mid-2000s.[129]

To recap: Since the 1970s, incomes have risen slowly for the broad middle of American households, despite sustained growth in the economy. With the top 1 percent getting a larger and larger portion, household income growth for the middle has become decoupled from economic growth. America's middle class is fairly well off by comparative and historical standards, but it could, and should, be even better off.

Some of the most commonly voiced solutions won't do the trick. Reversing key economic shifts such as trade, technological advance, the shift from manufacturing to services, and immigration is neither likely nor desirable. Turning firms away from their shareholder value orientation would be difficult. Revitalizing unions is a very tall order. But we have other options. A tighter labor market would put more pressure on employers to raise wages. A public subsidy, such as a revised Earned Income Tax Credit, could supplement middle-class earnings. And enhanced government support for key services and insurance programs—early education, college, health insurance, sickness insurance, paid parental leave—would reduce big-ticket expenses for households and facilitate greater employment by parents and other caregivers.

We Can Do Better

In the past generation, ordinary Americans have had less economic security, less opportunity, and less income growth than they should in a country as prosperous as ours. We can do better. In the next chapter I explain how.

7

A Better America

Our historical experience and those of other rich democratic countries suggest that more expansive and generous social programs and employment-conducive public services would help in the United States, and they would do so without sacrificing other good outcomes, such as economic growth or individual freedom. These programs function as a floor, a safety net, and a springboard: they ensure a decent living standard for the least well-off, provide income security, and enhance opportunity. Properly formulated, they can also serve as an escalator, ensuring rising living standards over time.

It's worth emphasizing that this approach, which I call "social democratic capitalism," isn't itself the goal we seek. It's a means to an end. The reason why the United States should embrace social democratic capitalism is because it works well. Public insurance programs and employment-promoting services boost the living standards of the least well-off, improve economic security, and very likely enhance equality of opportunity, and they achieve these goals with little or no tradeoffs. That is the core message from Part 1 of this book.

The United States has a lot of public insurance programs already. For the most part they work very well. We should adjust and expand some of them and add others, because the experience of other rich democratic nations shows us that there are other policies and programs that would be good for Americans and because we face new economic and social challenges that didn't exist or were less consequential in earlier eras.

What exactly should we do? We should add or improve the following:

- Health insurance
- Paid parental leave
- Child allowance
- Unemployment insurance and wage insurance
- Sickness insurance
- Disability assistance
- Social assistance

- Criminal justice
- Pensions
- Eldercare
- Housing assistance
- Early education
- Apprenticeships
- College
- Affirmative action
- Full employment
- Minimum wage
- Earned Income Tax Credit
- Profit sharing
- Infrastructure and public spaces
- Paid vacation days and holidays

After outlining the details for each of these, I turn to how much it will cost and how to pay for it.

Health Insurance

In a rich nation such as the United States, everyone should have health insurance. We also should do better at controlling healthcare costs; while we won't go bankrupt spending 18 percent of our GDP on health, or even more, the fact that every other rich democratic country achieves equivalent or better health outcomes while spending far less suggests that we have considerable room for improvement.[1] How can we achieve these two goals?

The most straightforward path would be to expand coverage through Medicare, Medicaid, and a "public option": lower the age at which Americans can get Medicare, raise the income limit for Medicaid eligibility, and add a Medicare-like program that individuals and families can purchase on health insurance exchanges and that firms can purchase for their employees. Or simply allow any employer or individual to buy into Medicaid or Medicare, with subsidies for those who need them. Eventually, a large portion of the population would be covered by these public programs. This would achieve universal coverage, and the government, as the dominant payer, would be in a strong position to control healthcare costs.[2]

Canada's experience suggests that this type of arrangement can function quite effectively. Every Canadian has health insurance, and as Figure 7.1 indicates, over the past half century life expectancy has increased more in Canada than in the United States despite a far smaller rise in healthcare expenditures.

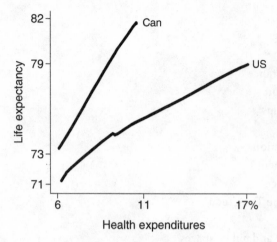

Figure 7.1 Life expectancy by health expenditures. The data points are years, from 1970 to 2016. Life expectancy: years at birth. Health expenditures: public plus private, as a share of GDP. Data source: OECD. The lines are loess curves.

Such a system wouldn't eliminate private insurers. There would be a market among the affluent for insurance plans better than the one(s) offered by the government. And employers and individuals might choose to supplement the basic health insurance plan with an additional one, as many elderly Americans who have Medicare currently do.

Over time, government has gradually increased its role in promoting access to health insurance in the United States. The Veterans Administration (VA) was created in 1865 and significantly reformed in 1930 and 1994. In the 1940s and 1950s the federal government created and expanded a tax deduction for firms that contribute to health insurance for their employees. Medicare was created in 1965 and extended to cover prescription drugs in 2004. Medicaid too was created in 1965, and the share of the population it covers was expanded in the 1980s, in 1999 with the S-CHIP program, and in 2010 via the Affordable Care Act (ACA). Figure 7.2 shows the rise in the share of Americans with Medicare or Medicaid since the mid-1960s. Together, these two programs now cover about 40 percent of the US population. The 2010 ACA also requires that medium-size and large firms offer health insurance to their employees, it provides subsidies for persons and families with modest incomes, it requires that health insurers allow people to remain on their parents' plan through age twenty-five, and it forbids insurers from denying insurance to persons with preexisting conditions. (Its mandate that individuals have health insurance was removed in 2017.)

Why not instead expand employer-based health insurance? America's employer-centered health insurance system was a historical accident.[3] It

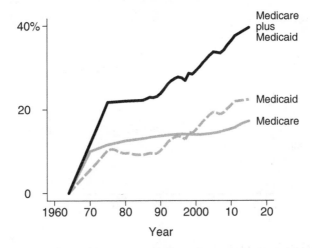

Figure 7.2 Health insurance via Medicare and Medicaid. Share of the US population. Data source: Centers for Medicare and Medicaid Services, "Medicare and Medicaid Statistical Supplement," tables 2.1 and 13.4.

originated during World War II, when wage controls made it difficult for firms to offer higher pay in order to attract and retain good employees. Some decided to offer health insurance instead. After the war, encouraged by a new tax break, this practice proliferated, and it has remained in place ever since. But in a society where people switch jobs frequently, it makes little sense for insurance against a potentially major and very costly risk to be tied to one's employer. Moreover, providing health insurance is expensive for firms, putting them at a disadvantage relative to small firms and foreign competitors. And it likely acts as a brake on wage increases.

Why does employer-based health insurance work well in some other countries, such as Germany and Japan? The reason is that if people quit or lose their job, they are automatically switched into a government ("community") health insurance plan. And the cost of healthcare is contained, so it's less of a burden for employers. This happens in part because health insurance firms and funds aren't for-profit, so they aren't inserting additional costs into the system, and partly via cost controls set by centralized agreements between insurers and providers, with government stepping in if that fails.[4]

Do Americans like government health insurance? Most say they do. Figure 7.3 shows that about two-thirds of Americans think Medicare and Medicaid are working well for the groups they serve. In 2015, Gallup asked a representative sample of US adults "Are you satisfied or dissatisfied with how the healthcare system is working for you?" As Figure 7.4 shows, satisfaction was higher among those getting their health insurance via the military, the Veterans Administration,

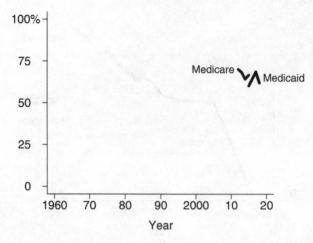

Figure 7.3 Medicare and Medicaid are working well. Share of US adults. Questions: "Would you say the current Medicare program is working well for most seniors, or not?" "Would you say the current Medicaid program is working well for most low-income people covered by the program, or not?" Response options: working well, not working well, don't know. The lines show the share responding working well, with "don't know" responses excluded. Data source: Kaiser Family Foundation.

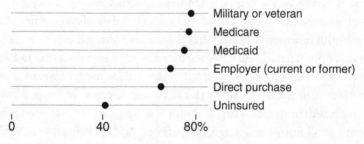

Figure 7.4 Satisfaction with how the healthcare system is working by insurance source. Share of US adults who say they are satisfied. The data are for 2015. Question: "Are you satisfied or dissatisfied with how the healthcare system is working for you?" Data source: Rebecca Riffkin, "Americans with Government Health Plans Most Satisfied," Gallup, 2015, gallup.com.

Medicare, or Medicaid than among those getting it via an employer or purchasing it directly themselves.

Should government not only pay for health insurance and oversee it but also be the provider? That's how countries such as the United Kingdom, Sweden, Finland, and some others do it, and it tends to work well. Indeed, the UK got top ranking in a recent Commonwealth Fund assessment of healthcare quality in 11 affluent nations.[5] But these might be isolated examples; there is no systematic evidence to support a conclusion that government provision is superior to mixed public and private provision. In any event, it's extremely unlikely that the United States will replace its existing array of private for-profit and nonprofit medical providers with a fully government-run physician and hospital system.

How much would a single-payer healthcare system cost, and where would the money come from? In 2015, the United States spent $3.2 trillion, 18 percent of the country's GDP, on healthcare. The government's share is a little less than half of this total. The tax benefit to employers costs about $250 billion, Medicare $650 billion, Medicaid $560 billion, healthcare for veterans $65 billion, and healthcare for current military personnel and their families $40 billion.

Medicare and Medicaid limit the amount they will pay to healthcare providers, and they have relatively low administrative costs. Even though they've been covering more and more of the population (Figure 7.2), the share of GDP spent on these two programs has been rising at about the same pace as the rest of the healthcare system, as Figure 7.5 shows. Their cost will continue to rise going forward, owing partly to population aging and expansion of Medicaid coverage and partly to the general rise in healthcare costs, but the projected increases are fairly small.[6]

A key obstacle facing proposals for a single-payer system is that taxes would have to increase significantly in order to pay for it. But this isn't insurmountable. A single-payer system likely would reduce total spending on healthcare. According to one estimate, adding coverage for the roughly 9 percent of Americans who now lack it and improving coverage for the 35 percent who currently are underinsured would increase costs by about 10 percent. But single-payer would reduce overall healthcare costs by approximately 18 percent: 7 percent from

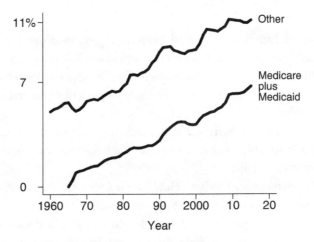

Figure 7.5 Health expenditures. Share of GDP. Data source: Centers for Medicare and Medicaid Services, "National Health Expenditures by Type of Service and Source of Funds." These numbers aren't adjusted for the share of the population covered, which has increased steadily and significantly for Medicare and Medicaid.

reduction in administrative costs, 3 percent from lower pharmaceutical prices, 3 percent from paying Medicare rates to healthcare providers, and 5 percent from improved service delivery (reduction in unnecessary services, inefficiently delivered services, missed prevention opportunities, and fraud).[7] If correct, this estimate suggests a single-payer healthcare system would cost roughly 90 percent of the current spending total, or about 16 percent of GDP. That means government expenditures on health would rise by about 8 percent of GDP.

Of current health spending, 45 percent is by government (federal, state, and local). The other 55 percent is private: 27 percent by households, 20 percent by private firms, and 8 percent by other private sources.[8] The cost of a single-payer system would need to come from taxes that replace these private expenditures. There are many possibilities, from a payroll tax paid by employers to an income tax and/or consumption tax on households. While the dollar figure will scare some Americans, such a system won't mean additional payments for healthcare; it will simply mean a different form of payment—public instead of private.

So is single-payer the solution for the United States? In the long run, probably yes. In the short run, it may be more sensible to focus on making health insurance universal and making sure all Americans have insurance that is minimally adequate. The most straightforward way to do this is by expanding access to Medicaid and/or Medicare, in one or more of the ways I described earlier. According to one estimate, this would increase government healthcare expenditures by approximately 10 percent, or about 1.75 percent of GDP.[9]

Paid Parental Leave

A 1993 law, the Family and Medical Leave Act, gives employees the right to twelve weeks of job-protected leave for the birth of a child or to care for a sick relative. But this only applies to companies with fifty or more employees. And there is no requirement that the leave be paid. Only 14 percent of American workers have employer-provided paid family leave.[10] Consequently, many Americans in middle- and low-income households take little time off. That's unfortunate, because outcomes for children tend to be best when they are with their parent(s) during the first year of life.[11]

In Sweden, parents of a newborn child have thirteen months of job-protected paid leave, with the benefit level set at approximately 80 percent of earnings. Two of those months are "use it or lose it" for the father; if he doesn't use them, the couple gets eleven months instead of thirteen. In addition, parents can take four months off per year to care for a sick child up to age twelve, paid at the same level as parental leave.[12] As Figure 7.6 shows, Sweden's policy is a generous one, but not exceptionally so by the standards of other rich nations.

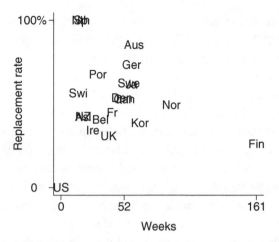

Figure 7.6 Paid parental leave. The data are for mothers. Includes both maternity and parental leave. Replacement rate is the share of wage or salary received. 2016. Data source: OECD, "Key Characteristics of Parental Leave Systems." "Asl" is Australia; "Aus" is Austria.

The United States is the only affluent democratic country without a paid parental leave program. A few states—California, New Jersey, New York, and Rhode Island—along with Washington DC have enacted small-scale programs. Results from California's, which has been in place since 2004, are encouraging.[13]

A new federal parental leave program for the United States should provide a minimum of six months of paid leave per child, with an incentive for the father to take a portion of the leave. The leave should be job-protected. The replacement rate should be at least 50 percent. All workers meeting minimum work history requirements, including those in small firms and self-employed persons, should be eligible.[14]

Sweden's policy costs about 0.75 percent of GDP per year.[15] With a slightly less generous version and our larger per capita GDP, an American counterpart might cost around 0.5 percent a year.[16]

Child Allowance

Many things affect children's well-being and life chances. Money is one of them.[17] An increase in family income of a mere $3,000 during a person's first five years of life is associated with nearly 20 percent higher earnings later in life.[18]

Most other affluent countries have a universal "child benefit" or "child allowance." In Canada, for instance, a family with two children under age six and an income below $30,000 receives an allowance of $10,000 (in US dollars). The amount is less for families with older children and/or higher income.[19]

The United States has a weaker version, the Child Tax Credit, which provides a maximum of $2,000 a year per child.[20] Families with no earnings don't qualify. Nor do those who don't file a federal income tax return. As a result, low-income households benefit far less than middle-income households.[21]

A team of researchers led by Luke Shaefer has offered a sensible proposal for improving this.[22] The Child Tax Credit would be replaced by a child allowance paid to all families with children. The amount would be $3,600 per year for younger children and $3,000 for older ones. It would be universal and unconditional—not contingent on employment or income or assets.[23] The money would be taxable, though that wouldn't affect its level for many households with low or lower-middle income. According to calculations by Shaefer and colleagues, this child allowance would reduce the child poverty rate in the United States by around 40 percent, and it would virtually eliminate extreme child poverty. The cost would be approximately $180 billion per year, or 1 percent of GDP. After subtracting the current cost of the Child Tax Credit and the child deduction (about $100 billion), the net additional cost would be around 0.5 percent of GDP.

Unemployment Insurance and Wage Insurance

Unemployment insurance is a key policy instrument for ensuring economic security. Our program was created in 1935 as part of the New Deal. The federal government pays for it, but states have considerable leeway in determining eligibility criteria and benefit levels.

The average share of prior earnings replaced by unemployment benefits is just 45 percent. A bigger problem is that only about 40 percent of unemployed Americans qualify for compensation. Particularly likely to not qualify are persons who have low wages, work part-time or intermittently, move frequently from one employer to another, are self-employed, or interrupt employment for childbirth or family care.[24] Two simple reforms would address these problems. The first is to federalize eligibility rules and benefit levels, as some states are too stingy. The second is to adjust eligibility criteria to accommodate nonstandard workers and nonstandard employment, which are more common now than in the past and will become even more common going forward.[25]

We also should add a wage insurance component to the program. Some Americans who get laid off can't find a job that pays as well and are forced to settle for less. For a year or two, wage insurance would fill half of the gap between the former pay and the new lower wage.[26]

Sickness Insurance

The United States is the only rich democratic nation without a public sickness insurance program.[27] Though many large private-sector firms offer employees some paid sickness days and five states (California, Hawaii, New Jersey, New York, and Rhode Island, along with Washington DC) have a public program, more than one in four employed Americans gets zero days of paid sick leave.[28]

Sweden's approach offers a useful model.[29] A person with illness, disease, or injury that causes her to miss work receives 80 percent of her pay. The amount of the benefit is capped at about $28,000 per year.[30] The benefit is taxed as ordinary income. Day 1 isn't reimbursed. Days 2 through 14 are paid by the employer, and after that the money comes from a public sickness insurance fund. Self-employed persons are paid from the public fund. The payments can last up to a year (longer for a serious disease). A certificate from a doctor is required after seven days and a detailed medical exam after one month. Eligibility begins after three months of employment for sickness and disease and immediately for workplace injury.

We need not begin with a program as generous as Sweden's, which has typically cost about 1.5 percent of GDP. A program spending about a third of that amount, 0.5 percent of GDP, would be a good start.

Disability Assistance

Disability is pervasive and varied:

> A baby is starved of oxygen during childbirth. A construction worker slices off a finger with a power saw. Another loses partial lung function after spending a year cleaning up dusty debris at Ground Zero. A retired professional football player forgets instructions he was given moments earlier. A nurse suffers back strain from helping an obese patient into bed. A young adult develops schizophrenia. An oncologist diagnoses an energy-depleted fifty-five-year-old salesman with multiple myeloma. A soldier in Iraq suffers a traumatic brain injury when an explosive device detonates underneath a transport vehicle. A Cornell student is paralyzed for life by a prescription drug-induced stroke. Another suffers the same fate as the result of an act of drunken horseplay.

> Disability may be innate, as in the cases of those born with developmental deficiencies. It may be total, as in the case of the worst traumatic brain injuries, but more often it is partial. It may be temporary or

permanent. It may lead to a shortened life span, but often it does not. It may occur on the job, but more often it happens away from work. Whatever its genesis and character, disability leaves the victim with a diminished capacity to work for a living. Through rehabilitation and retraining some can overcome the functional limitations engendered by their disabilities, but many cannot regain sufficient functioning to enter or reenter the workforce.[31]

About 20 percent of Americans are disabled. Approximately 30 percent will at some point in their career experience a disability significant enough to cause them to miss ninety or more days of work.

One-third of Americans have private disability insurance (short-term and/or long-term) through their employers, mostly in large or middle-sized firms. A few purchase disability insurance on their own. The chief source of disability compensation for most working-age Americans is three public programs: workers' compensation, Social Security Disability Insurance (SSDI), and Supplemental Security Income (SSI).

Workers' compensation covers about 85 percent of employed Americans. It pays out about $30 billion per year to people injured on the job, generally replacing two-thirds or less of a worker's earnings. The incidence of on-the-job injury requiring time off from work has decreased from about 3 percent of employees in the early 1990s to 1 percent as of 2010. As a result, workers' compensation claims and payments have decreased.

Persons who become severely disabled and have paid Social Security taxes in five of the previous ten years may, after a five-month lag, receive Social Security Disability Insurance payments. After two years, they also receive Medicare to cover healthcare costs. The average SSDI payment is $15,000 a year. About 40 percent of applicants qualify for the benefit. Recipients are reviewed every two to five years to determine whether they remain eligible.

Around 10 million Americans, including former workers, spouses, and children, receive SSDI benefits. The share of the population getting SSDI payments has increased over the past generation, due to the rise in the share of people employed, an increase in the retirement age for Social Security eligibility (from sixty-five to sixty-seven), the aging of the population, and an expansion of eligibility criteria to include musculoskeletal maladies and mood disorders.

Disabled Americans who don't qualify for SSDI, and who have assets of less than $2,000 excluding house and car, may be eligible to receive SSI payments. These average $7,000 per year. The number of recipients is approximately 6 million. About one in three applicants are deemed eligible. Recipients also typically qualify for Medicaid health insurance.

Some people who are disabled temporarily don't qualify for unemployment insurance, workers' compensation, SSDI, SSI, or veterans' compensation and don't have private disability insurance. Five states provide temporary disability insurance for such circumstances. Because this group of states includes heavily-populated California and New York, more than a third of Americans have this protection. In many states, however, it is easy to fall through this crack in the system.

There are three major deficiencies in our support for disabled Americans. One is the lack of short-term disability insurance for many Americans with partial or temporary disabilities. A second is our limited commitment to vocational rehabilitation for disabled persons who might be able to return to work. Such efforts have a low success rate, even in countries that dedicate more resources than we do. Yet the signal these efforts send—about our commitment to genuine inclusion for disabled persons and about our support for employment—arguably justifies the cost.[32]

The United States spends about 1.5 percent of GDP on "incapacity" programs. Adding an additional 0.5 percent would put us closer to the average of 2.5 percent in other rich democratic nations.[33]

A third problem with our current policy is the strict asset limit for SSI recipients. Many Medicaid recipients also are subject to this limit, and Medicaid is the only program that provides for long-term care needs, such as an in-home personal care assistant. This has the perverse effect of forcing people with significant disabilities to spend down their assets in order to qualify for the medical services and assistance they need.[34] Hardly any other rich democratic nations require this.

Social Assistance

What to do about working-age households that have no employed adult has long been the thorniest question in American social policy.[35] There is no optimal solution. If we are generous, some will cheat the system. If we are stingy, we cause avoidable suffering. Given this tradeoff, the best approach is a policy that vigorously promotes employment for those who are able, provides a decent minimum for those who aren't, and deals on a case-by-case basis with those who can work but don't.

This requires several modifications to what the United States has now. First, we should adjust our approach to caseworkers and the assistance they provide. In theory, caseworkers help Temporary Assistance for Needy Families (TANF) recipients find jobs, but in reality many caseworkers are undertrained, overworked, and have limited means to provide real help.[36]

For some Americans at the low end of the labor market, adulthood is a series of transitions between part-time or full-time employment, off-the-books work, government benefits, romantic relationships, childrearing, drug or alcohol addiction, and time in jail.[37] The best thing we can do is to provide support, guidance, cajoling, and the occasional threat. People who struggle to find a job after leaving school (whether at age twenty-two, eighteen, or earlier) should immediately get individualized assistance. This may include training, counseling, and cash support. Strugglers should be monitored as they move along in life, and helped when necessary. For this to be effective, we need caseworkers who are well trained, connected to local labor market needs, committed to their job, and not swamped with clients. They must be able to make realistic judgments about when clients can make it in the work force and when the best solution is to help them find a path to dignity and social inclusion that isn't premised on employment.[38]

Second, TANF's eligibility restrictions, including the five-year lifetime limit, should be eased. In bad economic times, such as the 2008–2009 recession and its aftermath, the five-year limit has proved too stringent, causing needless hardship.[39] We should allow more exemptions during economic downturns. But there is a strong case for relaxing the time limit even when the economy is doing well. Caseworkers should be allowed to make judgments about which clients can make it in the labor force and which ones can't, about what is best for clients and their children, and about what supports and requirements are most appropriate for them. Some observers don't like this because they don't trust caseworkers to be sufficiently strict. (This is akin to favoring "three strikes" laws on the grounds that judges who have discretion about sentencing are likely to be too lenient.) This is an understandable sentiment, but it leads to more suffering than is necessary, or justifiable, in a rich society.[40]

Third, TANF's benefit level should be increased. The average AFDC-TANF payment has fallen steadily since 1970, from about $12,000 per recipient family to just $5,000 today.[41] Current spending on TANF is about $30 billion per year. Doubling that amount would fund the needed changes. That would cost an additional 0.2 percent of GDP.

Food Stamps (SNAP) can be kept as is. It is effective, efficient, and widely appreciated.[42]

Criminal Justice

Bruce Western and his research team conducted extensive interviews with 122 Americans released from prison in the Boston area in the mid-2010s. Here is his summary description of their situations:

Aman was raised by his mother in a poor African American section of Dorchester. He was stabbed three different times during his teenage years, and by the onset of his schizophrenia, he had accumulated a long list of juvenile convictions. Eddie was an army veteran and had been a crack addict for most of his adult life. He worked periodically, but in the year after incarceration he lived mostly off his veteran's benefits and street scams. Patrick's mother was a heroin addict who died of AIDS when he was seventeen. A heroin user himself, Patrick had been a witness and victim of serious violence since early childhood. Carla was also a heavy drug user whose life was suffused by violence. Before she went to prison, she made a living by prostitution, selling drugs, and a government disability check for a bad back injured in a prison brawl. Juney was abandoned by his father and raised by his mother, left school at sixteen, and completed his GED in prison. Juney's parole was revoked when his brother got arrested and called him to the scene to help out. Celia was raised by her mother, who had fled an abusive husband who battered her for years. Celia periodically lived with her grandmother, but left home for good at age seventeen. Like her mother, Celia was a victim of domestic violence as a young parent of twenty and made her living as a drug dealer. Peter grew up in the housing projects of Roxbury, with a mother who was addicted to drugs and an abusive father. He was a runaway from the age of eleven. At fourteen, his head was split open with a crowbar in a racial brawl. From the age of seventeen, he spent more than half his life in prison.

These many different starting points all led to Massachusetts prisons, and then to prison release. . . .

Most [of the 122] had grown up poor in poor neighborhoods. . . . Two-thirds of those we interviewed had a history of mental illness or addiction to drugs or alcohol. Depression was common among them—and nearly universal among the women—and anxiety and post-traumatic stress were also frequently reported. Twenty percent of respondents used heroin or cocaine in the year after prison release, and about half of those with a history of addiction experienced a relapse to drug use, which regularly preceded a return to prison. Most of the regular users were the children of addicts. . . . Over 40 percent of the reentry study sample lived with chronic disease, like diabetes or hepatitis, and another one-third reported chronic pain, often related to accidents, fights, or heavy drug use. . . . By the time we interviewed them, the men and women of the reentry study had survived abusive childhood homes, grown up through teenage years filled with fighting, been stabbed or shot, and delivered their own share of violence too.[43]

As violent crime increased sharply and steadily in the 1960s and 1970s and then remained at a high level through the early 1990s, many US policy makers signed on to a "lock 'em up" response. At the time, social scientists had little systematic knowledge of the drivers of crime or how best to combat its rise. Given this ignorance, and in a context in which a "tough on crime" approach was popular with voters, their choice is perhaps understandable.

Today we can, and should, do better. There is broad agreement among experts that incarceration contributed to the drop in crime since the mid-1990s, but that its impact probably was fairly small.[44] A sensible approach to criminal behavior—not just low-level drug offenders but also persons convicted of violent crimes—would minimize time in jail and prison, ensure a decent living standard after release, and provide extensive, individualized support and monitoring.[45] Not only would this improve fairness; it also would be less expensive than incarceration, the direct cost of which averages around $30,000 per inmate per year.

Pensions

The poverty rate among elderly Americans has fallen steadily over the past half century, and the best available projections suggest that average incomes in the bottom 40 percent of elderly households will continue to rise in coming decades. Yet that rise is projected to be relatively slow, with incomes in old age falling farther and farther behind growth of the economy.[46]

Social Security benefits could be increased.[47] A modest, gradual rise over time is appropriate as the economy grows, and it surely is affordable. However, this is only a partial solution. We need one or more of the other retirement income security pillars—personal savings, employer pensions, home ownership, earnings—to increase as well.

We could try to encourage more saving. But previous attempts, such as offering tax advantages (IRAs), have had little impact on the savings behavior of most ordinary Americans.[48]

We should shore up employment-based pensions. Rather than allow Americans to contribute to defined-contribution plans if they have a steady job and if their employer offers a plan and if they know about it and if they feel they can afford to put some of their earnings in it, we could make contributing the default option and make it available to everyone. Employers that have an existing plan could continue that plan, but they would have to automatically enroll all employees and deduct a portion of earnings unless the employee elects to opt out. Employees who lack access to an employer plan would be automatically enrolled in a new universal retirement fund, and those who lack an employer match would be eligible for matching contributions from the government.[49]

In the absence of federal government action along these lines, some states have created their own programs. California's CalSavers program, the largest of these, requires firms with five or more employees to enroll them if it doesn't offer a company-sponsored pension program. The program deposits 5 percent of each paycheck, unless an employee chooses to opt out. But there is no matching contribution from the employer or the state.[50]

We also could facilitate greater employment among the elderly. The employment rate among Americans aged sixty-five and over dropped steadily in the 1960s, 1970s, and 1980s. Since the late 1990s it has slowly but steadily risen.[51] Later retirement isn't a good option for everyone, of course, especially those who have spent most of their working lives in stressful or physically taxing jobs. But for those who can manage it, it is doubly beneficial: it provides an additional source of income, and it allows people to delay receipt of Social Security, which in turn increases the benefit level they will receive.

Eldercare

An estimated 7 million elderly Americans, 14 percent of the elderly population, need help with everyday activities. The average yearly cost is about $30,000 for a home-health aide (30 hours per week, 50 weeks per year, $20 per hour), $45,000 for a room in an assisted living center, and $85,000 for a room in a nursing home. Few Americans have the resources to cover these costs for more than a few years, if that. Medicare doesn't cover long-term eldercare, so Medicaid is the principal provider of government funding. It funds mainly nursing home care and in-home care, though some money is available for care in assisted-living facilities. Medicaid has a stiff asset limit, which often forces recipients to spend down most of their assets in order to qualify. And Medicaid covers a comparatively small share of those who need support. About 3 percent of elderly Americans live in an eldercare institution, and another 3 percent receive in-home services. These shares are smaller than in most other rich democratic nations. Public expenditure on long-term care in the United States amounts to just 0.75 percent of GDP.[52]

Sweden has a more generous system. It spends a little over 3 percent of its GDP on long-term care. About 5 percent of elderly Swedes live in an eldercare institution, and another 12 percent receive "home-help services" in their home. In-home assistance may be for several hours, throughout the day, or round-the-clock if needed. Decisions about types and levels of provision are made by counties and municipalities. Providers of institutional care and in-home help are both public and private. There is a copayment, but it is capped at about $200 per month.

Increased funding for eldercare would improve financial security and quality of life for millions of older Americans. Spending an additional 0.5 percent of our GDP in this area would move us closer to the norm among affluent democratic countries.

Housing Assistance

Many ordinary Americans would like to live in a large city but can't afford to. Cities are attractive for a variety of reasons: they are where many jobs are located, particularly analytical professional positions; they are diverse; they provide lots of eating and entertainment choices; and unlike a generation ago, they are relatively safe and clean. Cities also are economically productive: they concentrate lots of economic activity in a small space, and by bringing people together they generate multiplier effects. And cities are environmentally friendly: they use far fewer cars and less heat and electricity per person than do suburbs and rural areas.[53]

But home prices and rents in some large cities—New York, Boston, Washington DC, San Francisco, San Jose, Los Angeles, San Diego, among others—exceed what many poor, working-class, and even middle-class Americans can afford. The chief cause is an inadequate supply of housing. When demand for something is high and supply is limited, the price tends to go up. In some instances, such as Manhattan and San Francisco, the inadequate supply of homes and rental units owes partly to physical constraints imposed by surrounding water, yet that can be overcome by additional vertical construction. The key obstacle is restrictions on new building stemming from zoning laws and historical preservation designations.[54]

We should loosen these restrictions. Local government is the ideal source of action, but where city councils and mayors are reluctant to act, state governments may have to step in. California's did so in 2017 with passage of SB35, which stipulates that if local ordinances or decisions needlessly prevent or delay construction of new affordable housing, the state will overrule the local authority.

Income among the bottom fifth of US households averages just $22,000 a year, so lower-income Americans need assistance with housing costs not only in large cities, but virtually everywhere.[55] The federal government currently spends around $50 billion a year on low-income housing assistance.[56] This assistance comes through a variety of programs. Since the 1930s the government has built public housing units, which are offered to low-income tenants at below-market rents. Though there has been little new public housing construction in recent decades, about 1 million such units remain across the country. Since the 1960s government has subsidized private construction of low-cost rental units and subsidized the rent that low-income tenants pay. Since 1986 it has provided a tax credit (the Low Income Housing Tax Credit, or LIHTC) to developers for construction or rehabilitation of rental housing in which at least 20 percent of tenants have incomes below half of the area's median income. And since 1974 the federal government has given "Section 8" housing vouchers to some low-income households who rent on the private market. Renters pay 30 percent of their income toward rent, and the voucher pays the difference between this amount and the rent amount (up to an allowable maximum).

These programs serve about 5 million households. Eligibility criteria have varied across the programs and over time within them. Roughly speaking, households with an income below 50 percent or sometimes 80 percent of the area median income tend to be eligible. Among eligible households, only one in four receives assistance from any of these programs. This isn't due to lack of interest; about 6 million households are on waiting lists for a housing voucher and/or a public housing unit.

On average, these programs have enhanced access to housing, reduced overcrowding, improved housing quality, and increased residential mobility for their low-income recipients.[57] There are run-down, violence-plagued public housing projects, such as Cabrini Green in Chicago, but these have been the exception, not the rule. Housing vouchers tend to boost housing quality more, and at lower cost, than public housing.[58]

We should expand housing assistance, via provision of a voucher, to the 15 million or so low-income American households who are eligible for such assistance but don't currently receive it. Doing so would cost about $75 billion a year.[59] The federal government spends (forgoes) about $80 billion each year on the mortgage interest tax deduction. The aim of this program is to boost home ownership, but many other affluent nations have home ownership rates comparable to ours or higher without a tax incentive. Moreover, most of the mortgage interest deduction goes to households in the top fifth of incomes; few in the middle or below benefit from it.[60] We could pay for the expansion of low-income housing assistance by ending the mortgage interest deduction. The additional cost to taxpayers would therefore be $0.

Early Education

Universal high-quality publicly-funded early education for children ages one to four would facilitate work-family balance for Americans, and the best available evidence, detailed in Chapter 2, suggests it would enhance opportunity for children who grow up in less-advantaged homes.[61]

Why can't we leave early education to the market? A good early education system will combine three features: accessibility, affordability, and quality. For Americans able and willing to pay a lot for childcare, our current market-based system typically delivers all three. But for those with low to moderate incomes, getting access to affordable care often means sacrificing quality.[62] A universal system with public funding and some direct public provision could change this, ensuring good-quality care to everyone at an affordable price.

Government already pays for some early education: the federal government funds Head Start, subsidizes childcare for some poor families via the Child Care and Development Fund (CCDF), allows a tax break for childcare, and funds some special education services; and some state and city governments offer preschool for four-year-olds. Yet current funding is nowhere near sufficient to ensure that everyone has access to good-quality childcare and preschool. Among three-year-olds, for instance, about 20 percent are covered by existing funding: state preschools enroll 5 percent, Head Start enrolls 10 percent, and the CCDF subsidizes care for another 5 percent. The shares are even smaller for children ages one and two.[63]

Should government not only pay for but also *provide* early education? Those who say yes contend that this is the only way to guarantee universal access to preschool and care that's above an acceptable quality threshold. On the other hand, it isn't necessary that government be the sole provider. Denmark and Sweden allow private providers, as long as they meet quality standards. In many districts across the United States we allow private providers for publicly-funded K–12 schooling (charter schools), and we allow private doctors and hospitals to provide medical care for Medicare and Medicaid recipients. What's the ideal mix? We don't know. Maybe it's 25 percent of kids in public early education centers, or perhaps it's 75 percent. This depends largely on how many private providers can combine good quality with a reasonable rate of return.

Why not increase access only for those with low incomes rather than for everyone? The argument for universal access is threefold. First, it isn't just low-income parents who struggle to find good quality care that's affordable. Middle-class parents do too. Second, family structure and parents' traits and behaviors are key sources of disadvantage, and they don't overlap perfectly with family income. If we target low-income households, we'll miss many children who need help. Third, development of cognitive and especially noncognitive skills is aided by peer interaction. Children from less advantaged homes gain by mixing with kids from middle-class homes, which doesn't happen in a program that exclusively serves the poor.[64]

Should we encourage parents to put their kids in out-of-home early education immediately after birth? Probably not. As noted in the "Paid Parental Leave" section, research suggests children tend to fare best staying with a parent during the first year of life.

Why not just give the money to parents and let them choose whether to use it on early education or on something else? The argument against doing so is that if early education has individual and social benefits, it makes sense to require that the money be used for that and only that. The same is true of safety (military, police), infrastructure (roads, bridges), health insurance (Medicare, Medicaid), and K–12 schooling, among others. It's worth emphasizing that no one would be forced to enroll their children in early education; parents who prefer to stay home with their children during the first five years would still be able to do so.

Some of the revenue needed to fund early education can come from user fees. Early education is different from police protection and healthcare, the kinds of services that almost no one opts to go without. Even if good early education programs were readily available, some families would choose not to use them because they prefer to provide stay-at-home parental care for their young children. And of course some American adults have no children. This argues for having parents who do want to use early education pay something—even parents with low incomes. Here too the Nordic approach is sensible; in Denmark and Sweden programs charge on a sliding scale, with the fee rising in proportion to family income but capped at 10 percent.

The bill to taxpayers will depend on specific details, but a rough estimate is 1 percent of GDP, or $190 billion, per year.[65] There are two ways to reach this number. First, suppose 75 percent of children age one to four enroll in early education. That's 12 million children. If we spend $12,500 per child, the same as for K–12 schools,[66] total expenditures would be around $150 billion. We'll want the teacher-child ratio for early education to be better than for K–12, which will increase the cost a bit.[67] Second, public expenditure on early education in Denmark and Sweden is about 1.5 percent of GDP.[68] We're likely to end up with more private provision and we have a larger per capita GDP, so 1 percent of our GDP might well be sufficient to create a system that approximates theirs in quality and accessibility. Government (federal, state, and local) currently spends about $30 billion per year on childcare and preschool,[69] so additional spending would amount to around $150 billion, or 0.8 percent of GDP.

K–12 Schools

Elementary and secondary schooling is important for capability development, and it's almost always a focal point of policy debate. How to make it better, for average students and particularly for the least advantaged, is one of the most heavily researched policy questions in the United States.

We need to improve. The high school graduation rate is just 84 per-cent.[70] According to a White House report, only 40 percent of high school graduates are prepared for college or work.[71] American fifteen-year-olds score lower than their counterparts in many other rich democratic nations on the Program for International Student Assessment (PISA) reading, math, and science tests.[72] And literacy and numeracy among American adults, as judged by the OECD's Survey of Adult Skills assessment, is lower than in many of those countries.[73]

Yet after thousands of studies, there is little agreement about how best to im-prove America's K–12 schools.[74] Candidates include equalizing school funding, better pay for teachers, more school choice, smaller class sizes, longer school days, longer school years, longer breaks in the school day, more standardized testing, less standardized testing, more homework, less homework, more use of modern technology, less use of modern technology, and better integration of individualized assistance into classrooms, among others.

We could afford to spend more on K–12 schooling. Public expenditures as a share of GDP have been flat for half a century, as Figure 7.7 shows. And we spend less than many other nations, though that's partly because private school expenditures are greater here than elsewhere. Yet while there is room for more spending, it might be better to allocate our scarce dollars to the other additions and expansions I propose in this chapter and wait on increasing elementary and secondary school spending until we have a better sense of which changes are most likely to yield improvement.

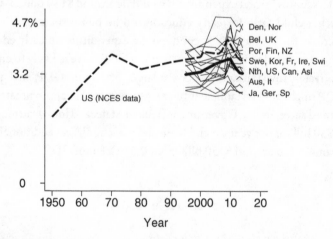

Figure 7.7 Public expenditures on K–12 education. Share of GDP. Data sources: OECD; National Center for Education Statistics, *Digest of Education Statistics*, 2016, table 236.10. Thick solid and dashed lines: United States. "Asl" is Australia; "Aus" is Austria.

Apprenticeships

Of the two-thirds of Americans who don't get a four-year college degree, some enter the labor market directly, others get some vocational training in high school or community college, and others complete a certificate program of some sort. Some among these two-thirds fare reasonably well, but the experience of other affluent nations suggests that a more robust approach to vocational education could help.

One option is an "apprenticeship" program that students would begin around age sixteen and that combines classroom and on-the-job training. The best such programs run for three or four years and are tightly integrated with employers and employer organizations to ensure that the skills being produced are needed ones rather than simply ones schools feel competent to provide.[75]

Federal government funding can be put to two particularly useful purposes here. One is to encourage and subsidize local or regional consortia of high schools, community colleges, universities, and employer associations with the aim of building career pathways.[76] The other is a tax credit for employers who create apprenticeships. Harry Holzer, for instance, recommends a credit of $1,000 per apprenticeship with a goal of 1 million new apprenticeships.[77] The total cost these efforts would likely be no more than 0.1 percent of GDP.

College

America's colleges and universities are among the country's greatest achievements. Taken as a whole, they've long been, and remain, the best in the world. Yet too few Americans from less-advantaged families enroll in college, too few of those who enroll end up getting a four-year degree, and our colleges and universities probably aren't doing as well as they should in educating students. These deficiencies have multiple causes, only one of which is the cost of college.[78] And yet Christopher Jencks is correct in pointing out that "Making college a lot more affordable is a challenge governments know how to meet, while making students learn a lot more is a challenge we do not currently know how to meet. Under those circumstances, starting with affordability is probably the best bet."[79]

What is the best way to make college more affordable? If we want to reduce the cost mainly for students from lower-income families, we ought to focus on room and board, because many such students already receive enough financial aid and grant money to cover most or all of the cost of tuition.[80] However, many American high schoolers and parents aren't aware of this, and the process of applying for school-based financial aid and federal grants can be complicated. Making two-year and four-year public colleges tuition-free for in-state students would send a clear, simple message that college is affordable for all Americans.[81] Another potential benefit of zero tuition at public colleges is that it could increase pressure on private colleges to lower their prices.

A common objection is that eliminating tuition is inefficient, in that students whose families can afford to pay the tuition now wouldn't have to. But this is true of all universal transfers and services, including elementary and secondary schooling. The key question isn't whether there is "waste." It's whether the benefits of the program outweigh the costs. With zero-tuition college, it seems likely they would.

Another concern has to do with the need for funding increases over time. The United Kingdom's experience illustrates the problem. Prior to 1998, public universities in the UK were tuition-free. But in the 1980s and 1990s the government proved unwilling to increase funding in order to keep up with rising enrollments. Eventually it chose instead to cap the number of students colleges could admit. In 1998 the zero tuition policy was ended.[82] If a zero tuition policy leads to an increase in the share of people who apply to college but universities don't increase the quantity they admit, students from less-advantaged circumstances could conceivably be harmed rather than helped by the policy, since fewer of them might end up being admitted to any college. It's impossible to know whether this dynamic would play out in the US context, but this is an important caution.

What would be the price tag for tuition-free public college? About 12 million Americans attend in-state public colleges every year, a majority of them in community colleges. Average tuition is $6,000 per year.[83] So the total yearly cost would be approximately $75 billion, or about 0.4 percent of GDP.

The cost of room and board averages about $10,000 per year for US college students, and tuition-free college won't do away with these costs. Moreover, many Americans will to want to attend private colleges, which won't be tuition-free and may continue to get more expensive.[84] Consequently, many American students will still have to take out loans. (The same is true in Sweden, where students pay no tuition and yet the average college graduate owes about $20,000 in student loans.[85]) In the late 1990s we created a program that allows income-based repayment of student loans: the lower the student's income after college, the smaller the portion of their loan debt they are required to pay back. This program was enhanced in 2007 and 2010, and it could be expanded further. We also could lengthen the loan repayment period to twenty or perhaps even thirty years.[86] And it would help to automatically enroll college students in this program, rather than requiring them to find out about it on their own and then wade through a complicated application process in order to utilize it.

The total cost of these two efforts to increase college affordability would be around 0.5 percent of GDP.

Affirmative Action

Since the late 1960s, affirmative action programs for university admissions and employment have promoted opportunity for women and for members of racial and ethnic minority groups.[87] Not surprisingly, as these programs have been cut back or ended in recent decades, some of that progress has been reversed.[88] Affirmative action should continue, but with family background as the focal criterion.[89]

Full Employment

Employment is front and center in the American ethos. Self-sufficiency and self-realization via paid work are at the core of the "Protestant ethic" that shaped the country in its early years and the "American dream" that has animated it since the mid-1800s. As I noted in Chapter 2, employment has significant benefits for individuals, from mental stimulation to social integration to self-esteem and beyond. We also need a significant majority of people in paid work to help fund government programs. High employment allows for hefty tax revenues without requiring overly high tax rates. High employment eases the fiscal crunch another way too, by reducing the number of people fully or heavily reliant on government benefits.

From the mid-1940s to 2000, the employment rate among working-age Americans rose steadily, from 60 percent to nearly 78 percent, as Figure 7.8 shows. But since 2000 we've moved in the opposite direction. Our employment rate currently stands at about 74 percent. This is partly a product of the deep 2008–2009 recession, but sluggish employment growth began before the crash. And in the meantime many other rich nations have increased employment sharply, suggesting the problem isn't something endemic to modern affluent societies.[90]

There are a number of things we can do to address this. One is better family-friendly policies, particularly childcare and preschool, paid parental leave, and sickness insurance, as described above.

We should strive to improve schooling, from early education to K–12 to apprenticeships to college and beyond.

We should commit more resources to active labor market policy. Sweden and Denmark have used retraining and job placement assistance to help improve the

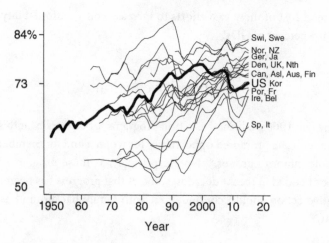

Figure 7.8 Employment rate. Employed persons aged 25–64 as a share of all persons aged 25–64. The vertical axis doesn't begin at zero. Data source: OECD. Thick line: United States. "Asl" is Australia; "Aus" is Austria.

efficiency of the private-sector labor market and public employment to increase demand for labor.[91] These two countries have committed 1.5 to 2 percent of GDP to such programs.[92] Swedish firms must notify their local board in advance when employees are to be laid off and when they have job openings that have lasted more than ten days. Workers who are displaced or who leave their job by choice can receive subsidized training through the employment service. Officials in local labor market boards keep in close communication with firms and with officials in other areas regarding trends in skill needs. The training programs are full-time and range in duration from two weeks to more than a year. The service then helps to place workers in new positions. If necessary, an employer subsidy may be used to encourage a private-sector employer to hire, or a public-sector job may be created. Denmark increased pursuit of active labor market programs in the mid-1990s, with apparently beneficial effects. A recent meta-analysis of research on such programs concludes that they tend to improve medium-term employment outcomes.[93]

It helps if monetary policy authorities prioritize labor market tightness. The Federal Reserve, like independent central banks in other rich nations, is charged with maintaining both price stability and low unemployment. Its choices about which to prioritize, particularly during periods in which the unemployment rate is low and there are worries about the potential for a jump in inflation, impacts not just the business cycle but also the long-run employment rate. The longer the labor market can remain tight, the stronger the pressure on employers to increase wages and salaries, which tends to attract more people into paid work. And the boost to wages is a good thing apart from its effect on employment rates.[94]

Government should serve as employer of last resort.[95] "Make-work" has a mixed history in the United States. It played a prominent role in the 1930s, and subsequent smaller-scale programs have boosted employment rates of low-end workers.[96] These programs are often criticized because they have not tended to improve long-term labor market success of participants. But we should think of make-work not as a route to "real" employment, but rather as a worth-while expense. If we believe people who are able and willing to work should be employed, the fact that make-work might not provide a ladder to a good job shouldn't discourage us.

That doesn't mean we should guarantee everyone a job in the place where they currently live. Doing that would prevent sensible shrinkage of some towns or cities that are no longer economically viable. Instead, government can provide support for job creation in a variety of ways: public infrastructure investment, place-specific investment funds, regional employer consortiums, and temporary wage subsidies for new private-sector jobs.[97] An additional potentially helpful strategy is to provide assistance for job losers to move out and incentives for others (including immigrants) to move in.[98]

Employee Voice

Downward pressure on wages is a signature feature of our modern economic era, as I've noted in several earlier chapters. Labor unions are the principal insti-tutional mechanism available to counteract this pressure. Their strength during the "golden age" following the Second World War was integral to the sustained pay growth that occurred during those three decades. Today, only 10 percent of employed Americans are union members. Increasing that share significantly probably would be the most effective way to ensure regular wage increases for middle- and low-paid workers.

But accomplishing this is a very tall order. As Figure 7.9 makes clear, America's declining unionization rate isn't a recent phenomenon. Nor is it mainly a function of Reagan administration hostility in the 1980s. Unionization in the United States has been falling steadily for more than half a century. Indeed, union de-cline isn't a peculiarly American problem. As we saw in Chapter 3, unionization rates have been falling in almost all affluent nations. Only five still have a rate above 40 percent, and four of those (Belgium, Denmark, Finland, and Sweden) are helped by the fact that access to unemployment insurance hinges on union membership. It's well and good to wish for bigger, stronger unions, but no one has yet figured out an effective strategy to achieve that.[99]

Are there alternatives to stronger unions? One possibility is "employee board-level representation" (also called "codetermination"), whereby employees elect a

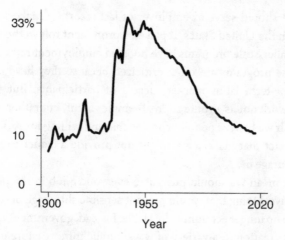

Figure 7.9 Unionization. Share of employees who are union members. Data sources: 1900–82 are from Richard B. Freeman, "Spurts in Union Growth: Defining Moments and Social Processes," in *The Defining Moment: The Great Depression and the American Economy in the Twentieth Century*, edited by Michael D. Bordo et al., University of Chicago Press, 1998, table 8A.2. 1982ff are from Bureau of Labor Statistics, data.bls.gov, series LUU0204899600, using Current Population Survey data.

portion of their company's board of directors. Shareholder obsession with short-run profits is one of the key obstacles to wage growth. Giving employees more voice in firms' decision making might mitigate this.[100]

Opponents of employee board-level representation tend to argue that it will weaken firms' performance. However, it appears to have had no such adverse effect in the European countries where large firms operate under codetermination requirements.[101]

Few companies will opt for employee board-level representation unless they are legally obligated to, so Democratic lawmakers have introduced legislation—the Reward Work Act and the Accountable Capitalism Act, both in 2018—requiring employee election of 33 percent or 40 percent of the board of directors in large US corporations. Such proposals have no hope of becoming law at the moment, but the political environment will shift at some point.

It's worth noting that even if such a requirement eventually is enacted, employee board-level representation's reach would be limited. In the Accountable Capitalism Act, the requirement would apply to companies with annual revenues of $1 billion or more. The roughly 1,300 firms that meet this criterion employ approximately 45 million Americans, or about one-third of the workforce.[102]

Germany is a helpful test case for gauging employee board-level representation's impact on wages in a country that doesn't have especially strong labor unions. While German unions and collective bargaining remain powerful in some manufacturing industries, they have weakened considerably in much

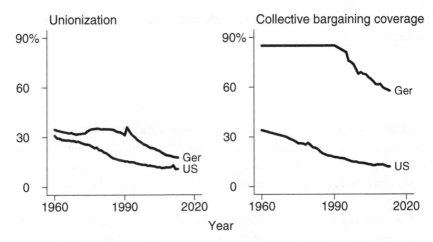

Figure 7.10 Unionization and collective bargaining coverage in Germany and the United States. Unionization: share of employees who are labor union members. Collective bargaining coverage: share of employees whose wages are determined by a collective agreement. Data source: Jelle Visser, "ICTWSS: Database on Institutional Characteristics of Trade Unions, Wage Setting, State Intervention, and Social Pacts," version 5.1, 2016, Amsterdam Institute for Advanced Labour Studies, series ud, ud_s, adjcov.

of the rest of the economy, as Figure 7.10 suggests. But employee board-level representation is solidly entrenched.[103] German workers have been able to elect half of the directors in firms with 2,000 or more employees since the early 1950s and one-third of the directors in firms with 500 to 2,000 employees since the mid-1970s.[104] About one-quarter of German workers are employed in such firms.[105]

So has Germany had healthy wage growth? No, it hasn't. As Figure 3.16 in Chapter 3 shows, Germany's record has been similar to that of the United States: growth of median compensation has been much slower than growth of the economy, and it has lagged well behind compensation growth in most other affluent democratic countries.[106] Germany's slow wage growth owes partly to its reunification with the former East Germany in 1990 and its intentional creation of a low-wage ("mini-jobs") segment of the labor market in the early 2000s. Still, its wage performance gives us little reason for optimism about employee board-level representation's ability to boost wages in the United States.

There is a good case on fairness grounds for enhancing employees' ability to influence decision making in the company they work for.[107] However, most proponents of strengthened labor unions and employee board-level representation see them mainly as mechanisms to boost pay. Unfortunately, neither looks especially promising in the American context. We don't know how to significantly increase the size and strength of unions, and employee board-level representation in a weak-union environment may turn out to have little impact on wages.

Minimum Wage

The federal minimum wage in the United States is low, and it has been flat for half a century, as Figure 7.11 shows. We should increase it to around $12 per hour and index it to inflation. States and localities with thriving economies or a higher cost of living could set their own minimum wage at a higher level, as many currently do.

The chief worry about increasing the minimum wage is that doing so will reduce employment. The best available evidence, however, suggests that modest increases in the statutory minimum in the past have not reduced employment. The best test, because it is closest to an experimental design, is a "difference in differences" approach.[108] The fact that many of the US states have set minimum wages higher than the federal minimum, in varying degrees and at different times, is helpful for analytical purposes. In the early 1990s David Card and Alan Krueger compared changes in employment in fast food restaurants on either side of the New Jersey–Pennsylvania border after one state increased its minimum wage while the other didn't. Arindrajit Dube and colleagues pursued this strategy for every pair of adjacent counties straddling state borders in which one increased its minimum wage between 1990 and 2006. They, like Card and Krueger, found no adverse employment effect of minimum wage increases.[109]

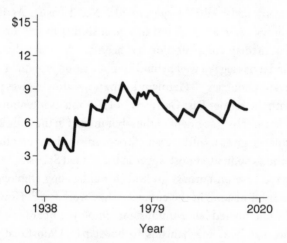

Figure 7.11 Minimum wage. Federal minimum wage. 2015 dollars; inflation adjustment is via the CPI-U-RS. Data source: Economic Policy Institute, stateofworkingamerica.org/data.

This suggests reason for optimism that raising the wage floor to $10 an hour, and perhaps to $12, is likely to cause little or no employment decline.

The real question is whether the federal minimum wage should be even higher. California, the state of New York, and the city of Seattle, among others, have passed legislation to raise their statutory minimum to $15 an hour by the early 2020s. Some argue that we should do this for the nation as a whole.[110] That would be a big increase, and it would affect a lot of Americans. Half of employed Americans currently earn less than $36,500 a year, and a person working full-time year-round at a $15 minimum wage would have annual earnings of $30,000.[111]

As Figure 7.11 suggests, we have no prior historical experience with a federal minimum wage anywhere close to $15 an hour. Nor is cross-country comparison of much help. Figure 7.12 shows that among the fourteen rich democratic nations that have a statutory minimum, none is above the equivalent of $11 per hour in US dollars.

Even some prominent advocates of a significantly higher wage floor fear that $15 an hour might cause substantial job loss, particularly in less-affluent parts of the country.[112] Given this concern, coupled with the lack of empirical evidence on which to base a policy conclusion, the wise approach probably is to increase the federal minimum to something below $15 per hour, index it to inflation, monitor its impact, and then adjust as needed.[113]

There are several other regulatory changes we should implement in order to boost wages for ordinary Americans: protect employees from being improperly classified as independent contractors; improve employees' ability to recover

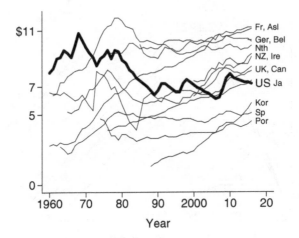

Figure 7.12 Minimum wage. 2015 US dollars. Currencies converted using purchasing power parities. Austria, Denmark, Finland, Italy, Norway, Sweden, and Switzerland don't have a statutory minimum wage. Data source: OECD. Thick line: United States. "Asl" is Australia.

wages their employer has illegally withheld from them; ensure that workers in retail, food service, and cleaning sectors be paid for at least four hours per shift; require that all workers paid less than $50,000 per year be paid at an overtime rate if they work more than 40 hours in a week.

Earned Income Tax Credit

The Earned Income Tax Credit (EITC) is a very effective program, encouraging employment while boosting the incomes of households who struggle in the labor market.[114] The EITC subsidizes earnings by as much as 45 percent, providing up to $6,300 (for a household with three or more children). It is paid to households rather than to individuals, and the money comes in a lump sum once a year.[115] Households with at least one employed adult and earnings below $54,000 are eligible. The credit functions like a cash benefit; if it amounts to more than the household owes in federal income taxes, the household receives the difference as a cash refund.

As Figure 7.13 shows, the amount of the EITC increases with earnings up to a certain level, then plateaus, and then decreases with earnings.

The average amount recipient households get is $2,300 per year. The benefit level increased sharply between 1987 and 1996. Since then it has been flat. Nearly one in four Americans receives the EITC. This share rose significantly between the late 1980s and the mid-1990s and again in the 2000s, a result of changes in eligibility criteria, increases in the benefit amount, and stagnant wage levels for Americans on the lower rungs of the wage ladder.[116]

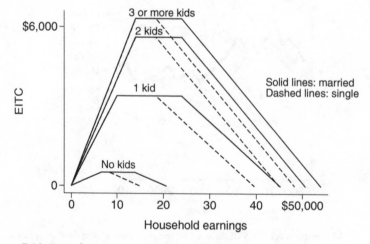

Figure 7.13 Earned Income Tax Credit benefit structure. The benefit levels shown are for 2017. Source: Tax Policy Center, "Earned Income Tax Credit Parameters."

The United States and the United Kingdom were the first countries to introduce an EITC-type program, both in the 1970s. In recent decades many other rich longstanding-democratic countries have adopted some version of it. A number of US states and a few cities have their own EITC; most are small, but some supplement the national EITC by as much as 75 percent.[117]

We can improve on the existing federal Earned Income Tax Credit in four respects.

First, the EITC is far too small for Americans who don't have any children, as Figure 7.13 makes clear. A household with one child can receive up to $3,400, but the maximum for a childless household is just $500. Childless households are 25 percent of EITC recipients, but they receive only 5 percent of total EITC payments. The EITC thus creates little employment incentive for childless adults, and it provides very little income support for them.

Second, the fact that the size of the EITC credit depends on household earnings (actually pretax income) and that it has a phase-out range creates some employment disincentives for a potential second earner in a household whose earnings are likely to be relatively low.

A way to address these two problems is to give the EITC to employed persons, rather than households, and to give it to all or most such persons, rather than only those with low earnings. Sweden has an EITC, first introduced in 2007, that works like this, as Figure 7.14 shows.

Third, we could increase the amount of the EITC credit.

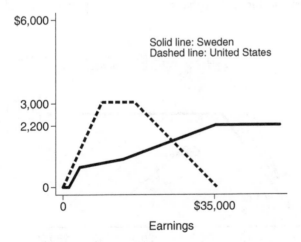

Figure 7.14 Swedish and US Earned Income Tax Credit benefit structures. The benefit levels shown are for 2010, in US dollars. United States: single unmarried adult with one child. Sweden: one earner (not contingent on the presence or number of children). PPP conversion: 1 US dollar = 9 Swedish kroner. Data sources: Karin Edmark et al., "Evaluation of the Swedish Earned Income Tax Credit," Working Paper 2012:1, Institute for Labor Market Policy Evaluation, 2012, figure 1; Tax Policy Center.

Fourth, we could use the EITC to help compensate for wage stagnation. As we saw in Chapter 6, pay for ordinary American workers hasn't increased since the late 1970s. In the absence of a resurgence of union strength, which is unlikely, there is little reason to expect this to change. To ensure that incomes rise over time as the economy grows, we could index the EITC to GDP per capita, rather than to inflation. This won't compensate fully for stagnant pay: the EITC is a fraction of the $30,000 a year earned by a typical middle-class American, so if the EITC rises in line with the economy but earnings don't, income (earnings plus EITC) growth will lag behind growth of the economy. It's a partial remedy, not a full solution. But it will help.

How much would an expanded federal EITC cost? A fully universal version would give it to all 145 million employed Americans. If the credit averages $3,500 per person, the cost would be approximately 2.8 percent of GDP. (Sweden's EITC costs 2.4 percent of GDP.) That's a sizable increase over current expenditure on the program, which is 0.3 percent of GDP.[118] The cost could be reduced by tapering the credit for those at the top of the distribution—the top tenth or the top fifth. The added cost might then be around 2.25 percent of GDP.

Figure 7.15 shows what this proposed EITC might look like.

There are two main objections to an expanded EITC as a centerpiece of strategies to boost incomes. First, it might cause wage levels to fall. In the presence of the EITC, employers may offer a lower wage than they otherwise would, and workers may be willing to accept a lower wage. Also, the EITC might increase the supply of less-educated people seeking jobs, and without an increase in employer demand for such workers, this rise in supply could push wages

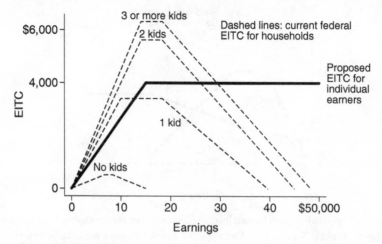

Figure 7.15 EITC benefit structure: actual and proposed. For discussion of the proposed benefit levels, see the text. The actual benefit levels shown are for 2017. Source: Tax Policy Center, "Earned Income Tax Credit Parameters."

down. Existing studies suggest that the EITC may indeed reduce wages somewhat, but the evidence is thin and the effect is likely fairly small.[119] The best way to address this danger is with a moderate to high minimum wage.[120]

Second, some object to taxpayers rather than employers bearing the cost of ensuring that household incomes rise. This is an understandable sentiment. But consider how we think about health insurance, pensions, unemployment insurance, and sickness insurance. Like income, these contribute to material well-being. In all affluent nations, including the United States, they are financed at least partly by taxes. Few object to the fact that firms aren't the sole funders.

Profit Sharing

Another potential way to boost household incomes is profit sharing, whereby employees receive part of their compensation in the form of a portion of the firm's profit rather than as a guaranteed wage or salary. For owners, the advantage is that when the firm is struggling, for example during a recession, its labor costs will fall, because workers will absorb part of the reduction in profits in the form of lower take-home pay. For workers, the advantage is that if profits rise, their pay automatically will too. Over time, their pay will be higher than it would have been without profit sharing.[121]

There's also a risk for employees: they will bear part of the cost of falling profits during bad economic times. Then again, the enhanced flexibility in labor costs makes it less likely that firms will need to fire employees during rough times.[122] In this respect, workers' security is increased.

How could we encourage profit sharing? In 2016, Hillary Clinton's presidential campaign proposed offering firms that implement profit sharing a two-year tax credit equal to 15 percent of the amount they share (higher for small businesses).[123] The credit would apply to shared profits up to 10 percent of a worker's salary or wage. For instance, if a new profit share program in a firm added $5,000 to the pay of someone making $50,000 a year, the firm would receive a subsidy of $750. The cost of this subsidy would be in the neighborhood of 0.01 percent of GDP per year, or about $2 billion.

Infrastructure and Public Spaces

Public spaces and services matter directly for people's lived experience. Think of roads, bridges, stoplights, enforcement of speed limits, air traffic control, sidewalks, museums, parks, sports fields, forests, campgrounds, beaches, oceans, lakes, swimming pools, zoos, weather forecasts, phone lines, broadband, the

Internet, public television and radio programming, subsidization of free private TV and radio networks, libraries, festivals, and more.

Infrastructure also underpins a successful economy. America's firms, and citizens, face significant hurdles and risks due to our failure to maintain and improve our roads, bridges, plane and rail systems, city layouts, broadband networks, and water systems. In 2013, the American Society of Civil Engineers reported that one-third of US roads are in poor or mediocre condition. According to the Federal Highway Administration, one-quarter of America's bridges are deficient or functionally obsolete. The cost of traffic congestion in fuel and lost time is estimated to be nearly 1 percent of GDP. Delayed and canceled plane flights cost another 0.25 percent of GDP. We have an efficient freight-rail system for transporting products, but high-speed rail to move people around is nonexistent. The California drought in the mid-2010s exposed, once again, the inadequacy of our water supply systems. Four thousand dams are in need of repair. Ten percent of Americans report not using the Internet, and 12 percent lack access to a high-speed connection.[124]

This isn't to say that America's infrastructure is worse than it used to be. That notion is based largely on anecdote.[125] Nor is it to suggest that our infrastructure is far behind that of other affluent nations. We do lag behind some of them, according to the most recent assessment by the World Economic Forum, but the gap isn't enormous.[126] The point, rather, is that our infrastructure isn't as good as it could and should be.

The needed amounts of money aren't huge. One proposal, from a progressive think tank, estimates that to bring our roads, bridges, mass transit, rail, ports, airports, inland waterways, drinking water, wastewater, and energy infrastructure up to par would require additional expenditures by the federal government of about 0.5 percent of GDP per year.[127]

Investment in infrastructure doesn't only grease the wheels of the economy. It also increases employment.[128] Boosting employment is helpful in the aggregate, but it's also vital, in the contemporary era, to the pursuit of geographical fairness. As production of food and goods has become steadily more automated and as more of it has moved abroad, smaller cities and towns across the United States have struggled economically. Places that suffer a sudden loss of a major employer experience particularly acute economic and social pain. Large job losses tend to have ripple effects, as unemployed households reduce their spending and thereby reduce employment at retail stores, restaurants, and other potential sources of substitute employment.

According to one study, counties with fewer than 100,000 residents accounted for 32 percent of the new businesses created during the 1992–1996 economic recovery, but just 15 percent during in the 2002–2006 recovery and 0 percent during the 2010–2014 recovery. The pattern was similar for jobs: in the 1992–1996 recovery, counties with population below 100,000 got 27 percent of the net increase in the nation's jobs, while in 2010–2014 they got just 9 percent.[129]

If these recent patterns continue, there is no easy long-term fix for small cities and towns.[130] But the building and repair of infrastructure can help in the short run.[131] Given that a good infrastructure is directly beneficial for quality of life, and given that it can kick-start economic development, it tends to be money well spent.

Paid Vacation Days and Holidays

In other rich democratic countries, the law requires that companies give their employees between ten and thirty-eight paid vacation days and holidays. The average in these nations is twenty-seven days.[132] In the United States, the number is zero. Most public employees get some paid days off, and 77 percent of private-sector employers offer some to their workers. Yet some employees get none, and the average number of paid days off for those who get any is just eighteen.[133]

We should make the provision of paid vacation days and holidays mandatory. And it would make sense to increase the number to ten paid holidays and fifteen days (three weeks) of paid vacation, for a total of twenty-five.

How Much Will It Cost?

The additional expenditures needed to fund these various programs would total around 10 percent of GDP. Figure 7.16 provides a breakdown. Details for each area or policy are provided above.

How to Pay for It

Increasing tax revenues by 10 percent of GDP would be a significant change for the United States, but it wouldn't be unprecedented. During the course of the twentieth century, government revenues' share of America's GDP rose by about 25 percentage points. And an increase of 10 percentage points would put the United States merely in the middle of the pack—not at the top—among the world's rich democratic countries.[134]

What would be the best way to get the money? Broadly speaking, there are two options: "Soak the rich" or "Spread the burden." Other affluent democratic nations tend to do the latter. They have a relatively proportional tax system, with

2.25%	Earned Income Tax Credit
1.75	Health insurance
1.0	Full employment
0.8	Early education
0.5	Paid parental leave
0.5	Child allowance
0.5	Sickness insurance
0.5	Disability assistance
0.5	Eldercare
0.5	College
0.5	Infrastructure and public spaces
0.25	Pensions
0.2	Unemployment insurance and wage insurance
0.2	Social assistance
0.1	Apprenticeships
0.01	Profit sharing
0	Housing assistance
0	Minimum wage
0	Criminal justice reform
0	Affirmative action
0	Paid vacation days and holidays

Figure 7.16 Cost of proposed government program additions and expansions. The numbers are percentages of GDP. They total 10.06 percent. All are estimates.

everyone paying roughly the same share of their pretax income in taxes.[135] They do this instead of soaking the rich—taxing the rich at much higher rates than everyone else—for two reasons. One is to minimize tax resistance by the rich. The other is the need to go where the money is; even if the rich have very high incomes, there aren't that many of them, so in order to generate a lot of revenue it's usually necessary to spread the tax burden up and down the income ladder.

America too has a relatively flat tax system. Figure 7.17 shows average effective tax rates in the United States at various points along the pretax income distribution (hollow circles). An "effective tax rate" is calculated as taxes paid divided by pretax income. These calculations include all types of taxes at all levels of government. The effective tax rates paid by Americans are fairly similar up and down the income ladder.

However, the distribution of pretax income is quite unequal. Households at the top get a much larger portion of the income than those in the middle or bottom.[136] As a result, the distribution of tax payments (dark circles in Figure 7.17) also is very unequal. Households in the top quintile pay about 65 percent

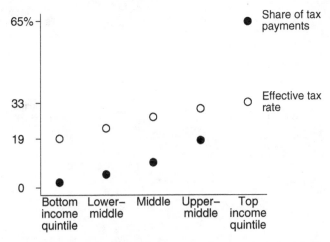

Figure 7.17 Effective tax rates and shares of tax payments by pretax income quintile. Includes all types of taxes (personal and corporate income, payroll, property, sales, excise, estate, other) at all levels of government (federal, state, local). 2016. Effective tax rates: taxes paid as a share of pretax income. Data source: Institute on Taxation and Economic Policy (ITEP), "Who Pays Taxes in America: 2016."

of all tax dollars, the middle fifth pay about 10 percent, and the bottom fifth pay 2 percent. Each is paying a similar percentage of their income in taxes, but the affluent end up paying a lot of the tax dollars because they have so much of the income.

Suppose we were to increase taxes for everyone, keeping the distribution of tax payments exactly the same as it is now while increasing revenues by 10 percent of GDP. What would that change look like for households at various points along the income distribution? Households in lowest fifth of incomes would account for about 2 percent of these added revenues, households in the middle around 10 percent, and households in the top quintile 65 percent. In dollar terms, households in the bottom fifth of incomes would pay, on average, about $1,400 more per year, those in the lower-middle fifth $3,600, those in the middle fifth $7,000, those in the upper-middle fifth $13,100, and those in the top fifth $46,200 more.[137]

As a presidential candidate in 2008, Barack Obama pledged to not increase taxes for households in the bottom 95 percent of incomes. The Democratic nominee in 2016, Hillary Clinton, made the same pledge. In the contemporary US context, there is some sense in focusing on the top in the search for more revenue. The chief rationale for progressive taxation is that those with more income can afford to pay a larger share of that income than those with less.[138] While the incomes of Americans in the middle and below have risen slowly over the past few decades, for those at the top incomes have soared, so it's reasonable to ask them to contribute a larger share of those incomes.

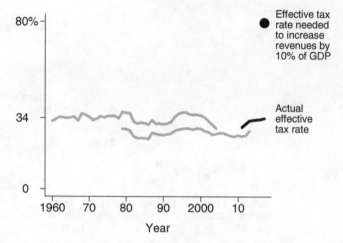

Figure 7.18 Effective tax rate on the top 5 percent of incomes. Effective tax rate: tax payments as a share of pretax income. The chart has three estimates of the actual rate. The gray lines are for federal taxes. The black line is for all taxes (federal, state, and local). Data source for the top gray line: Thomas Piketty and Emmanuel Saez, data set for "How Progressive Is the US Federal Tax System?," *Journal of Economic Perspectives*, 2007, elsa.berkeley.edu/~saez. Data source for the lower gray line: Congressional Budget Office, "The Distribution of Household Income and Federal Taxes, 2011," data set, alternative income definition, worksheet 13. Data source for the black line: Institute on Taxation and Economic Policy (ITEP), "Who Pays Taxes in America," various years. Calculation of the rate needed to increase tax revenues by 10 percent of GDP is as follows: Get the total pretax income of the top 5 percent of households by multiplying this group's average pretax income (from ITEP) by its number of households (from the Census Bureau). Then divide 10 percent of GDP by the group's total pretax income.

However, there's a limit to how much additional tax revenue we can get from those at the top. Figure 7.18 shows the effective tax rate on the top 5 percent of households going back to 1960. We have three estimates of this tax rate (two of the three include only federal taxes, not state and local). The dot for the year 2016 indicates what the effective tax rate on this group would need to have been in that year in order to increase tax revenues by 10 percent of GDP.[139] It's a very high rate, and one far above the actual rate at any point in the past half century. This seems neither desirable nor likely to find favor among policy makers.

What, then, should we do to increase government revenues by 10 percent of GDP? A multipronged approach might work. Figure 7.19 shows one possibility.

Begin with a national consumption tax. The United States raises the least revenue from consumption taxes of any rich nation, as Figure 7.20 shows. Currently we collect only about 5 percent of GDP in consumption taxes, almost entirely at the state and local levels. Most other affluent countries collect 10 percent or more.[140] A value-added tax (VAT) at a rate of 12 percent, with limited deductions, would likely bring in about 5 percent of GDP in revenue.[141]

Because of its regressivity, the idea of a large consumption tax has yet to be embraced by America's left.[142] The degree of regressivity can be lessened by

5.0%	Add a national consumption tax (VAT) at a rate of 12%, with limited deductions or a small flat rebate
1.4	Improve collection of unpaid taxes and reduce use of tax havens
1.0	Return to the 2000 (pre-Bush) federal income tax rates for taxpayers with incomes below $450,000
0.7	Increase the effective tax rate for the top 1% by 6 percentage points (from 34% to 40%)
0.3	Return the estate tax exemption threshold and rates to their 1965-75 levels
0.7	Add a carbon tax
0.5	Add a financial transactions tax of 0.5% on trades
0.3	Increase the payroll tax by 1 percentage point
0.2	Increase the cap on the Social Security payroll tax so the tax covers 90% of total earnings, as it did in the early 1980s
0.2	End the real estate tax credit

Figure 7.19 How to increase tax revenues by 10 percent of GDP. The numbers are percentages of GDP. They total 10.3 percent. All are estimates.

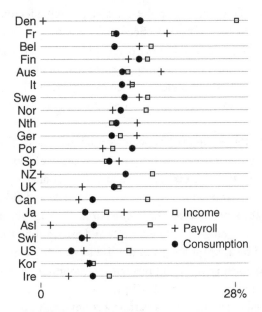

Figure 7.20 Income tax revenues, payroll tax revenues, and consumption tax revenues. Share of GDP. The data are for 2016. The countries are ordered according to total tax revenues as a share of GDP. "Payroll" includes both payroll taxes proper and social security contributions. For Italy, the symbol for payroll taxes isn't visible because income and payroll taxes each account for the same share of GDP. Data source: OECD. "Asl" is Australia; "Aus" is Austria.

exempting more items from the tax[143]; but the greater the exemptions, the less revenue the tax will bring in. A better strategy might be to offset the regressivity of a new consumption tax with other changes to the tax system.

Those on the political right tend to object to a VAT for fear it will become a "money machine"—a tax that can be steadily increased over time. But this fear is based on a misreading of the experience of other rich nations. Some countries have decreased their VAT rate, some have held it constant, and most of those that have increased it did so mainly in the 1970s and early 1980s, when high inflation made such increases less noticeable.[144] Some argue that tax increases in rich countries since the 1960s have come mainly via VAT increases, but they've in fact come as much or more via increases in income and payroll taxes.[145]

Where would the rest of the new revenues come from? By improving collection of unpaid taxes and reducing the use of tax havens, we could raise, as a conservative estimate, 1.4 percent of GDP.[146]

We could return to the pre-Bush income tax rates for taxpayers with incomes below $450,000. (We did so in 2013 for incomes above that amount.) This would increase revenues by about 1 percent of GDP.[147]

We could raise income tax rates for those in the top 1 percent a bit more.[148] This might entail increasing the tax rate on personal income or capital income, or both. The effective tax rate on the top 1 percent currently is around 34 percent.[149] An increase of 6 percentage points, to a 40 percent effective rate, would hardly be confiscatory. Increasing the effective tax rate for this group by 6 percentage points would generate about 0.7 percent of GDP.[150] A common worry is that raising taxes on the rich will cause them to flee, or at least to park their money elsewhere. The best available evidence suggests that while high earners are indeed responsive to changes in tax rates, the magnitude of this effect is small.[151]

Since the 1970s, the estate tax has been steadily decreased. The exemption threshold—the amount of the estate beyond which the tax kicks in—has been reduced to the point where the tax applies to just two out of every thousand estates. And the tax rate has been lowered. Since 2010 estate and gift tax revenues have totaled just 0.13 percent of GDP, compared to 0.45 percent between 1965 and 1975.[152] Returning the estate tax rate and exemption threshold to the earlier levels would be appropriate given the rise in wealth inequality in recent decades.[153] It could boost government revenues by around 0.3 percent of GDP.

A carbon tax could generate about 0.7 percent of GDP in revenues.[154] The United States arguably should have a carbon tax anyway, in order to shift resources away from activities that contribute to climate change.[155]

A modest tax on financial transactions, such as purchases of stock shares, would bring in about 0.5 percent of GDP. Every rich democratic nation other than the United States has a tax on financial transactions. On average those taxes yield about 0.5 percent of GDP in revenue.[156]

Increasing the payroll tax by 1 percentage point (half a percentage point on employees and half a point on employers) would add about 0.3 percent to revenues.[157] This would leave the payroll tax rate well below that in many

European countries, and almost certainly below the level at which it would be a significant deterrent to employment.

We could increase the cap on earnings that are subject to the Social Security payroll tax. A person's earnings above $128,400 (as of 2018) aren't subject to this tax. Because a growing share of total earnings in the US economy has gone to those at the top, a growing share has been exempt from the Social Security payroll tax. In the early 1980s, about 90 percent of earnings was subject to the tax; this has dropped to below 85 percent. Raising the cap to get back to 90 percent would increase tax revenues by about 0.2 percent of GDP.[158]

Finally, we could do away with the real estate tax credit, which allows homeowners to deduct their state and local property tax payments from the income on which they pay federal income tax. The evidence suggests this credit does nothing to increase home ownership, and it mainly goes to affluent taxpayers. This would increase revenues by about 0.2 percent of GDP.[159]

This set of proposed changes is just one of many possible ways to increase tax revenues.[160] The point is that the technical details of getting an additional 10 percent of GDP are not difficult.

A Partial but Valuable Fix

The recommendations I offer in this chapter won't solve every problem we face. We also need to deal with climate change, foreign policy challenges, prevention of future financial crises, reform of our electoral process, and much more. But the new programs and expansions of existing ones outlined here would improve the lives of lots of Americans. We know from our own experience and from the experiences of other rich democratic nations that public insurance programs help, and that they do so without impeding the economy, breaking the bank, or curtailing individual freedom.

The question is whether our policy makers and our political system are up to the task. I turn to this in Chapter 8.

8

How to Get There

I expect the scope and size of American public social programs will expand significantly in coming decades. My reasoning can be stated simply:

- Experience here and abroad suggests that government social programs can improve well-being, so policy makers will regularly propose new programs and expansion of existing ones.
- On occasion they will succeed in getting their proposals enacted. (The hypothesis doesn't specify when or why. It's probabilistic.)
- Those successes will tend to stick.

This is how social policy in the United States has evolved over the past century. It has expanded in fits and starts, with bursts and lulls. Movement has been largely forward. Backsliding has been rare.[1]

Analysts of social programs in rich democratic nations often treat the difference between the US welfare state and that of the leading social democratic countries as a categorical one—a difference in type.[2] However, the core difference is one of degree, rather than of kind. The United States has fewer public social programs than nations such as Sweden and Denmark, and our programs tend to cover fewer people and to be less generous. Yet we do already have many of the same programs as the leading countries. And while our welfare state lags behind, it has been advancing for most of the past century. Figure 8.1 shows expenditures on public social programs as a share of GDP in Denmark, Sweden, and the United States since the late 1800s. While the two Nordic countries spend significantly more, the difference between these countries and the United States today is much smaller than the difference between the United States today and the United States a century ago.

The expansion of public insurance that has occurred over the past century in the United States is what we should expect for the future. Further advance won't necessarily happen right away, and progress almost certainly won't be

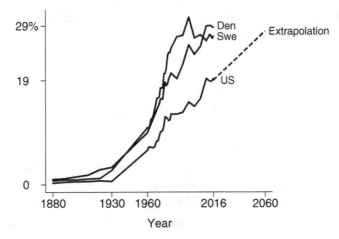

Figure 8.1 Public social expenditures. Share of GDP. Gross public social expenditures. Data source: Esteban Ortiz-Ospina and Max Roser, "Public Spending," *Our World in Data*, using data for 1880–1930 from Peter Lindert, *Growing Public*, volume 1, Cambridge University Press, 2004, data for 1960–1979 from OECD, "Social Expenditure 1960–1990: Problems of Growth and Control," OECD Social Policy Studies, 1985, and data for 1980ff from OECD, Social Expenditures Database. The dashed portion of the line for the United States is an extrapolation, based on the average increase over the period 1930–2016.

steady. But if we think in terms of decades, or better yet half a century, the most reasonable projection is for a significant increase in public social programs along the lines of what I describe in Chapter 7. Simple extrapolation suggests that at that point America's welfare state will look similar to those of Sweden and Denmark today.

Is it sensible to extrapolate? I consider eleven reasons for skepticism. First, Americans don't like big government. Second, America's welfare state isn't very universalistic. Third, opponents of public social programs are effective at deploying the rhetoric of reaction. Fourth, America's "left" political party, the Democrats, isn't especially progressive. Fifth, the left might increasingly struggle to get elected. Sixth, the balance of organized power in the United States has shifted to the right. Seventh, the structure of our political system impedes progressive policy change. Eighth, we might not have the money to fund significant expansions of public insurance. Ninth, conservative states can take advantage of our federalist system to weaken government social programs. Tenth and eleventh, a sustained economic growth slowdown or an increase in racial and ethnic diversity might weaken popular support for government social programs.

While each of these is a potential obstacle to progress, none is likely to derail America's slow but steady movement toward an expanded government role in improving economic security, enhancing opportunity, and ensuring decent and rising living standards for all.

Potential Obstacle 1: Americans Don't Like Big Government

A longstanding view holds that the United States lags behind many other rich democracies in the expansiveness and generosity of its government social programs because that's what Americans want. More than our counterparts in other affluent nations, we tend to believe individual effort, rather than luck, determines success in life, and we therefore see a need for only minimal government assistance.

One of the best expositions of this view is by Seymour Martin Lipset, who helped to popularize the notion of American exceptionalism. Lipset argues that Americans' belief in individualism and liberty and their hostility to government are the source of many differences between the United States and other rich countries.[3]

In the early 2000s, John Micklethwait and Adrian Woolridge, a British editor and writer for the *Economist* magazine, took a close look at the peculiarities of American politics and political culture. In their book *The Right Nation*, they conclude that "The United States has always been a conservative country, marinated in religion, in love with business, and hostile to the state. . . . Americans are exceptionally keen on limiting the size of the state and the scope of what it does."[4]

A more recent statement of this view comes from Alberto Alesina and Edward Glaeser, who argue that differences in the generosity of government social programs across the world's rich nations stem from differing popular views of the causes of poverty. Alesina and Glaeser find that in countries in which a larger share of the population believes people's effort is the key determinant of their income, government spending on social programs tends to be lower. In nations where people deem luck more important, social program expenditures tend to be higher. The United States is among the former. Only about 35 percent of Americans in the survey feel luck is more important than effort, compared to 60 percent of Danes.[5]

Americans Are Ideologically Conservative but Programmatically Progressive

Public opinion data support the notion that Americans don't like big government. Surveys conducted since the mid-1970s have asked representative samples of American adults "If you had to choose, would you rather have a smaller government providing fewer services or a bigger government providing more services?" In only a few years has the share choosing "bigger government providing more services" reached 50 percent; in most years it has hovered between 30 and 45 percent.[6] Gallup periodically asks "In your opinion, which of the following will be the biggest threat to the country in the future—big business, big labor, or big government?" Since the early 1980s, 50 to 70 percent of Americans have said "big government" is the largest threat.[7] For more than twenty years, the Pew Research Center has asked Americans whether they agree or disagree that "When something is run by the government, it is usually inefficient and wasteful." In each year 55 to 75 percent have said they completely agree or mostly agree.[8] The American National Election Study (ANES) regularly asks "Do you think that people in government waste a lot of the money we pay in taxes, waste some of it, or don't waste very much of it?" In most years 60 to 75 percent have said "a lot."[9] Since the early 1970s, the General Social Survey (GSS) has asked Americans if they have "a great deal of confidence, only some confidence, or hardly any confidence at all" in various organizations and institutions. For Congress and the president, the share responding "a great deal of confidence" has been below 30 percent in every year.[10]

Public opinion data like these buttress the impression that Americans are averse to activist government. Yet they hide a deeper truth: while Americans are ideologically conservative when it comes to the size and scope of government, we're programmatically progressive. We're averse to big government in the abstract, but we like a lot of the things government actually does.

The General Social Survey regularly asks a set of questions prefaced by the following statement: "We are faced with many problems in this country, none of which can be solved easily or inexpensively. I'm going to name some of these problems, and for each one I'd like you to tell me whether you think we're spending too much money on it, too little money, or about the right amount." Since the late 1970s a large majority, always over 80 percent and often more than 90 percent, has said current spending is too little or about right on "assistance to the poor," on "improving the nation's education system," on "improving and protecting the nation's health," and on "Social Security."[11] An irregular series of polls since 1980 has asked "Do you favor or oppose national health insurance, which would be financed by tax money, paying for most forms of healthcare?" In almost every instance 50 to 65 percent have said they are in favor, with 25 to 40 percent opposed.[12] In 2011 the Pew Research Center found 61 percent of Americans saying "people on Medicare already pay enough of the cost of their healthcare" versus 31 percent saying "people on Medicare need to be more responsible for the cost of their healthcare in order to keep the program financially secure."[13] In 2007, Benjamin Page and Lawrence Jacobs asked a representative sample of Americans "Would you be willing to pay more taxes in order to provide health coverage for everyone?" Nearly 60 percent were willing, versus just 40 percent who were unwilling.[14] They asked the same question about paying more in taxes for "early childhood education in kindergarten and nursery school." Here 64 percent were willing, versus 33 percent unwilling.[15] Page and Jacobs also asked whether the Earned Income Tax Credit (EITC) should be increased, decreased, or kept about the same. More than 90 percent wanted it increased or kept the same.[16]

There is only one significant exception to the popularity of existing social programs in America: "welfare." In the GSS surveys, between 40 and 60 percent of Americans say we spend too much on welfare.[17] Though the question doesn't specify the particular program, it's likely that most respondents have in mind Aid to Families with Dependent Children (AFDC), which was replaced in the mid-1990s by Temporary Assistance for Needy Families (TANF). As Martin Gilens has documented, AFDC was a uniquely unpopular program with the American public.[18] This owes to a variety of factors, according to Gilens, prominent among them race and media portrayals. This perception is deeply ingrained.

Have opinions about government's role or about specific programs shifted? For the most part, no. Views about government effectiveness and how much we should be spending on particular policies have remained remarkably constant.[19]

So yes, many Americans dislike the idea of big government. But when we think about government in terms of specific programs, we're not at all averse to a government that is medium-sized or even large.[20]

Is Public Support Necessary to Get Social Programs Adopted?

When the American public favors a proposed policy change, it is more likely to be adopted. When the public opposes a change, it is less likely to be adopted. That's the finding of a study titled "Effects of Public Opinion on Policy" by Benjamin Page and Robert Y. Shapiro, published in 1983.[21] Page and Shapiro find considerable congruence in public opinion and policy changes in the United States from 1935 to 1979. They also find that public opinion influences policy changes rather than the other way around.

In a book published thirty years later, Martin Gilens looks at patterns between the mid-1960s and the mid-2000s.[22] His findings echo those of Page and Shapiro. When only 5 percent of Americans favored a proposed policy change, as gauged by public opinion surveys, the change was adopted just 10 percent of the time. When 45 to 55 percent favored the change, it was adopted about 25 to 30 percent of the time. When 95 percent were in favor, the proposed change was adopted 60 percent of the time.

Robert Erikson, Michael MacKuen, and James Stimson conducted a similar test but in a slightly different way.[23] Rather than examine the relationship between public opinion and policy change for each specific issue, they constructed an index of public opinion liberalism and an index of policy liberalism and looked at how these indexes correlate over time. They too find strong indication of an association between public opinion and policy, and they too conclude that the relationship is causal.

What these types of studies can tell us is constrained by the limits of available survey data. For some issues public opinion data don't exist, and for others the questions don't effectively tap the issue at stake. Still, these findings suggest a basic harmony between what Americans want and what their policy makers give them.

From the perspective of democracy, that's a reassuring conclusion. But it raises a question about my expectation that government social policy will expand in coming decades: Do we need strong public support beforehand in order to get new programs adopted or existing ones expanded?

No, we don't. Consider Martin Gilens' recent findings. In his data, if public support for a proposed policy change is in the neighborhood of 45 to 55 percent, the likelihood that the change will be adopted is about 25 to 30 percent. In other words, even if public opinion is split, the change has a one in four chance of getting passed. Public support helps, but it isn't necessary.

Additional evidence comes from a study by Katherine Newman and Elisabeth Jacobs.[24] Examining public opinion on the major social policy innovations of the 1930s and the 1960s, they find evidence of considerable ambivalence and/or opposition among ordinary Americans to the proposed programs. The public, according to Newman and Jacobs, had "mixed and contentious attitudes about activist government."[25] Policy advance owed mainly to the efforts of political leaders, particularly presidents Roosevelt and Johnson, who "moved boldly into a policy vacuum or forged on against growing antagonism. They pushed and pulled legislators into creating and then sustaining the progressive history of the 1930s and 1960s that we now—mistakenly—see as a sea change in popular political culture."[26] Here too, the message is that while public support increases the likelihood of policy advance, it isn't a necessary condition.

Public Opinion Impedes Policy Reversal

Often, ordinary Americans aren't sure what they think about a social program until it has been around for a while. That's hardly surprising; it's difficult to know ahead of time how, and how well, a program will function. Once people see a program in action, they are better able to form an opinion. If a program works well and there don't appear to be any major adverse side effects, they tend to like it.

Since public views about a program tend to be stronger after the program is put in place, we might expect public opinion to have more influence on changes to existing programs than on creation of new programs. And since the public tends to like existing social programs, we might expect public opinion to act as a brake on proposals to cut back or remove such programs. That's exactly what the historical pattern suggests. For example, Paul Pierson examined changes in social policy in the United Kingdom during the Thatcher years and in the United States during the Reagan years.[27] Both administrations were committed to reducing the size and scope of government, including social programs. Both put forward multiple proposals for such cutbacks. Both were in power for a fairly lengthy period. Yet neither Thatcher nor Reagan had much success. A similar story played out in 2005 when the Bush administration proposed to partially privatize Social Security and in recent years when Republicans attempted to overturn the 2010 Medicaid expansion.

Popularity doesn't make a program invulnerable to retrenchment or removal. But it reduces the likelihood of that happening. This is a key reason why the trajectory of American social policy has been forward, and why we might reasonably expect that to continue.

Potential Obstacle 2: America's Welfare State Isn't Universalistic

"Targeted" government programs are directed (sometimes disproportionately, sometimes exclusively) to persons with low income and assets, whereas "universal" programs are available to those with low, middle, or high income. The Earned Income Tax Credit and Medicaid are examples of targeted programs; only people or households with limited income are eligible. Social Security and Medicare are examples of universal programs; they go to persons of retirement age regardless of their income.

Targeted programs are more efficient at helping the least well-off, since each dollar transferred or spent on service provision is more likely to go a person with low income. But targeted programs tend to have political constituencies that are smaller and less cohesive, engaged, and influential. This may weaken their prospects for expansion and increase their vulnerability to cutbacks.[28]

Compared to the norm among rich democratic nations, America's welfare state features few universal programs. In the eyes of some, that makes it harder to expand in moments of opportunity and more difficult to defend when conservatives have the political upper hand.

The reasoning here is sensible. But what do we see in practice? One piece of evidence is the pattern across countries. A generation ago, in the 1980s, it was true that among the affluent democracies, those with greater universalism in their public transfer programs tended to spend more on their welfare states.[29] However, over the ensuing decades that pattern eroded, and by the mid-2000s it had disappeared.[30]

What if we look over time within countries? All of the rich countries have faced pressure to reduce social policy generosity over the past several decades, due to economic globalization and to changes in the balance of power between unions and left parties on one side and employers and right parties on the other. If universalism is better for redistribution, nations with more universal social policy should have fared better in resisting this pressure for cutbacks. However, Kenneth Nelson's examination of eighteen rich countries finds little difference between the trajectories of means-tested benefits (mainly social assistance) and social insurance benefits (old-age pensions, unemployment insurance, and sickness insurance) during the 1990s and early 2000s.[31] And my own analysis yields a similar conclusion: nations with greater targeting haven't experienced larger declines (or smaller increases) in redistribution in recent decades.[32]

The same is true if we compare developments in targeted programs versus universal programs in the United States. Robert Greenstein and Paul Pierson examined the pattern of attempted cuts and successful cuts to targeted programs by the Reagan administration in the 1980s. Both concluded that these programs fared surprisingly well.[33] Christopher Howard has updated the US story through the mid-2000s, and his conclusion echoes those of Greenstein and Pierson.[34] Subsequent developments have continued in this vein. Social program expansions in 2009 and 2010 were mainly for targeted programs such as Medicaid and the Earned Income Tax Credit, and the 2017 Republican attempt to roll back Medicaid was the least popular major legislative proposal in recent decades.[35]

The hypothesis that targeting in social policy weakens political support and thereby reduces the size and generosity of public social programs is compelling in its logic. Yet the experience of the rich countries in recent decades suggests little support for it. Countries with more universalistic social policy don't (any longer) tend to be more redistributive. Nor do we observe a systematic tendency for universal programs to grow and targeted programs to shrink over time.

Potential Obstacle 3: The Rhetoric of Reaction

Proponents of small government are adept at deploying what Albert Hirschman has termed the "rhetoric of reaction"—arguments suggesting that efforts to enhance justice and fairness are misguided.[36] Hirschman identifies three types: futility arguments, perversity arguments, and jeopardy arguments. Futility arguments hold that government programs fail to have any impact. For instance, public schools fail to educate, because they face little or no competition. Perversity arguments contend that government programs worsen the problem they aim to address. Here an example is the notion that generous government benefits discourage work and thereby increase poverty instead of reducing it. Jeopardy arguments claim that government programs threaten some other desirable outcome. For instance, if we increase government spending, we'll get less economic growth.

Will these types of arguments block future progress in American social policy? I suspect not.

Futility, perversity, and jeopardy arguments seem compelling. That's what makes them rhetorically effective. Sometimes they are empirically true, but often they aren't. Hirschman points out that in centuries past these types of claims were made in opposition to the introduction of democracy. It was suggested, for instance, that if voting rights were extended to the "ignorant masses" they would elect a tyrant, who would subsequently abolish democracy (futility). Or democracy would result in expropriation and redistribution of property, thereby wrecking the economy and making everyone poorer (jeopardy).

In principle, such claims are testable. But prior to democracy's introduction, there was no evidence. The absence of evidence underpins the effectiveness of the rhetoric of reaction. An incorrect hypothesis can hold sway for a long time if it's plausible and scientists don't have the evidence needed to show it's wrong.

Until recently we've lacked data to subject claims about the futility, perversity, or jeopardy of generous government social programs to empirical scrutiny. But this is changing. We're now in a much better position to evaluate these hypotheses, and our ability to do so will improve even more going forward. Hardly anyone today argues that nations should avoid democracy on the grounds that it leads to tyranny. That argument doesn't square with the facts. For the same reason, half a century from now few will claim that government taxing and spending at 45 percent of GDP will damage the American economy.

At a moment when Donald Trump is the US president and many Republican lawmakers still claim that we don't know whether greenhouse gas emissions cause climate change, my confidence that evidence will win out may seem naive. But historical experience suggests that this, too, will pass. Denialism and

Trump-style dishonesty can find an audience. But in the long run they're unlikely to carry the day.

Potential Obstacle 4: Does America Have a Progressive Political Party?

Unlike most other rich democratic nations, the United States doesn't have an avowedly "labor" or "social democratic" political party. The Democratic Party has tended to be more centrist than its counterparts abroad.[37] This is partly a function of America's winner-take-all electoral system, which makes it difficult for a third party to compete successfully. In a two-party context, each party has an incentive to position itself as close to the center as possible in order to maximize its vote share. In addition, for much of the twentieth century conservative Southerners were a core component of the Democratic Party, due to the legacy of the Civil War.

Even so, most major advances in American social policy have occurred when Democrats held the presidency and one or both bodies of Congress. And those advances have been significant, even if they haven't matched those of Denmark, Sweden, and other welfare state leaders.

A common refrain among leftist activists and pundits holds that the Democrats have shifted even further toward the political center in recent decades. That would be surprising, given that conservative Southerners have been steadily moving from the Democratic Party to the Republicans during this time. But perhaps the growing need for large private campaign contributions coupled with the rising concentration of income and wealth has forced Democrats to cater more and more to the preferences of America's rich.[38] Or maybe Democrats have been seduced by neoliberal ideology in this "age of Reagan."[39]

The data suggest that Democrats haven't shifted to the center. Figure 8.2 shows trends in voting behavior on economic issues by Democrats in the House and Senate. What we see is a slow but steady movement to the left.[40]

Focusing on voting might be misleading. After all, much of the important decision making by policy makers occurs before proposals come to a final vote. If we could measure this, it's conceivable we would find there has in fact been a move toward the center by Democrats. But if that shift has happened, it has yet to be documented.

There is at least one reason to expect the Democrats' movement to the left to not only continue but perhaps accelerate: the growing prominence of women in top positions in the party. Hillary Clinton's success in becoming the first-ever female major-party presidential nominee in 2016 was just the tip of

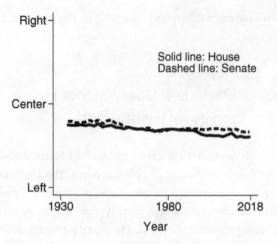

Figure 8.2 Voting by Democrats in the House and Senate. Average "DW-nominate dimension 1" scores for Democratic legislators. The range shown here is −1 to +1 (left to right). Data source: Jeffrey B. Lewis, Keith Poole, Howard Rosenthal, Adam Boche, Aaron Rudkin, and Luke Sonnet, *Voteview: Congressional Roll-Call Votes Database*, voteview.com, series dem.mean.d1.

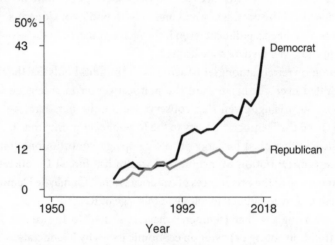

Figure 8.3 Women's share of party nominees for House of Representatives elections. Nominees for general elections. Data source: Center for American Women and Politics.

the iceberg. More important is the sharp rise in women running for Congress in the Democratic Party, shown in Figure 8.3. Female legislators are more likely than their male counterparts to support and vote for women-friendly and child-friendly policies.[41] A Democratic congressional bloc that is half or more female will quicken the push for affordable early education, paid parental leave, paid sickness insurance, and a more generous child tax credit (or allowance).

Potential Obstacle 5: Can the Left Continue to Get Elected?

Most major advances in American social policy have occurred when Democrats held the presidency and one or both bodies of Congress, and that's likely to continue. As Figure 8.4 shows, Democrats dominated the House of Representatives and the Senate from 1930 to 1980, though the presidency swung back and forth. Since 1980, control of the presidency and both chambers of Congress have been split fairly evenly between the two parties. To achieve social policy advances in coming decades, the Democrats need to avoid a lengthy period of sustained minority status of the kind suffered by the Republicans during the New Deal era.

Two hypotheses predict this worst-case scenario may well come to pass. The first says Democrats will struggle because working-class whites, the party's traditional base, now are guided in their party preference by social and cultural issues rather than economic ones, and that leads them to vote for Republicans. The second says we are entering a period when enormous quantities of private money will flow into election campaigns, with Republicans the chief beneficiaries.

Do the Democrats Lack an Electoral Base?

Working-class whites have moved away from the Democrats. In the mid-1970s, about 60 percent of white Americans who self-identified as working class said they preferred the Democratic Party. That fell steadily from the late 1970s,

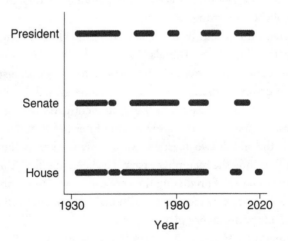

Figure 8.4 Democratic control of the presidency, the Senate, and the House of Representatives. Lines indicate Democratic control. Blank spaces indicate Republican control.

bottoming out at 40 percent in the early 1990s, where it has remained since.[42] The same trend is evident among whites with less than a college degree and among whites on the lower third of the income ladder.[43] In the four presidential elections since 2004, whites with less than a four-year college degree favored the Republican candidate over the Democratic one by 20 percentage points or more.[44]

Why has this happened? As we saw in Chapter 1, as a society gets wealthy, issues other than those connected to material self-interest become more important to people.[45] There is no clear working-class interest in being either pro-choice or pro-life on abortion or in favoring or opposing equal rights for homosexuals. Hence, as material issues fade in centrality, working-class identification with the party that better serves its material interests is likely to decline. To the extent that white working-class voters perceive themselves to be closer to Republicans on issues such as crime, immigration, family, religion, racial diversity, gay rights, abortion, guns, or others, they are more likely now than in the past to let those issues determine their vote choice.[46]

Will this consign the Democrats to regular electoral defeat? That seems unlikely. As Ruy Teixeira and his collaborators have shown, the Democratic Party has a new electoral base centered on women, the highly educated, urban professionals, African Americans, Latinos, Asians, singles (nonmarried), seculars, and the young.[47] These groups are large and most are growing. In addition, geographic trends will help the Democrats to remain competitive in national elections for the foreseeable future. The Northeast, the West Coast, and Illinois are now solidly Democratic, and parts of the upper Midwest lean in that direction. None of this guarantees presidential victories or congressional majorities, but it does suggest that forecasts of impending electoral disaster for the Democrats probably are wrong.

Equally important, the health of the economy is the chief determinant of the outcome of national elections. Douglas Hibbs and Larry Bartels point out that presidential election outcomes can be predicted fairly well with just a single measure of economic performance—per capita income growth.[48] This is displayed in Figure 8.5. On the vertical axis is the incumbent-party candidate's vote margin. On the horizontal axis is the growth rate of per capita real disposable personal income in the middle two quarters (April to September) of the election year, adjusted for how long the incumbent party has been in office. This simple model does a very good job of predicting the vote outcome. Other models can predict even more accurately by including additional factors, but in all of them, measures of economic performance play a central role.[49]

What about Congress? House and Senate elections are more idiosyncratic than presidential elections. Yet the condition of the national economy has

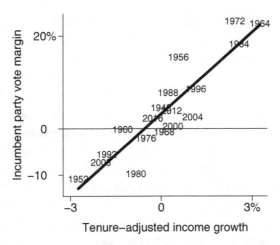

Figure 8.5 Income growth and presidential election outcomes. Vertical axis: incumbent-party candidate's popular vote margin. Data source: Wikipedia. Horizontal axis: growth rate of real disposable personal income per capita in the second and third quarters of the election year, adjusted for incumbency (−1.29 for each consecutive term, beyond the first, that the incumbent party has held the White House). Data source: Bureau of Economic Analysis, bea.gov, table 7.1, line 12. The correlation is +.91. This replicates and extends Larry Bartels' chart in "Obama Toes the Line," *The Monkey Cage* blog, 2013. For more detail, see Christopher Achen and Larry Bartels, *Democracy for Realists*, Princeton University Press, 2016, ch. 6.

consistently been a good predictor of the outcome, and congressional elections increasingly are influenced by the popularity of the current president, which in turn hinges on the economy.[50]

The implication is clear: if the Democrats do reasonably well (or Republicans fare poorly) at managing the economy, they'll remain competitive in elections.

Does Citizens United Spell Electoral Doom for the Left?

The second hypothesis predicting electoral struggles for the American left suggests that the Supreme Court's 2010 *Citizens United* decision will allow private money to flood into Republican campaign coffers. That ruling prohibited restrictions on political campaign spending by organizations such as firms and unions, opening the door to unlimited expenditures by outside groups on behalf of their preferred candidate or party.

It's too soon to be able to render an informed judgment on the *Citizens United* decision's impact, but the degree to which it altered the legal landscape is sometimes overstated. Before the super PACs and 501(c)(4)s that sprang up after *Citizens United*, individuals and corporations already could make unlimited donations to 527s. The difference is that the new organizations are less constrained in naming candidates they favor or oppose in advertisements running during the two months prior to the election.[51]

Figure 8.6 shows campaign expenditures for Democrats and Republicans in presidential-year elections and in off-year elections since 1998 (the earliest for which data are available). In 2010, 2012, and 2014, Republican candidates had a money advantage, just as pessimists predicted.[52] But that advantage was small, and in 2016 and 2018 Democrats regained the upper hand. This back-and-forth is consistent with the pattern of campaign finance in national elections over the past four decades, with each party and its backers seeking new ways to raise and spend large amounts of money in spite of existing regulations. In the 1970s, the Democrats had the advantage. By the end of the 1980s the Republicans had the upper hand. Toward the end of the 2000s it shifted back to the Democrats, then back to Republicans in the first half of the 2000s. This history suggests Democrats and their supporters will figure out ways to offset the advantage Republicans gain from *Citizens United*, or at least to mitigate its impact.[53]

Moreover, even if money totals favor Republicans going forward, it's unclear what the effect will be. Money clearly matters in American elections,[54] but there are diminishing returns to money in influencing election outcomes. When a lot already is being spent, additional amounts have limited impact.

The Left Can Continue to Get Elected

Since Ronald Reagan was elected president in 1980, a significant portion of the American left has been in a state of despair about the electoral future of the

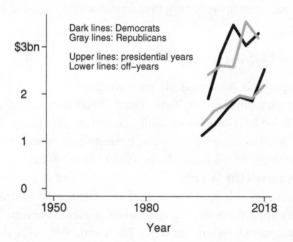

Figure 8.6 Campaign expenditures by and for Democrats and Republicans. Billions of inflation-adjusted dollars. Includes expenditures by candidates, parties, and outside groups. Data source: Center for Responsive Politics, "Cost of Election," opensecrets.org.

Democratic Party. The party had drifted too far to the left, according to some. It had moved too far to the right, said others. It was incapable of nominating effective candidates. It couldn't keep up with the Republicans' fundraising. It had lost touch with ordinary Americans. It was disorganized. It was too liberal on social issues. It was too dependent on big finance for campaign funding.

Each of these concerns is understandable. But the Democratic Party and its major candidates have, at least to this point, proven more resilient than pessimists expected. The Democratic candidate has won the popular vote in six of the last seven presidential elections, and in the past seven Congresses Democrats have held a majority in the House three times and in the Senate three times. The recent past isn't necessarily a useful guide to the future. It's not inconceivable that American politics is on the verge of a sea change, with the Democrats' electoral fortunes dwindling. But while that's possible, it does not seem especially likely.

Potential Obstacle 6: The Balance of Organized Power Has Shifted to the Right

According to a distinguished line of political analysis, from E. E. Schattschneider to Thomas Ferguson and Joel Rogers to Jacob Hacker and Paul Pierson, the scope and generosity of government social policy in the United States is determined less by election outcomes than by the relative strength of organized interest groups.[55] Since the mid-1970s, American businesses and America's rich have mobilized, while the groups on the left have fragmented and weakened.[56] Will this altered balance of power inhibit further progress in social policy?

There are two versions of this line of thinking. Figure 8.7 displays a stylized depiction of each. According to the first, the change was a one-off shift in the level of organizational strength. It happened in the late 1970s and/or the early 1980s, and since then there has been no change. According to the second, the shift is a trend. It began in the late 1970s, has been ongoing since then, and will continue into the future.

If the change in the balance of interest group strength was a one-off shift, its impact on social policy advance should already be apparent, given that the shift occurred quite a while ago. Has progress in social policy stopped?

No. It has slowed, but it hasn't ceased.[57] Advances since the 1970s include:

- Healthcare: Increases in Medicaid benefits and expansion of access (1984-1988, S-CHIP 1998, 2010). COBRA policy allowing people who lose their job to continue with employer-provided health insurance (1986). Emergency Medical Treatment and Labor Act requiring most hospitals to

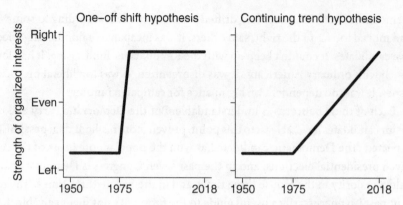

Figure 8.7 "One-off shift" and "continuing trend" hypotheses about the relative strength of organized interest groups. The vertical scale indicates the relative strength of organized interest groups. Higher on the axis indicates the right is stronger; lower indicates the left is stronger.

provide emergency treatment to anyone who needs it, even if they don't have health insurance (1986). Free immunization of children in low-income families (Vaccines for Children 1993). Expansion of Medicare to include prescription drugs (2004). Subsidies and regulation of private insurers aimed at expanding access (2010).

- Childcare, preschool, after-care: Subsidy for low-income families' childcare expenses (Child Care and Development Fund 1990, 2009). Expansions of Head Start (1984, 1990, 1995, 2009). Expansion of public kindergarten to full day in most states and establishment of age-four and age-three pre-kindergarten in some states and cities. Public funding of after-school activities in schools in low-income communities (21st Century Community Learning Centers program 1998).
- K–12 and college education: Reduction of funding inequality across elementary and secondary schools in most states. Increases in college student loan funding (Pell Grant, Lifetime Learning Credit, Hope Credit).
- Employment assistance: Expansions of retraining, job placement assistance, access to healthcare, and income support for people who lose a job due to international trade (1997, 2002, 2009).
- Parental-family leave: Right to unpaid family leave (1993). Introduction of paid leave in a few states (2004ff).
- Unemployment insurance: Expansion of eligibility in thirty-eight states (2009)
- Disability: Expansion of eligibility to include musculoskeletal (e.g. back pain) and mental health conditions (1984). Antidiscrimination protection for persons with disabilities (1990). Increase in disability benefits and

expansion of access over the ensuing decades. For instance, expansion of children's access to SSI (1990); Medicaid provision of services extended beyond institutions to include disabled persons' homes and communities (1991); a broad continuum of community-based prevention, early intervention, and other services for residents with severe mental illnesses established in California (2005); money for states to expand services and access to healthcare for disabled persons provided by the Affordable Care Act (2010).

- Earned Income Tax Credit: Increases in benefit level and expansion of access (1984, 1986, 1990, 1993, 2009).
- Child Tax Credit: Created and expanded (1997, 2003, 2017).
- Housing: Increase in subsidy for construction of low-income housing (Low-Income Housing Tax Credit 1987).
- Energy assistance: Established and increased (Low-Income Energy Assistance 1981, 2009).
- Social assistance: Reversal of earlier tightening of AFDC eligibility criteria (1984). Expansion of AFDC eligibility to two-parent families (1988). Increases in food stamp access and benefit level (1985, 1987, 1993, 2002, 2008, 2009).

Cuts during this period include the following:

- Social assistance: Continuation of the 1970s reduction of AFDC benefit levels in inflation-adjusted terms. Reduction in AFDC eligibility (1981). Establishment of time limits on benefit receipt (1996). Reductions in Food Stamp eligibility and/or benefit level (1981, 1982, 1996).
- Disability assistance: Tightening of eligibility criteria for disability insurance (1980s).
- Employment assistance: Elimination of Public Service Employment (1983).
- Social Security: Increase in retirement age, payroll tax, and taxation of benefits (1983).
- Immigrant access to benefits: Reduction in food stamp and SSI benefits (1996).

Of these cutbacks, the biggest was to social assistance. But AFDC was a uniquely unpopular social program. In fact, "welfare" is the lone public social program consistently disliked by a majority of Americans.[58]

Other indicators also tell a story of expansion. The generosity of public insurance programs aimed at risks during childhood, working age, and old age increased between 1980 and 2010, according to calculations by researchers at the Swedish Institute for Social Research.[59] Net government transfers (transfers received minus taxes paid, adjusted for inflation) to households in the bottom fifth of incomes increased from an average of $7,300 in the 1980s to $9,400 in the 2010s.[60] And government expenditures on social programs increased from 13 percent of GDP in 1980 to 19 percent in 2016.[61]

There have been noteworthy qualitative shifts in American social policy in recent decades alongside the expansion in scope and generosity. One is a turn from cash payments to tax expenditures.[62] The Earned Income Tax Credit is illustrative. Instead of providing a check (or bank transfer) to a low-income household, it reduces the household's federal income tax payment (though it does pay the household if the EITC is larger than the taxes the household owes). This shift has consequences. Tax expenditures that aren't refundable aren't very helpful to those who pay little or no income tax. And as Suzanne Mettler points out, tax expenditures are less visible to Americans, which contributes to people's impression that government does little to help them.[63] Despite their drawbacks, however, tax expenditures such as the EITC do represent expansions of US public insurance.

Another shift has been toward boosting supports for working-age Americans who are employed and reducing them for persons who aren't—for example, the expansion of the Earned Income Tax Credit alongside the reduction in AFDC-TANF.[64] In one respect this mimics social democrats' turn from the 1970s pursuit of decommodification toward an embrace of employment, though in the US context this change has had a less benign impact because of the absence of a robust social assistance benefit.[65]

If the shift in organized interest group power was a one-off, the fact that public social policy has continued to advance despite the shift implies that we are likely to see further advance in the future.

The second version of the shift-in-the-balance-of-organized-power hypothesis, depicted in the second chart in Figure 8.7, posits that the shift is a trend. It began in the late 1970s and has been ongoing since then, with the strength of the right relative to that of the left steadily increasing. This paints a worrisome picture, in that it suggests we haven't yet reached the point of maximum strength in the organized power of the right.

If this hypothesis is correct, what might the impact be on advances in social policy? We can glean some information by comparing policy change in the two decades between 1980 and 2000 with change in the nearly two decades since 2000. If the "continuing trend" hypothesis is correct, there should have been less social policy advance in the latter period than in the former. But the above list of changes in the size and scope of social programs suggests that isn't the case.

Here too, then, the most reasonable conclusion is that the pattern of progress in social policy over the past century will continue.

Potential Obstacle 7: The Structure of the US Political System Impedes Progressive Policy Change

Even if the obstacles I've considered so far can be overcome, progress toward more expansive and generous social policy might be impeded by our political system's abundance of "veto points": a legislature and executive each elected directly by the people, two coequal legislative bodies, and the filibuster in the Senate.[66] These offer a determined minority multiple ways to block proposed policy changes.

On the one hand, these features of America's political system have been in place for some time, and while they surely have slowed the pace of social policy advance in the United States, they haven't prevented it. On the other hand, recent years have seen an increase in the cohesiveness, discipline, and confrontational posture of Republicans in Congress, making it very difficult for Democrats to get legislation passed unless they hold the presidency, a majority in the House, and 60 seats in the Senate. Does this spell the end of social policy advance?

Cohesive Parties in a Veto-Point-Heavy Political System

The extensiveness of veto points has taken on new importance in American politics because the Democratic and Republican parties have become much more cohesive. Until recently, both were loose collections of individuals with varying orientations and policy preferences. This was largely a legacy of the Civil War and the New Deal. Many Southerners viewed the Civil War as a military invasion engineered by the Republican Party. For the better part of the following century, political competition in the South occurred entirely within the Democratic Party rather than between Democrats and Republicans. With the New Deal legislation in the 1930s, the Democrats became the party in favor of government intervention to enhance security and opportunity. Although this conflicted with the conservative orientation of many Southern Democrats, they remained in the party until the Civil Rights Act of 1964 aligned the national Democratic Party with equal rights for African Americans.

While conservative Southerners have been moving to the Republican Party, liberals in the rest of the country have been switching to the Democratic Party.[67] The ideological purification of the two parties is now complete: in both the House of Representatives and the Senate, the leftmost Republican is to the right of the rightmost Democrat.[68]

In prior eras, proponents of policy change often succeeded by fashioning a coalition across party lines. While this was seldom an easy task, it is now an extremely difficult one.[69]

From the perspective of democracy, there is a benefit to party cohesiveness: it provides voters with clear information about how a candidate will behave in office. But in a political system with multiple veto points, party cohesiveness increases the likelihood of gridlock. As long as the minority party controls one of the three lawmaking bodies—the presidency, the House, or the Senate—it can veto virtually any proposed policy change. Given the filibuster rule in the Senate, the minority doesn't actually need to control any of the three; it simply needs 41 of the 100 seats in the Senate. The majority can circumvent the filibuster via a procedure known as "reconciliation," but this can be used only for a narrow range of bills.

Republican Obstructionism

The polarization of America's two political parties has been asymmetrical: the Republicans have moved farther to the right than the Democrats have moved to the left. Figure 8.8 shows the average voting position on economic issues (broadly defined) among members of each party in the House of Representatives and

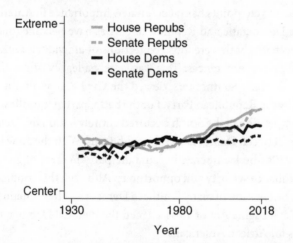

Figure 8.8 Voting by Republicans and Democrats in the House and Senate. Average "DW-nominate dimension 1" scores for Republican and Democratic legislators. The range shown here is 0 (center) to –1 or +1 (extreme left or extreme right). Data source: Jeffrey B. Lewis, Keith Poole, Howard Rosenthal, Adam Boche, Aaron Rudkin, and Luke Sonnet, *Voteview: Congressional Roll-Call Votes Database*, voteview.com, series rep.mean.d1 and dem.mean.d1.

Senate. Both parties have shifted away from the center as they've become more co-hesive. But Republicans have moved farther from the center than have Democrats.

Republicans have become more unified in voting as well. Keith Poole has measured the share of party members who follow their party on votes in which a majority in one party votes opposite to a majority in the other party (in other words, leaving out votes on which there is significant bipartisan sup-port). The share has risen from 75 percent in 1970 to 90–95 percent in recent years.[70]

In the Senate, both parties have made more frequent use of the filibuster to block legislative proposals when they are in the minority. The best indicator of filibuster use is the number of cloture motions—motions to cut off filibuster attempts—that are filed. As Figure 8.9 shows, the rise in filibustering began in the 1970s. Large jumps occurred in 1971, 1991, and 2007, with the latter being especially pronounced. In each instance, Republicans initiated the rise.

Have these developments made it more difficult to pass legislation? Figure 8.10 shows the number of laws passed by Congress in each term since the early 1930s. Although there has been a decline, it began before the 1970s. And there was no acceleration in the 1970s when the polarization of the parties and increased use of the filibuster began, nor in the 1990s when Republicans in the House began their sharp turn to the right and filibuster use jumped, nor in the past few years when Republicans became especially obstructionist.

Even if we don't see a clear effect of the new Republican obstructionism, it will have an impact going forward unless the party moves back toward the

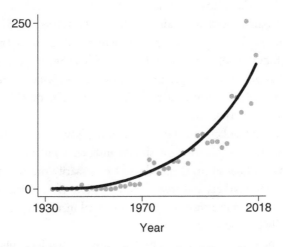

Figure 8.9 Use of the filibuster in the Senate. Number of cloture filings. Data source: www.senate.gov, "Senate Action on Cloture Motions." The line is a loess curve.

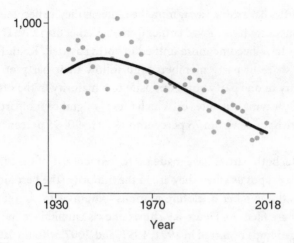

Figure 8.10 Number of laws passed by Congress. Data sources: Tobin Grant, personal communication; GovTrack.us, "Statistics and Historical Comparison: Bills by Final Status." The line is a loess curve.

center. In the long run, such a turn is the most likely scenario. Republicans will abandon the staunch antigovernment orientation that has dominated their approach of late, and the center of gravity in the party probably will be similar to that of center-right parties in western Europe, most of which accept a generous welfare state and relatively high taxes.

How will this come about? One push toward Republican moderation could come from the growing importance of working-class whites as a constituency for the party. Some thoughtful and prominent voices on America's right—David Brooks, Oren Cass, Ross Douthat, David Frum, Charles Murray, Ramesh Ponnuru, Reihan Salam, Michael Strain—have noted that this group is struggling economically and could benefit from government help.[71] Donald Trump's populist pledges to focus on job creation and to keep Social Security, Medicare, and Medicaid intact appealed to this group, and were part of what helped him win the Republican presidential nomination in 2016, even if he quickly abandoned those pledges upon entering office.

In addition, clear thinkers on the right eventually will realize that the key question isn't how *much* government should intervene but *how* it should do so.[72] An expansion of social programs doesn't necessarily mean more government interference in markets and weaker competition. If Americans want protection and support and the choice is between social insurance and regulation, the former usually is preferable.

Another potential cause of a return to the center among Republican elites is a series of Democratic election wins. Since the turn of the century, the United

States has been close to a "50-50" nation, with Democrats and Republicans each supported by about half of the population. Democrats have an advantage in party affiliation, but this is neutralized by the fact that Republican supporters are more likely to vote. Even so, Democratic candidates have won the popular vote in six of the past seven presidential elections. And as Figure 8.11 shows, while the Silent Generation, the baby boom generation, and Generation X each tilt only mildly toward the Democrats, millennials prefer the Democrats by a wide margin. This could change, as it has for each of the other generations at various points in the past. But thus far millennials have shown no sign of moving away from the Democratic Party. If they don't, Republicans will struggle electorally as millennials come to account for a larger and larger share of voters.[73]

Veto Points Impede Backsliding

In the race to the good society, America is a tortoise.[74] We advance slowly, but we do advance. The long-run trend in American social policy has been one of slow but steady ratcheting upward. Part of the reason for this advance, ironically, is our veto-point-heavy political system. For while our extensive array of veto points impedes progressive change, it also makes it difficult for opponents of

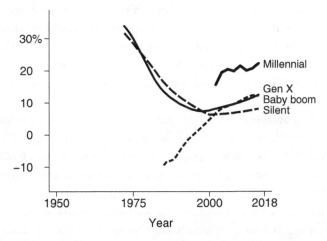

Figure 8.11 Democratic advantage in party affiliation by cohort. Share of US adults identifying as Democrat (strong Democrat, not strong Democrat, or independent leaning Democrat) minus share identifying as Republican (strong Republican, not strong Republican, or independent leaning Republican). Question: "Generally speaking, do you usually think of yourself as a Republican, Democrat, independent, or what?" Silent generation: born 1928–1945. Baby boom generation: born 1946–1964. Generation X: born 1965–1980. Millennial generation: born 1981–2000. Data source: General Social Survey, sda.berkeley.edu/archive.htm, series partyid, cohort. The lines are loess curves.

government social programs to dilute or do away with them. This is a key reason why social policy advances tend to endure.

Potential Obstacle 8: Conservative States in a Federalist Political System

In America's political system, state and local governments have considerable discretion in policy adoption and implementation. When it comes to social policy, in some instances this doesn't have much impact. Social Security, for example, operates uniformly throughout the country; state governments aren't involved in setting eligibility conditions or benefit levels or in implementation. But for some programs—Medicaid, unemployment insurance, SNAP (food stamps), TANF, and more—state governments make a big difference.[75]

Will this matter going forward? In the past two decades we've seen growing variation in state rules, benefit levels, and on-the-ground implementation of programs over which states have decision-making authority, with conservative states tending to be much less generous than progressive ones. A notable recent example is nineteen states refusing the Medicaid expansion offered by the 2010 Affordable Care Act. Even though the federal government provides nearly all of the money to pay for an expansion of health insurance to low-income households, Republican legislatures and/or governors in these states decided to forgo this opportunity. Given the growing distance between Democratic and Republican policy makers, it's likely we will see more of this going forward.

But while federalism means less generous social policy for Americans who live in conservative states, it also allows governments in progressive states to jump ahead of the federal government. For instance, since 1999 California has enacted paid sick leave, paid parental leave, an automatic-enrollment pension system for people whose employer doesn't offer a plan, a large Medicaid expansion (it now covers one in three Californians), an expansion of TANF eligibility, a phased-in $15 per hour minimum wage indexed to inflation, a state Earned Income Tax Credit to supplement the federal EITC, increased money for K–12 schooling funded by two tax increases on high-income households, an array of services for residents with severe mental illnesses, low-cost public auto insurance for persons with low income, new funds for roads and high-speed rail, a significant reduction in incarceration, and more.[76] (In addition, in 2018 California passed a law requiring an end to the use of fossil-fuel-based electricity by 2045, and the governor issued an executive order committing the state to full carbon neutrality by that same year. It is the largest economy in the world to enact such a pledge.[77])

It isn't only California. The state of New York recently adopted zero-tuition public college for in-state students from middle- and lower-income households and a $15 minimum wage, and its largest city now has universal preschool for four-year-olds and is on track to expand that to three-year-olds. Washington, Oregon, and Massachusetts have been moving in a similar direction. Nearly 80 million people, one in four Americans, live in these five states.

Potential Obstacle 9: Will There Be Enough Money to Pay for It?

In the past twenty years a lot of ink has been spilled pondering the implications of population aging for the welfare state in the US and other rich democratic countries. As the baby boom generation retires, the cost of public pensions (Social Security) and public health insurance (Medicare) will rise. Will that crowd out any possibility for spending on the new and expanded programs I outline in Chapter 7?

Not likely. The best projections suggest that the total increase in cost for these programs will be about 3.5 percent of GDP—1 percent for Social Security and 2.5 percent for Medicare—as we see in Figures 8.12 and 8.13. While that's a large amount, it's smaller than the increase in these two programs between 1970

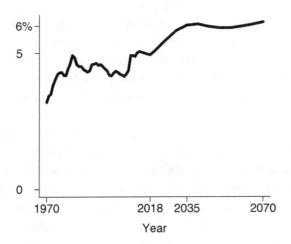

Figure 8.12 Social Security expenditures. Share of GDP. Social Security (OASI) plus Disability Insurance (SSDI). Data source: *2018 OASDI Trustees Report*, "Table VI.G4. OASDI and HI Annual and Summarized Income, Cost, and Balance as a Percentage of GDP."

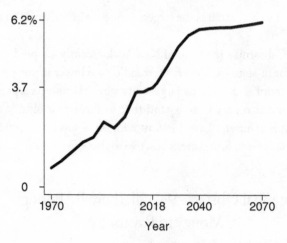

Figure 8.13 Medicare expenditures. Share of GDP. HI and SMI (including part D). Data source: *2018 Medicare Trustees Report,* "Table V.B2. HI and SMI Incurred Expenditures as a Percentage of the Gross Domestic Product."

and today. The estimated total cost for the proposals I advance in Chapter 7 is 10 percent of GDP. One possibility is that we choose to drop or delay some of these proposals in order to ensure adequate funding for Social Security and Medicare. Another is that we raise additional revenues.

What about Americans' hatred of taxes? To what extent does that threaten our ability to pay for expanded public insurance programs? There was some truth to this axiom in the late 1970s and early 1980s, when revolts against local property taxes were spreading across the country and Ronald Reagan was elected president on a tax-cutting agenda. Yet that moment has long since passed. Public opinion surveys now frequently find support for higher taxes, particularly on rich Americans.[78] The 2017 Republican tax cut was the second least popular major legislative proposal since 1990.[79] And state and local referendums proposing tax hikes have grown steadily more popular since the 1980s. They now are as likely to pass as those proposing cuts.[80]

Republican legislators and presidents remain committed to opposing tax increases, as they have since the early 1980s. This owes partly to their overall small-government orientation, partly to the preferences of their wealthy individual and corporate donors, and partly to tax cuts' usefulness as a goody they can offer voters to counter Democrats' promise of new and expanded government programs.[81] But the most important cause is party political culture. The tax-cutting success of Reagan and the local property tax revolts shaped the thinking of a new generation of Republican leaders, advisors, and voters, creating an image of the modern Republican Party as the party of tax cuts. Just as a generation of Democrats identified theirs as the party of the New Deal following

Franklin D. Roosevelt's success and popularity in the 1930s and early 1940s, tax reductions became the core element of the political culture of post-1980 Republicans. Fox News, conservative talk radio, and anti-tax organizations such as Grover Norquist's Americans for Tax Reform have helped to keep this at the center of the party's ideology.

Eventually, however, ideologies lose their grip and organizational priorities change. This will happen to the Republicans at some point, as it did to the Democrats by the late 1980s.

Potential Obstacle 10: Slower Economic Growth

Over the past century, America's GDP per capita has grown at an average rate of 1.9 percent per year. But between 2000 and 2007, the rate dipped to 1.5 percent, and from 2007 through 2017 it fell further, to an average of just 0.6 percent.[82] The great recession is the chief culprit: its arrival in 2008 cut short the economic expansion of the early-mid 2000s, and its depth dug a big hole from which the US economy has yet to fully emerge. Yet some analysts believe that the United States has entered not a moment but an era of slow growth.

One version of this story points to weak demand, perhaps due to the rising share of income that goes to the rich, who tend to spend a smaller fraction of their earnings than do ordinary households.[83] Others contend that the problem is a decline in competition in important sectors, such as high tech, or a slowdown in the formation of new businesses.[84] The most pessimistic assessment suggests that inventions such as electricity, railroads, and the assembly line boosted productivity and growth in earlier eras to a degree that more recent innovations cannot match.[85]

Economic growth facilitates the expansion of public social programs. For one thing, it makes them more affordable; as the economy grows, so do tax revenues. Economic growth also increases public support for the welfare state.[86] Most people are loss-averse and altruistic, so as they get richer, they tend to want more protections for themselves and more fairness in their society. If the United States suffers years of slow growth, Americans' embrace of generous public insurance programs might wane. One worrisome sign: perceptions of economic trouble, including slow recovery from the 2008–2009 economic crisis, have fueled support for anti-immigrant "populists" across the rich democracies.[87] Although many populists support the safety net itself, nativism could undermine the public's commitments to the fairness and inclusivity on which social democratic policies depend.

Still, the most likely scenario is that growth will return to a higher rate in coming decades. There have been previous periods, such as the 1930s, when the economy slowed down before returning to the long-run trend. And the productivity benefits of new technologies such as the Internet may take years to appear; after all, the period of strongest productivity growth stemming from electricity and other nineteenth-century innovations occurred decades later, between the mid-1940s and the mid-1970s.

Moreover, even if the slowdown in the rate of economic growth persists, the United States will still become far richer in coming decades. Over the last 70 years, America's per capita GDP, adjusted for inflation, has increased by about $40,000. The country is now wealthy enough that securing the same increase over the next 70 years would require a yearly growth rate of only 0.8 percent.

Potential Obstacle 11: Racial Anxiety and Fear

Racial and ethnic diversity can be an obstacle to social progress, including to the expansion of government social programs.[88] One reason is that people are less likely to empathize with those they see as different. While skin color is in principle an unimportant difference, for some it is a real or imagined marker of distinct norms, behaviors, and values. Members of a racial or ethnic group may therefore feel threatened by members of other groups. That can be particularly true when one group historically has held a dominant position vis-à-vis another, as with whites and African Americans in the United States, or where racial/ethnic difference is coupled with a sharp difference in religion, as with native populations in rich countries and Muslim immigrants. Difference can prompt not just uncertainty and discomfort but fear.

When this happens, people's thinking can turn—or return—to a scarcity orientation. Findings by Ronald Inglehart, Christian Welzel, and others suggest that this means less sentiment for fairness, personal freedom, and government programs that insure against loss. Instead, people tend to focus on protecting what they have, including the cultural norms and values that they see as integral to their way of life. If they perceive these norms and values to be threatened by another group that is growing in size or newly prominent or assertive, they turn to a protective mode.[89] Sometimes difference has nothing to do with race; American Protestants reacted the same way against white Catholics and Jews in the early twentieth century, and middle-aged and elderly Americans reacted this way against white hippies and teenagers in the late 1960s and 1970s.

When threats to existing patterns of life are coupled with a perceived threat to economic well-being and/or physical safety, the reaction may be even more intense. When large numbers of African Americans migrated to the northern parts of the United States during the twentieth century, they encountered hostility that sometimes was fiercer than they had experienced in the South. This was partly due to white worry that migrating blacks might compete for their jobs. The same is true of the wave of migrants, many from Mexico and other parts of Latin America, that arrived in the United States following the immigration law reform in 1965. The increase in violent crime in American cities in the 1960s, 1970s, and 1980s compounded the anxiety of suburban and rural whites. Terrorist acts by radical Islamists have had a similar effect in recent years.

In the short term, diversity therefore militates against an expansion of public insurance in the United States. What about the long run? Here our most informative guide may be California's experience. California has long been seen as America's bellwether state, and as Peter Leyden, Ruy Teixeira, and Manuel Pastor have suggested, it's likely to prove exactly that for politics and policy in coming decades.[90]

In the first two-thirds of the twentieth century, California's economy grew rapidly—propelled by natural resources, heavy investment in public goods (water, roads, ports, education), population inflow from other states, and emerging manufacturing industries. In the 1970s, however, the state struggled, like the nation as a whole, with rising unemployment and inflation. A decade later the decline of manufacturing jobs, also a nationwide phenomenon, began to bite, and in the 1990s California's defense-oriented manufacturing sector was hit hard by the end of the Cold War. During this period the state also experienced an enormous rise in immigration. In 1960, California was home to 9 percent of America's population and 13 percent of its immigrants. By 1990, California had 12 percent of the nation's population and 32 percent of its immigrants.[91]

These changes created, in Pastor's words, "a perfect stew of racial anxiety and economic drift."[92] In concert with other developments—the 1960s counterculture and antiwar movement, urban riots, surging crime, and rapidly rising property taxes—they sparked a popular backlash.[93] In the 1980s, 1990s, and early 2000s, Californians elected law-and-order, tough-on-immigration Republicans to the governorship and prominent mayoral positions, and they voted in favor of a series of referendums to reduce taxes and limit supports for immigrants and minorities. In 1978, Californians passed Proposition 13, which reduced property tax revenues and limited future property tax increases, putting a crimp in funding for K–12 schools. It also hampered the state government's ability to raise general tax revenues by requiring that any proposed revenue increase get a two-thirds majority, rather that a simple majority, in both legislative bodies. Other referendums affirmed by California voters banned school busing and reversed other school desegregation mechanisms (1972, later ruled unconstitutional by the state's Supreme Court); banned affirmative action by the state government and other public entities, including in university admissions (1996); restricted bilingual education in schools (1998); prohibited unauthorized immigrants from having access to public services (1994, also later ruled unconstitutional);

mandated a minimum sentence of twenty-five years for persons with a third felony conviction (1994); required juveniles accused of certain crimes to be treated as adults (2000); and imposed term limits on state legislators (1990).

By the mid-2000s, however, California's economy had found a new footing, led by the success of digital tech firms in Palo Alto and San Francisco. And while the state's population had become even more diverse, its white inhabitants had had more time to come to terms with this reality. The last gasp of the conservative backlash came in 2005, when Republican governor Arnold Schwarzenegger called a special election aimed at passing a set of propositions limiting state spending, labor union power, and teacher tenure. All of his initiatives were voted down.

Over the past two decades Californians have turned away from a politics of traditionalism and fear. And the state's Republican Party, which mirrors national Republicans in hewing to small-government orthodoxy and to traditional views on many social issues, has steadily lost electoral ground, giving Democrats more opportunity to shape state policy. As noted earlier in this chapter, since the early 2000s California has enacted an array of public social programs that put it well ahead of the federal government.

Will the rest of the country follow suit? There is no guarantee it will, but one of the biggest potential obstacles, whites' discomfort with growing diversity, is certain to diminish. As Figure 8.14 shows, the nation's demographic mix is following California's. As it does so, whites' electoral influence will decrease, and so too will the degree to which racial anxiety shapes their political orientation.

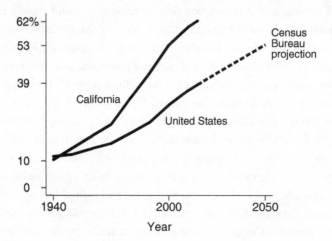

Figure 8.14 Population that is nonwhite and/or Hispanic. Share of the total population. The dashed portion of the line for the US as a whole is a projection. Data source: Census Bureau.

Political Changes That Would Help

The message of this chapter is that despite the significant political obstacles that exist in the United States, progress toward a social democratic future is likely. A few upgrades to our democracy's rules and practices would make it even more likely.[94]

We should make it easier to vote. Voter registration should be automatic. Elections should be on a weekend day. Voting by mail should be available everywhere. Efforts to suppress voter eligibility should be thwarted. And people with criminal convictions should be permitted to vote.

We should reform campaign finance. Many who rightly decry the influence of private money from interest groups and wealthy individuals in our elections focus on ways to restrict the flow of this money. A better strategy is to increase transparency, allowing everyone to know what interests are supporting which parties and candidates, and to offset the impact of private money with public money.

We should end gerrymandering of House of Representatives districts. Each decade, following the census, these districts are redrawn to reflect population shifts. To ensure that this process doesn't intentionally tilt the playing field toward one of the two parties, it should be handled by independent commissions rather than by state governments.

The Senate should pare back the filibuster. As I noted earlier, the filibuster helps to safeguard America's public insurance programs in periods when conservatives hold the presidency and a majority in both houses of Congress. However, requiring a supermajority to pass most legislation is fundamentally anti-democratic. It should be reserved for only a small number of Senate decisions.

Progress is Probable

The notion of a social democratic America will strike some observers of US politics as a pipe dream. But in the realm of public social policy, the distance between the United States today and Denmark or Sweden today is smaller than the distance between the United States a century ago and the United States today. In the past 100 years we've put in place a host of public programs that contribute to a decent income floor, economic security, equality of opportunity, and shared prosperity. Getting closer to the good society doesn't require a radical break from our historical path. It simply requires continuing along that path. In all likelihood, that is exactly what we will do.

This doesn't mean the future is predetermined. The trajectory I've laid out here is the most likely one, in my view, but it's by no means the only possibility. Moreover, even if we do move toward expanded government social programs, there will be plenty of space for actors to shape the timing, scope, and nature of future policy. My aim in writing this book is, above all else, to help inform those who seek to do so.

ACKNOWLEDGMENTS

This book builds on a large body of research on the world's rich longstanding-democratic nations. My most important debt is to researchers who have helped to advance our knowledge about these countries—their policies and institutions, their successes and failures, their similarities and differences. Especially influential in shaping my thinking and understanding over the past three decades have been Rolf Aaberge, Daron Acemoglu, Art Alderson, Alberto Alesina, Bruno Amable, Klaus Armingeon, Anthony Atkinson, David Autor, Lucio Baccaro, Dean Baker, Larry Bartels, Tim Bartik, William Baumol, Pablo Beramendi, Suzanne Berger, Barbara Bergmann, Jared Bernstein, Anders Björklund, Rebecca Blank, Fran Blau, Giuliano Bonoli, Heather Boushey, Samuel Bowles, Robert Boyer, Bruce Bradbury, David Brady, Andrea Brandolini, Mike Brewer, Brian Burgoon, Gary Burtless, David Cameron, Andrea Louise Campbell, John Campbell, Maria Cancian, Bea Cantillon, David Card, Francis Castles, Mary Corcoran, Miles Corak, Colin Crouch, Janet Currie, Tom Cusack, Sheldon Danziger, Brad DeLong, Tom DiPrete, Ronald Dore, Greg Duncan, Bernhard Ebbinghaus, Kathy Edin, Thomas Edsall, Werner Eichhorst, Patrick Emmenegger, Paula England, Gøsta Esping-Andersen, Tommy Ferrarini, Maurizio Ferrera, Claude Fischer, Michael Forster, Robert H. Frank, Richard Freeman, Milton Friedman, Duncan Gallie, Steffen Ganghof, Markus Gangl, Irv Garfinkel, Geoffrey Garrett, Andrew Gelman, Martin Gilens, John Goldthorpe, Janet Gornick, Ian Gough, Jørgen Goul Andersen, Peter Gourevitch, Bob Greenstein, Paul Gregg, David Grusky, Jacob Hacker, Peter Hall, Bjorn Hallerod, Knut Halvorsen, Bob Hancke, Ron Haskins, Anke Hassel, Silja Hausermann, Robert Haveman, Anton Hemerijck, Doug Hibbs, Alex Hicks, John Hills, Barbara Hobson, Mike Hout, Christopher Howard, Evelyne Huber, Ronald Inglehart, Torben Iversen, Larry Jacobs, Markus Jäntti, Sandy (Christopher) Jencks, Jane Jenson, Larry Kahn, Arne Kalleberg, Olli Kangas, Lawrence Katz, Peter Katzenstein, Bernhard Kittel, Mike Konczal, Tomas Korpi, Walter Korpi, Paul Krugman, Bob Kuttner, Jon Kvist, Peter Lange, Christian Albrekt Larsen,

Richard Layard, William Lazonick, Frank Lechner, Stephan Leibfried, Frank Levy, Leon Lindberg, Peter Lindert, Claudio Lucifora, Angus Maddison, Philip Manow, Jeff Madrick, Per Kongshøj Madsen, Katherine Magnuson, Jeff Manza, Theodore Marmor, Cathie Jo Martin, Isaac Martin, Ive Marx, Jerry Mashaw, Susan Mayer, Leslie McCall, Sara McLanahan, Suzanne Mettler, Bruce Meyer, Larry Mishel, Joya Misra, Deborah Mitchell, Karl Ove Moene, Robert Moffitt, Stephanie Moller, Kimberly Morgan, Charles Murray, John Myles, Kenneth Nelson, David Neumark, Katherine Newman, Stephen Nickell, Brian Nolan, Pippa Norris, Mancur Olson, Ann Orloff, Lars Osberg, Paul Osterman, Ben Page, Bruno Palier, Joakim Palme, Ove Pedersen, Paul Pierson, Thomas Piketty, Michael Piore, Niels Ploug, Jonas Pontusson, Michael Porter, Monica Prasad, Adam Przeworski, Bob Putnam, Charles Ragin, Lee Rainwater, Mark Rank, Marino Regini, Robert Reich, Philipp Rehm, Martin Rhodes, Dani Rodrik, John Roemer, Joel Rogers, Stephen Rose, Bo Rothstein, David Rueda, Christopher Ruhm, Charles Sabel, Emmanuel Saez, Diane Sainsbury, Reihan Salam, Wiemer Salverda, Peter Saunders, Isabel Sawhill, Stefano Scarpetta, Fritz Scharpf, Ronald Schettkat, Philippe Schmitter, Marc Schneiberg, Günther Schmid, John Schmitt, John Schwarz, Lyle Scruggs, Theda Skocpol, Tim Smeeding, Robert Solow, David Soskice, Sven Steinmo, John Stephens, Joseph Stiglitz, Wolfgang Streeck, Robin Stryker, Holly Sutherland, Stefan Svallfors, Duane Swank, Peter Taylor-Gooby, Ruy Teixeira, Kathy Thelen, Wim van Oorschot, Frank Vandenbroucke, Gerlinde Verbist, Jelle Visser, Jane Waldfogel, Michael Wallerstein, Niels Westergard-Nielsen, Bruce Western, Christopher Whelan, Peter Whiteford, Harold Wilensky, William Julius Wilson, Scott Winship, Justin Wolfers, Edward Wolff, Anne Wren, Erik Olin Wright, Jonathan Zeitlin, and John Zysman. There are no doubt others I've missed. My apologies to them.

Just as important has been the work of the Organization for Economic Cooperation and Development (OECD), the Luxembourg Income Study (LIS), the World Values Survey, and other organizations in collecting and disseminating data on these countries.

I've presented earlier versions of some of the book's chapters at various venues, and I'm grateful to participants who asked questions, provided corrections, and offered other types of feedback. For written comments on part or all of the manuscript, I thank Angus Deaton, Peter Gourevitch, Anton Hemerijck, Alexander Hicks, Christian Albrekt Larsen, Jeff Madrick, John Myles, Kenneth Nelson, Brian Nolan, and the reviewers for Oxford University Press.

Portions of Chapters 6 through 8 draw on my earlier book, *Social Democratic America*. I've benefited from critical commentary on that book, particularly by Jeff Manza and Joel Rogers.

Last but not least, special thanks to the major source of happiness in my life— Kim, Mia, Hannah, Noah, and Josh.

NOTES

The data used in this book are available at lanekenworthy.net.

Introductory Quotations

Martin Luther King Jr.: Commencement Address, Wesleyan University, 1964
Abraham Lincoln: Fragment on Government, July 1, 1854
Steven Pinker: *Enlightenment Now*, Viking, 2018, p. 11

Chapter 1
Sources of Successful Societies

1. Throughout this book I focus on Australia (abbreviated Asl in charts), Austria (Aus), Belgium (Bel), Canada (Can), Denmark (Den), Finland (Fin), France (Fr), Germany (Ger), Ireland (Ire), Italy (It), Japan (Ja), Korea (Kor), the Netherlands (Nth), New Zealand (NZ), Norway (Nor), Portugal (Por), Spain (Sp), Sweden (Swe), Switzerland (Swi), the United Kingdom (UK), and the United States (US). "Germany" prior to 1990 refers to West Germany. "Korea" refers to South Korea.
2. I borrow the term "successful societies" from Hall and Lamont 2009.
3. Maddison 2007.
4. Acemoglu and Robinson 2012.
5. Tversky and Kahneman 1992; *Wikipedia*, "Loss Aversion."
6. Marmor, Mashaw, and Harvey 1990; Barr 2001; Lindert 2004; Marmor, Mashaw, and Pakutka 2014.
7. Friedman 2005; Welzel 2013; Inglehart 2018.
8. Welzel 2013; Inglehart 2018.
9. Welzel 2013, ch. 3; Inglehart 2018.
10. Welzel 2013; Inglehart 2018.
11. See also Knight and Brinton 2017.
12. Welzel 2013; Inglehart 2018.
13. See also Barber 2011.
14. Kenworthy 2019, "Families" chapter.
15. Kenworthy 2019, "Religion" chapter.
16. Welzel 2013; Inglehart 2018.
17. Friedman 2005; Welzel 2013; Inglehart 2018; Vaisey and Lizardo 2018.
18. How can we be sure that both affluence and attitudes contribute to these good outcomes? In some instances, simple statistical analyses suggest that both matter. For example, both GDP per capita and the share of people who disagree that when jobs are scarce men should have

more right to a job than women predict countries' scores on the women, peace, and security index. The same is true for education, life expectancy, immigrants' life satisfaction, and personal freedom. Democracy is a more complicated case, though here too it appears that both affluence and citizen attitudes have a causal impact. See Welzel 2013, chs. 8–9; Inglehart 2018, ch. 7.

19. See also Deaton 2013; Pinker 2011.
20. Collier 2007; Rodrik 2014.
21. Dollar, Kleineberg, and Kraay 2016; Norberg 2016; Pinker 2018, ch. 8.
22. Sen 1999; Deaton 2013; Andrews, Pritchett, Woolcock 2017; Lutz and Kebede 2018.
23. Population data are from the Organization for Economic Cooperation and Development (OECD).

Chapter 2

Social Democratic Capitalism and the Good Society

1. Goodin et al. 1999; Esping-Andersen et al. 2002; Madsen 2006; Goul Andersen 2007; Huo, Nelson, and Stephens 2008; Esping-Andersen 2009; Morel, Palier, and Palme 2012; Pontusson 2011; Christoffersen et al. 2014; Dolvik 2014; Kenworthy 2014; Hemerijck 2017; Pedersen and Kuhnle 2017.
2. Przeworski 1985; Esping-Andersen 1990; Berman 2006; Sejerstad 2011.
3. Madsen 2006; Morel, Palier, and Palme 2012; Hemerijck 2017.
4. I adjust for the share of the population that is elderly or unemployed. There are other ways to measure welfare state comprehensiveness and generosity, but they don't significantly alter the picture. See Kenworthy 2019, "Social Programs" chapter.
5. See also van Kersbergen and Kraft 2017.
6. Esping-Andersen 1990, pp. 153, 156.
7. Korpi 1991 and Pontusson 2011 argue that the emphasis on high employment came earlier.
8. Jahoda 1982; Esping-Andersen et al. 2002; Layard 2005; Huo, Nelson, and Stephens 2008; Kenworthy 2008a; Morel, Palier, and Palme 2012; Kleven 2014; Krueger 2016; Hemerijck 2017.
9. This reasoning underlies arguments for an unconditional basic income. See Chapter 5.
10. If a key rationale for high employment is the tax revenues it brings, why not focus on average hours worked per person rather than the share of persons in employment? Unfortunately, available data on work hours aren't comparable across countries (OECD 2017, statistical annex, table L, footnote A). Even if we had those data, they wouldn't necessarily be our best indicator, because many people are paid an annual salary rather than an hourly wage, so their taxable earnings are the same whether they work thirty hours a week or fifty. Also, it probably wouldn't be desirable for most people to have very long work weeks and years even if that would generate more taxable earnings. So while the employment rate isn't a perfect measure, it may be the best one, both conceptually and in terms of data availability.
11. Deaton 2010; Ravallion 2012.
12. Kenworthy 2011c; Kenworthy 2019, "How Do We Know?" and "Is Income Inequality Harmful?" chapters.
13. Kenworthy 2011c; Kenworthy 2019, "Is Income Inequality Harmful?" chapter.
14. Kenworthy 2019, "Social Programs" chapter.
15. Rawls 1971.
16. Rawls 1996.
17. *Wikipedia*, "Loss Aversion."
18. Layard 2005, p. 168.
19. This was Rawls's view.
20. The figure for the United States is similar to food insecurity estimates from the US Department of Agriculture. See Keith-Jennings 2018.
21. The pattern is similar using other indicators of material hardship. One is the share of households experiencing one or more of the following: arrears in mortgage or rent payment, arrears in utility bill payment, inability to adequately heat home, constrained food choices,

overcrowding, poor environmental conditions (e.g., noise, pollution), difficulty in making ends meet (OECD 2008, pp. 186–8). These data are available for only seventeen of the twenty-one countries and only for the mid-2000s. A second alternative hardship indicator is the share of the population living in households who say they cannot afford at least four of the following nine items: mortgage or rent payments, utility bills, hire purchase installments, or other loan payments; one week's holiday away from home, a meal with meat, chicken, fish, or vegetarian equivalent every second day, unexpected financial expenses, a telephone (including mobile telephone), a color television, a washing machine, a car, heating to keep the home adequately warm (Eurostat 2017). These data are available for years since 2012 but only for fifteen European countries.

22. Goodin, Headey, Muffels, and Dirven 1999; Kenworthy 1999, 2004, 2011; Moller et al. 2003; Misra, Moller, and Budig 2007; Brady 2009; Garfinkel, Rainwater, and Smeeding 2010; Wang and Caminada 2011; Nelson 2012; Bailey and Danziger 2013; Jencks 2015; Brady, Finnigan, and Hübgen 2016; Ferrarini, Nelson, and Palme 2016; Birnbaum, Ferrarini, Nelson, and Palme 2017; McKernan, Ratcliffe, and Iceland 2018; Kenworthy 2019, "A Decent and Rising Income Floor" and "Public Insurance and the Least Well-Off" chapters.

23. Kenworthy 2011b; Kenworthy 2019, "Public Insurance and the Least Well-Off" chapter.

24. Murray 1984.

25. Jencks 2015; Kenworthy 2019, "Employment" and "Public Insurance and the Least Well-Off" chapters.

26. Cantillon and Vandenbroucke 2013; Bonoli, Cantillon, and Van Lancker 2017.

27. Figure 2.1 above; Van Vliet and Wang 2015; Noël forthcoming.

28. Marx, Vandenbroucke, and Verbist 2012; Cantillon and Vandenbroucke 2013; Taylor-Gooby, Gumy, and Otto 2014; Seikel and Spannagel 2018; Van Lancker and Horemans 2018.

29. Kenworthy 2011b, ch. 2.

30. Odendahl 2017; Kenworthy 2019, "A Decent and Rising Income Floor: Additional Data" appendix.

31. Andress and Lohmann 2008; Kenworthy 2011b, ch. 2; Thévenot 2017; Lohmann and Marx 2018; Nieuwenhuis, van Lancker, Collado, and Cantillon 2018; Kenworthy 2019, "A Decent and Rising Income Floor: Additional Data" appendix.

32. Hacker 2006; Garfinkel, Rainwater, and Smeeding 2010.

33. Kenworthy 2019, "Early Education" chapter.

34. Heckman 2008; Reardon 2011, figure 5.5; Ermisch, Jäntti, and Smeeding 2012, pp. 465–8; Bradbury, Corak, Waldfogel, and Washbrook 2015, chs. 4–6; von Hippel, Workman, and Downey 2018.

35. Downey, von Hippel, and Broh 2004; Alexander, Entwisle, and Olson 2007; Quinn and Polikoff 2017. For discussion of additional findings from natural experiments in which children go without schooling, see Nisbett 2009, ch. 3.

36. Brooks-Gunn 2003; Heckman 2008; Almond and Currie 2010; von Hippel, Workman, and Downey 2018.

37. Heckman 2008; Deming 2009; Reynolds et al. 2011; Esping-Andersen, Garfinkel, Han, Magnuson, Wagner, and Waldfogel 2012; Duncan and Magnuson 2013; Herbst 2013; Yoshikawa, Weiland, et al. 2013; Bartik 2014; Carneiro and Ginja 2014; Havnes and Mogstad 2015; Magnuson and Duncan 2016. Skeptics point to findings of little apparent impact of existing universal preschool programs for four-year-olds in Oklahoma and Georgia. But these programs are too new to assess long-run effects. See Barnett 2013; Duncan and Magnuson 2013.

38. Kenworthy 2019, "How Do We Know?" chapter.

39. Esping-Andersen 2009, pp. 135–6.

40. Kenworthy 2019, "Equality of Opportunity" chapter.

41. Berlin 1958; Sen 1999, 2009; Nussbaum 2011; Hick and Burchardt 2016; Robeyns 2018.

42. Renwick 2017.

43. Partanen 2016. See also Schall 2016, ch. 3.

44. Kenworthy 2019, "Equality of Opportunity" chapter.

45. In ordinary least squares regressions.

NOTES

46. A regression of relative poverty on public insurance and employment yields statistically significant coefficients for both variables and an r-squared of .70. A regression of p10 household income on public insurance and employment yields statistically significant coefficients for both variables and an r-squared of .64. A regression of material hardship on public insurance and employment yields statistically significant coefficients for both variables and an r-squared of .49. A regression of income decline on public insurance and employment yields statistically significant coefficients for both variables and an r-squared of .65. A regression of intergenerational mobility on early education and employment yields nearly statistically significant coefficients for both variables and an r-squared of .49. A regression of freedom to make life choices on public insurance and employment yields statistically significant coefficients for both variables and an r-squared of .60.
47. The replacement rate scores aren't available for Portugal, Spain, and South Korea, so for these countries I substitute their scores for public expenditures on social programs.
48. Kenworthy 2019, "Economic Freedom" chapter.
49. Friedman 1962; Friedman and Friedman 1979.
50. This line of reasoning follows Stokey and Rebelo 1995; Myles 2000.
51. Stiglitz 2012 argues that income inequality is an impediment to economic growth.
52. Kahn 2010; Oreopoulos, von Wachter, and Heisz 2012; Giuliano and Spilimbergo 2014.
53. See also Atkinson and Morelli 2010; Morelli and Atkinson 2015.
54. Autor, Dorn, and Hanson 2016; Goldstein 2017.
55. Kolko 2017.
56. Guiso, Herrera, Morelli, and Sonno 2017; Colantone and Stanig 2018.
57. Figures 2.5, 2.6, and 2.7.
58. Nolan 2018a, 2018b.
59. Kenworthy 2019, "Longevity" chapter.
60. Crimmins, Preston, and Cohen 2011.
61. Landersø and Heckman 2017.
62. Miliband 2017.
63. Traub 2016; Kenworthy 2018.
64. Waters and Pineau 2015.
65. Polakow-Suransky 2017; Goodwin 2018.
66. Traub 2016; Fasani, Frattini, and Minale 2018; Kenworthy 2018.
67. See also Hooijer and Picot 2015; Kesler 2015.
68. Children who grow up with both of their original parents tend to fare better on a range of outcomes, from school completion and performance to crime to earnings and income to maintaining lasting relationships. See McLanahan and Sandefur 1994; McLanahan, Tach, and Schneider 2013.
69. Murray 2012.
70. Castles 2003.
71. Levin 2012. See also Murray 2012.
72. In earlier eras inflation was a way to get around this problem, but this is more difficult to pursue in the modern era of global capital.
73. Kenworthy 2019, "Climate Stability" chapter.
74. Bentham 1843; Layard 2005; Murray 2012.
75. Stephens-Davidowitz 2013.
76. See also Radcliff 2013; Anderson and Hecht 2015.
77. Bergh 2014; Sanandaji 2016.
78. Kenworthy 2011b, ch. 6; Van Lancker and Van Mechelen 2014; Palme and Cronert 2015; Van Kersbergen and Kraft 2017.
79. Palier 2010; Hemerijck 2013, 2017.
80. Streeck 2016.
81. See Chapter 3.
82. Iversen and Soskice 2019.
83. See Chapter 4.
84. Welzel 2013; Inglehart 2018.
85. Goodman 2017.
86. DeLong 2015; Summers 2016.

Chapter 3

Is Its Success Generalizable?

1. See Chapter 8.
2. Sanandaji 2016.
3. Agell 1996, p. 1767. See also Esping-Andersen 1990, ch. 6.
4. OECD.Stat, "Absence from Work Due to Illness," https://stats.oecd.org/index. aspx?queryid=30123
5. Dahl, Kostøl, and Mogstad 2014.
6. Putnam 1993, 2000; Fukuyama 1995. See also Christoffersen et al. 2014, p. 136.
7. Larsen 2013.
8. Cowell 2006.
9. Kenworthy 2001.
10. Rothstein and Stolle 2008; Rothstein 2017.
11. Sønderskov and Dinesen 2014.
12. Brewer, Oh, and Sharma 2014; Kumlin and Haugsgjerd 2017.
13. Alesina et al. 2003.
14. Cameron 1978; Katzenstein 1985; Campbell, Hall, and Pedersen 2006.
15. Cowen 2016a.
16. Alesina, Spolare, and Wacziarg 2005; Alesina, Harnoss, and Rapoport 2013; Kenworthy 2019, "Economic Growth" chapter.
17. Hall and Soskice 2001; Hall and Gingerich 2009. Coherence applies both within and across economic spheres. A country's institutional mix is deemed more coherent to the extent that its institutions within each sphere are closer to one or the other of the two poles (liberal market or coordinated market) rather than in between and its institutions are consistent across spheres. Incoherence can be a product of being in the middle within each sphere or having liberal market institutions in some spheres and coordinated market institutions in others.
18. For suggestive arguments in this vein, see Pontusson 2011; Barth, Moene, and Willumsen 2014.
19. Kenworthy 2006; Campbell and Pedersen 2007; Hall and Gingerich 2009; Kristensen and Lilja 2011.
20. Kenworthy 2006.
21. Rothstein 2011; Steinmo 2013; Wooldridge 2013.
22. Micklethwait and Wooldridge 2014.
23. Ornston 2018.
24. Friedman 1962; Niskanen 1971; Friedman and Friedman 1979; Buchanan 1988; Wilson 1989; Chubb and Moe 1990; Scott 1998; Tanzi 2011; Zingales 2012.
25. Social Security Administration, "Social Security Administrative Expenses," https://www.ssa. gov/OACT/STATS/admin.html
26. Greenstein et al. 2012.
27. Buffie 2017; Tobias 2017; Frakt 2018.
28. Greenstein et al. 2012.
29. Andrews, Pritchett, and Woolcock 2017.
30. Roosevelt 1932.
31. Marmor, Mashaw, and Pakutka 2014.
32. Katzenstein 1985; Hicks and Kenworthy 1998; Wilensky 2002; Ornston 2012.
33. Kenworthy 2002; Kenworthy 2019, "Economic Growth" chapter.
34. Krugman 2009.
35. Galbraith 1967.
36. Kenworthy 2019, "Good Government: Additional Data" appendix. See also Boix 1998; Pontusson 2011. "The boom, not the slump, is the right time for austerity at the Treasury," wrote Keynes in 1937. See Krugman 2018.
37. Kleven et al. 2009; Kleven et al. 2011; Pampel, Andrighetto, and Steinmo 2019.
38. Kleven 2014.
39. Korpi 1983; Hicks 1999; Huber and Stephens 2001; Ebbinghaus 2010.
40. Kenworthy 2002.

41. Baker and Bernstein 2013; Bernstein 2016a.
42. Freeman and Medoff 1984; Kenworthy 2004; Pontusson 2011; Barth, Moene, and Willumsen 2014; Huber, Huo, and Stephens 2017; Kenworthy 2019, "Income Distribution" chapter.
43. Baccaro and Howell 2017.
44. Influential statements of this view include Wilkinson and Pickett 2009; Reich 2010; Stiglitz 2012.
45. Kenworthy 2019, "Is Income Inequality Harmful?" chapter.

Chapter 4
Is There an Attractive Small-Government Alternative?

1. Friedman 1962; Friedman and Friedman 1979; Murray 1984, 2012; Tanzi 2011; Levin 2012, 2016.
2. Polanyi 1957; Stiglitz 1989; Gough 1996; Moss 2002; Lindert 2004; Madrick 2009; Huang 2012; Bartlett 2012; Saez, Slemrod, and Giertz 2012; Bakija, Kenworthy, Lindert, and Madrick 2016.
3. Bakija, Kenworthy, Lindert, and Madrick 2016; Kenworthy 2019, "Is Big Government Bad for the Economy?" chapter.
4. Konczal 2014, 2016.
5. Ellwood and Jencks 2004; McLanahan 2004; Edin and Kefalas 2005; Cherlin 2009, ch. 7, 2014; England and Edin 2009; Haskins and Sawhill 2009, ch. 10; Wilson 2009, ch. 4; Conger, Conger, and Martin 2010; Isen and Stevenson 2010; England, McClintock, and Shafer 2012; England, Wu, and Shafer 2012; Murray 2012, ch. 8; Nelson and Edin 2013; McLanahan and Jacobsen 2015; Putnam 2015.
6. Kenworthy 2019, "Civic Engagement" chapter. Theda Skocpol offers a more optimistic interpretation. She looks farther back in time and identifies six clusters of high associational activity in the United States: the 1820s to 1850s, the 1850s to 1890s, the middle-to-late 1910s, the 1930s, the 1940s, and the 1960s to 1970s. According to Skocpol, many of the clusters appear to center around events of "nationalizing impact," such as the Civil War, the two World Wars, and the Cold War, and during periods when mobilization of voters was high. It's conceivable, then, that what appears to be a collapse of civic engagement since 1960 actually is just another valley between participatory peaks. Skocpol 1997.
7. Nisbet 1953; Douthat 2010.
8. Levin 2012. See also Nisbet 1953; Hayek 1960; Wolfe 1989; Douthat 2010.
9. Levin 2016. See also Nisbet 1953; Douthat 2010.
10. Kenworthy 2019, "Health Care" chapter.
11. Kenworthy 2019, "A Decent and Rising Income Floor" and "Health Care" chapters.
12. Alexander 2010.
13. Pension payments are a significant portion of government transfers in all rich countries. In one interpretation, counting public pensions in a measure of targeting-universalism or redistribution is misleading, because pension programs are best conceptualized as forced saving. The government requires employed citizens to put money away during their working years and then returns it to them (with interest) in their retirement years. In retirement, many people have no income from employment, so the pension they receive appears in the calculations as though it is going to a very poor household. According to this view, the measures therefore overstate the degree of targeting and the degree of redistribution achieved by transfers. Peter Whiteford (2008, 2009) has attempted to address this concern by calculating targeting-universalism and redistribution using households' position in the income distribution *after* transfers are added and taxes subtracted, rather than before. If a retired couple's income consists solely of a public pension payment, they will be at the very bottom of the distribution according to the calculations in Figure 4.10's second chart. In Whiteford's calculations they instead might be at the 20th percentile or even higher, depending on the size of their pension. In these calculations, Australia remains the most targeting-heavy of the rich nations, but it ranks higher on redistribution than in the second chart in Figure 4.10.

14. See also Saunders 2002; Korpi and Palme 2004; McClelland and Smyth 2014; Bradbury, Jäntti, and Lindahl 2017.
15. Korpi and Palme 1998; Kim 2000; Pontusson 2005.
16. Kenworthy 2011b, ch. 6; Marx, Salanauskaite, and Verbist 2016.
17. Whiteford, Phillips, Bradbury, Stanton, Gray, and Stewart 2018.
18. Christoffersen et al. 2014.
19. See Chapter 2.
20. Boaz 1998.
21. See also Bartlett 2015; Wilkinson 2017a, 2017b.
22. Friedman 1962; Niskanen 1971; Friedman and Friedman 1979; Buchanan 1988; Wilson 1989; Chubb and Moe 1990; Tanzi 2011; Zingales 2012.
23. Rothstein 2011.
24. Using other measures of the quality of government, such as Transparency International's corruption perceptions index, doesn't change the story.
25. Teles 2012.
26. IRS Taxpayer Advocate Service, *2010 Annual Report to Congress,* volume 1, cited in Teles 2012.
27. Milward and Provan 2000; DiIulio 2014.
28. Zingales 2012, p. 6. See also Friedman 1962; Friedman and Friedman 1979.
29. Baker 2011, ch. 10.
30. Weeden 2002; Carpenter, Knepper, Erickson, and Ross 2012.
31. Avent 2011; Glaeser 2011; Yglesias 2013.
32. Baker and Moss 2009; Stiglitz 2009; Baker 2011, ch. 9; Zingales 2012.
33. In the US context, see, for example, Haskins and Margolis 2014; Strain 2014; Lindsey and Teles 2017.

Chapter 5

Why Not A Basic Income?

1. Friedman 1962; Tobin 1966; Steensland 2007; Standing 2017; Van Parijs and Vanderborght 2017.
2. Hayek 1979; Galbraith 1998; Van Parijs 2001; Murray 2006, 2008; Wright 2010; Matthews 2014; Atkinson 2015; Reich 2015; Tanner 2015; Zwolinski 2015; Stern 2016; Standing 2017; Van Parijs and Vanderborght 2017; Lowrey 2018.
3. Van Parijs 2001, pp. 3, 19.
4. Van Parijs and Vanderborght 2017.
5. Murray 2008.
6. Ford 2015.
7. Bergmann 2006.
8. Ben-Galim and Dal 2009; Scrivener et al. 2015.
9. Standing 2017; Van Parijs and Vanderborght 2017.
10. Moffitt 1981; Burtless 1986; Calnitsky and Latner 2017.
11. Calnitsky and Latner 2017.
12. Kenworthy 2019, "Employment" chapter.
13. Kenworthy 2008.
14. Galston 2001; Cowen 2016b.
15. Krugman 2017.
16. Frank 2014.
17. Greenstein 2017.
18. Kenworthy 2019, "Social Programs" chapter.
19. Stern 2016; Lowrey 2018.
20. Van Parijs and Vanderborght 2017, ch. 6.
21. Chapter 2.

Chapter 6

America is Underachieving

1. Posttransfer-posttax income. Data source: Luxembourg Income Study, series DHI, using Current Population Survey data. Household income is adjusted for household size (each household's income is divided by the square root of the number of persons in the household) and then rescaled to reflect a three-person household.
2. OECD 2008, ch. 7. See also Kenworthy 2007; Nolan and Whelan 2010; Whelan and Maitre 2012.
3. Is this due to the fact that the US data are from a different survey than those for most of the other countries? Probably not. The Pew Research Center conducted a survey in the early 2000s that included the following material deprivation question: "Have there been times during the last year when you did not have enough money (a) to buy food your family needed, (b) to pay for medical and health care your family needed, (c) to buy clothes your family needed?" Among the seven affluent countries included in the Pew survey, measured material hardship was highest in the United States. See Boarini and Mira d'Ercole 2006, p. 18.
4. Rector 2007; Eberstadt 2008.
5. Edin and Lein 1997; Ehrenreich 2001; DeParle 2004; Shipler 2004; Abramsky 2013.
6. Jencks 2016, table 1.
7. Edin and Shaefer 2015; Desmond 2016.
8. Corporation for Enterprise Development 2013, using Survey of Income and Program Participation (SIPP) data. The original measure of asset poverty is Caner and Wolff 2004.
9. Mayer and Jencks 1993; Edin and Lein 1997.
10. Rank, Hirschl, and Foster 2014, table 3.1, using Panel Study of Income Dynamics (PSID) data. See also Hills 2017.
11. Siebens 2013.
12. Boushey, Brocht, Gundersen, and Bernstein 2001. See also Gould, Hething, Sabadish, and Finio 2013.
13. United Way 2014.
14. McMahon and Horning 2013.
15. Board of Governors of the Federal Reserve System 2015, pp. 18–19.
16. Dollar and Kraay 2002; Dollar, Kleineberg, and Kraay 2016.
17. For more detail, see Kenworthy 2011b.
18. For the most part, increases in government transfers hasn't meant increasing the share of GDP allocated to public transfers. Such increases were common in the 1960s and 1970s, but in many of the rich democratic countries increases in the share of GDP going to public transfers slowed or stopped after the 1970s. In recent decades, the distinction has been between countries that have kept transfers rising in line with GDP versus those that haven't. See Kenworthy 2019, "Social Programs" chapter.
19. Many elderly Americans have no income from earnings, but Social Security benefits, payments from employer-based retirement programs (company pension or 401k), and other income (from the sale of a house, for instance) combine to keep them out of poverty.
20. Kenworthy 2011e, figure 2.
21. Stevens 2018.
22. Calculations by the Congressional Budget Office (2018) suggest a much larger increase. This owes partly to the use of a different price index to adjust for inflation. Figure 6.5 uses the CPI-U-RS, while the CBO uses the PCE. The main cause of the difference is that the CBO adds an estimated income value of government-provided health insurance (Medicaid, S-CHIP, Medicare), and healthcare costs have increased dramatically in recent decades. This is problematic in three respects. First, the income value of other government services and public goods—education, safety, transportation, parks, and so on—isn't similarly included. Second, while surely beneficial to the poor, public health insurance probably doesn't free up income for them in the way that some other noncash benefits do. Christopher Jencks (2015) explains: "Medical care is by far the most expensive of today's noncash benefits, and Medicaid and veterans' benefits now pay for most of the big medical bills that poor families

incur. However, incorporating these programs' value into poverty calculations is more difficult than incorporating food and housing subsidies. Most of what Medicaid spends on the
poor is for 'big ticket' items, like nursing homes, heart surgery, and cancer treatments, that
poor families have never been able to pay for out of their own income. Before Medicaid
was created, the poor sometimes got such care from state and municipal programs or from
doctors and private hospitals that offered 'uncompensated' care. Medicaid coverage has un-
doubtedly made such care available to many poor families that previously went without it,
saving some lives and improving many others. But it has not had the same effect as food
stamps or rent subsidies on poor families' nonmedical standard of living. When a poor
family gets food stamps or a rent subsidy, it spends less of its cash on food and shelter and has
more to spend on the phone bill, fixing the family car, or taking a child to McDonald's for her
birthday. Medicaid frees up far less money for such uses than food stamps or a rent subsidy,
because poor families without Medicaid cannot afford to set aside enough money for major
medical emergencies. They know that if they need expensive care they will somehow have to
get it free or else do without. . . . The best estimates I have seen suggest that in 2010 Medicaid
reduced the average poor family's out-of-pocket medical spending by about $500." Third,
given that other countries have achieved similar improvements in health despite much
smaller increases in healthcare costs, it isn't clear whether the cost increases in the United
States reflect improved living standards for America's poor or simply additional income for
healthcare providers and insurance companies.
23. Kenworthy 2019, "Employment" chapter.
24. Kenworthy 2019, "Social Programs" chapter.
25. This is evident in poverty rates as well. See Fox et al. 2014, figure 6a; Danziger and Wimer
    2014, figure 6.
26. Sefton, Hills, and Sutherland 2009; Waldfogel 2010.
27. Murray 1984.
28. Jencks 1992; Edin and Lein 1997; Blank 1997; Nelson 2004; Ben-Shalom, Moffitt, and
    Scholz 2011; Fox et al. 2014, figure 9; Kenworthy 2019, "Social Programs" chapter.
29. Blank 2002; Blank 2006; Jencks 2005; Myles, Hou, Picot, and Myers 2009.
30. See Chapter 2.
31. U.S. Financial Diaries Project 2014b.
32. Moss 2002; Castles, Leibfried, Lewis, Obinger, and Pierson 2010.
33. Osterman 1999; Baumol, Blinder, and Wolff 2003; Fligstein and Shin 2003; Hacker 2006;
    Uchitelle 2006; Gosselin 2008; Blinder 2009; Farber 2010; Kalleberg 2011; Boushey and
    Ansel 2016; Katz and Krueger 2016; Schneider and Harknett 2016.
34. Gosselin 2008.
35. Western, Bloome, Sosnaud, and Tach 2012; Kenworthy 2019, "Families" chapter.
36. Hacker 2004; Kenworthy 2019, "Social Programs" chapter.
37. Hacker, Rehm, and Schlesinger 2010, figure 4; Marketplace-Edison Economic Anxiety
    Research Poll 2016, questions 7B, 8, 24.
38. Layard 2005.
39. Rose and Winship 2009, figure 6.
40. Marmor, Mashaw, and Pakutka 2014, pp. 22, 100.
41. Rose and Winship 2009, figure 2. For additional estimates based on the PSID data, see
    Gosselin and Zimmerman 2008; Hacker and Jacobs 2008; Dynan 2010; Dynan, Elmendorf,
    and Sichel 2012; Jensen and Shore 2015.
42. Winship 2012, figure 1. For additional estimates based on the SIPP data, see Acs, Loprest, and
    Nichols 2009.
43. US Congressional Budget Office 2008, figure 5, p. 10.
44. Hacker et al. 2013.
45. See also Dynan, Elmendorf, and Sichel 2012.
46. Morduch and Schneider 2014, p. 6.
47. Pofeldt 2014.
48. General Social Survey (GSS), sda.berkeley.edu/archive.htm, series wrksched; Golden 2015.
49. Katz and Krueger 2016; Horowitz 2015.

50. Morduch and Schneider 2014; U.S. Financial Diaries Project 2014a.
51. JPMorgan Chase Institute 2016. This report analyzed a sample of one million bank account holders between 2012 and 2015.
52. Mazumder and Miller 2016.
53. Kenworthy 2019, "Health Care" chapter.
54. Barnett and Berchick 2017, figure 2.
55. Families USA 2009.
56. Rosenthal 2015.
57. Gallup, "Healthcare System," gallup.com.
58. Carroll 2016.
59. Collins, Rasmussen, Doty, and Beutel, 2015, p. 6. See also Hamel et al. 2016.
60. Hamel et al. 2016, p. 14.
61. Jacoby 2014.
62. Kenworthy 2019, "Stable Income and Expenses" chapter.
63. Kenworthy 2019, "Wealth Distribution" chapter.
64. Caner and Wolff 2004, using Survey of Consumer Finances data; Corporation for Enterprise Development 2013, using Survey of Income and Program Participation (SIPP) data.
65. Economic Security Index, "The ESI: Contributions of Income, Medical Costs, Debt, and Wealth, 1986–2011."
66. Pew Research Center 2012, p. 147.
67. Pew Research Center 2011.
68. Sen 1999; Nussbaum 2011.
69. Noah 2012.
70. Kenworthy 2019, "Inclusion: Women" chapter.
71. Kenworthy 2019, "Inclusion: African Americans" chapter.
72. There are other types of mobility. See Kenworthy 2008b.
73. Economic Mobility Project 2012, figure 3. See also Harding, Jencks, Lopoo, and Mayer 2005; Jäntti et al. 2006; Ratcliff and McKernan 2010.
74. Currie 2011.
75. McLanahan, Tach, and Schneider 2013; McLanahan and Jencks 2015.
76. Duncan, Ziol-Guest, and Kalil 2010; Kaushal, Magnuson, and Waldfogel 2011; Cooper and Stewart 2013.
77. Mayer 1999; Lareau 2003; Phillips 2011; Cooper and Stewart 2013; Kalil 2015.
78. Jencks and Mayer 1990; Wilson 1987, 1996; Sampson 2012; Sharkey 2013.
79. Vandell and Wolfe 2000; Waldfogel 2006; Chaudry, Morrissey, Weiland, and Yoshikawa 2017.
80. Jacob and Ludwig 2008; Altonji and Mansfield 2011.
81. Economic Mobility Project 2012.
82. Bailey and Dynarski 2011.
83. MacLeod 2009.
84. Western 2006.
85. Wilson 1987, 1996; Wright and Dwyer 2003; Blinder 2009; Autor 2010; Western and Rosenfeld 2011.
86. Schwartz and Mare 2005.
87. Hauser, Warren, Huang, and Carter 2000.
88. A good overview is Putnam 2015.
89. Cherlin 2009; Kenworthy 2019, "Families" chapter.
90. Kenworthy 2019, "Income Distribution" chapter.
91. Kornrich and Furstenberg 2013, table 3, using data from the Consumer Expenditure Survey.
92. Lareau 2003; Putnam 2015, ch. 3.
93. Sean Reardon, personal communication.
94. Putnam 2015.
95. Bailey and Dynarski 2011.
96. Schwartz and Mare 2005.

97. Harding, Jencks, Lopoo, and Mayer 2005; Lee and Solon 2009; Winship 2013; Chetty et al. 2014; Hout 2018.
98. Aaronson and Mazumder 2008; Bloome and Western 2011; Davis and Mazumder 2017.
99. Corak, Lindquist, and Mazumder 2014; Schnitzlein 2015.
100. Jäntti and Jenkins 2015.
101. Rawls 1971; Kenworthy 2011b.
102. See also Leonhardt and Quealy 2014.
103. This figure uses income data for families rather than households. A family is defined by the Census Bureau as a household with two or more related persons. Defined this way, families don't include adults who live alone or with others to whom they aren't related. It's odd to exclude this group, but that's what the Census Bureau did until the late 1960s. Only then did it begin tabulating data for all households. I use families in this figure in order to begin earlier, in the mid-1940s. Note also that the same price deflator is used for both GDP per capita and family income in the figure. Using different deflators would exaggerate the divergence since the late 1970s. See Nolan, Roser, and Thewissen 2016.
104. For individual country graphs showing this pattern, see Kenworthy 2019, "Shared Prosperity: Additional Data" appendix.
105. Kenworthy 2019, "Is Income Inequality Harmful?" chapter.
106. Kenworthy 2019, "Is Income Inequality Harmful?" chapter.
107. Bailey, Coward, and Whittaker 2011, figure A1, using OECD data.
108. Bailey et al. 2011, figure A2, using OECD data.
109. Bailey et al. 2011, figure A3, using OECD data; Mishel et al. 2012, pp. 180–3, using Bureau of Labor Statistics Employer Costs for Employee Compensation (ECEC) survey data.
110. I use households rather than persons as the denominator for GDP because the number of households has increased faster than the number of persons since the late 1970s. Note also that I use the same price deflator for both GDP and median income. See Nolan, Roser, and Thewissen 2016.
111. See, for instance, Samuelson 1995; Cox and Alm 1999; Easterbrook 2003; Rose 2010; Burkhauser, Larrimore, and Simon 2011; Meyer and Sullivan, 2011.
112. See also Guvenen, Kaplan, Song, and Weidner 2017.
113. Actually, it's worse than the trend for all families. That's because median income among the retired has been growing at a slightly faster pace than median income among prime-working-age families, due to rising Social Security benefit levels. The data are at US Census Bureau, "Historical Income Data," table F-11.
114. US Census Bureau, "Foreign Born."
115. The data are at US Census Bureau, "Historical Income Data," table F-5.
116. Johnson 2004; Meyer and Sullivan 2011. See also Attanasio, Hurst, and Pistaferri 2012.
117. Wolff 2012.
118. Martin and Niedt 2015.
119. The data in the following paragraphs come from a variety of sources, including Lebergott 1976; Cox and Alm 1999; Easterbrook 2003; Fischer 2010.
120. Isaacson 2011.
121. For an argument that the pace of innovation has been *less* rapid since the mid-1970s, see Cowen 2011.
122. See in particular Warren and Tyagi 2003; Lesmerises 2007; Blank 2010.
123. US Census Bureau, "Historical Income Data," table F-12.
124. Jacobs and Gerson 2004.
125. Presser 2003.
126. McKenzie and Rapino 2011.
127. Some suggest that the cost of goods and services consumed by low income households has risen less rapidly than that of the bundle used to adjust for inflation. See Broda and Romalis 2008. Others argue that this is wrong. See Meyer and Sullivan 2011.
128. Lesmerises 2007, figure 12, using data from Warren and Tyagi 2003. See also DeLong 2012.
129. Kenworthy 2019, "College Education" chapter.

Chapter 7

A Better America

1. Kenworthy 2019, "Health Care" chapter.
2. Hacker 2016, 2018; Matthews 2017; Kliff and Klein 2017; Starr 2017, 2018; Sparer 2018.
3. Carroll 2017.
4. Klein 2012.
5. Kenworthy 2019, "Health Care" chapter.
6. Elmendorf 2014.
7. Pollin, Heintz, Arno, and Wicks-Lim 2017.
8. Keehan et al. 2017, exhibit 4.
9. Pollin, Heintz, Arno, and Wicks-Lim 2017.
10. US Department of Labor 2016, table 32.
11. Waldfogel 2006, ch. 2; Brooks-Gunn, Han, and Waldfogel 2010; Huerta et al. 2011; AEI-Brookings Working Group on Paid Family Leave 2017.
12. Ferrarini and Duvander 2010; Swedish Ministry of Health and Social Affairs 2016; US Social Security Administration 2016.
13. Rossin-Slater, Ruhm, and Waldfogel 2013.
14. For a sample proposal, see Ruhm 2017.
15. Kenworthy 2019, "Work-Family-Leisure Balance" chapter.
16. According to one estimate, a program with six months of leave and a replacement rate of 66 percent would cost about 0.5 percent of GDP. AEI-Brookings Working Group on Paid Family Leave 2017, p. 25.
17. Kenworthy 2019, "Equality of Opportunity" chapter.
18. Duncan, Ziol-Guest, and Kalil 2010.
19. Sturgeon 2016.
20. Prior to 2018, the maximum amount was $1,000.
21. Chikhale 2016, figure 3. Prior to 2018, there also was an exemption on federal income taxes of $4,000 per child ("child deduction"). This too was worth little to those with low incomes, many of whom owe no federal income tax, and even for households in the middle of the income distribution it is of limited value. See Marmor, Mashaw, and Pakutka 2014.
22. Shaefer et al. 2016.
23. It would be paid monthly via electronic transfer in order to ensure a high take-up rate.
24. Graetz and Mashaw 1999; Marmor, Mashaw, and Pakutka 2014, ch. 8; Stone and Chen 2014.
25. Marmor, Mashaw, and Pakutka 2014.
26. Kletzer and Litan 2001; LaLonde 2007.
27. Heymann, Rho, Schmitt, and Earle 2009; Kenworthy 2019, "Social Programs" chapter.
28. US Bureau of Labor Statistics 2017, table 6 ("Selected Paid Leave Benefits"), using data from the National Compensation Survey.
29. Swedish Ministry of Health and Social Affairs 2016; US Social Security Administration 2016.
30. 706 Swedish kroner per day. This cap is indexed to inflation.
31. Marmor, Mashaw, and Pakutka 2014, p. 153. The descriptive information and data in this section draw heavily from chapter 9 of this book.
32. Autor and Duggan 2010; Burkhauser and Daly 2012; Reno and Ekman 2012.
33. Kenworthy 2019, "Social Programs" chapter.
34. Campbell 2014.
35. Harrington 1962; Murray 1984; Ellwood 1988; Marmor, Mashaw, and Harvey 1990; Jencks 1992; Skocpol 1992; Blank 1997; Gilens 1999; DeParle 2004; Haskins and Sawhill 2009; Thiebaud Nicoli 2012; Danziger, Danziger, Seefeldt, and Shaefer 2016.
36. Hays 2003; DeParle 2004, ch. 14; Morgen, Acker, and Weigt 2010.
37. Edin and Lein 1997; Newman 1999, 2006; DeParle 2004; Edin and Kefalas 2005; England and Edin 2009; Nelson and Edin 2013; Edin and Shaefer 2015; Desmond 2016; Western 2018.
38. Ben-Galim and Dal 2009; Scrivener et al. 2015; Rice, Fuertes, and Monticelli 2018.
39. DeParle 2012; Edin and Shaefer 2015.
40. Edin and Shaefer 2015.
41. Kenworthy 2019, "Social Programs" chapter.

42. Center on Budget and Policy Priorities 2018.
43. Western 2018, pp. 174–7.
44. Travis, Western, and Redburn 2014.
45. Western 2018, ch. 11.
46. Kenworthy 2019, "Inclusion: The Elderly" chapter.
47. Geoghegan 2011; Lind, Hill, Hiltonsmith, and Freedman 2013.
48. Ghilarducci 2008.
49. Graetz and Mashaw 1999; Munnell 2012; U.S. Senate Committee on Health, Education, Labor, and Pensions 2012.
50. Farrell 2016; Walsh 2016; Olson 2017; Munnell 2018.
51. The United States has one of the highest elderly employment rates among affluent nations. Kenworthy 2019, "Inclusion: The Elderly" chapter.
52. U.S. National Center for Health Statistics 2013; Nguyen 2017.
53. Glaeser 2011.
54. Avent 2011; Glaeser 2011; Yglesias 2013.
55. Kenworthy 2019, "A Decent and Rising Income Floor" chapter.
56. The following description and data draw from Collinson, Ellen, and Ludwig 2015; US Congressional Budget Office 2015; Desmond 2016; Center on Budget and Policy Priorities 2017.
57. Collinson, Ellen, and Ludwig 2015.
58. Haveman 2013; Fischer 2014; Collinson, Ellen, and Ludwig 2015.
59. The Congressional Budget Office estimates that providing a voucher to the eight million households with incomes below 50 percent of the area median and that don't currently receive one would cost about $40 billion. US Congressional Budget Office 2015.
60. Carasso, Reynolds, and Steurle 2008; Toder, Turner, Lim, and Getsinger 2010; Bourassa, Haurin, Hedershott, and Hoesli 2015; Chikhale 2017.
61. Kenworthy 2019, "Early Education" chapter.
62. Laughlin 2013, table 6, using data from the Survey of Income and Program Participation (SIPP). See also Chaudry et al. 2011; ChildCare Aware of America 2012.
63. Cascio 2017b, table 1.
64. Hanushek, Kain, Markman, and Rivkin 2001; Heckman 2008; Bauchmüller, Gørtz, and Rasmussen 2011; Barnett 2013; Cascio 2017a.
65. Timothy Bartik proposes an alternative that he estimates would cost half as much, or about 0.5 percent of GDP. It includes universal pre-K available to all four-year-olds, targeted full-time full-year childcare and pre-K available for all disadvantaged children from birth to age five, and targeted parenting services for first-time disadvantaged mothers and their children from the prenatal period until age two. See Bartik, 2011, ch. 7. Other proposals for smaller-scale programs include the Obama administration's 2014 budget proposal (US Department of Education 2013) and Brown et al. 2013.
66. National Center for Education Statistics, "Expenditures."
67. New York City and Boston each spend about $10,000 per child on their well-regarded public pre-kindergarten programs. Kirp 2016.
68. OECD 2011, figure 1.11.
69. Chaudry, Morrissey, Weiland, and Yoshikawa 2017.
70. U.S. National Center for Education Statistics 2018. This doesn't count persons who get a degree via a GED (General Educational Development) exam.
71. Cited in Sawhill 2018, ch. 3, note 62.
72. See Chapter 2.
73. Kenworthy 2019, "What Good Is Education?" chapter.
74. OECD 2016; Dynarski 2017; What Works Clearinghouse 2019.
75. Holzer 2015; Rosenbaum, Ahern, Becker, and Rosenbaum 2015; Schwartz and Hoffman 2015.
76. Schwartz and Hoffman 2015.
77. Holzer 2015.
78. Kenworthy 2019, "College Education" chapter.
79. Jencks 2009.
80. Chingos 2016; Kenworthy 2019, "College Education" chapter.

81. Leonhardt 2011. The Tennessee Promise program, which made community college tuition-free for students, seems to have yielded a significant enrollment response. Carruthers and Fox 2016.
82. Murphy, Scott-Clayton, and Wyness 2017.
83. College Board, "Trends in College Pricing," various years, https://trends.collegeboard.org/college-pricing
84. Davidson 2016.
85. Phillips 2013.
86. Carey 2015; Dynarski 2016a, 2016b.
87. Bowen and Bok 1998; Reskin 1998.
88. Ashkenas, Park, and Pearce 2017.
89. Kahlenberg 1996; Kahlenberg and Porter 2013; Alon 2015. This won't work as well at elite universities; see Dynarski 2018.
90. Kenworthy 2019, "Employment" chapter.
91. Rehn 1952, 1985; Ginsburg 1983; Björklund and Freeman 1987; Kvist and Ploug 2003; OECD 2003; Madsen 2006.
92. Kenworthy, "Social Programs" chapter.
93. Card, Kluve, and Weber 2018. See also Brown and Koettl 2015; Manoli, Michaelides, and Patel 2018.
94. Pollin 2011; Baker and Bernstein 2013; Bernstein 2016a.
95. Gregg and Layard 2009; Harvey 2011; Matthews 2018.
96. Gottschalk 1998.
97. Long 2018.
98. Cohen 2017; Porter 2018.
99. Western and Rosenfeld 2012; Usmani 2018.
100. Holmberg 2017; Warren 2018; Yglesias 2018.
101. Vitols 2010; Fox 2018.
102. This is an estimate. As of 2015, the 1,000 companies in the "Fortune 1000" had 34 million employees in total, and the firm at the bottom of the list had revenue of $1.8 billion.
103. Silvia 2013.
104. There is only one other rich democratic nation, the Netherlands, that has strong employee board-level representation and a moderate-to-low unionization rate. But unlike in Germany, in the Netherlands collective bargaining coverage remains very high—85 percent as of 2014.
105. Sigurt Vitols, personal communication.
106. This is true for household income as well. See Kenworthy 2019, "Shared Prosperity: Additional Data" appendix.
107. Walzer 1978; Dahl 1985.
108. Kenworthy 2019, "How Do We Know?" chapter.
109. Card and Krueger 1995; Dube, Lester, and Reich 2010; Schmitt 2013; Cengiz, Dube, Lindner, and Zipperer 2019.
110. Howell, Fiedler, and Luce 2016; Hanuer 2016.
111. US Census Bureau, "Historical Income Tables: People," table P-43.
112. Dube 2013; Krueger 2015.
113. For further discussion of this debate, see Kenworthy 2014, pp. 134–41.
114. Kenworthy 2015; Nichols and Rothstein 2016.
115. This may affect its attractiveness to recipients, the degree to which it incentivizes employment, and the ways recipients spend the benefit money. Halpern-Meekin, Edin, Tach, and Sykes 2014.
116. Kenworthy 2019, "Social Programs" chapter.
117. Center on Budget and Policy Priorities 2014.
118. The current federal EITC averages $2,300 per household.
119. Kenworthy 2015.
120. Even if it does reduce wages, it's worth noting that this kind of hazard exists with all insurance. Public pension programs encourage people to save less during their working years than they otherwise would. Unemployment insurance encourages people to remain out of work longer than they otherwise might. Affordable healthcare encourages people to use more

health services than they truly need. In each case, we judge the likely cost to be smaller than the gain in economic security, psychological well-being, and social justice. Arguably, the same is true here.

121. Kruse, Freeman, and Blasi 2008.
122. Weitzman 1984.
123. Chozick 2015.
124. Cooper 2012; American Society of Civil Engineers 2013; US Federal Highway Administration 2014; Kanter 2015; Anderson, Perrin, Jiang, and Kumar 2019; US Federal Communications Commission 2019, figure 4.
125. Soltas 2013.
126. World Economic Forum 2015.
127. Cooper 2012.
128. US Congressional Budget Office 2011; Zandi 2011; Leduc and Wilson 2012.
129. Economic Innovation Group 2016.
130. Krugman 2019.
131. Meyerson 2017.
132. *Wikipedia*, "List of Minimum Annual Leave by Country"; Ray, Sanes, and Schmitt 2013.
133. Van Giezen 2013; Society for Human Resource Management 2016.
134. Kenworthy 2014.
135. Kenworthy 2019, "Taxes" chapter.
136. Kenworthy 2019, "Income Distribution" chapter.
137. The amount paid by households in the bottom fifth is calculated as $1.8 trillion (the total tax revenue needed) multiplied by .02 (this group will account for 2 percent of the revenues) divided by 25.2 million (the number of households in this group) = $1,428. The calculation is analogous for the other four groups. With the top fifth, we can go further and break it down into subgroups. Those between the 80th and 90th percentiles would pay $21,100 more per year, those between the 90th and 95th percentiles $30,600, those between the 95th and 99th percentiles (average income $320,000) $54,600, and those in the top 1 percent (average income $1.8 million) $340,000.
138. Kenworthy 2011a. As Adam Smith put it in *The Wealth of Nations* (book 5, ch. 2, part 2), "The subjects of every state ought to contribute toward the support of the government, as nearly as possible, in proportion to their respective abilities; that is, in proportion to the revenue which they respectively enjoy under the protection of the state."
139. This assumes high income households don't alter their behavior in response to the increase in the effective tax rate.
140. Kenworthy 2008a, figure 8.12.
141. This estimate is based on information in Krueger 2009; Toder and Rosenberg 2010; Barro 2011; Campbell 2011; Sawhill 2018.
142. See, for instance, Kuttner 2010.
143. In fact, a consumption tax can be made progressive. See Frank 2008.
144. Bartlett 2012.
145. Kenworthy 2011b, ch. 8.
146. Zucman 2015; Avi-Yonah 2016; Bernstein 2016b.
147. Kenworthy 2011d.
148. Surowiecki 2010.
149. Wamhoff and Gardner 2019 .
150. In 2016, average pretax income of households in the top 1 percent was $1.827 million, according to the Institute for Taxation and Economic Policy. There were about 1.26 million households in this group. Six percent of their total income is about 0.7 percent of the country's $18 trillion GDP.
151. Young 2017.
152. Data source: OECD, Revenue Statistics Database.
153. Kenworthy 2019, "Wealth Distribution" chapter.
154. Rorke, Moylan, and Semelsberger 2016; Carbon Tax Center 2018.
155. Kenworthy 2019, "Climate Stability" chapter.
156. Data source: OECD, Revenue Statistics Database.

157. The total payroll (Social Security and Medicare) tax rate is about 15 percent, and since the mid-1980s it has consistently collected 6.6 to 7.0 percent of GDP.
158. US Congressional Budget Office 2016; Romig 2016.
159. Chikhale 2017.
160. For more, see Bernstein 2016b.

Chapter 8
How to Get There

1. Cogan 2017.
2. Esping-Andersen 1990.
3. Lipset 1996.
4. Micklethwait and Woolridge 2004, pp. 382, 303.
5. Alesina and Glaeser 2004. See also Brooks and Manza 2007.
6. Pew Research Center, ABC/*Washington Post*, CBS/*New York Times*, *Los Angeles Times*, reported in Pew Research Center 2012, pp. 109–110. "Depends" and "don't know" responses omitted.
7. Fishman and Davis 2017. "No opinion" responses omitted.
8. Pew Research Center 2012, p. 147.
9. American National Election Study, sda.berkeley.edu/archive.htm.
10. General Social Survey, sda.berkeley.edu/archive.htm, series conlegis and confed.
11. General Social Survey, sda.berkeley.edu/archive.htm, series natfarey, nateduc, natheal, and natsoc.
12. Reported in the data set for Page and Jacobs 2009, variable qhc2.
13. Pew Research Center 2011b, p. 24.
14. Data set for Page and Jacobs 2009, variable qtaxl.
15. Data set for Page and Jacobs 2009, variable qtaxm.
16. Data set for Page and Jacobs 2009, variable qjob4.
17. General Social Survey, sda.berkeley.edu/archive.htm, series natfare.
18. Gilens 1999.
19. Manza, Heerwig, and McCabe 2012; Kenworthy 2019, "How Much Public Insurance Do Americans Want?" and "Is America Too Polarized?" chapters. This includes "welfare." Despite the pronounced changes introduced by the 1996 welfare reform—strict time limits on benefit receipt, reduced benefit levels, stronger employment requirements—the General Social Survey responses suggest little, if any, shift in public opinion about "welfare" since then.
20. See also Ellis and Stimson 2012.
21. Page and Shapiro 1983.
22. Gilens 2012.
23. Erikson, MacKuen, and Stimson 2002.
24. Newman and Jacobs 2010.
25. Newman and Jacobs 2010, p. 7.
26. Newman and Jacobs 2010, p. 5.
27. Pierson 1994.
28. Korpi 1980; Rainwater 1982; Ringen 1987; Esping-Andersen 1990; Skocpol 1991; Gelbach and Pritchett 1995; Korpi and Palme 1998; Rothstein 1998; Moene and Wallerstein 2001; Van Oorschot 2002; Wilensky 2002; Pontusson 2005; Campbell 2007; Larsen 2008.
29. Korpi and Palme 1998.
30. Kenworthy 2011b, ch. 6; Marx, Salanauskaite, and Verbist 2016. To measure the size of the redistributive budget I use government social expenditures as a share of GDP, adjusted for the size of the elderly population and the unemployment rate. This is similar to the measure used by Korpi and Palme 1998, table 3.
31. Nelson 2007, figure 1.
32. Kenworthy 2011b, ch. 6.
33. Greenstein 1991; Pierson 1994.
34. Howard 2007, p. 106.

35. Sides 2017.
36. Hirschman 1991.
37. Brady, Huber, and Stephens 2016.
38. Feingold 2013; Page and Gilens 2017.
39. Reich 1999; Wilentz 2008.
40. This is partly because Democratic senators and representatives from the South, who tended to be the most conservative Democrats in Congress, have been disappearing. But even among non-Southern Democratic lawmakers, there is no sign of a move to the center. See Keith Poole, "Party Polarization: 1879–2010," polarizedamerica.com/Polarized_America.htm. A measure of the views of Democratic Party nominees for House of Representatives seats based on the ideological preferences of donors also suggests a movement to the left from 1980 to 2018. See *Economist* 2018.
41. Swers 2013; Mendelberg, Karpowitz, and Goedert 2014.
42. Kenworthy, Barringer, Duerr, and Schneider 2007.
43. Larry Bartels finds no decline in the share of whites in the bottom income third that voted Democratic in presidential elections between 1952 and 2004. But in eight of those fourteen elections a majority of this group voted for the Republican candidate, so it can't really be considered to have been the electoral base of the Democrats. See Bartels 2008.
44. Teixeira 2017.
45. Welzel 2013; Inglehart 2018.
46. Frank 2004.
47. Judis and Teixeira 2002; Browne, Halpin, and Teixeira 2011; Teixeira 2017; Pew Research Center 2018.
48. Hibbs 2009; Bartels 2013; Achen and Bartels 2016.
49. Bartels and Zaller 2000; Fair 2012; Silver 2012; Sides and Vavreck 2013.
50. Hibbs 2012; McGhee 2012; Jacobsen 2018; Masket 2018.
51. Persily 2010.
52. Center for Responsive Politics, "Outside Spending," opensecrets.org.
53. See, for example, Burns 2018.
54. Jacobs et al. 2004; Drutman 2012.
55. Schattschneider 1960; Ferguson and Rogers 1986; Hacker and Pierson 2010.
56. Ferguson and Rogers 1986; Vogel 1989; Hacker and Pierson 2010.
57. Blank 1997; Garfinkel, Rainwater, and Smeeding 2010; Ben-Shalom, Moffitt, and Scholz 2011; Howard 2011; Edelman 2012; Meyer and Sullivan 2012; Kenworthy 2019, "Social Programs" chapter.
58. Gilens 1999; Kenworthy 2019, "How Much Public Insurance Do Americans Want?" chapter.
59. Birnbaum et al. 2017, using data from the Social Policy Indicators (SPIN) database. See also Kenworthy 2019, "Social Programs" chapter.
60. Lane Kenworthy 2019, "A Decent and Rising Income Floor" chapter, using Luxembourg Income Study data.
61. OECD, Social Expenditures database. See also Kenworthy 2019, "Social Programs" chapter.
62. Howard 2007, 2011; Mettler 2011.
63. Mettler 2011.
64. Howard 2011; Moffitt 2015.
65. Edin and Shaefer 2015.
66. Huber, Ragin, and Stephens 1993; Tsebelis 1995; Amenta 1998. There is the additional possibility of veto by the judicial branch. Lobbying, too, plays a role in minimizing policy change; see Baumgartner et al. 2009.
67. Baldassarri and Gelman 2008; Bartels 2008.
68. Poole and Hare 2012.
69. On top of ideological purification, the leadership in both parties has taken to using an array of rewards and punishments—from allocation of committee positions to backing of reelection campaigns—to get backbenchers to vote the party line.
70. Keith Poole, "Party Unity Votes," polarizedamerica.com.
71. Douthat and Salam 2008; Frum 2008; Brooks 2012; Murray 2012; Ponnuru 2013; Strain 2014; Cass 2018.

72. Lindsey, Wilkinson, Teles, and Hammond 2018.
73. See also Bonica 2018.
74. See "The Tortoise and the Hare," one of Aesop's fables.
75. Parolin 2016; Björklund 2017.
76. Perry 2017; Pastor 2018.
77. *Wikipedia*, "Carbon Neutrality."
78. Fingerhut 2017; Gallup 2018.
79. Sides 2017.
80. Williamson 2017.
81. Prasad 2018.
82. My calculations using Maddison Project data.
83. DeLong 2015; Summers 2016.
84. Stiglitz et al. 2015.
85. Cowen 2011; Gordon 2016.
86. Friedman 2005; Teixeira 2017.
87. Kolko 2017; Guiso et al. 2017; Colantone and Stanig 2018; Inglehart 2018, ch. 9.
88. Alesina and Glaeser 2004; Hochschild 2016.
89. Welzel 2013; Inglehart 2018. See also Abrajano and Hajnal 2015; Hochschild 2016; Polakow-Suransky 2017; Mutz 2018.
90. Leyden and Teixeira 2017; Pastor 2018.
91. Pastor 2018, p. 51, using data from the US Census Bureau.
92. Pastor 2018, p. 59.
93. Martin 2008; Abrajano and Hajnal 2015; Pastor 2018.
94. Hacker and Pierson 2016; Keisling 2016; Page and Gilens 2017; Wang and Remlinger 2017; Brennan Center 2018a, 2018b, 2018c.

REFERENCES

Aaronson, Daniel and Bhashkar Mazumder. 2008. "Intergenerational Economic Mobility in the U.S., 1940 to 2000." *Journal of Human Resources* 43, 139–72.

Abrajano, Marisa and Zoltan L. Hajnal. 2015. *White Backlash: Immigration, Race, and American Politics*. Princeton University Press.

Abramsky, Sasha. 2013. *The American Way of Poverty: How the Other Half Still Lives*. Nation Books.

Acemoglu, Daron and James Robinson. 2012. *Why Nations Fail: The Origins of Power, Prosperity, and Poverty*. Crown.

Achen, Christopher and Larry Bartels. 2016. *Democracy for Realists*. Princeton University Press.

Acs, Gregory, Pamela Loprest, and Austin Nichols. 2009. "Risk and Recovery: Understanding the Changing Risks to Family Incomes." Urban Institute.

AEI-Brookings Working Group on Paid Family Leave. 2017. "Paid Family and Medical Leave: An Issue Whose Time Has Come." Brookings Institution.

Agell, Jonas. 1996. "Why Sweden's Welfare State Needed Reform." *Economic Journal* 106, 1760–71.

Alesina, Alberto, Arnaud Devleeschauwer, William Easterly, Sergio Kurlat, and Romain Wacziarg. 2003. "Fractionalization." *Journal of Economic Growth* 8, 155–94.

Alesina, Alberto and Edward L. Glaeser. 2004. *Fighting Poverty in the US and Europe*. Oxford University Press.

Alesina, Alberto, Johann Harnoss, and Hillel Rapoport. 2013. "Birthplace Diversity and Economic Prosperity." Working Paper 18699. National Bureau of Economic Research.

Alesina, Alberto, Enrico Spolaore, and Roman Warczarg. 2005. "Trade, Growth, and the Size of Countries." In *Handbook of Economic Growth*, volume 1B, edited by P. Aghion and S.N. Durlauf, 1499–1542. North-Holland.

Alexander, David. 2010. "Free and Fair: How Australia's Low-Tax Egalitarianism Confounds the World." *Policy* (Summer), 3–14.

Alexander, Karl L., Doris R. Entwisle, and Linda Steffel Olson. 2007. "Lasting Consequences of the Summer Learning Gap." *American Sociological Review* 72, 167–80.

Almond, Douglas and Janet Currie. 2010. "Human Capital Development Before Age Five." Working Paper 15827. National Bureau of Economic Research.

Alon, Sigal. 2015. *Race, Class, and Affirmative Action*. Russell Sage Foundation.

Altonji, Joseph G. and Richard K. Mansfield. 2011. "The Role of Family, School, and Community Characteristics in Inequality in Education and Labor-Market Outcomes." In *Whither Opportunity?*, edited by Greg J. Duncan and Richard J. Murnane. Russell Sage Foundation and Spencer Foundation.

Amenta, Edwin. 1998. *Bold Relief: Institutional Politics and the Origins of Modern American Social Policy*. Princeton University Press.

American Society of Civil Engineers. 2013. "Report Card for America's Infrastructure." infrastructurereportcard.org.

Anderson, Christopher J. and Jason D. Hecht. 2015. "Happiness and the Welfare State: Decommodification and the Political Economy of Subjective Well-Being." In *The Politics of Advanced Capitalism,* edited by Pablo Beramendi, Silja Hausermann, Herbert Kitcschelt, and Hanspeter Kriesi, 357–80. Cambridge University Press.

Anderson, Monica, Andrew Perrin, Jingjing Jiang, and Madhumitha Kumar. 2019. "10% of Americans Don't Use the Internet. Who Are They?" Pew Research Center.

Andress, Hans-Jürgen and Henning Lohmann, eds. 2008. *The Working Poor in Europe.* Edward Elgar.

Andrews, Matt, Lant Pritchett, and Michael Woolcock. 2017. *Building State Capacity.* Oxford University Press.

Ashkenas, Jeremy, Haeyoun Park, and Adam Pearce. 2017. "Even with Affirmative Action, Blacks and Hispanics Are More Underrepresented at Top Colleges Than 35 Years Ago." *New York Times,* August 24.

Atkinson, Anthony B. 2015. *Inequality: What Can Be Done?* Harvard University Press.

Atkinson, Anthony B. and Salvatore Morelli. 2010. "Inequality and Banking Crises: A First Look." Report for the International Labour Organization (ILO).

Attanasio, Orazio, Erik Hurst, and Luigi Pistaferri. 2012. "The Evolution of Income, Consumption, and Leisure Inequality in the US, 1980–2010." Working Paper 17982. National Bureau of Economic Research.

Autor, David H. 2010. "The Polarization of Job Opportunities in the U.S. Labor Market." Center for American Progress and the Hamilton Project.

Autor, David H., David Dorn, and Gordon H. Hanson. 2016. "The China Shock: Learning from Labor Market Adjustment to Large Changes in Trade." Working Paper 21906. National Bureau of Economic Research.

Autor, David H. and Mark Duggan. 2010. "Supporting Work: A Proposal for Modernizing the U.S. Disability Insurance System." Center for American Progress and the Hamilton Project.

Avent, Ryan. 2011. *The Gated City.* Amazon Digital Services.

Avi-Yonah, Reuven S. 2016. "International Tax Evasion and Avoidance: What Can Be Done?" *The American Prospect,* Spring, 63–67.

Baccaro, Lucio and Chris Howell. 2017. *Trajectories of Neoliberal Transformation: European Industrial Relations Since the 1970s.* Cambridge University Press.

Bailey, Jess, Joe Coward, and Matthew Whittaker. 2011. "Painful Separation: An International Study of the Weakening Relationship between Economic Growth and the Pay of Ordinary Workers." Commission on Living Standards. Resolution Foundation.

Bailey, Martha J. and Sheldon Danziger, eds. 2013. *Legacies of the War on Poverty.* Russell Sage Foundation.

Bailey, Martha J. and Susan Dynarski. 2011. "Gains and Gaps: A Historical Perspective on Inequality in College Entry and Completion." In *Whither Opportunity?,* edited by Greg J. Duncan and Richard J. Murnane. Russell Sage Foundation and Spencer Foundation.

Baker, Dean. 2011. *The End of Loser Liberalism: Making Markets Progressive.* Center for Economic and Policy Research.

Baker, Dean and Jared Bernstein. 2013. *Getting Back to Full Employment.* Center for Economic and Policy Research.

Baker, Tom and David Moss. 2009. "Government as Risk Manager." In *New Perspectives on Regulation,* edited by David Moss and John Cisternino. Tobin Project.

Bakija, Jon, Lane Kenworthy, Peter Lindert, and Jeff Madrick. 2016. *How Big Should Our Government Be?* University of California Press.

Baldassarri, Delia and Andrew Gelman. 2008. "Partisans Without Constraint: Political Polarization and Trends in American Public Opinion." *American Journal of Sociology* 114, 408–46.

Barber, Nigel. 2011. "A Cross-National Test of the Uncertainty Hypothesis of Religious Belief." *Cross-Cultural Research* 45, 318–33.

Barnett, Jessica C. and Edward R. Berchick. 2017. "Health Insurance Coverage in the United States: 2016." U.S. Census Bureau.

Barnett, W. Steven. 2013. "Getting the Facts Right on Pre-K and the President's Pre-K Proposal." National Institute for Early Education Research.

Barr, Nicholas. 2001. *The Welfare State as Piggy Bank*. Oxford University Press.

Barro, Robert J. 2011. "How to Really Save the Economy." *New York Times*, September 10.

Bartels, Larry. 2008. *Unequal Democracy*. Russell Sage Foundation and Princeton University Press.

Bartels, Larry. 2013. "Obama Toes the Line." *The Monkey Cage* blog, January 8.

Bartels, Larry and John Zaller. 2000. "Presidential Vote Models: A Recount."

Barth, Erling, Karl O. Moene, and Fredrik Willumsen. 2014. "The Scandinavian Model—an Interpretation." *Journal of Public Economics* 117, 60–72.

Bartik, Timothy. 2011. *Investing in Kids: Early Childhood Programs and Local Economic Development*. Upjohn Institute for Employment Research.

Bartik, Timothy J. 2014. *From Preschool to Prosperity*. Upjohn Institute for Employment Research.

Bartik, Timothy J. 2014. "Grading the Pre-K Evidence." *Investing in Kids*.

Bartlett, Bruce. 2012. *The Benefit and the Burden: Tax Reform—Why We Need It and What It Will Take*. Simon and Schuster.

Bartlett, Bruce. 2012. "Tax Reform That Works: Building a Solid Fiscal Foundation with a VAT." New America Foundation.

Bartlett, Bruce. 2015. "A Conservative Case for the Welfare State." *Dissent*, April 24.

Bauchmüller, Robert, Mette Gørtz, and Astrid Würtz Rasmussen. 2011. "Long-Run Benefits from Universal High-Quality Preschooling." AKF Working Paper.

Baumgartner, Frank R., Jeffrey M. Berry, Marie Hojnacki, David C. Kimball, and Beth L. Leech. 2009. *Lobbying and Policy Change*. University of Chicago Press.

Baumol, William J., Alan S. Blinder, and Edward N. Wolff. 2003. *Downsizing in America*. Russell Sage Foundation.

Ben-Galim, D. and A. Sachraida Dal, eds. 2009. *Now It's Personal: Learning from Welfare-to-Work Approaches Around the World*. Institute for Public Policy Research.

Ben-Shalom, Yonatan, Robert A. Moffitt, and John Karl Scholz. 2011. "An Assessment of Anti-Poverty Programs in the United States." Working Paper 17042. National Bureau of Economic Research.

Bentham, Jeremy. 1843. *The Complete Works of Jeremy Bentham*. Volume 10. Online Library of Liberty.

Bergh, Andreas. 2014. "What Are the Policy Lessons from Sweden? On the Rise, Fall, and Revival of a Capitalist Welfare State." *New Political Economy* 19, 662–94.

Bergmann, Barbara R. 1996. *Saving Our Children from Poverty: What the United States Can Learn from France*. Russell Sage Foundation.

Bergmann, Barbara R. 2006. "A Swedish-Style Welfare State or Basic Income: Which Should Have Priority?" In *Redesigning Redistribution*, edited by Erik Olin Wright, 130–42. Verso.

Berlin, Isaiah. 1958. *Two Concepts of Liberty*. Oxford University.

Berman, Sheri. 2006. *The Primacy of Politics*. Cambridge University Press.

Bernstein, Jared. 2016a. *The Reconnection Agenda: Reuniting Growth and Prosperity*. CreateSpace Independent Publishing Platform.

Bernstein, Jared. 2016b. "We're Going to Need More Tax Revenue. Here's How to Raise It." *The American Prospect*, June 13.

Birnbaum, Simon, Tommy Ferrarini, Kenneth Nelson, and Joakim Palme. 2017. *The Generational Welfare Contract*. Edward Elgar.

Björklund, Anders and Richard B. Freeman. 1987. "Generating Equality and Eliminating Poverty, the Swedish Way." In *The Welfare State in Transition: Reforming the Swedish Model*, edited by Richard B. Freeman, Robert Topel, and Birgitta Swedenborg. University of Chicago Press.

Bjorklund, Eric. 2017. "Out of Many, One? U.S. Sub-National Political Economies in the Post-Welfare Reform Era." *Socio-Economic Review*, doi org/10.1093/ser/mwx018.

Blank, Rebecca M. 1997. *It Takes a Nation: A New Agenda for Fighting Poverty*. Russell Sage Foundation and Princeton University Press.

Blank, Rebecca M. 2002. "Evaluating Welfare Reform in the United States." *Journal of Economic Literature* 40, 1105–1166.

Blank, Rebecca M. 2006. "Was Welfare Reform Successful?" *Economists Voice*, March, 1–5.

Blank, Rebecca M. 2010. "Middle Class in America." U.S. Department of Commerce.

Blinder, Alan S. 2009. "How Many U.S. Jobs Might Be Offshorable?" *World Economics* 10(2), 41–78.

Bloome, Dierdre and Bruce Western. 2011. "Cohort Change and Racial Differences in Educational and Income Mobility." *Social Forces* 90, 375–395.

Board of Governors of the Federal Reserve System. 2015. "Report on the Economic Well-Being of U.S. Households in 2014."

Boarini, Romina and Marco Mira d'Ercole. 2006. "Measures of Material Deprivation in OECD Countries." OECD Social, Employment, and Migration Working Paper 37.

Boaz, David, ed. 1998. *The Libertarian Reader*. Free Press.

Boix, Carles. 1998. "Partisan Governments, the International Economy, and Macroeconomic Policies in Advanced Nations, 1960–93." *World Politics* 53, 38–73.

Bonica, Adam. 2018. "What's Good for Democracy Is Also Good for Democrats." *New York Times*, July 26.

Bonoli, Giuliano, Bea Cantillon, and Wim Van Lancker. 2017. "Social Investment and the Matthew Effect: Limits to a Strategy." In *The Uses of Social Investment*, edited by Anton Hemerijck, 66–76. Oxford University Press.

Bourassa, Steven C., Donald R. Haurin, Patric H. Hedershott, and Martin Hoesli. 2015. "Mortgage Interest Deductions and Homeownership: An International Survey." Swiss Finance Institute Research Paper 12–06.

Boushey, Heather and Bridget Ansel. 2016. "Working by the Hour: The Economic Consequences of Unpredictable Scheduling Practices." Washington Center on Equitable Growth.

Boushey, Heather, Chauna Brocht, Bethney Gundersen, and Jared Bernstein. 2001. *Hardships in America*. Economic Policy Institute.

Bowen, William G. and Derek Bok. 1998. *The Shape of the River*. Princeton University Press.

Bradbury, Bruce, Miles Corak, Jane Waldfogel, and Elizabeth Washbrook. 2015. *Too Many Children Left Behind*. Russell Sage Foundation.

Bradbury, Bruce, Markus Jäntti, and Lena Lindahl. 2017. "Labour Income, Social Transfers, and Child Poverty." Working Paper 707. Luxembourg Income Study.

Brady, David. 2009. *Rich Democracies, Poor People*. Oxford University Press.

Brady, David, Ryan M. Finnigan, and Sabine Hübgen. 2016. "Rethinking the Risks of Poverty: A Framework for Analyzing Prevalences and Penalties." *American Sociological Review* 123, 740–86.

Brady, David, Evelyne Huber, and John D. Stephens. 2016. "Comparative Welfare States Data Set," version 2014. Luxembourg Income Study.

Brennan Center. 2018a. "Automatic Voter Registration." brennancenter.org.

Brennan Center. 2018b. "Money in Politics." brennancenter.org.

Brennan Center. 2018c. "Redistricting." brennancenter.org.

Brewer, Kathryne B., Hans Oh, and Shilpi Sharma. 2014. "'Crowding In' or 'Crowding Out'? An Examination of the Impact of the Welfare State on Generalized Social Trust." *International Journal of Social Welfare* 23, 61–68.

Broda, Christian and John Romalis. 2008. "Inequality and Prices: Does China Benefit the Poor in America?" conference.nber.org/conferences/2008/si2008/ITI/romalis.pdf.

Brooks, Clem and Jeff Manza. 2007. *Why Welfare States Persist: The Importance of Public Opinion in Democracies*. University of Chicago Press.

Brooks, David. 2012. "The Party of Work." *New York Times*, November 8.

Brooks-Gunn, Jeanne. 2003. "What We Can Expect from Early Education Childhood Intervention Programs." Society for Research in Child Development.

Brooks-Gunn, Jeanne, Wen-Jui Han, and Jane Waldfogel. 2010. "First-Year Maternal Employment and Child Development in the First Seven Years." *Monographs of the Society for Research in Child Development* 75(2), vii–145.

Brown, Alessio J. G. and Johannes Koettl. 2015. "Active Labor Market Programs—Employment Gain or Fiscal Drain?" *IZA Journal of Labor Economics* 4, 1–36.

Brown, Cynthia G., Donna Cooper, Juliana Herman, Melissa Lazarín, Michael Linden, Sasha Post, and Neera Tanden. 2013. "Investing in Our Children: A Plan to Expand Access to Preschool and Child Care." Center for American Progress.

Browne, Matt, John Halpin, and Ruy Teixeira. 2011. "Building a Progressive Center: Political Strategy and Demographic Change in America." Center for American Progress.

Buchanan, James M. 1988. "The Economic Theory of Politics Reborn." *Challenge* March–April, 4–10.

Buffie, Nick. 2017. "Overhead Costs for Private Health Insurance Keep Rising, Even as Costs Fall for Other Types of Insurance." Center for Economic Policy Research.

Burkhauser, Richard V. and Mary C. Daly. 2012. "Social Security Disability Insurance: Time for Fundamental Change." *Journal of Public Policy Analysis and Management* 31, 454–61.

Burkhauser, Richard V., Jeff Larrimore, and Kosali I. Simon. 2011. "A 'Second Opinion' on the Economic Health of the American Middle Class." Working Paper 17164. National Bureau of Economic Research.

Burns, Alexander. 2018. "With $30 Million, an Obscure Democratic Group Blitzes House Races." *New York Times*, November 1.

Burtless, Gary. 1986. "The Work Response to a Guaranteed Income: A Survey of Experimental Evidence." In *Lessons from the Income Maintenance Experiments*, edited by Alicia H. Munnell, 22–59. Federal Reserve Bank of Boston and Brookings Institution.

Calnitsky, David and Jonathan P. Latner. 2017. "Basic Income in a Small Town: Understanding the Elusive Effects on Work." *Social Problems* 64, 373–397.

Cameron, David R. 1978. "The Expansion of the Public Economy: A Comparative Analysis." *American Political Science Review* 72, 1243–61.

Campbell, Andrea Louise. 2007. "Universalism, Targeting, and Participation." In *Remaking America: Democracy and Public Policy in an Age of Inequality*, edited by Joe Soss, Jacob S. Hacker, and Suzanne Mettler. Russell Sage Foundation.

Campbell, Andrea Louise. 2011. "The 10 Percent Solution." *Democracy*, Winter.

Campbell, Andrea Louise. 2014. *Trapped in America's Safety Net*. University of Chicago Press.

Campbell, John L., John A. Hall, and Ove K. Pedersen, eds. 2006. *National Identity and the Varieties of Capitalism: The Danish Experience*. McGill-Queen's University Press.

Campbell, John L. and Ove K. Pedersen. 2007. "The Varieties of Capitalism and Hybrid Success: Denmark in the Global Economy." *Comparative Political Studies* 40, 307–32.

Caner, Asa and Edward Wolff. 2004. "Asset Poverty in the United States, 1984-1999." *Challenge* 47(1), 5–52.

Cantillon, Bea and Frank Vandenbroucke, eds. 2013. *Reconciling Work and Poverty Reduction*. Oxford University Press.

Carasso, Adam, Gillian Reynolds, and C. Eugene Steurle. 2008. "How Much Does the Federal Government Spend to Promote Economic Mobility and for Whom?" Economic Mobility Project.

Carbon Tax Center. 2018. "FAQs."

Card, David, Jochen Kluve, and Andrea Weber. 2018. "What Works? A Meta Analysis of Recent Active Labor Market Program Evaluations." *Journal of the European Economic Association* 16, 894–931.

Card, David and Alan B. Krueger. 1995. *Myth and Measurement: The New Economics of the Minimum Wage*. Princeton University Press.

Carey, Kevin. 2015. "A Quiet Revolution in Helping Lift the Burden of Student Debt." *New York Times*, January 24.

Carneiro, Pedro and Rita Ginja. 2014. "Long-Term Impacts of Compensatory Preschool on Health and Behavior: Evidence from Head Start." *American Economic Journal: Economic Policy* 6(4), 135–73.

Carpenter, Dick M., Lisa Knepper, Angela E. Erickson, and John K. Ross. 2012. *License to Work: A National Study of the Burdens from Occupational Licensing*. Institute for Justice.

Carroll, Aaron E. 2016. "When Having Insurance Still Leaves You Dangerously Uncovered." *New York Times*, November 28.

Carroll, Aaron E. 2017. "The Real Reason the U.S. Has Employer-Sponsored Health Insurance." *New York Times: The Upshot*, September 5.

Carruthers, Celeste and William Fox. 2016. "Aid for All: College Coaching, Financial Aid, and Post-Secondary Persistence in Tennessee." *Economics of Education Review* 51, 97–112.

Cascio, Elizabeth U. 2017a. "Does Universal Preschool Hit the Target? Program Access and Preschool Impacts." Working Paper 23215. National Bureau of Economic Research.

Cascio, Elizabeth U. 2017b. "Public Investments in Child Care." In *The 51%: Driving Growth through Women's Economic Participation*, edited by Diane Whitmore Schanzenbach and Ryan Nunn. Brookings Institution.

Cass, Oren. 2018. *The Once and Future Worker*. Encounter Books.

Castles, Francis G. 2003. "The World Turned Upside Down: Below Replacement Fertility, Changing Preferences and Family-Friendly Public Policy in 21 OECD Countries." *Journal of European Social Policy* 13, 209–27.

Castles, Francis G., Stephan Leibfried, Jane Lewis, Herbert Obinger, and Christopher Pierson, eds. 2010. *The Oxford Handbook of the Welfare State*. Oxford University Press.

Cengiz, Doruk, Arindrajit Dube, Attila Lindner, and Ben Zipperer. 2019. "The Effect of Minimum Wages on the Total Number of Jobs: Evidence from the United States Using a Bunching Estimator." Working Paper 25434. National Bureau of Economic Research.

Center on Budget and Policy Priorities. 2014. "Policy Basics: State Earned Income Tax Credits." cbpp.org.

Center on Budget and Policy Priorities. 2017. "Policy Basics: Federal Rental Assistance." cbpp.org.

Center on Budget and Policy Priorities. 2018. "Policy Basics: The Supplemental Nutrition Assistance Program (SNAP)." cbpp.org.

Chaudry, Ajay, et al. 2011. "Child Care Choices of Low-Income Working Families." Urban Institute.

Chaudry, Ajay, Taryn Morrissey, Christina Weiland, and Hirokazu Yoshikawa. 2017. *Cradle to Kindergarten*. Russell Sage Foundation.

Cherlin, Andrew. 2009. *The Marriage-Go-Round*. Knopf.

Cherlin, Andrew. 2014. *Love's Labor Lost: The Rise and Fall of the Working-Class Family in America*. Russell Sage Foundation.

Chetty, Raj, et al. 2014. "Is the United States Still the Land of Opportunity? Recent Trends in Intergenerational Mobility." Working Paper 19844. National Bureau of Economic Research.

Chikhale, Nisha. 2016. "A Child Tax Credit Primer. " Washington Center on Equitable Growth.

Chikhale, Nisha. 2017. "U.S. Homeownership Tax Policies Are Expensive and Inequitable." Washington Center for Equitable Growth.

ChildCare Aware of America. 2012. "Parents and the High Cost of Child Care." childcareaware. org.

Chingos, Matthew M. 2016. "Who Would Benefit Most from Free College? " Brookings Institution.

Chozick, Amy. 2015. "Hillary Clinton Proposes Tax Credit for Businesses That Share Profits." *New York Times*, July 16.

Christoffersen, Henrik, Michelle Beyeler, Reiner Eichenberger, Peter Nannestad, and Martin Paldam. 2014. *The Good Society: A Comparative Study of Denmark and Switzerland*. Springer.

Chubb, John E. and Terry M. Moe. 1990. *Politics, Markets, and America's Schools*. Brookings Institution Press.

Cogan, John F. 2017. *The High Cost of Good Intentions: A History of U.S. Federal Entitlement Programs*. Stanford University Press.

Cohen, Patricia. 2017. "Immigrants Keep Iowa Meatpacking Town Alive and Growing." *New York Times*, May 29.

Colantone, Italo and Piero Stanig. 2018. "The Trade Origins of Economic Nationalism: Import Competition and Voting Behavior in Western Europe." *American Journal of Political Science*, doi 10.1111/ajps.12358.

Collier, Paul. 2007. *The Bottom Billion*. Oxford University Press.

Collins, Sara R., Petra W. Rasmussen, Michelle M. Doty, and Sophie Beutel. 2015. "The Rise in Health Care Coverage and Affordability Since Health Reform Took Effect: Findings from the Commonwealth Fund Biennial Health Insurance Survey, 2014." The Commonwealth Fund.

Collinson, Robert, Ingrid Gould Ellen, and Jens Ludwig. 2015. "Low-Income Housing Policy." Working Paper 21071. National Bureau of Economic Research.

Conger, Rand D., Katherine J. Conger, and Monica J. Martin. 2010. "Socioeconomic Status, Family Processes, and Individual Development." *Journal of Marriage and the Family* 72, 685–704.

Cooper, Donna. 2012. *Meeting the Infrastructure Imperative*. Center for American Progress.

Cooper, Kerris and Kitty Stewart. 2013. *Does Money Affect Children's Outcomes? A Systematic Review*. Joseph Rowntree Foundation.

Corak, Miles, Matthew J. Lindquist, and Bhashkar Mazumder. 2014. "A Comparison of Upward and Downward Intergenerational Mobility in Canada, Sweden, and the United States." *Labour Economics* 30, 185–200.

Corporation for Enterprise Development. 2013. "Assets and Opportunity Scorecard." prosperitynow.org.

Cowell, Alan. 2006. "An Economy with Safety Features, Sort of Like a Volvo." *New York Times*, May 10.

Cowen, Tyler. 2011. *The Great Stagnation*. Penguin.

Cowen, Tyler. 2016a. "Denmark's Nice, Yes, But Danes Live Better in U.S." *Bloomberg View*, August 16.

Cowen, Tyler. 2016b. "My Second Thoughts About Universal Basic Income." *Bloomberg View*, October 27.

Cox, W. Michael and Richard Alm. 1999. *Myths of Rich and Poor*. Basic Books.

Crimmins, Eileen M., Samuel H. Preston, and Barney Cohen, eds. 2011. *Explaining Divergent Levels of Longevity in High-Income Countries*. National Academies Press.

Currie, Janet. 2011. "Inequality at Birth: Some Causes and Consequences." *American Economic Review* 100 (Papers and Proceedings), 1–22.

Dagan, David and Steven M. Teles. 2016. "Conservatives and Criminal Justice." *National Affairs*, Spring, 118–36.

Dahl, Gordon B., Andreas Ravndal Kostøl, and Magne Mogstad 2014. "Family Welfare Cultures." *Quarterly Journal of Economics* 129, 1711–52.

Dahl, Robert A. 1985. *A Preface to Economic Democracy*. University of California Press.

Danziger, Sandra K., Sheldon Danziger, Kristin S. Seefeldt, and H. Luke Shaefer. 2016. "From Welfare to a Work-Based Safety Net: An Incomplete Transition." *Journal of Policy Analysis and Management* 35, 231–38.

Danziger, Sheldon and Christopher Wimer. 2014. "Poverty." *Pathways: The Poverty and Inequality Report*, 13–18.

Davidson, Adam. 2016. "Is College Tuition Really Too High?" *New York Times*, September 12.

Davis, Jonathan and Bhashkar Mazumder. 2017. "The Decline in Intergenerational Mobility After 1980." Working Paper 2017-05. Federal Reserve Bank of Chicago.

Deaton, Angus. 2010. "Instruments, Randomization, and Learning about Development." *Journal of Economic Literature* 48, 424–55.

Deaton, Angus. 2013. *The Great Escape: Health, Wealth, and the Origins of Inequality*. Princeton University Press.

DeLong, J. Bradford. 2012. "The Changing Structure of Prices Since 1960." *Grasping Reality with Both Invisible Hands* blog, December 8.

DeLong, J. Bradford. 2015. "The Scary Debate over Secular Stagnation." *Milken Institute Review*, Fourth Quarter, 34–51.

Deming, David. 2009. "Early Childhood Intervention and Life-Cycle Skill Development: Evidence from Head Start." *American Economic Journal: Applied Economics* 1(3), 111–34.

DeParle, Jason. 2004. *American Dream*. Penguin.

DeParle, Jason. 2012. "Welfare Limits Left Poor Adrift as Recession Hit." *New York Times*, April 7.

Desmond, Matthew. 2016. *Evicted*. Crown Books.

DiIulio, Jr., John J. 2014. *Bring Back the Bureaucrats*. Templeton Press.

Dollar, David, Tatjana Kleineberg, and Aart Kraay. 2016. "Growth Still Is Good for the Poor." *European Economic Review* 81, 68–85.

Dollar, David and Aart Kraay. 2002. "Growth is Good for the Poor." *Journal of Economic Growth* 7, 195–225.

Dolvik, Jon Erik. 2014. "The Social Foundations of the Nordic Models: A Review of the Labour and Welfare Regime's Evolution and Distinctions." *NordMod2030: Summaries of Project Reports*, 7–14. Fafo.

Douthat, Ross. 2010. "Introduction to the Background Edition" of Robert Nisbet's *The Quest for Community*. Intercollegiate Studies Institute.

Douthat, Ross and Reihan Salam. 2008. *Grand New Party*. Doubleday.

Downey, Douglas B., Paul T. von Hippel, and Beckett A. Broh. 2004. "Are Schools the Great Equalizer? Cognitive Inequality During the Summer Months and the School Year." *American Sociological Review* 69, 613–35.

Drutman, Lee. 2012. "Why Money Still Matters." *The Monkey Cage* blog, November 14.

Dube, Arindrajit. 2013. "Designing Thoughtful Minimum Wage Policy at the State and Local Levels." Hamilton Project.

Dube, Arindrajit, T. William Lester, and Michael Reich. 2010. "Minimum Wage Effects Across State Borders: Estimates Using Contiguous Counties." *Review of Economics and Statistics* 92, 945–964.

Duncan, Greg J. and Katherine Magnuson. 2013. "Investing in Preschool Programs." *Journal of Economic Perspectives* 27(2), 109–32.

Duncan, Greg J., Kathleen M. Ziol-Guest, and Ariel Kalil. 2010. "Early-Childhood Poverty and Adult Attainment, Behavior, and Health." *Child Development* 81, 306–25.

Dynan, Karen. 2010. "The Income Rollercoaster: Rising Income Volatility and Its Implications." *Pathways*, Spring, 2–6.

Dynan, Karen E., Douglas W. Elmendorf, and Daniel E. Sichel. 2012. "The Evolution of Household Income Volatility." *B.E. Journal of Economic Analysis and Policy* 12(2).

Dynarski, Mark. 2017. "What We Don't Know About High Schools Can Hurt Us." Brookings Institution.

Dynarski, Susan. 2016a. "America Can Fix Its Student Loan Crisis. Just Ask Australia." *New York Times*, July 9.

Dynarski, Susan. 2016b. "What Does Cutting Rates on Student Loans Do?" Brookings Institution.

Dynarski, Susan. 2018. "At Elite Colleges, Racial Diversity Requires Affirmative Action." *New York Times*, September 28.

Easterbrook, Gregg. 2003. *The Progress Paradox*. Random House.

Eberstadt, Nicholas. 2008. "The Poverty of the Official Poverty Rate." American Enterprise Institute.

Ebbinghaus, Bernhard. 2010. "Unions and Employers." In *The Oxford Handbook of the Welfare State*, edited by Francis G. Castles, Stephan Leibfried, Jane Lewis, Herbert Obinger, and Christopher Pierson, 196–210. Oxford University Press.

Economic Innovation Group. 2016. "The New Map of Economic Growth and Recovery." eig.org.

Economic Mobility Project. 2012. "Pursuing the American Dream: Economic Mobility Across Generations." Pew Charitable Trusts.

Economist, The. 2018. "The Centre Can Hold." September 22.

Edelman, Peter. 2012. *So Rich, So Poor*. New Press.

Edin, Kathryn and Maria J. Kefalas. 2005. *Promises I Can Keep: Why Poor Women Put Motherhood Before Marriage.* University of California Press.

Edin, Kathryn and Laura Lein. 1997. *Making Ends Meet.* Russell Sage Foundation.

Edin, Kathryn J. and Luke K. Shaefer. 2015. *$2.00 a Day: Living on Almost Nothing in America.* Houghton Mifflin.

Ehrenreich, Barbara. 2001. *Nickel and Dimed: On (Not) Getting By in America.* Henry Holt and Company.

Ellis, Christopher and James A. Stimson. 2012. *Ideology in America.* Cambridge University Press.

Ellwood, David T. 1988. *Poor Support.* Basic Books.

Ellwood, David T. and Christopher Jencks. 2004. "The Uneven Spread of Single-Parent Families: What Do We Know? Where Do We Look for Answers?" In *Social Inequality,* edited by Kathryn M. Neckerman. Russell Sage Foundation.

Elmendorf, Doug. 2014. "Revisions to CBO's Projections of Federal Health Care Spending." Congressional Budget Office.

England, Paula and Kathryn Edin, eds. 2009. *Unmarried Couples with Children.* Russell Sage Foundation.

England, Paula, Elizabeth McClintock, and Emily Fitzgibbons Shafer. 2012. "Birth Control Use and Early, Unintended Births: Evidence for a Class Gradient." In *Social Class and Changing Families in an Unequal America,* edited by Marcia Carlson and Paula England.

England, Paula, Lawrence L. Wu, and Emily Fitzgibbons Shafer. 2012. "Cohort Trends in Premarital First Births: What Roles for Premarital Conceptions and the Retreat from Preconception and Postconception Marriage?" New York University and Harvard University.

Erikson, Robert S., Michael B. MacKuen, and James A. Stimson. 2002. *The Macro Polity.* Cambridge University Press.

Ermisch, John, Markus Jäntti, and Timothy Smeeding, eds. 2012. *From Parents to Children: The Intergenerational Transmission of Advantage.* Russell Sage Foundation.

Esping-Andersen, Gøsta. 1990. *The Three Worlds of Welfare Capitalism.* Princeton University Press.

Esping-Andersen, Gøsta. 2009. *The Incomplete Revolution.* Polity.

Esping-Andersen, Gøsta, with Duncan Gallie, Anton Hemerijck, and John Myles. 2002. *Why We Need a New Welfare State.* Oxford University Press.

Esping-Andersen, Gøsta, Irwin Garfinkel, Wen-Jui Han, Katherine Magnuson, Sander Wagner, and Jane Waldfogel. 2012. "Child Care and School Performance in Denmark and the United States." *Children and Youth Services Review* 34, 576–89.

Eurostat. 2017. "Material Deprivation Statistics." ec.europa.eu.

Fair, Ray. 2012. *Predicting Presidential Elections and Other Things.* 2nd edition. Stanford University Press.

Families USA. 2009. "Americans at Risk: One in Three Uninsured." familiesusa.org.

Farber, Henry S. 2010. "Job Loss and the Decline in Job Security in the United States." In *Labor in the New Economy,* edited by Katharine G. Abraham, James R. Spletzer, and Michael Harper. University of Chicago Press.

Farrell, Chris. 2016. "No 401(k)? Your State May Come to the Rescue." *NextAvenue.*

Fasani, Francesco, Tommaso Frattini, and Luigi Minale. 2018. "(The Struggle for) Refugee Integration into the Labour Market: Evidence from Europe." Discussion Paper 11333. Institute of Labor Economics (IZA).

Feingold, Russ. 2013. "Building a Permanent Majority for Reform." *Democracy,* Winter.

Ferguson, Thomas and Joel Rogers. 1986. *Right Turn: The Decline of the Democrats and the Future of American Politics.* Hill and Wang.

Ferrarini, Tommy and Ann-Zofie Duvander. 2010. "Earner-Carer Model at the Cross-Roads: Reforms and Outcomes of Sweden's Family Policy in Comparative Perspective." *International Journal of Health Services* 40, 373–98.

Ferrarini, Tommy, Kenneth Nelson, and Joakim Palme. 2016. "Social Transfers and Poverty in Middle- and High-Income Countries." *Global Social Policy* 16, 22–46.

Fingerhut, Hannah. 2017. "More Americans Favor Raising Than Lowering Tax Rates on Corporations, High Household Incomes." Pew Research Center, September 27.

Fischer, Claude S. 2010. *Made in America*. University of Chicago Press.

Fischer, Will. 2014. "Research Shows Housing Vouchers Reduce Hardship and Provide Platform for Long-Term Gains Among Children." Center on Budget and Policy Priorities.

Fishman, Noam and Alyssa Davis. 2017. "Americans Still See Big Government as Top Threat." Gallup.

Fligstein, Neil and Taek-Jin Shin. 2003. "The Shareholder-Value Society." *Indicators*.

Ford, Martin. 2015. *Rise of the Robots: Technology and the Threat of a Jobless Future*. Basic Books.

Fox, Justin. 2018. "Why German Corporate Boards Include Workers." *Bloomberg Opinion*, August 24.

Fox, Liana, Irwin Garfinkel, Neeraj Kaushal, Jane Waldfogel, and Christopher Wimer. 2014. "Waging War on Poverty: Historical Trends in Poverty Using the Supplemental Poverty Measure." Working Paper 19789. National Bureau of Economic Research.

Frakt, Austin. 2018. "Is Medicare for All the Answer to Sky-High Administrative Costs?" *New York Times*, October 16.

Frank, Robert H. 2008. "Progressive Consumption Tax." *Democracy*.

Frank, Robert H. 2014. "Let's Try a Basic Income and Public Work." Cato Institute.

Frank, Thomas. 2004. *What's the Matter with Kansas?* Metropolitan Books.

Freeman, Richard B. and James L. Medoff. 1984. *What Do Unions Do?* Basic Books.

Friedman, Benjamin M. 2005. *The Moral Consequences of Economic Growth*. Knopf.

Friedman, Milton. 1962. *Capitalism and Freedom*. University of Chicago Press.

Friedman, Milton and Rose Friedman. 1979. *Free to Choose*. Harcourt Brace Jovanovich.

Frum, David. 2008. "The Vanishing Republican Voter." *New York Times*, September 7.

Fukuyama, Francis. 1995. *Trust: The Social Virtues and the Creation of Prosperity*. The Free Press.

Galbraith, John Kenneth. 1998 (1958). *The Affluent Society*. 40th anniversary edition. Houghton Mifflin.

Galbraith, John Kenneth. 2007 (1967). *The New Industrial State*. Princeton University Press.

Gallup. 2018. "Taxes." In Depth: Topics A to Z.

Galston, William A. 2001. "What About Reciprocity? " In *What's Wrong with a Free Lunch?* edited by Joshua Cohen and Joel Rogers, 29–33. Beacon Press.

Garfinkel, Irwin, Lee Rainwater, and Timothy Smeeding. 2010. *Wealth and Welfare States*. Oxford University Press.

Gelbach, Jonah B. and Lant H. Pritchett. 1995. "Does More for the Poor Mean Less for the Poor?" Working Paper 1523. Policy Research Department, Poverty and Human Resources Division. World Bank.

Geoghegan, Thomas. 2011. "Get Radical: Raise Social Security." *New York Times*, June 19.

Ghilarducci, Teresa. 2008. *When I'm Sixty-Four*. Princeton University Press.

Gilens, Martin. 1999. *Why Americans Hate Welfare*. University of Chicago Press.

Gilens, Martin. 2012. *Affluence and Influence*. Princeton University Press.

Ginsburg, Helen. 1983. *Full Employment and Public Policy: The United States and Sweden*. D.C. Heath.

Giuliano, Paola and Antonio Spilimbergo. 2014. "Growing Up in a Recession." *Review of Economic Studies* 81, 787–817.

Glaeser, Edward. 2011. *Triumph of the City*. Penguin.

Golden, Lonnie. 2015. "Irregular Work Scheduling and Its Consequences." Briefing Paper 394. Economic Policy Institute.

Goldstein, Amy. 2017. *Janesville: An American Story*. Simon and Schuster.

Goodin, Robert E., Bruce Headey, Ruud Muffels, and Henk-Jan Dirven. 1999. *The Real Worlds of Welfare Capitalism*. Cambridge University Press.

Goodman, Peter S. 2017. "The Robots Are Coming, and Sweden Will Be Fine." *New York Times*, December 27.

Goodwin, Matthew. 2018. "Why a Far-Right Party with White Supremacist Roots Is on the Rise—in Sweden." *Washington Post: The Monkey Cage*, September 10.

Gordon, Robert G. 2016. *The Rise and Fall of American Growth*. Princeton University Press.

Gosselin, Peter. 2008. *High Wire*. Basic Books.

Gosselin, Peter and Seth Zimmerman. 2008. "Trends in Income Volatility and Risk, 1970–2004." Urban Institute.

Gottschalk, Peter. 1998. "The Impact of Changes in Public Employment on Low-Wage Labor Markets." In *Generating Jobs: How to Increase Demand for Less-Skilled Workers*, edited by Richard B. Freeman and Peter Gottschalk. Russell Sage Foundation.

Gough, Ian. 1996. "Social Welfare and Competitiveness." *New Political Economy* 1, 209–32.

Goul Andersen, Jørgen. 2007. "The Danish Welfare State as 'Politics for Markets': Combining Equality and Competitiveness in a Global Economy." *New Political Economy* 12, 71–78.

Gould, Elise, Hilary Hething, Natalie Sabadish, and Nicholas Finio. 2013. "What Families Need to Get By." Issue Brief 368. Economic Policy Institute.

Graetz, Michael J. and Jerry L. Mashaw. 1999. *True Security: Rethinking American Social Insurance*. Yale University Press.

Greenstein, Robert. 1991. "Universal and Targeted Approaches to Relieving Poverty: An Alternative View." In *The Urban Underclass*, edited by Christopher Jencks and Paul E. Peterson. Brookings Institution.

Greenstein, Robert. 2017. "Universal Basic Income May Sound Attractive But, If It Occurred, Would Likelier Increase Poverty Than Reduce It." Center on Budget and Policy Priorities.

Greenstein, Robert and CBPP Staff. 2012. "For Major Low-Income Programs, More Than 90 Percent Goes to Beneficiaries." Center on Budget and Policy Priorities.

Gregg, Paul and Richard Layard. 2009. "A Job Guarantee." Centre for Economic Performance. London School of Economics.

Guiso, Luigi, Helios Herrera, Massimo Morelli, and Tommaso Sonno. 2017. "Demand and Supply of Populism." Einaudi Institute for Economics and Finance.

Guvenen, Faith, Greg Kaplan, Jae Song, and Justin Weidner. 2017. "Lifetime Incomes in the United States over Six Decades." Working Paper 23371. National Bureau of Economic Research.

Hacker, Jacob S. 2004. "Privatizing Risk without Privatizing the Welfare State: The Hidden Politics of Social Policy Retrenchment in the United States." *American Political Science Review* 98, 243–60.

Hacker, Jacob S. 2006. *The Great Risk Shift*. Oxford University Press.

Hacker, Jacob S. 2016. "Stronger Policy, Stronger Politics." *The American Prospect*, October 17.

Hacker, Jacob S. 2018. "The Road to Medicare for Everyone." *The American Prospect*, January 3.

Hacker, Jacob S., Gregory A. Huber, Austin Nichols, Philipp Rehm, Mark Schlesinger, Rob Valletta, Stuart Craig. 2013. "The Economic Security Index: A New Measure for Research and Policy Analysis." *Review of Income and Wealth*, doi 10.1111/roiw.12053.

Hacker, Jacob S. and Elizabeth Jacobs. 2008. "The Rising Instability of American Family Incomes, 1969–2004." Economic Policy Institute.

Hacker, Jacob S. and Paul Pierson. 2010. *Winner-Take-All Politics*. Simon and Schuster.

Hacker, Jacob S. and Paul Pierson. 2016. *American Amnesia*. Simon and Schuster.

Hacker, Jacob S., Philipp Rehm, and Mark Schlesinger. 2010. "Standing on Shaky Ground." Economic Security Index.

Hall, Peter A. and Daniel W. Gingerich. 2009. "Varieties of Capitalism and Institutional Complementarities in the Political Economy: An Empirical Analysis." *British Journal of Political Science* 39, 449–82.

Hall, Peter A. and Michele Lamont, eds. 2009. *Successful Societies*. Cambridge University Press.

Hall, Peter A. and David Soskice. 2001. "An Introduction to Varieties of Capitalism." In *Varieties of Capitalism*, edited by Peter A. Hall and David Soskice, 1–68. Oxford University Press.

Halpern-Meekin, Sarah, Kathryn Edin, Laura Tach, and Jennifer Sykes. 2014. *It's Not Like I'm Poor: How Working Families Make Ends Meet in a Post-Welfare World*. University of California Press.

Hamel, Liz, et al. 2016. "The Burden of Medical Debt: Results from the Kaiser Family Foundation/ *New York Times* Medical Bills Survey." Kaiser Family Foundation.

Hanuer, Nick. 2016. "Confronting the Parasite Economy." *The American Prospect*, May 16.

Hanushek, Eric A., John F. Kain, Jacob M. Markman, and Steven G. Rivkin. 2001. "Does Peer Ability Affect Student Achievement?" Working Paper 8502. National Bureau of Economic Research.

Harding, David J., Christopher Jencks, Leonard M. Lopoo, and Susan E. Mayer. 2005. "The Changing Effect of Family Background on the Incomes of American Adults." In *Unequal Chances: Family Background and Economic Success*, edited by Samuel Bowles, Herbert Gintis, and Melissa Osborne Groves. Russell Sage Foundation and Princeton University Press.

Harrington, Michael. 1962. *The Other America: Poverty in the United States*. Simon and Schuster.

Harvey, Philip. 2011. "Back to Work: A Public Jobs Proposal for Economic Recovery." Demos.

Haskins, Ron and Greg Margolis. 2014. *Show Me the Evidence: Obama's Fight for Rigor and Results in Social Policy*. Brookings Institution.

Haskins, Ron and Isabel V. Sawhill. 2009. *Creating an Opportunity Society*. Brookings Institution.

Hauser, Robert M., John Robert Warren, Min-Hsiung Huang, and Wendy Y. Carter. 2000. "Occupational Status, Education, and Social Mobility in the Meritocracy." In *Meritocracy and Economic Inequality*, edited by Kenneth Arrow, Samuel Bowles, and Steven Durlauf. Princeton University Press.

Haveman, Robert. 2013. "Do Housing Vouchers Work?" *Pathways*, Spring, 15–17.

Havnes, Tarjei and Magne Mogstad. 2015. "Is Universal Child Care Leveling the Playing Field?" *Journal of Public Economics* 127, 100–14.

Hayek, Friedrich A. 1960. *The Constitution of Liberty*. University of Chicago Press.

Hayek, Friedrich A. 1979. *Law, Legislation, and Liberty*. Volume 3. University of Chicago Press.

Hays, Sharon. 2003. *Flat Broke with Children*. Oxford University Press.

Heckman, James J. 2008. "Schools, Skills, and Synapses." Working Paper 14064. National Bureau of Economic Research.

Hemerijck, Anton. 2013. *Changing Welfare States*. Oxford University Press.

Hemerijck, Anton, ed. 2017. *The Uses of Social Investment*. Oxford University Press.

Herbst, Chris M. 2013. "Universal Child Care, Maternal Employment, and Children's Long-Run Outcomes: Evidence from the U.S. Lanham Act of 1940." Discussion Paper 7846. Institute for the Study of Labor (IZA).

Heymann, Jody, Hye Jin Rho, John Schmitt, and Alison Earle. 2009. "Contagion Nation: A Comparison of Paid Sick Day Policies in 22 Countries." Center for Economic Development Research.

Hibbs, Douglas. 2009. "The Bread and Peace Model Applied to the 2008 US Presidential Election." douglas-hibbs.com.

Hibbs, Douglas. 2012. "The Partisan Division of House Seats in 2012: Implications of the 'Bread and Incumbency' Model." douglas-hibbs.com.

Hick, Rod and Tania Burchardt. 2016. "Capability Deprivation." In *Oxford Handbook of the Social Science of Poverty*, edited by David Brady and Linda M. Burton, 75–92. Oxford University Press.

Hicks, Alexander. 1999. *Social Democracy and Welfare Capitalism*. Cornell University Press.

Hicks, Alexander and Lane Kenworthy. 1998. "Cooperation and Political Economic Performance in Affluent Democratic Capitalism." *American Journal of Sociology* 103, 1631–72.

Hills, John. 2017. *Good Times, Bad Times: The Welfare Myth of Them and Us*. Revised edition. Policy Press.

Hirschman, Albert O. 1991. *The Rhetoric of Reaction*. Harvard University Press.

Hochschild, Arlie Russell. 2016. *Strangers in Their Own Land: Anger and Mourning on the American Right*. New Press.

Holmberg, Susan R. 2017. "Fighting Short-Termism with Worker Power." Roosevelt Institute.

Holzer, Harry. 2015. "Creating New Pathways into Middle Class Jobs." Progressive Policy Institute.

Hooijer, Gerda and Georg Picot. 2015. "European Welfare States and Migrant Poverty: The Institutional Determinants of Disadvantage." *Comparative Political Studies* 48, 1879–904.

Horowitz, Sara. 2015. "Help for the Way We Work Now." *New York Times*, September 7.

Hout, Mike. 2018. "Occupational Change in a Generation in the United States, 1994–2016." Population Center, New York University.

Howard, Christopher. 2007. *The Welfare State Nobody Knows.* Princeton University Press.

Howard, Christopher. 2011. "Party Politics and the American Welfare State." In *What's Left of the Left?*, edited by James Cronin, George Ross, and James Shoch, 188–209. Duke University Press.

Howell, David R., Kea Fiedler, and Stephanie Luce. 2016. "What's the Right Minimum Wage?" Washington Center for Equitable Growth.

Huang, Chye-Ching. 2012. "Recent Studies Find Raising Taxes on High-Income Households Would Not Harm the Economy." Center on Budget and Policy Priorities.

Huo, Jingjing, Moira Nelson, and John D. Stephens. 2008. "Decommodification and Activation in Social Democratic Policy: Resolving the Paradox." *Journal of European Social Policy* 18, 5–20.

Huber, Evelyne, Jingling Huo, and John D. Stephens. 2017. "Power, Markets, and Top Income Shares." *Socio-Economic Review*, doi 10.1093/ser/mwx027.

Huber, Evelyne, Charles Ragin, and John D. Stephens. 1993. "Social Democracy, Christian Democracy, Constitutional Structure and the Welfare State." *American Journal of Sociology* 99, 711–49.

Huber, Evelyne and John D. Stephens. 2001. *Development and Crisis of the Welfare State.* Chicago: University of Chicago Press.

Huerta, Maria del Carmen, et al. 2011. "Early Maternal Employment and Child Development in Five OECD Countries." OECD Social, Employment, and Migration Working Paper 118.

Inglehart, Ronald F. 2018. *Cultural Evolution.* Cambridge University Press.Isaacson, Walter. 2011. *Steve Jobs.* Simon and Schuster.

Isen, Adam and Betsey Stevenson. 2010. *Women's Education and Family Behavior: Trends in Marriage, Divorce, and Fertility.* Wharton School, University of Pennsylvania.

Iversen, Torben and David Soskice. 2019. *Democracy and Prosperity.* Princeton University Press.

Jacob, Brian and Jens Ludwig. 2008. "Improving Educational Outcomes for Poor Children." Working Paper 14550. National Bureau of Economic Research.

Jacobs, Jerry A. and Kathleen Gerson. 2004. *The Time Divide.* Harvard University Press.

Jacobs, Lawrence R. et al. 2004. "American Democracy in an Age of Rising Inequality." *Perspectives on Politics* 2, 651–66.

Jacobsen, Gary C. 2018. "Donald Trump and the 2018 Midterm Elections." Paper presented at the American Political Science Association annual meeting.

Jacoby, Melissa. 2014. "Financial Fragility, Medical Problems, and the Bankruptcy System." In *Working and Living in the Shadow of Economic Fragility*, edited by Marion Crain and Michael Sherraden. Oxford University Press.

Jahoda, Marie. 1982. *Employment and Unemployment: A Social Psychological Analysis.* Cambridge University Press.

Jäntti, Markus, et al. 2006. "American Exceptionalism in a New Light: A Comparison of Intergenerational Earnings Mobility in the Nordic Countries, the United Kingdom, and the United States." Discussion Paper 1938. Institute for the Study of Labor (IZA).

Jäntti, Markus and Stephen P. Jenkins. 2015. "Income Mobility." In *Handbook of Income Distribution.* Volume 2A. Elsevier.

Jencks, Christopher. 1992. *Rethinking Social Policy.* Harvard University Press.

Jencks, Christopher. 2005. "What Happened to Welfare?" *New York Review of Books,* December 15.

Jencks, Christopher. 2009. "The Graduation Gap." *The American Prospect,* October 22.

Jencks, Christopher. 2015. "The War on Poverty: Was It Lost?" *New York Review of Books*, April 2.

Jencks, Christopher. 2016. "Why the Very Poor Have Become Poorer." *New York Review of Books*, June 9.

Jencks, Christopher and Susan Mayer. 1990. "The Social Consequences of Growing Up in a Poor Neighborhood." In *Inner-City Poverty in the United States*, edited by Laurence Lynn and Michael McGeary. National Academy Press.

Jensen, Shane T. and Stephen H. Shore. 2015. "Changes in the Distribution of Income Volatility." *Journal of Human Resources* 50, 811–36.

Johnson, David S. 2004. "Using Expenditures to Measure the Standard of Living in the United States: Does It Make a Difference?" In *What Has Happened to the Quality of Life in the Advanced Industrialized Nations?*, edited by Edward N. Wolff. Edward Elgar.

JPMorgan Chase Institute. 2016. "Paychecks, Paydays, and the Online Platform Economy." jpmorganchase.com

Judis, John B. and Ruy Teixeira. 2002. *The Emerging Democratic Majority*. Scribner.

Kahlenberg, Richard. 1996. *The Remedy: Class, Race, and Affirmative Action*. Basic Books.

Kahlenberg, Richard and Halley Porter. 2013. *A Better Affirmative Action*. Century Foundation.

Kahn, Lisa. 2010. "The Long-Term Labor Market Consequences of Graduating from College in a Bad Economy." *Labour Economics* 17, 303–16.

Kalil, Ariel. 2015. "Inequality Begins at Home: The Role of Parenting in the Diverging Destinies of Rich and Poor Children." In *Families in an Era of Increasing Inequality*, edited by Paul R. Amato, Alan Booth, Susan M. McHale, and Jennifer Van Hook. Springer.

Kalleberg, Arne. 2011. *Good Jobs, Bad Jobs*. Russell Sage Foundation.

Kanter, Rosabeth Moss. 2015. *Move: Putting America's Infrastructure Back in the Lead*. W. W. Norton.

Katz, Lawrence F. and Alan B. Krueger. 2016. "The Rise and Nature of Alternative Work Arrangements in the United States, 1995–2015." Working Paper 22667. National Bureau of Economic Research.

Katzenstein, Peter J. 1985. *Small States in World Markets*. Cornell University Press.

Kaushal, Neeraj, Katherine Magnuson, and Jane Waldfogel. 2011. "How Is Family Income Related to Investments in Children's Learning?" In *Whither Opportunity?*, edited by Greg J. Duncan and Richard J. Murnane. Russell Sage Foundation and Spencer Foundation.

Keehan, Sean P., John A. Poisal, Gigi A. Cuckler, Andrea M. Sisko, Sheila D. Smith, Andrew J. Madison, Devin A. Stone, Christian J. Wolfe, and Joseph M. Lizonitz. 2017. "National Health Expenditure Projections, 2015–25: Economy, Prices, and Aging Expected to Shape Spending and Enrollment." *HealthAffairs*, doi 10.1377/hlthaff.2016.0459.

Keisling, Phil. 2016. "Vote from Home, Save Your Country." *Washington Monthly*, January–February.

Keith-Jennings, Brynne. 2018. "Millions Still Struggling to Afford Food." Center on Budget and Policy Priorities.

Kenworthy, Lane. 1999. "Do Social-Welfare Policies Reduce Poverty? A Cross-National Assessment." *Social Forces* 77, 1119–39.

Kenworthy, Lane. 2001. "Social Capital, Cooperation, and Economic Performance." In *Beyond Tocqueville: Civil Society and the Social Capital Debate in Comparative Perspective*, edited by Bob Edwards, Michael W. Foley, and Mario Diani, 125–35. University Press of New England.

Kenworthy, Lane. 2002. "Corporatism and Unemployment in the 1980s and 1990s." *American Sociological Review* 67, 367–88.

Kenworthy, Lane. 2004. *Egalitarian Capitalism*. Russell Sage Foundation.

Kenworthy, Lane. 2006. "Institutional Coherence and Macroeconomic Performance." *Socio-Economic Review* 4, 69–91.

Kenworthy, Lane. 2007. "Measuring Poverty and Material Deprivation." lanekenworthy.net.

Kenworthy, Lane. 2008a. *Jobs with Equality*. Oxford University Press.

Kenworthy, Lane. 2008b. "Types of Mobility." *Consider the Evidence* blog, July 4.

Kenworthy, Lane. 2009. "The Conscience of a Modern Conservative." *Consider the Evidence* blog, November 11.

Kenworthy, Lane. 2011a. "Are Progressive Income Taxes Fair?" *Consider the Evidence* blog, April 2.

Kenworthy, Lane. 2011b. *Progress for the Poor*. Oxford University Press.

Kenworthy, Lane. 2011c. "Step Away from the Pool." *Newsletter of the American Political Science Association Organized Section for Qualitative and Multi-Method Research,* Fall, 26–28.

Kenworthy, Lane. 2011d. "Were the Bush Tax Cuts Worse for Progressivity or for Revenues?" *Consider the Evidence* blog, November 2.

Kenworthy, Lane. 2011e. "When Does Economic Growth Benefit People on Low to Middle Incomes—and Why?" Commission on Living Standards. Resolution Foundation.

Kenworthy, Lane. 2014. *Social Democratic America.* Oxford University Press.

Kenworthy, Lane. 2015. "Do Employment-Conditional Earnings Subsidies Work?" ImPRovE Working Paper 15–10. Herman Deleeck Centre for Social Policy. University of Antwerp.

Kenworthy, Lane. 2018. "Is Sweden Failing on Immigration?" *Consider the Evidence* blog, September 8.

Kenworthy, Lane. 2019. *The Good Society.* lanekenworthy.net.

Kenworthy, Lane, Sondra Barringer, Daniel Duerr, and Garrett Andrew Schneider. 2007. "The Democrats and Working-Class Whites." lanekenworthy.net.

Kesler, Christel. 2015. "Welfare States and Immigrant Poverty: Germany, Sweden, and the United Kingdom in Comparative Perspective." *Acta Sociologica* 58, 39–61.

Kim, Hwanjoon. 2000. "Anti-Poverty Effectiveness of Taxes and Income Transfers in Welfare States." *International Social Security Review* 53(4), 105–29.

Kirp, David. 2016. "How New York Made Pre-K a Success." *New York Times,* February 13.

Klein, Ezra. 2012. "Why an MRI Costs $1,080 in America and $280 in France." *Washington Post: Wonkblog,* March 15.

Kletzer, Lori G. and Robert E. Litan. 2001. "A Prescription to Relieve Worker Anxiety." Policy Brief 01–2. Peterson Institute for International Economics.

Kleven, Henrik Jacobsen. 2014. "How Can Scandinavians Tax So Much?" *Journal of Economic Perspectives* 28(4), 77–98.

Kleven, Henrik Jacobsen, Martin B. Knudsen, Claus Thustrup Kreiner, Søren Pedersen, and Emmanuel Saez. 2011. "Unwilling or Unable to Cheat? Evidence from a Tax Audit Experiment in Denmark." *Econometrica* 79, 651–92.

Kleven, Henrik Jacobsen, Claus Thustrup Kreiner, and Emmanuel Saez. 2009. "Why Can Modern Governments Tax So Much? An Agency Model of Firms as Fiscal Intermediaries." Working Paper 15218. National Bureau of Economic Research.

Kliff, Sarah and Ezra Klein. 2017. "The Lessons of Obamacare." *Vox,* March 15.

Knight, Carly R. and Mary C. Brinton. 2017. "One Egalitarianism or Several? Two Decades of Gender-Role Attitude Change in Europe." *American Journal of Sociology* 122, 1485–532.

Kolko, Jed. 2016. "Trump Was Stronger Where the Economy Is Weaker." *FiveThirtyEight,* November 10.

Konczal, Mike. 2014. "The Voluntarism Fantasy." *Democracy Journal,* Spring.

Konczal, Mike. 2016. "The Forgotten State." *Boston Review,* July 18.

Kornrich, Sabino and Frank Furstenberg. 2013. "Investing in Children: Changes in Spending on Children, 1972 to 2007." *Demography* 50, 1–23.

Korpi, Walter. 1980. "Approaches to the Study of Poverty in the United States: Critical Notes from a European Perspective." In *Poverty and Public Policy,* edited by V.T. Covello. Schenkman.

Korpi, Walter. 1983. *The Democratic Class Struggle.* Routledge and Kegan Paul.

Korpi, Walter. 1991. "Political and Economic Explanations for Unemployment: A Cross-National and Long-Term Analysis." *British Journal of Political Science* 21, 315–48.

Korpi, Walter and Joakim Palme. 1998. "The Paradox of Redistribution and Strategies of Equality: Welfare State Institutions, Inequality, and Poverty in the Western Countries." *American Sociological Review* 63, 661–87.

Korpi, Walter and Joakim Palme. 2004. "Robin Hood, St. Matthew, or Simple Egalitarianism? Strategies of Equality in Welfare States." In *A Handbook of Comparative Social Policy,* edited by P. Kennett, 153–79. Edward Elgar.

Kristensen, Peer Hull and Kari Lilja, eds. 2011. *Nordic Capitalisms and Globalization.* Oxford University Press.

Krueger, Alan B. 2009. "A Future Consumption Tax to Fix Today's Economy." *New York Times: Economix*, January 12.

Krueger, Alan B. 2015. "The Minimum Wage: How Much Is Too Much?" *New York Times*, October 10.

Krueger, Alan B. 2016. "Where Have All the Workers Gone?" Brookings Institution.

Krugman, Paul. 2009. *The Return of Depression Economics and the Crisis of 2008*. W. W. Norton.

Krugman, Paul. 2017. "Interview with Ezra Klein." *Vox*, December 14.

Krugman, Paul. 2018. "The Fraudulence of the Fiscal Hawks." *New York Times*, February 9.

Krugman, Paul. 2019. "Getting Real About Rural America. " *New York Times*, March 18.

Kruse, Douglas, Richard Freeman, and Joseph Blasi. 2008. "Do Workers Gain by Sharing? Employee Outcomes under Employee Ownership, Profit Sharing, and Broad-Based Stock Options." Working Paper 14233. National Bureau of Economic Research.

Kumlin, Staffan and Atle Haugsgjerd. 2017. "The Welfare State and Political Trust: Bringing Performance Back In." In *Handbook of Political Trust*, edited by Tom van der Meer and Sonja Zmerli. Edward Elgar.

Kuttner, Robert. 2010. "Progressive Revenue as the Alternative to Caps, Commissions, and Cuts." Prepared for the Scholars Strategy Network.

Kvist, Jon and Niels Ploug. 2003. "Active Labour Market Policies: When Do They Work—and Where Do They Fail?" Danish National Institute of Social Research.

LaLonde, Robert J. 2007. "The Case for Wage Insurance." Council on Foreign Relations.

Landersø, Rasmus and James J. Heckman. 2017. "The Scandinavian Fantasy: The Sources of Intergenerational Mobility in Denmark and the U.S." *Scandinavian Journal of Economics* 119, 178–230.

Lareau, Annette. 2003. *Unequal Childhoods*. University of California Press.

Larsen, Christian Albrekt. 2008. "The Institutional Logic of Welfare Attitudes: How Welfare Regimes Influence Public Support." *Comparative Political Studies* 41, 145–68.

Larsen, Christian Albrekt. 2013. *The Rise and Fall of Social Cohesion*. Oxford University Press.

Laughlin, Lynda. 2013. "Who's Minding the Kids? Child Care Arrangements: Spring 2011." U.S. Census Bureau.

Layard, Richard. 2005. *Happiness*. Penguin.

Lebergott, Stanley. 1976. *The American Economy*. Princeton University Press.

Leduc, Sylvain and Daniel Wilson. 2012. "Highway Grants: Roads to Prosperity." *Federal Reserve Bank of San Francisco Economic Letters*.

Lee, Chul-In and Gary Solon. 2009. "Trends in Intergenerational Income Mobility." *Review of Economics and Statistics* 91, 766–792.

Leonhardt, David. 2011. "Why Does College Cost So Much?" *New York Times*, February 18.

Leonhardt, David and Kevin Quealy. 2014. "The American Middle Class Is No Longer the World's Richest." *New York Times*, April 22.

Lesmerises, Monica. 2007. *The Middle Class at Risk*. Century Foundation.

Levin, Yuval. 2012. "The Real Debate." *Weekly Standard*, October 8.

Levin, Yuval. 2016. *The Fractured Republic*. Basic Books.

Leyden, Peter and Ruy Teixeira. 2017. "California Is the Future of American Politics." *Medium*, October 4.

Lind, Michael, Steven Hill, Robert Hiltonsmith, and Joshua Freedman. 2013. "Expanded Social Security." New America Foundation.

Lindert, Peter. 2004. *Growing Public: Social Spending and Economic Growth since the Eighteenth Century*. Two volumes. Cambridge University Press.

Lindsey, Brink and Steven M. Teles. 2017. *The Captured Economy: How the Powerful Enrich Themselves, Slow Down Growth, and Increase Inequality*. Oxford University Press.

Lindsey, Brink, Will Wilkinson, Steven M. Teles, and Samuel Hammond. 2018. "The Center Can Hold: Public Policy for an Age of Extremes." Niskanen Center.

Lipset, Seymour Martin. 1996. *American Exceptionalism*. W. W. Norton.

Lohmann, Henning and Ive Marx, eds. 2018. *Handbook on In-Work Poverty*. Edward Elgar.

Long, Heather. 2018. "America's Forgotten Towns: Can They Be Saved or Should People Just Leave?" *Washington Post: Wonkblog.* January 2.

Lowrey, Annie. 2018. *Give People Money: How a Universal Basic Income Would End Poverty, Revolutionize Work, and Remake the World.* Crown.

Lutz, Wolfgang and Endale Kebede. 2018. "Education and Health: Redrawing the Preston Curve." *Population and Development Review,* doi 10.1111/padr.12141.

MacLeod, Jay. 2009. *Ain't No Makin' It.* 3rd edition. Westview.

Maddison, Angus. 2007. *Contours of the World Economy, 1–2030 AD.* Oxford University Press.

Madrick, Jeff. 2009. *The Case for Big Government.* Princeton University Press.

Madsen, Per Kongshøj. 2006. "How Can It Possibly Fly? The Paradox of a Dynamic Labour Market in a Scandinavian Welfare State." In *National Identity and the Varieties of Capitalism: The Danish Experience,* edited by John L. Campbell, John A. Hall, and Ove K. Pedersen. McGill-Queen's University Press.

Magnuson, Katherine and Greg J. Duncan. 2016. "Can Early Childhood Interventions Decrease Inequality of Economic Opportunity?" *RSF: The Russell Sage Foundation Journal of the Social Sciences* 2(2), 123–41.

Manoli, Dayanand S., Marios Michaelides, and Ankur Patel. 2018. "Long-Term Effects of Job-Search Assistance: Experimental Evidence Using Administrative Tax Data." Working Paper 24422. National Bureau of Economic Research.

Manza, Jeff, Jennifer A. Heerwig, and Brian J. McCabe. 2012. "Public Opinion in the 'Age of Reagan.'" In *Social Trends in American Life,* edited by Peter V. Marsden, 117–45. Princeton University Press.

"Marketplace-Edison Economic Anxiety Index Research Poll." 2016. Marketplace.org, February.

Marmor, Theodore R., Jerry L. Mashaw, and Philip L. Harvey. 1990. *America's Misunderstood Welfare State.* Basic Books.

Marmor, Theodore R., Jerry L. Mashaw, and John Pakutka. 2014. *Social Insurance.* CQ Press.

Martin, Isaac William. 2008. *The Permanent Tax Revolt.* Stanford University Press.

Martin, Isaac William and Christopher Niedt. 2015. *Foreclosed America.* Stanford University Press.

Marx, Ive, Pieter Vandenbroucke, and Gerlinde Verbist. 2012. "Can Higher Employment Levels Bring Down Relative Income Poverty in the EU? Regression-Based Simulations of the Europe 2020 Target." *Journal of European Social Policy* 22, 472–86.

Marx, Ive, Lina Salanauskaite, and Gerlinde Verbist. 2016. "For the Poor, but Not Only the Poor: On Optimal Pro-Poorness in Redistributive Policies." *Social Forces* 95, 1–24.

Masket, Seth. 2018. "A House Forecast Holds Good News for Democrats." *Vox,* February 12.

Matthews, Dylan. 2014. "A Guaranteed Income for Every American Would Eliminate Poverty—and It Wouldn't Destroy the Economy. *Vox,* July 23.

Matthews, Dylan. 2017. "This Old Bill Could Be the Secret to Affordable Universal Health Care." *Vox,* September 11.

Matthews, Dylan. 2018. "Corey Booker's New Big Idea: Guaranteeing Jobs for Everyone Who Wants One." *Vox,* April 20.

Mayer, Susan E. 1999. *What Money Can't Buy.* Harvard University Press.

Mayer, Susan E. and Christopher Jencks. 1993. "Recent Trends in Economic Inequality in the United States: Income versus Expenditures versus Material Well-being." In *Poverty and Prosperity in the USA in the Late Twentieth Century,* edited by Dimitri B. Papadimitriou and Edward N. Wolff. St. Martin's Press.

Mazumder, Bhaskar and Sarah Miller. 2016. "The Effects of the Massachusetts Health Reform on Household Financial Distress." *American Economic Journal: Economic Policy* 8(3), 284–313.

McClelland, Alison and Paul Smyth, eds. 2014. *Social Policy in Australia.* 3rd edition. Oxford University Press.

McGhee, Eric. 2012. "Forecasting House Elections." *The Monkey Cage,* September 17.

McKenzie, Brian and Melanie Rapino. 2011. "Commuting in the United States: 2009." U.S. Census Bureau.

McKernan, Signe-Mary, Caroline Ratcliffe, and John Iceland. 2018. "Policy Efforts to Reduce Material Hardship for Low-Income Families." Urban Institute.

McLanahan, Sara. 2004. "Diverging Destinies: How Children Are Faring Under the Second Demographic Transition." *Demography* 41, 607–27.

McLanahan, Sara and Christopher Jencks. 2015. "Was Moynihan Right? What Happens to Children of Unmarried Mothers?" *Education Next*, Spring, 15–20.

McLanahan, Sara and Gary Sandefur. 1994. *Growing Up with a Single Parent*. Harvard University Press.

McLanahan, Sara, Laura Tach, and Daniel Schneider. 2013. "The Causal Effects of Father Absence." *Annual Review of Sociology* 39, 399–427.

McLanahan, Sara and Wade Jacobsen. 2015. "Diverging Destinies Revisited." In *Families in an Era of Increasing Inequality*, edited by Paul R. Amato, Alan Booth, Susan M. McHale, and Jennifer Van Hook. Springer.

McMahon, Shawn and Jessica Horning. 2013. "Living Below the Line: Economic Insecurity and America's Families." Wider Opportunities for Women.

Mendelberg, Tali, Christopher F. Karpowitz, and Nicholas Goedert. 2014. "Does Descriptive Representation Facilitate Women's Distinctive Voice? How Gender Composition and Decision Rules Affect Deliberation." *American Journal of Political Science* 58, 291–306.

Mettler, Suzanne. 2011. *The Submerged State*. University of Chicago Press.

Meyer, Bruce D. and James X. Sullivan. 2011. "The Material Well-Being of the Poor and the Middle Class Since 1980." Working Paper 2011-04. American Enterprise Institute.

Meyer, Bruce D. and James X. Sullivan. 2012. "Dimensions of Progress: Poverty from the Great Society to the Great Recession." Presented at the Fall 2012 Brookings Panel on Economic Activity.

Meyerson, Harold. 2017. "Place Matters." *The American Prospect*, June 22.

Micklethwait, John and Adrian Wooldridge. 2004. *The Right Nation*. Penguin.

Micklethwait, John and Adrian Wooldridge. 2014. *The Fourth Revolution: The Global Race to Reinvent the State*. Penguin.

Miliband, David. 2017. *Rescue: Refugees and the Political Crisis of Our Time*. Simon and Schuster.

Milward, Brinton and Keith G. Provan. 2000. "Governing the Hollow State." *Journal of Public Administration Research and Theory* 10, 359–79.

Mishel, Lawrence, Josh Bivens, Elise Gould, and Heidi Shierholz. 2012. *The State of Working America*. 12th edition. Economic Policy Institute.

Misra, Joya, Stephanie Moller, and Michelle J. Budig. 2007. "Work-Family Policies and Poverty for Partnered and Single Women in Europe and North America." *Gender and Society* 21, 804–27.

Moene, Karl Ove and Michael Wallerstein. 2001. "Targeting and Political Support for Welfare Spending." *Economics of Governance* 2, 3-24.

Moffitt, Robert A. 1981. "The Negative Income Tax: Would It Discourage Work?" *Monthly Labor Review*, April, 23–27.

Moffitt, Robert A. 2015. "The Deserving Poor, the Family, and the U.S. Welfare System." *Demography* 52, 729–49.

Moller, Stephanie, David Bradley, Evelyne Huber, François Nielsen, and John D. Stephens. 2003. "Determinants of Relative Poverty in Advanced Capitalist Democracies." *American Sociological Review* 68, 22–51.

Morduch, Jonathan and Rachel Schneider. 2014. "Spikes and Dips: How Income Uncertainty Affects Households." U.S. Financial Diaries.

Morel, Nathalie, Bruno Palier, and Joakim Palme, eds. 2012. *Towards a Social Investment Welfare State?* Policy Press.

Morelli, Salvatore and Anthony Atkinson. 2015. "Inequality and Crises Revisited." *Economia Politica* 32, 31–51.

Morgen, Sandra, Joan Acker, and Jill Weigt. 2010. *Stretched Thin: Poor Families, Welfare Work, and Welfare Reform*. Cornell University Press.

Moss, David A. 2002. *When All Else Fails: Government as the Ultimate Risk Manager.* Harvard University Press.

Munnell, Alicia H. 2012. "Bigger and Better: Redesigning Our Retirement System in the Wake of the Financial Collapse." In *Shared Responsibility, Shared Risk,* edited by Jacob S. Hacker and Ann O'Leary. Oxford University Press.

Munnell, Alicia H. 2018. "The United States." In *Towards a New Pension Settlement: The International Experience,* edited by Gregg McClymont and Andy Tarrant. Rowman and Littlefield.

Murphy, Richard, Judith Scott-Clayton, and Gillian Wyness. 2017. *Lessons from the End of Free College in England.* Brookings Institution.

Murray, Charles. 1984. *Losing Ground: American Social Policy, 1950–1980.* Basic Books.

Murray, Charles. 2006. *In Our Hands: A Plan to Replace the Welfare State.* AEI Press.

Murray, Charles. 2008. "Guaranteed Income as a Replacement for the Welfare State." *Basic Income Studies* 3(2), 1–12.

Murray, Charles. 2012. *Coming Apart: The State of White America, 1960-2010.* Crown Forum.

Mutz, Diane C. 2018. "Status Threat, Not Economic Hardship, Explains the 2016 Presidential Vote." *PNAS,* doi 10.1073/pnas.1718155115.

Myles, Gareth D. 2000. "Taxation and Economic Growth." *Fiscal Studies* 21, 141–68.

Myles, John, Feng Hou, Garnett Picot, and Karen Myers. 2009. "The Demographic Foundations of Rising Employment and Earnings among Single Mothers in Canada and the United States, 1980–2000." *Population Research and Policy Review,* doi 10.1007/s11113-008-9125-2.

Nelson, Kenneth. 2004. "The Formation of Minimum Income Protection." Working Paper 373. Luxembourg Income Study.

Nelson, Kenneth. 2007. "Universalism versus Targeting: The Vulnerability of Social Insurance and Means-Tested Minimum Income Protection in 18 Countries, 1990-2002." *International Social Security Review* 60, 33–58.

Nelson, Kenneth. 2012. "Counteracting Material Deprivation: The Role of Social Assistance in Europe." *Journal of European Social Policy* 22, 148–63.

Nelson, Timothy J. and Kathryn Edin. 2013. *Doing the Best I Can: Fathering in the Inner City.* University of California Press.

Newman, Katherine S. 1999. *No Shame in My Game: The Working Poor in the Inner City.* Vintage Books and Russell Sage Foundation.

Newman, Katherine S. 2006. *Chutes and Ladders: Navigating the Low-Wage Labor Market.* Russell Sage Foundation and Harvard University Press.

Newman, Katherine S. and Elisabeth S. Jacobs. 2010. *Who Cares? Public Ambivalence and Government Activism from the New Deal to the Second Gilded Age.* Princeton University Press.

Nguyen, Vivian. 2017. "Long-Term Support and Services." AARP Public Policy Institute.

Nichols, A. and J. Rothstein. 2016. "The Earned Income Tax Credit." In *Economics of Means-Tested Transfer Programs in the United States,* volume 1, edited by R. Moffitt. University of Chicago Press.

Nieuwenhuis, Rense, Wim van Lancker, Diego Collado, and Bea Cantillon. 2018. "Has the Potential for Compensating Poverty by Women's Employment Growth Been Depleted?" lisdatacenter.org.

Nisbet, Robert A. 1953. *The Quest for Community.* Oxford University Press.

Nisbett, Richard E. 2009. *Intelligence and How to Get It.* W. W. Norton.

Niskanen, William A. 1971. *Bureaucracy and Representative Government.* Aldine.

Noah, Timothy. 2012. "The Mobility Myth." *The New Republic,* March 1, 14–17.

Noël, Alain. Forthcoming. "Is Social Investment Inimical to the Poor?" *Socio-Economic Review,* doi 10.1093/ser/mwy038.

Nolan, Brian, ed. 2018a. *Generating Prosperity for Working Families in Affluent Countries.* Oxford University Press.

Nolan, Brian, ed. 2018b. *Inequality and Inclusive Growth in Rich Countries.* Oxford University Press.

Nolan, Brian and Christopher T. Whelan. 2010. "Using Non-Monetary Deprivation Indicators to Analyze Poverty and Social Exclusion: Lessons from Europe?" *Journal of Policy Analysis and Management* 29, 305–25.

Nolan, Brian, Max Roser, and Stefan Thewissen. 2016. "GDP Per Capita Versus Median Household Income: What Gives Rise to Divergence Over Time?" Working Paper 672. Luxembourg Income Study.

Norberg, Johan. 2016. *Progress*. Oneworld Publications.

Nussbaum, Martha C. 2011. *Creating Capabilities*, Harvard University Press.

Odendahl, Christian. 2017. "The Hartz Myth: A Closer Look at Germany's Labour Market Reforms." Centre for European Reform.

OECD. 2003. "Benefits and Employment, Friend or Foe? Interactions between Passive and Active Social Programmes." In *OECD Employment Outlook*.

OECD. 2008. *Growing Unequal? Income Distribution and Poverty in OECD Countries*. OECD.

OECD. 2011. *Doing Better for Families*. OECD.

OECD. 2016. *PISA 2015 Results: Policies and Practices for Successful Schools*. OECD.

OECD. 2017. *OECD Employment Outlook 2017*. OECD.

Olson, Elizabeth. 2017. "In Oregon, You Can Now Save for Retirement. Unless You Object." *New York Times*, November 17.

Oreopoulos, P., T. von Wachter, and A. Heisz. 2012. "The Short- and Long-Term Career Effects of Graduating in a Recession: Hysteresis and Heterogeneity in the Market for College Graduates." *American Economic Journal: Applied Economics* 4, 1–29.

Ornston, Darius. 2012. "Creative Corporatism: The Politics of High-Technology Competition in Nordic Europe." *Comparative Political Studies* 46, 702–29.

Ornston, Darius. 2018. *Good Governance Gone Bad: How Nordic Adaptability Leads to Excess*. Cornell University Press.

Osterman, Paul. 1999. *Securing Prosperity*. Princeton University Press.

Page, Benjamin I. and Martin Gilens. 2017. *Democracy in America?* University of Chicago Press.

Page, Benjamin I. and Lawrence Jacobs. 2009. *Class War? What Americans Really Think about Economic Inequality*. University of Chicago Press.

Page, Benjamin I. and Robert Y. Shapiro. 1983. "Effects of Public Opinion on Policy." *American Political Science Review* 77, 175–90.

Palier, Bruno, ed. 2010. *A Long Goodbye to Bismarck? The Politics of Welfare Reform in Continental Europe*. University of Chicago Press.

Palme, Joakim and Axel Cronert. 2015. "Trends in the Swedish Social Investment Welfare State: 'The Enlightened Path' or 'The Third Way' for 'the Lions'?" ImPRovE Working Paper 15–12. Herman Deleeck Centre for Social Policy. University of Antwerp.

Pampel, Fred, Giulia Andrighetto, and Sven Steinmo. 2019. "How Institutions and Attitudes Shape Tax Compliance: a Cross-National Experiment and Survey." *Social Forces* 97, 1337–64.

Parolin, Zachary. 2016. "The Sum of Its Parts? Assessing Variation and Trends in Family Income Support Across the 48 Contiguous United States." Working Paper 16–05. Herman Deleeck Centre for Social Policy. University of Antwerp.

Partanen, Anu. 2016. *The Nordic Theory of Everything*. HarperCollins.

Pastor, Manuel. 2018. *State of Resistance: What California's Dizzying Descent and Remarkable Resurgence Mean for America's Future*. New Press.

Pedersen, Axel West and Stein Kuhnle. 2017. "The Nordic Welfare State Model." In *The Nordic Models in Political Science: Challenged, but Still Viable?*, edited by Oddbjorn Knutsen. Fagbokforlage.

Perry, Ian. 2017. "The Effects of California's Public Policy on Jobs and the Economy Since 2011." Working Paper 108–17. Institute for Research on Labor and Employment.

Persily, Nathaniel. 2010. "The Floodgates Were Already Open." *Slate*, January 25.

Pew Research Center. 2011. "The Elusive 90% Solution." March 11.

Pew Research Center. 2012. "Trends in American Values: 1987–2012." pewresearch.org.

Pew Research Center. 2018. "White Millennial Voters Are More Democratic Than White Voters in Older Generations." March 20.

Pierson, Paul. 1994. *Dismantling the Welfare State? Reagan, Thatcher, and the Politics of Retrenchment.* Cambridge University Press.

Phillips, Matt. 2013. "College in Sweden Is Free but Students Still Have a Ton of Debt. How Can That Be?" *Quartz,* May 30.

Phillips, Meredith. 2011. "Parenting, Time Use, and Disparities in Academic Outcomes." In *Whither Opportunity?,* edited by Greg J. Duncan and Richard J. Murnane. Russell Sage Foundation and Spencer Foundation.

Pinker, Steven. 2011. *The Better Angels of Our Nature: Why Violence Has Declined.* Penguin.

Pinker, Steven. 2018. *Enlightenment Now.* Viking.

Pofeldt, Elaine. 2014. "Is the Job of the Future a Freelance One?" CNBC, January 29.

Polakow-Suransky, Sasha. 2017. *Go Back to Where You Came From: The Backlash Against Immigration and the Fate of Western Democracy.* PublicAffairs.

Polanyi, Karl. 1957 (1944). *The Great Transformation.* Beacon Press.

Pollin, Robert. 2011. "Back to Full Employment." *Boston Review,* bostonreview.net.

Pollin, Robert, James Heintz, Peter Arno, and Jeannette Wicks-Lim. 2017. "Economic Analysis of the Healthy California Single-Payer Health Care Proposal (SB-562)." Political Economy Research Institute (PERI). University of Massachusetts–Amherst.

Ponnuru, Ramesh. 2013. "Reaganism after Reagan." *New York Times,* February 17.

Pontusson, Jonas. 2005. *Inequality and Prosperity.* Cornell University Press.

Pontusson, Jonas. 2011. "Once Again a Model: Nordic Social Democracy in a Globalized World." In *What's Left of the Left?,* edited by James Cronin, George Ross, and James Shoch, 89–115. Duke University Press.

Poole, Keith T. and Christopher Hare. 2012. "An Update on Political Polarization (through 2011)." *Voteview Blog,* January 30.

Porter, Eduardo. 2018. "The Hard Truths of Trying to 'Save' Rural America." *New York Times,* December 14.

Prasad, Monica. 2018. *Starving the Beast: Ronald Reagan and the Tax Cut Revolution.* Russell Sage Foundation.

Presser, Harriet. 2003. *Working in a 24/7 Economy.* Russell Sage Foundation.

Przeworski, Adam. 1985. *Capitalism and Social Democracy.* Cambridge University Press.

Putnam, Robert D. 1993. "The Prosperous Community: Social Capital and Public Life." *The American Prospect,* Spring, 35–42.

Putnam, Robert D. 2000. *Bowling Alone: The Collapse and Revival of American Community.* Simon and Schuster.

Putnam, Robert D. 2015. *Our Kids: The American Dream in Crisis.* Simon and Schuster.

Quinn, David M. and Morgan Polikoff. 2017. "Summer Learning Loss: What Is It, and What Can We Do about It?" Brookings Institution.

Radcliff, Benjamin. 2013. *The Political Economy of Human Happiness.* Cambridge University Press.

Rainwater, Lee. 1982. "Stigma in Income-Tested Programs." In *Income-Tested Transfer Programs,* edited by Irwin Garfinkel. Academic Press.

Rank, Mark, Thomas Hirschl, and Kirk Foster. 2014. *Chasing the American Dream.* Oxford University Press.

Ratcliff, Caroline and Signe-Mary McKernan. 2010. "Childhood Poverty Persistence: Facts and Consequences." Urban Institute.

Ravallion, Martin. 2012. "Fighting Poverty One Experiment at a Time." *Journal of Economic Literature* 50, 103–14.

Rawls, John. 1971. *A Theory of Justice.* Harvard University Press.

Rawls, John. 1996. *Political Liberalism.* Columbia University Press.

Ray, Rebecca, Milla Sanes, and John Schmitt. 2013. *No-Vacation Nation Revisited.* Center for Economic and Policy Research.

Reardon, Sean F. 2011. "The Widening Academic-Achievement Gap Between the Rich and the Poor: New Evidence and Possible Explanations." In *Whither Opportunity?*, edited by Greg J. Duncan and Richard J. Murnane. Russell Sage Foundation.

Rector, Robert. 2007. "How Poor Are the Poor?" Backgrounder 2064. Heritage Foundation.

Rehn, Gosta. 1952. "The Problem of Stability: An Analysis of Some Policy Proposals." In *Wages Policy under Full Employment*, edited by Ralph Turvey. William Hodge.

Rehn, Gosta. 1985. "Swedish Active Labor Market Policy: Retrospect and Prospect." *Industrial Relations* 24, 62–89.

Reich, Robert B. 1999. "We Are All Third-Wayers Now." *The American Prospect*, March-April.

Reich, Robert B. 2010. *Aftershock*. Knopf.

Reich, Robert B. 2015. *Saving Capitalism*. Knopf.

Reno, Virginia P. and Lisa D. Ekman. 2012. "Social Security Disability Insurance: Essential Protection When Work Incapacity Strikes." *Journal of Public Policy Analysis and Management* 31, 461–69.

Renwick, Chris. 2017. *Bread for All: The Origins of the Welfare State*. Allen Lane.

Reskin, Barbara F. 1998. *The Realities of Affirmative Action in Employment*. American Sociological Association.

Reynolds Arthur J., et al. 2011. "Age 26 Cost-Benefit Analysis of the Child-Parent Center Early Education Program." *Child Development* 82, 379–404.

Rice, Deborah, Vanesa Fuertes, and Lara Monticelli. 2018. "Does Individualized Employment Support Deliver What Is Promised? Findings from Three European Cities." *International Social Security Review* 71, 91–109.

Ringen, Stein. 1987. *The Possibility of Politics: A Study in the Political Economy of the Welfare State*. Clarendon Press.

Robeyns, Ingrid. 2018. *Well-Being, Freedom, and Social Justice: The Capabilities Approach Reexamined*. Open Book Publishers.

Rodrik, Dani. 2014. "The Past, Present, and Future of Economic Growth." *Challenge* 57(3), 5–39.

Romig, Kathleen. 2016. "Increasing Payroll Taxes Would Strengthen Social Security." Center on Budget and Policy Priorities.

Roosevelt, Franklin D. 1932. "Address at Oglethorpe University in Atlanta, Georgia." May 22.

Rorke, Catrina, Andrew Moylan, and Daniel Semelsberger. 2016. "Swapping the Corporate Income Tax for a Price on Carbon." Policy Study 79. R Street.

Rose, Stephen J. 2010. *Rebound*. St. Martin's Press.

Rose, Stephen J. and Scott Winship. 2009. "Ups and Downs: Does the American Economy Still Promote Upward Mobility?" Economic Mobility Project.

Rosenbaum, James, Caitlin Ahern, Kelly Becker, and Janet Rosenbaum. 2015. "The New Forgotten Half and Research Directions to Support Them." William T. Grant Foundation.

Rosenthal, Elizabeth. 2015. "Insured, But Not Covered." *New York Times*, February 7.

Rossin-Slater, Maya, Christopher J. Ruhm, and Jane Waldfogel. 2013. "The Effects of California's Paid Family Leave Program on Mothers' Leave-Taking and Subsequent Labor Market Outcomes." *Journal of Public Policy Analysis and Management*.

Rothstein, Bo. 1998. *Just Institutions Matter: The Moral and Political Logic of the Universal Welfare State*. Cambridge University Press.

Rothstein, Bo. 2011. *The Quality of Government*. University of Chicago Press.

Rothstein, Bo. 2017. "Solidarity, Diversity, and the Quality of Government." In *The Strains of Commitment: The Political Sources of Solidarity in Diverse Societies*, edited by Keith Banting and Will Kymlicka. Oxford University Press.

Rothstein, Bo and Dietlind Stolle. 2008. "The State and Social Capital: An Institutional Theory of Generalized Trust." *Comparative Politics* 40, 441–59.

Ruhm, Christopher J. 2017. "A National Paid Parental Leave Policy for the United States." In *The 51%: Driving Growth through Women's Economic Participation*, edited by Diane Whitmore Schanzenbach and Ryan Nunn. Brookings Institution.

Saez, Emmanuel, Joel Slemrod, and Seth H. Giertz. 2012. "The Elasticity of Taxable Income with Respect to Marginal Tax Rates: A Critical Review." *Journal of Economic Literature* 50, 3–50.

Samuelson, Robert J. 1995. *The Good Life and Its Discontents*. Times Books.

Sampson, Robert. 2012. *Great American City*. University of Chicago Press.

Sanandaji, Nima. 2016. *Debunking Utopia: Exposing the Myth of Nordic Socialism*. WND Books.

Saunders, Peter. 2002. *The Ends and Means of Welfare: Coping with Economic and Social Change in Australia*. Cambridge University Press.

Sawhill, Isabel. 2018. *The Forgotten Americans: An Economic Agenda for a Divided Nation*. Yale University Press.

Schall, Carly Elizabeth. 2016. *The Rise and Fall of the Miraculous Welfare Machine: Immigration and Social Democracy in Twentieth-Century Sweden*. ILR University Press.

Schattschneider, E. E. 1960. *The Semisovereign People*. Holt, Rinehart, and Winston.

Schmitt, John. 2013. "Why Does the Minimum Wage Have No Discernible Effect on Employment?" Center for Economic and Policy Research.

Schneider, Daniel and Kristen Harknett. 2016. "Schedule Instability and Unpredictability and Worker and Family Health and Wellbeing." Washington Center on Equitable Growth.

Schnitzlein, Daniel D. 2015. "A New Look at Intergenerational Mobility in Germany Compared to the US." *Review of Income and Wealth* 62, 650–67.

Schwartz, Christine R. and Robert D. Mare. 2005. "Trends in Educational Assortative Marriage from 1940 to 2003." *Demography* 42, 621–46.

Schwartz, Nancy and Robert Hoffman. 2015. "Pathways to Upward Mobility." *National Affairs*, Summer.

Scott, James C. 1998. *Seeing Like a State: How Certain Schemes to Improve the Human Condition Have Failed*. Yale University Press.

Scrivener, Susan, Michael J. Weiss, Alyssa Ratledge, Timothy Rudd, Colleen Sommo, and Hannah Fresques. 2015. "Doubling Graduation Rates: Three-Year Effects of CUNY's Accelerated Study in Associate Programs (ASAP) for Developmental Education Students." MDRC.

Sefton, Tom, John Hills, and Holly Sutherland. 2009. "Poverty, Inequality, and Redistribution." In *Towards a More Equal Society? Poverty, Inequality, and Policy since 1997*, edited by John Hills, Tom Sefton, and Kitty Stewart. Policy Press.

Seikel, Daniel and Dorothee Spannagel. 2018. "Activation and In-Work Poverty." In *Handbook on In-Work Poverty*, edited by Henning Lohmann and Ive Marx, 245–60. Edward Elgar.

Sejersted, Francis. 2011. *The Age of Social Democracy*. Princeton University Press.

Sen, Amartya. 1999. *Development as Freedom*. Oxford University Press.

Sen, Amartya. 2009. *The Idea of Justice*. Harvard University Press.

Shaefer, H. Luke, Greg Duncan, Kathryn Edin, Irwin Garfinkel, David Harris, Timothy Smeeding, Jane Waldfogel, Christopher Wimer, and Hiro Yoshikawa. 2016. "A Universal Child Allowance: A Plan to Reduce Poverty and Income Instability among Children in the United States." *RSF: The Russell Sage Foundation Journal of the Social Sciences* 4(2), 22–42.

Sharkey, Patrick. 2013. *Stuck in Place: Urban Neighborhoods and the End of Progress Toward Racial Equality*. University of Chicago Press.

Shipler, David K. 2004. *The Working Poor*. Knopf.

Sides, John. 2017. "Here's the Incredibly Unpopular GOP Tax Reform Plan—in One Graph." *Washington Post: Wonkblog*, November 18.

Sides, John and Lynn Vavreck. 2013. *The Gamble: Choice and Chance in the 2012 Presidential Election*. Princeton University Press.

Siebens, Julie. 2013. "Extended Measures of Well-Being: Living Conditions in the United States: 2011." Household Economic Studies P70–136. U.S. Census Bureau.

Silver, Nate. 2012. "Measuring the Effect of the Economy on Elections." *FiveThirtyEight*, July 5.

Silvia, Stephen J. 2013. *Holding the Shop Together: German Industrial Relations in the Postwar Era*. Cornell University Press.

Skocpol, Theda. 1991. "Targeting within Universalism: Politically Viable Policies to Combat Poverty in the United States." In *The Urban Underclass*, edited by Christopher Jencks and Paul E. Peterson. Brookings Institution.

Skocpol, Theda. 1992. *Protecting Soldiers and Mothers*. Harvard University Press.

Skocpol, Theda. 1997. "The Tocqueville Problem: Civic Engagement in American Democracy." *Social Science History* 21, 455–79.

Society for Human Resource Management. 2016. "SHRM Survey Findings: 2017 Holiday Schedules." shrm.org.

Soltas, Evan. 2013. "The Myth of the Falling Bridge." *Bloomberg View*, April 8.

Sønderskov, Kim Mannemar and Peter Thisted Dinesen. 2014. "Danish Exceptionalism: Explaining the Unique Increase in Social Trust Over the Past 30 Years." *European Sociological Review* 30, 782–95.

Sparer, Michael S. 2018. "Buying into Medicaid: A Viable Path for Universal Coverage." *The American Prospect*, January 10.

Standing, Guy. 2017. *Basic Income: A Guide for the Open-Minded*. Yale University Press.

Starr, Paul. 2017. "The Next Progressive Health Agenda." *The American Prospect*, March 23.

Starr, Paul. 2018. "A New Strategy for Health Care." *The American Prospect*, January 4.

Steensland, Brian. 2007. *The Failed Welfare Revolution: America's Struggle Over Guaranteed Income Policy*. Princeton University Press.

Steinmo, Sven. 2013. "Governing as an Engineering Problem: The Political Economy of Swedish Success." In *Politics in the Age of Austerity*, edited by Armin Schäfer and Wolfgang Streeck. Polity Press.

Stephens-Davidowitz, Seth. 2013. "Dr. Google Will See You Now." *New York Times*, August 9.

Stern, Andy, with Lee Kravitz. 2016. *Raising the Floor: How a Universal Basic Income Can Renew Our Economy and Rebuild the American Dream*. PublicAffairs.

Stevens, Ann Huff. 2018. "Employment and Poverty." *EconoFact*, January 7.

Stiglitz, Joseph E. 1989. "On the Economic Role of the State." In *The Economic Role of the State*, edited by Arnold Heertje. Basil Blackwell.

Stiglitz, Joseph E. 2009. "Regulation and Failure." In *New Perspectives on Regulation*, edited by David Moss and John Cisternino. Tobin Project.

Stiglitz, Joseph E. 2012. *The Price of Inequality*. W. W. Norton.

Stiglitz, Joseph E., et al. 2015. *Rewriting the Rules of the American Economy*. Roosevelt Institute.

Stokey, Nancy L. and Sergio Rebelo. 1995. "Growth Effects of Flat Tax Rates." *Journal of Political Economy* 103, 519–50.

Stone, Chad and William Chen. 2014. "Introduction to Unemployment Insurance." Center on Budget and Policy Priorities.

Strain, Michael R. 2014. "A Jobs Agenda for the Right." *National Affairs*, Winter.

Streeck, Wolfgang. 2016. *How Will Capitalism End? Essays on a Failing System*. Verso.

Sturgeon, Jamie. 2016. "Here's How Much the New Canada Child Benefit Will Give You Each Month." *Global News*, March 23.

Summers, Lawrence H. 2016. "The Age of Secular Stagnation." *Foreign Affairs*, February 15.

Surowiecki, James. 2010. "Soak the Very, Very Rich." *The New Yorker*, August 9.

Swedish Ministry of Health and Social Affairs. 2016. "Social Insurance in Sweden." government.se.

Swers, Michele L. 2013. *Women in the Club*. University of Chicago Press.

Tanner, Michael. 2015. "The Pros and Cons of a Guaranteed National Income." Policy Analysis 773. Cato Institute.

Tanzi, Vito. 2011. *Government Versus Markets*. Cambridge University Press.

Taylor-Gooby, Peter, Julia M. Gumy, and Adeline Otto. 2014. "Can 'New Welfare' Address Poverty Through More and Better Jobs?" *Journal of Social Policy* 44, 83–104.

Teixeira, Ruy. 2017. *The Optimistic Leftist*. St. Martin's Press.

Teles, Steven M. 2012. "Kludgeocracy: The American Way of Policy." New America Foundation.

Thévenot, Céline. 2017. "Exits from Poverty and Labour Market Changes: Taking Up a Job Does Not Always Help to Get Out of Poverty." In *Monitoring Social Inclusion in Europe*, edited by Anthony B. Atkinson, Anne-Catherine Guio, and Eric Marlier, 419–34. European Union.

Thiebaud Nicoli, Lisa. 2012. *Half a Loaf: Generosity in Cash Assistance to Single Mothers Across U.S. States, 1911–1996*. PhD dissertation. Department of Sociology, University of Arizona.

Tobias, Manuela. 2017. "Comparing Administrative Costs for Private Insurance and Medicare." *PolitiFact*, September 20.

Tobin, James. 1966. "The Case for an Income Guarantee." *The Public Interest*, Summer.

Toder, Eric and Joseph Rosenberg. 2010. "Effects of Imposing a Value-Added Tax to Replace Payroll Taxes or Corporate Taxes." Tax Policy Center.

Toder, Eric, Marjery Austin Turner, Katherine Lim, and Liza Getsinger. 2010. "Reforming the Mortgage Interest Deduction." Urban Institute and Tax Policy Center.

Traub, James. 2016. "The Death of the Most Generous Nation on Earth." *Foreign Policy*, February 10.

Travis, Jeremy, Bruce Western, and Steve Redburn, eds. 2014. *The Growth of Incarceration in the United States*. National Academies Press.

Tsebelis, George. 1995. "Decision Making in Political Systems." *British Journal of Political Science* 25, 289–325.

Tversky, Amos and Daniel Kahneman. 1992. "Advances in Prospect Theory: Cumulative Representation of Uncertainty." *Journal of Risk and Uncertainty* 5, 297–323.

Uchitelle, Louis. 2006. *The Disposable American*. Knopf.

United Way. 2014. "United Way ALICE Report: Six-State Summary." unitedforalice.org

US Bureau of Labor Statistics. 2017. "Employee Benefits in the United States." bls.gov.

US Congressional Budget Office. 2008. "Recent Trends in the Variability of Individual Earnings and Household Incomes." cbo.gov.

US Congressional Budget Office. 2011. "Estimated Impact of the American Recovery and Reinvestment Act on Employment and Economic Output." cbo.gov.

US Congressional Budget Office. 2015. "Federal Housing Assistance for Low-Income Households." cbo.gov.

US Congressional Budget Office. 2016. "Increase the Maximum Taxable Earnings for the Social Security Payroll Tax." cbo.gov.

US Department of Education. 2013. "Obama Administration 2014 Budget Prioritizes Key Education Investments to Provide Opportunities for All Americans." ed.gov.

US Department of Labor. 2016. "National Compensation Survey: Employee Benefits in the United States, March 2016." Bulletin 2785.

US Federal Communications Commission. 2019. "2019 Broadband Deployment Report." fcc.gov.

US Federal Highway Administration. 2014. "Deficient Bridges by State and Highway System." fhwa.dot.gov.

US Financial Diaries Project. 2014a. "Hardest for Poorest Households to Predict Income and Expenses." *83 Charts to Describe the Hidden Financial Lives of Working Americans*.

US Financial Diaries Project. 2014b. "Households Broadly Prefer Stability to Higher Income." *83 Charts to Describe the Hidden Financial Lives of Working Americans*.

US National Center for Education Statistics. 2018. "Public High School Graduation Rates." nces.ed.gov.

US National Center for Health Statistics. 2013. "Long-Term Care Services in the United States: 2013 Overview." nces.ed.gov.

US Senate Committee on Health, Education, Labor, and Pensions. 2012. "The Retirement Crisis and a Plan to Solve It." cov.com.

US Social Security Administration. 2016. "Social Security Programs Throughout the World: Europe, 2016." ssa.gov.

Usmani, Adaner. 2018. "The Rise and Fall of Labor." Unpublished.

Vaisey, Stephen and Omar Lizardo. 2018. "Cultural Fragmentation or Acquired Dispositions? A New Approach to Accounting for Patterns of Cultural Change." *Socius* 2, 1–15.

Van Giezen, Robert W. 2013. "Paid Leave in Private Industry Over the Past 20 Years." Bureau of Labor Statistics.

Van Kersbergen, Kees and Philip Kraft. 2017. "De-universalization and Selective Social Investment in Scandinavia?" In *The Uses of Social Investment*, edited by Anton Hemerijck, 216–26. Oxford University Press.

Van Lancker, Wim and Natascha Van Mechelen. 2014. "Universalism under Siege? Exploring the Association between Targeting, Child Benefits, and Child Poverty across 26 Countries." Working Paper 14–1. Herman Deleeck Centre for Social Policy. University of Antwerp.

Van Lancker, Wim and Jeroen Horemans. 2018. "Childcare Policies and In-Work Poverty." In *Handbook on In-Work Poverty*, edited by Henning Lohmann and Ive Marx, 261–76. Edward Elgar.

Van Oorschot. 2002. "Targeting Welfare: On the Functions and Dysfunctions of Means Testing in Social Policy." In *World Poverty*, edited by Peter Townsend and David Gordon. Policy Press.

Van Parijs, Philippe. 2001. "A Basic Income for All." In *What's Wrong with a Free Lunch?* edited by Joshua Cohen and Joel Rogers, 3–26. Beacon Press.

Van Parijs, Philippe and Yannick Vanderborght. 2017. *Basic Income*. Harvard University Press.

Van Vliet, Olaf and Chen Wang. 2015. "Social Investment and Poverty Reduction: A Comparative Analysis across Fifteen European Countries." *Journal of Social Policy* 44, 611–38.

Vandell, Deborah Lowe and Barbara Wolfe. 2000. "Child Care Quality: Does It Matter and Does It Need to Be Improved?" Special Report 78. Institute for Research on Poverty. University of Wisconsin–Madison.

Vitols, Sigurt. 2010. "Board Level Employee Representation, Executive Remuneration, and Firm Performance in Large European Companies." Hans Böckler Foundation.

Vogel, David. 1989. *Fluctuating Fortunes: The Political Power of Business in America*. Basic Books.

von Hippel, Paul T., Joseph Workman, and Douglas B. Downey. 2018. "Inequality in Reading and Math Skills Forms Mainly before Kindergarten: A Replication, and Partial Correction, of 'Are Schools the Great Equalizer?'" *Sociology of Education* 91, 323–57.

Waldfogel, Jane. 2006. *What Children Need*. Harvard University Press.

Waldfogel, Jane. 2010. *Britain's War on Poverty*. Russell Sage Foundation.

Walsh, Mary Williams. 2016. "California Aims Retirement Plan at Those Whose Jobs Offer None." *New York Times*, August 25.

Walzer, Michael. 1978. "Town Meetings and Workers' Control." *Dissent*, Summer, 325–33.

Wamhoff, Steve and Matthew Gardner. 2019. "Who Pays Taxes in America in 2019?" Institute on Taxation and Economic Policy.

Wang, Chen and Koen Caminada. 2011. "Disentangling Income Inequality and the Redistributive Effect of Social Transfers and Taxes in 36 LIS Countries." Working Paper 567. Luxembourg Income Study.

Wang, Sam and Brian Remlinger. 2017. "Slaying the Partisan Gerrymander." *The American Prospect*, September 25.

Warren, Elizabeth. 2018. "Companies Shouldn't Be Accountable Only to Shareholders." *Wall Street Journal*, August 14.

Warren, Elizabeth and Amelia Warren Tyagi. 2003. *The Two-Income Trap*. Basic Books.

Waters, Mary C. and Marisa Gerstein Pineau, eds. 2015. *The Integration of Immigrants into American Society*. National Academies Press.

Weeden, Kim A. 2002. "Why Do Some Occupations Pay More Than Others? Social Closure and Earnings Inequality in the United States." *American Journal of Sociology* 108, 55–101.

Weitzman, Martin L. 1984. *The Share Economy*. Harvard University Press.

Welzel, Christian. 2013. *Freedom Rising: Human Empowerment and the Quest for Emancipation*. Cambridge University Press.

Western, Bruce. 2006. *Punishment and Inequality in America*. Russell Sage Foundation.

Western, Bruce. 2018. *Homeward: Life in the Year After Prison*. Russell Sage Foundation.

Western, Bruce and Jake Rosenfeld. 2011. "Unions, Norms, and the Rise in U.S. Wage Inequality." *American Sociological Review* 76, 513–37.

Western, Bruce, Dierdre Bloome, Benjamin Sosnaud, and Laura Tach. 2012. "Economic Insecurity and Social Stratification." *Annual Review of Sociology*, 38, 341–59.

Western, Bruce and Jake Rosenfeld. 2012. "Workers of the World Divide: The Decline of Labor and the Future of the Middle Class." *Foreign Affairs*, May–June.

What Works Clearinghouse. 2019. "Find What Works Based on the Evidence." ies.ed.gov/ncee/wwc.

Whelan, Christopher T. and Bertrand Maitre. 2012. "Understanding Material Deprivation: A Comparative European Analysis." *Research in Social Stratification and Mobility* 30, 489–503.

Whiteford, Peter. 2008. "How Much Redistribution Do Governments Achieve? The Role of Cash Transfers and Household Taxes." In *Growing Unequal?* OECD.

Whiteford, Peter. 2009. "Transfer Issues and Directions for Reform: Australian Transfer Policy in Comparative Perspective." Social Policy Research Center, University of New South Wales.

Whiteford, Peter, Ben Phillips, Bruce Bradbury, David Stanton, Matthew Gray, and Miranda Stewart. 2018. "It's Not Just Newstart. Single Parents Are $271 per Fortnight Worse Off. Labor Needs an Overarching Welfare Review. " *The Conversation*, December 2.

Whitehurst, Grover J. 2013. "Can We Be Hard-Headed About Preschool? A Look at Universal and Targeted Pre-K." Brookings Institution.

Whitehurst, Grover J. 2014. "Does Pre-K Work? It Depends on How Picky You Are." Brookings Institution.

Wilensky, Harold L. 2002. *Rich Democracies*. University of California Press.

Wilentz, Sean. 2008. *The Age of Reagan*. Harper.

Wilkinson, Richard and Kate Pickett. 2009. *The Spirit Level: Why Greater Equality Makes Societies Stronger*. Bloomsbury Press.

Wilkinson, Will. 2017a. "For Trump and GOP, the Welfare State Shouldn't Be the Enemy." *New York Times*, May 27.

Wilkinson, Will. 2017b. "Public Policy After Utopia." Niskanen Center.

Williamson, Vanessa S. 2017. *Read My Lips: Why Americans Are Proud to Pay Taxes*. Princeton University Press.

Wilson, James Q. 1989. *Bureaucracy*. Basic Books.

Wilson, William Julius. 1987. *The Truly Disadvantaged*. University of Chicago Press.

Wilson, William Julius. 1996. *When Work Disappears*. Vintage.

Wilson, William Julius. 2009. *More Than Just Race*. W. W. Norton.

Winship, Scott. 2012. "Bogeyman Economics." *National Affairs*, Winter.

Winship, Scott. 2013. "The Dream Abides: Economic Mobility in America from the Golden Age to the Great Recession." Policy Brief. Brookings Institution.

Winship, Scott. 2016. "Poverty After Welfare Reform." Manhattan Institute.

Wolfe, Alan. 1989. *Whose Keeper? Social Science and Moral Obligation*. University of California Press.

Wolff, Edward N. 2012. "The Asset Price Meltdown and the Wealth of the Middle Class." Russell Sage Foundation.

Wooldridge, Adrian. 2013. "The Secret of Their Success." *The Economist*, February 2.

World Economic Forum. 2015. *The Global Competitiveness Report 2013–2014*. weforum.org.

Wright, Erik Olin. 2010. *Envisioning Real Utopias*. Verso.

Wright, Erik Olin and Rachel Dwyer. 2003. "The Patterns of Job Expansions in the United States: A Comparison of the 1960s and 1990s." *Socio-Economic Review* 1, 289–325.

Yglesias, Matthew. 2013. *The Rent Is Too Damn High*. Simon and Schuster.

Yglesias, Matthew. 2018. "Elizabeth Warren Has a Plan to Save Capitalism." *Vox*, August 15.

Yoshikawa, Hirokazu, Christina Weiland, et al. 2013. *Investing in Our Future: The Evidence Base on Preschool*. Society for Research in Child Development and Foundation for Child Development.

Young, Cristobal. 2017. *The Myth of Millionaire Tax Flight*. Stanford University Press.

Zandi, Mark. 2011. "An Analysis of the Obama Jobs Plan." *Moody's Analytics: Dismal Scientist*, September 9.

Zingales, Luigi. 2012. *A Capitalism for the People*. Basic Books.

Zucman, Gabriel. 2015. *The Hidden Wealth of Nations: The Scourge of Tax Havens*. University of Chicago Press.

Zwolinski, Matt. 2015. "Property Rights, Coercion, and the Welfare State: The Libertarian Case for a Basic Income for All." *Independent Review* 19, 515–29.

INDEX

For the benefit of digital users, indexed terms that span two pages (e.g., 52–53) may, on occasion, appear on only one of those pages.